THE MANLY ART

THE MANLY ART

Bare-Knuckle Prize Fighting in America

ELLIOTT J. GORN

CORNELL UNIVERSITY PRESS   Ithaca, New York

Copyright © 1986 by Cornell University

First published 1986 by Cornell University Press
First printing, Cornell Paperbacks, 1989

Printed in the United States of America

Library of Congress Cataloging-in-Publication Data

Gorn, Elliott J., 1951–
   The Manly art.

   Includes index.
   1. Boxing—United States. 2. Boxing—United States—Matches—History. I. Title
GV1125.G67   1986   796.8'3'0973   86-6410
ISBN 0-8014-9582-2 (pbk. : alk. paper)

Cornell University Press strives to use environmentally responsible suppliers and materials to the fullest extent possible in the publishing of its books. Such materials include vegetable-based, low-VOC inks and acid-free papers that are recycled, totally chlorine-free, or partly composed of nonwood fibers. Books that bear the logo of the FSC (Forest Stewardship Council) use paper taken from forests that have been inspected and certified as meeting the highest standards for environmental and social responsibility. For further information, visit our website at www.cornellpress.cornell.edu.

Paperback printing   10 9 8 7 6

Frontispiece
John Lawrence Sullivan and Jake Kilrain battle for the championship on July 8, 1889, in Richburg, Mississippi. The fight took seventy-five rounds lasting two hours and fifteen minutes. From *The Modern Gladiator* (1892).

For Max Gorn, 1910–1979,
and Anne Francis Gorn

Contents

Illustrations

Preface

My father was a boxing fan. Before he married, he attended weekly fights with his buddies in New York City. I suspect that his interest in the ring originated during his youth; although he never formally boxed, Montreal's anti-Semitism in the 1920s drew him and his brothers into countless fistfights. Later, when he served in the merchant marine during World War II, similar provocations had similar results.

Growing up in Los Angeles during the fifties and sixties, his children were heir to tales about his occasional need to defend his integrity. These stories merged imperceptibly into accounts of famous boxers—"Gentleman" Gene Tunney, who taught a class at Yale, Jewish champions such as Benny Leonard and Max Baer, and the greatest fighter of them all, Joe Louis. These, in turn, blurred into childhood lessons on how to deal with a bully or an anti-Semite, as our tiny fists punched my father's open hands.

I never asked him, but I am sure that he found boxing the most compelling of all sports. The agility, cleverness, and ferocity of great boxers, the courage displayed in the ring, and the drama of two men stalking each other fascinated him. So here is a paradox: my father—a union member who considered himself a political radical—believed that boxing should be outlawed. Countless times I heard him say that if given the chance, he would vote to abolish the sport. Yet this was not a chastened man atoning for old mistakes. He enjoyed watching televised bouts until he died (he was the only person I know who correctly predicted the outcomes of both Ali-Spinks fights), but he believed that boxers were victims of racial and class discrimination, that the ring encouraged violence, and that pugilism appealed to all that was barbarous in man.

While I am neither as pugnacious nor as knowledgeable about boxing as my father was, I share his ambivalence. Prize fighting glorifies violence, exploits the poor, exalts force over reason, glamorizes atavism. It is these very horrors, however, so reprehensible by themselves, which highlight all that is noble in the ring. Courage, the quest for excellence, the overcoming of fear, dreams of transcending one's social and physical handicaps, boxers' poetic harmony of mind and body, their competitive strivings past all reasonable human limits—the ring's dark barbarism makes such qualities glow like fireflies on a Southern night.

As I try to indicate throughout this book, the morality of the ring, its simultaneous attraction and repulsion, was a theme central to boxing history; the ambivalence my father and I shared had deep roots. But in these pages, I tend to take the part of the lions over the Christians.

My specific subject is American bare-knuckle prize fighting in the nineteenth century. I seek to rescue from oblivion the deeds of men who were extraordinarily well known in their day. The colorful nature of the subject makes the historian's most ancient role, that of storyteller, particularly important. I have attempted, as far as my abilities and the historical sources allow, to capture the lives and times of early heroes.

But my emphasis on narrative is more than simply a desire to tell a good story. To understand prize fighting, to capture the layered and changing meanings that the sport had for its practitioners, fans, and opponents, we must become enmeshed in the culture of the ring. Only when we observe boxing's pageantry, rituals, and ceremonies—only, that is, when we reconstruct the history and experience of the ring—can we begin to grasp its social and cultural significance.

Prize fighting was one of the most popular sports among working-class males in the nineteenth century, and great championship battles galvanized men like few other events. It was also illegal. Pugilism elicited passionate responses from its partisans and from its opponents, and these responses grew out of deeply felt assumptions concerning man and society. Boxing is *not* about instincts or innate aggressiveness; it *is* about values, social relationships, and culture. To understand bare-knuckle prize fighting, I have discovered, is necessarily to understand something about nineteenth-century America. Ideology, ethnicity, social class formation, violence, urbanization, gender roles, religious world views, productive relationships, all are part of sports history in general and boxing history in particular.

I begin with the English origins of the ring, then discuss the earliest manifestations of pugilism in the young United States. By the antebellum era, as old artisan ways of life dissolved and a modern working class began to emerge in American cities, bare-knuckle fighting entered its golden age. Boxing encountered stiff opposition during these early Victorian years, for the forces transforming labor—entrepreneurial capitalism, specialization of tasks, industrialization—were driven by powerful bourgeois and evangelical ideologies that militated against the "sloppy" habits of laboring men. After the Civil War, however, prize fighting was reformed. From a fugitive, outlaw sport—the very words "sport" and "sporting" implied social deviance during much of the nineteenth century—it became a more businesslike, quasi-respectable recreation, one that upper- and middle-class men found fascinating. My last chapters explore the social basis of this transformation and its meaning for Victorian culture.

The Manly Art is of mixed academic parentage, though the disciplines from which it springs might not recognize their offspring. Still, one can detect genetic strains from folklore, anthropology, sociology, and American studies, as well as labor, social, and sports history. I have been deliberately eclectic; I am a partisan of no particular school of thought. But I do have some axes to grind.

This is gender history. It could not have been written without the crucial insights of the women's studies movement, that sexual definitions are a critical part of consciousness, and that they change with social, cultural, and economic circumstances. To write about prize fighting is necessarily to describe important rituals of manhood. But awareness of the potential malleability of gender roles gives added significance to the study of sports. Bare-knuckle boxing expressed a particular male ethos that grew out of specific historical conditions.

This is also social history or, more precisely, folk history. I attempt here, as historians have for the past couple of decades, to understand the lives of those who left few records but who nevertheless were important historical actors. The same biases that rendered women voiceless in the writing of history simultaneously excluded the majority of men, in particular workers, ethnic minorities, and the poor. *The Manly Art* is a small contribution toward rectifying that imbalance.

Finally, this is labor history. If in the 1950s scholars assumed that America's working class was merely an extension of the petit bourgeoisie, then those of the 1970s and 80s threaten to reduce culture to politics. I will state this baldly: most workers did not spend their free time reading the *Rights of Man*, toasting Tom Paine, and struggling to resist oppression. Probably more hours were consumed at cockfights than at union meetings during the nineteenth century. Radicals there were, of course, and they have been studied brilliantly. But if historians are to understand working-class people, they must look closely at their folklore and recreations, their pastimes and sports, for it has been in leisure more than in politics or in labor that many men and women have found the deepest sense of meaning and wholeness.

The Manly Art is not a complete history of the prize ring, nor a "genealogy" of champions and their battles. The names of some important fighters do not even appear here. Because my intent is to interpret boxing, not merely to describe it, I have had to be selective in the events I discuss. Besides, the sources—mostly newspapers and popular pamphlets—contain detailed and reliable information on a limited number of fights. It is on these bouts that I have dwelled in order to reconstruct the culture of the ring.

It is almost embarrassing to acknowledge all of those who helped bring this project to fruition, for the results seem so meager when measured against their talents and generosity. I have benefited from important institutional support. Yale University, where I attended graduate school in American Studies, nurtured me intellectually. The Harry Frank Guggenheim Foundation funded a one-year leave of absence from my teaching duties at the University of Alabama, allowing me to revise the work. The offices of the deans of arts and sciences at Alabama and at my new professional home, Miami University, have been very supportive, especially with aid for travel to collections and for preparation of the manuscript.

I also thank the staffs of the Sterling and Beinecke libraries at Yale University, the Widener Library at Harvard University, the New York Public Library, the New-York Historical Society, the Amelia Gayle Gorgas Library at the University of Alabama, and Miami University's King Library. Warren Platt of the New York Public Library and Bonnie Collier at Yale provided bibliographical aid beyond the call of duty. Jim Jacobs kindly lent me photocopied materials compiled thirty-five years ago by Paul Magriel, a bibliographer and chronicler of the ring. William Schutte of the University of Wisconsin, Whitewater, provided most of the illustrations. Several typists also contributed their skills, often under tight deadlines, among them Helen and Alison Genua, Jan Wilson, Rhonda Johnson, Margaret Vines, Tracy Noel, J. R. Ford, and especially Kathleen Grondin. I thank them all.

Alan Dundes and Lawrence Levine, my mentors at the University of California, Berkeley, for the first half of my career as a college student, taught by their example not only how to do humanistic scholarship but why. Several of my fellow graduate students—Joel Bernard, Edward

Ayers, Jane Hunter, John Endean, Gerald Burns, and Michael Smith—helped me get this project going. David Brion Davis encouraged my work even when neither of us had much idea where it would lead. His critical judgment improved the text immeasurably. More, he gave me the confidence to test my abilities, to try out ideas, and to seek the broadest meanings in history, but always within the boundaries of rigorous scholarship. Kai Erikson also brought crucial insights to the manuscript (and wry humor to our discussions), and Jean Agnew asked questions that helped frame the intellectual structure of this book while he offered personal supportiveness that aided its completion.

I also acknowledge my fellow "professors of pugilism." Randy Roberts has led the way for all of us who write sports history; his good advice proved indispensable on numerous occasions. Benjamin Rader also read the entire manuscript and added important suggestions. Jeffrey Sammons has been a constant source of aid, and his forthcoming book on twentieth-century boxing will be invaluable. Melvin Adelman kindly lent me early drafts of his path-breaking study of sports in nineteenth-century New York City. Fred Harvey Harrington provided a detailed critique of chapter three based on a biography he is writing on John Morrissey. Michael T. Isenberg read chapter seven and also lent me drafts of his fine biography-in-progress of John L. Sullivan, another work that promises a bright future for histories of the prize ring.

My colleagues in the American Studies Department at the University of Alabama were always there as I revised the work. Let me specifically name three Alabama faculty members who read the entire manuscript. Ralph Bogardus brought his breadth of knowledge and skill as a cultural critic to bear on the text; Fred Hobson of the English Department cast a literary scholar's eye on my prose and improved it greatly; and John Kneebone asked a social historian's keen questions. All contributed with their insight and even more with their friendship. Three editors helped bring a young writer through the shoals: Lawrence Malley bolstered me with early confidence in my work; Peter Agree contributed his copious skills to the final product; and Roger Haydon saved me from countless errors with a masterly job of copy editing. As the manuscript neared completion, John Kasson added important words of criticism and encouragement. My good friend Allen Tullos always reminded me by his example that writing history is as much a passion as a craft. I learned lessons in courage and humor and human decency simply by knowing Margaret Vines. And my brother Michael Gorn and kindred spirit Frank Travisano helped keep me going throughout the research and writing.

My wife of twelve years, Anna Yee, laughed at my spelling, ridiculed my grammar, and belittled my verbal pomposity. From deleting stray commas to expanding central ideas, she contributed to every draft of this work. More important, she sustained my spirits in good times and bad. Thank you for being my wife and letting me be your husband. And thank you, Jade, our two-year-old daughter, for reminding us constantly of what is important in life.

Shortly after I began graduate school, my father suggested that no one had ever written seriously about boxing. I assumed that a man with a seventh-grade education did not understand the complexities of scholarly work, so I paid little attention. He and a cousin, Manny Cole, persisted in telling me that prize fighting was just the thing a student should think about. I remained aloof—until I needed a topic for a seminar paper. As I keep discovering, my father knew more than I ever gave him credit for. My mother was not much interested in athletics, but she taught her children a sportsmanlike desire to do their best. If she loathed boxing, she still could sympathize with a prize fighter's ambition. Both of my parents nurtured me and sacrificed for me. They taught me the value of knowledge and inculcated a desire to understand the world and to help others understand it. This book is theirs in more ways than I can express.

ELLIOTT J. GORN

Oxford, Ohio

THE MANLY ART

Prologue: The English Prize Ring

The marquis of Queensberry, Sir Henry Smith, Lord Yarmouth, The Honourable Berkeley Craven, Major Mellish, General Grosvenor, Lord Pomfret, Sir Charles Alton, and countless other men of rank stood shoulder to shoulder at the ropes, waiting for the fighters to appear. Behind them, the motley crowd known as "the fancy" pressed forward. Professional gamblers, tavern keepers, and young dandies out for a grand time; prostitutes, costermongers, pugilists, and pickpockets; wealthy "Corinthians" who patronized lower-class recreations; cockfighters, dog trainers, butchers, weavers, and chimney sweeps; high and low, rich and poor—twenty thousand Englishmen mingled at Thistleton Gap, outside London, on September 28, 1811.[1]

Shortly after noon Tom Crib, a bellhanger turned tavern keeper and now champion of England, sprang upon the stage and bowed to the crowd. Three months of training on the estate of Captain Barclay—an old patron of the ring who allegedly staked ten thousand pounds on his man—had steeled the champion's frame with muscle. Thirty years old, five-feet-ten-inches tall, weighing thirteen stone six (one hundred and eighty-eight pounds), Crib was at the height of his pugilistic powers.

Tom Molineaux, an American and a black man, followed the champion into the ring. Almost the same size as Crib, Molineaux had astonished Englishmen over the previous year with spectacular displays of power and craft. Ringside betting stood at three-to-one for Crib, but many feared that the title was in jeopardy. Molineaux's foreignness disturbed the fancy even more than his color, for it raised the prospect that England might lose the championship, a symbol of national virility.[2]

These fears seemed well founded. Crib and Molineaux had met almost a year before, on a cold, wet December day. Pierce Egan, the great chronicler of sporting life, declared that interest in previous contests paled beside this one because, for the first time, national honor was at stake. Fancymen slogged through ankle-deep mud on their way to Copthall Common, thirty miles north of London, a trek that was rewarded with an outstanding fight. The American began as a four-to-one underdog, but by the ninth round the champion was in trouble. "Both the combatants appeared dreadfully *punished*," Egan wrote, "and Crib's head was terribly swelled on the left side. . . . Molineaux rallied with a spirit unexpected, bored in upon Crib, and by a strong blow through the Champion's Guard, which he planted in his face, brought him down."[3]

By the thirteenth round, the odds had turned to six-to-four on Molineaux. Three rounds later, they were roughly even, and the momentum shifted back and forth until the twenty-ninth round, when Crib, retreating and counterpunching, caught Molineaux with a blow to the right eye that seriously impaired his vision. The challenger carried the fight for ten more rounds, continuing to punish Crib, but he finally collapsed from exhaustion. "Molineaux," Egan concluded, "proved himself as courageous a man as ever an adversary contended with. . . . The Black astonished everyone, not only by his extraordinary power of hitting, and his gigantic strength, but also by his acquaintance with the science, which was far greater than any had given him credit for." Indeed, rumors were rife that only chicanery by Crib's seconds and interference by the crowd kept the championship from Molineaux's grasp.[4]

So, as the rematch began, those at ringside eyed the challenger with deep apprehension. The two heroes picked up where they had left off in their first fight. Fourth round: "although [Crib] was bleeding from every wound, he smiled with confidence, and rallied in the first style of manliness. A number of good blows were exchanged. Crib *milling* away at the body and *Molineaux punishing* the head." Fifth round: "Molineaux commenced a rally, and the *punishment* was truly dreadful on both sides; but the *Moor* had the best of it and the champion fell from a hit."[5]

Molineaux, however, was not the same fighter as a year before. While Crib trained with Captain Barclay, the challenger was unable to find a wealthy backer, so he sparred and fought prize battles in order to support himself. He also frequented the taverns and flash houses patronized by the sporting fraternity, drinking too much and dissipating his strength. As a result, Molineaux's "bottom"—the fancy's word for endurance— betrayed him. Sixth round: "Crib now gave the *Moor* so severe a blow in the body with his right hand, that it not only appeared to *roll him up*,

The second Crib-Molineaux championship fight, September 28, 1811, in which the American black and the English champion battled for eleven rounds. Engraved by the celebrated illustrators George and Robert Isaac Cruikshank.

but seemed as if he had completely knocked the wind out of him.'' Ninth round: "It was so evident which way the battle would now terminate, that it was *'Lombard Street to a China Orange'* Crib was the conqueror. The *Moor* in running in, had his jaw broke, and he fell as if dead from a tremendous left-handed blow of the Champion." Molineaux managed to rise for two more rounds before giving in.[6]

Crib's return home was triumphant; grateful Englishmen mobbed his coach in every town. Back in London, several Corinthians raised a subscription for an engraved silver cup. "You are requested," Crib was told before a gathering of wealthy ring patrons, "to accept this cup as a tribute of respect for the uniform valor and integrity you have shewn in your several combats, but most particularly for the additional proofs of native skill and manly intrepidity displayed by you in your last memourable battle, when the cause rested not merely on individual fame, but for the pugilistic reputation of your native country, in contending with a formidable foreign antagonist.'' A sumptuous dinner followed, then toasts, songs, and general conviviality capped the celebration.[7]

Here was the English prize ring in its glory. ''I have known the time,'' George Borrow recalled of these days, ''when a pugilistic encounter between two noted champions was considered as a national affair; when tens of thousands of individuals, high and low, meditated and brooded upon it, the first thing in the morning and the last at night, until the great event was decided.'' Molineaux and Crib were beneficiaries of boxing's apotheosis. Patronage by the aristocracy and gentry, participation by less than genteel members of the lower class, a shared love of conviviality and high times, a shared admiration for courage, displays of honor, and physical prowess, and a shared fear of national decadence and effeminancy, all made prize fighting England's most popular sport from the last decades of the eighteenth through the first quarter of the nineteenth century.[8]

The precise origins of English pugilism are obscure. We know that fistic combat was an event in the ancient Greek Olympiad. Pindar, for example, celebrated Diagoras' victory in the games of 474 B.C.: ''But do thou, O father Zeus, that rulest over the height of Atabyrium, grant honour to the hymn ordained in praise of an Olympian victor, and to the hero who hath found fame for his prowess as a boxer; and do thou give him grace and reverence in the eyes of citizens and of strangers too. For he goeth in a straight course along a path that hateth insolence; he hath learnt full well all the lessons prompted by the prudence which he inheriteth from goodly ancestors.'' For Pindar, the boxer's achievement was not merely physical but moral as well, a sign of proper upbringing by a good family and a culmination of virtuous living worthy of Zeus' blessing.[9]

Even lords and warriors competed to win prizes, entertain each other, uphold their honor, demonstrate virility, and pay homage to the dead. For the ancient Greeks, gifted fighters personified important cultural values. A dangerous, bloody sport, boxing was considered good preparation for warfare, so men of great science and finesse received special praise. Boxers became exalted heroes, models of the agonistic ideal who celebrated the gods with their deeds and embodied the goal of unified mental, physical, and spiritual cultivation. Sports in general and boxing in particular were encouraged because they taught discipline while exemplifying Greek ideals of grace and beauty.[10]

The Greeks passed the idea of fistic combat on to the Romans, as the

Latin origins of our word *pugilism* testify, but boxing matches became ever more bloody spectacles during the ascendancy of Rome. Under the Empire, fighters took to new extremes the Greek practice of wearing a thong—called *caestus* by the Romans—to protect the hand. Sometimes metal spikes were embedded in the surface. Virgil describes a pair in *The Aeneid*:

> From somewhere he produced the gloves of Eryx
> And tossed them into the ring, all stiff and heavy,
> Seven layers of hide and insewn lead and iron....
> You can still see the blood and a splash of brains
> That stained them long ago....

Virgil goes on to recount a mythic boxing match, part of the funeral games honoring Anchises, in which the old champion Entellus triumphed over young Dares. The fight was stopped once the outcome became clear, and the vanquished man was carried off, spitting blood and teeth. Entellus then faced his prize, a steer,

> Drew back his right hand, poised it, sent it smashing
> Between the horns, shattering the skull and splashing
> Brains on the bones, as the great beast came down, lifeless.

The champion declared the steer a sacrifice to the god Eryx and vowed to lay aside the gloves forever.[11]

In both Greece and Rome, then, boxing was more than mere entertainment. It grew out of cultural sensibilities that made male prowess, violent competition, and personal ambition part of larger social and religious ideals. Thus fist-fighting took its place alongside other bloody, gladitorial spectacles.[12]

Pugilism may have been introduced to England during the Roman occupation, but if so, it disappeared shortly after the Christian era began and apparently did not return until the seventeenth century. Perhaps the idea of boxing reemerged as Englishmen rediscovered the classics, learning about it from Virgil and Homer.[13] Certainly the morally relaxed atmosphere following the Puritan ascendancy permitted the revival of rough sports, along with their attendant vices of drinking, gambling, and carousing. Indeed, during the Restoration of the mid-1600s, ancient rural recreations returned in full glory and bloodiness, among them cockfighting, bullbaiting, and football. Boxing drew strength from this sporting revival, but the ring did not have deep roots in the English countryside. Rather, it became an urban phenomenon, supported by city nobles, local squires migrating to the commercial centers, and growing numbers of working-class men.[14]

James Fig is generally credited as the father of the English ring, though others certainly boxed before him. The first manual on fistic exercise, Captain Godfrey's *A Treatise on the Useful Science of Defense* published in 1740, called Fig the greatest teacher of boxing of the early 1700s. In addition to founding his own school, Fig's Amphitheatre, he fought several prize battles and exhibited his pugilistic talents, along with the arts of swordsmanship and cudgel play (fighting with heavy sticks), at such seasonal gatherings as the Southwark Fair. Jack Broughton succeeded Fig, receiving the duke of Cumberland's patronage and reigning as the second great founding father of the ring. Broughton also fought prize battles and taught "the theory and practice of that truly British Art" in his London Academy. Above all, he brought a more refined tone to the ring and promulgated the sport's first rules, a code that guided prize fighting from 1743 through 1838. In one of his championship bouts, Fig had been strangled for half a minute before extricating himself from his opponent's grip. Broughton's rules helped eliminate such brutality; they also outlawed hitting below the belt and striking a fallen opponent. The new code further specified that a round ended when a man was punched or thrown down, that the next round began thirty seconds later with both boxers toeing a mark called the "scratch" in the middle of the ring, and that each side appoint seconds to assist between rounds, umpires to settle disputes, and a referee whose decisions were final.[15]

These precedents were important, but it was not until near the end of the eighteenth century that boxing would grow so popular as to be deemed the national sport of England. The reasons were complex. Pugilism's rise was part of a larger flowering of commercialized leisure and popular recreations. Leading the way were newly reorganized spectator sports such as cricket and horse racing, with their formal rules, sophisticated betting, and powerful clubs comprised of influential patrons. The emergence of several skilled, colorful champions, moreover, was crucial to the ring's development—Daniel Mendoza, the quick and clever Jew; Bill Richmond, an American black who pioneered counterpunching and other defensive strategies; "Gentleman" John Jackson, teacher of the manly art for a whole generation of English aristocrats; John Gully, a butcher's son who rose from debtors' prison to champion, wealthy bookmaker, and member of Parliament; as well as Jem Belcher, Tom Spring, Richard Humphries, Bob Gregson, Tom Hickman, Jack Langan, and many others.[16]

"Gentleman" John Jackson's sparring rooms, 1821. Such notables as Lord Byron took lessons from the "sparring master to the aristocracy." Engraved by the Cruikshank brothers. Courtesy of the Print Collections, The New York Public Library, Astor, Lenox and Tilden Foundations.

The great English essayist William Hazlitt captured boxing's glory in "The Fight," his account of the championship battle in 1821 between Tom "The Gas-man" Hickman, and William Neate. Hazlitt described the taverns, bristling with excitement, as members of the fancy gathered the night before to discover the secret location of the battle and enjoy one another's company. He recounted his discussions with trainers, boxers, and other "knowing ones." Hazlitt painted the spectacle in colors still vivid today: "Reader, have you ever seen a fight? If not, you have a pleasure to come, at least if it is a fight like that between the Gas-man and Bill Neate. The crowd was very great when we arrived on the spot; open carriages were coming up, with streamers flying and music playing, and the country people were pouring in over hedge and ditch, in all directions, to see their hero beat or be beaten." Hazlitt sketched the young swells at ringside in their white box coats, the burly club-bearing ring keepers who kept the "magic circle" clear, the boxers themselves stripping off their garments, Neate quietly confident, Hickman strutting like the cock of the walk. At the last instant work-a-day time stopped, and the special rhythm of the ring began. "There was now a dead pause—attention was awe-struck. Who at that moment, big with a great event, did not draw his breath short—did not feel his heart throb? All was ready. . . . They were led up to the *scratch*—shook hands, and went at it."[17]

Hazlitt brilliantly evoked the ring's unique combination of lightheartedness and brutality. His words did not mask the violence but described the bloody ebb and flow of the battle until its chilling denouement: "[Neate] planted a tremendous blow on [Hickman's] cheek-bone and eyebrow, and made a red ruin of that side of his face. The Gas-man went down, and there was another shout—a roar of triumph as the waves of fortune rolled tumultuously from side to side. . . ." But the challenger would not give up. In the twelfth round Neate lunged again, striking Hickman with full force: "All traces of life, of natural expression, were gone from him. His face was like a human skull, a death's head, spouting blood. The eyes were filled with blood, the nose streamed blood, the mouth gaped blood. He was not like an actual man, but like a preternatural, spectral appearance, or like one of the figures in Dante's Inferno." Hickman came up for six more rounds, then lapsed into unconsciousness. Hazlitt chastened those critics of the ring who assumed superior airs yet could never replicate the courage and self-possession of one who lit gas lamps for a living. "The Fight" ended as it began, with descriptions of great conviviality and shared memories on the return trip to London.[18]

Hazlitt caught the prize ring at the peak of its grandeur, when men lived for the thrill of a good fight on which to wager; when remarkable writers, Vincent Dowling, John Badcock, and especially Pierce Egan, catered to the desire of the newly literate masses for fresh prose on exciting subjects; when dozens of the country's most distinguished gentlemen belonged to the Pugilistic Club, whose members arranged matches, put up stakes, and wore their distinctive blue-and-buff uniforms at ringside; when the czar of Russia and the king of Prussia, in celebration of their victory over Napoleon, were treated to an exhibition of the art of self-defense by the great English champions; when the Prince Regent, a patron of the ring, organized an honor guard of twenty leading pugilists to attend him at his coronation as George IV in 1821.[19]

Above all, boxing epitomized a cultural style. The pursuit of raucous sports had deep roots in the countryside, and many Britons reveled in the national love of rough play. Violent recreations affirmed masculine values such as prowess, valor, and physical courage. "The English claret had flowed so freely," Pierce Egan wrote of one fight, "that never before or since did I see two men so thoroughly and handsomely painted with the true blood red, from the crown of the head to the waistband. They would have made a rare subject for a painter.'' Boxing was one of several brutal pastimes—including cockfighting, bull- and bearbaiting, cudgel play, and dogfighting—long popular with the English people. On the simplest level, the bloodiness in ring and pit paralleled the bloodiness of society in the late eighteenth and early nineteenth centuries. Street violence threatened peace-loving citizens with assaults, robbery, gang attack, and murder. More, the era was rife with revolutionary bloodbaths, wars of unprecedented ferocity, public executions, grinding poverty, restive labor, and repressive capital.[20]

But boxing was far more than butchery turned spectacle. Prize fighting engendered a male aesthetic. For the fancy, a good bout was an artistic idealization of reality, displaying manliness, fair play, and finely developed physical skills. The ring, it was said, taught Englishmen bulldog courage, fostering a sense of national pride while countering effeminacy. Pugilism elevated honor over money-getting and martial valor over comfort. Equally important, the fancy found beauty in man's sheer physicality. The same Pierce Egan who evoked scenes drenched with blood also praised champion Richard Humphries for his "elegance of position," his "cool and prompt judgement," his "fortitude of manner," and his "manly and tasteful attitudes." Boxing, Egan argued, taught lessons in humanity, settling quarrels with the same finality as pistols and daggers but without the attendant loss of life. Bloodletting artfully performed, violence within explicit rules, brutality committed with style—the ring articulated an ideal of manhood that bound displays of sanguine passions within an aesthetic of restraint and decorum.[21]

The sons of the aristocracy and gentry were especially attracted to boxing. At Eton and Harrow, young gentlemen acquired black eyes and split lips along with courage, coolness under pressure, and a sense of leadership and command, the moral foundations of the landed classes' rule. Perhaps the aggressive masculinity of the ring was a defensive reaction for the men of an old upper class whose relative power and wealth—the very basis of their patriarchal prerogatives—were declining. Prize fights and other popular recreations momentarily reestablished elite authority among the masses. They allowed gentlemen at once to mingle with the multitude, cementing the loyalty of their social inferiors, but simultaneously to distance themselves through displays of wealth and largesse. Equally important, sports reasserted gentry values, especially love of pageantry, bold risk taking, and martial courage.[22]

Though boxing was nourished by the same ethos as other traditional

"A visit to the fives court," London, 1825. Here boxers sparred, matches were made, stakes deposited, and benefits given. Engraved by Robert Isaac Cruikshank for Pierce Egan's *Sporting Anecdotes* (1825). Courtesy of the Print Collection, The New York Public Library, Astor, Lenox and Tilden Foundations.

recreations, it was not a venerable country amusement like cockfighting. The ring was a product of those social and economic forces transforming England, and it grew from tensions endemic in society. The fancy was a large and heterogeneous club, replicating the diversity of the burgeoning metropolis. It was this very heterogeneity which was so appealing, giving the ring its colorful blend of rich and poor, well-born and debased, resplendent and ragged. Great men and small now migrated in unprecedented numbers to booming new centers of commerce and manufacturing. Urban life provided the fancy with a multitude of watering holes, including dozens of taverns run by former boxers, where the sporting crowd could drink, sing, and recall famous battles.[23]

Equally important, the city held a large working-class population, men for whom a purse of ten or fifty or one hundred pounds, along with the chance to become a hero among one's peers, was worth the risk of permanent injury, even death.[24] Boxers came from the ranks of coal heavers, canal diggers, brickmakers, chair carriers, butchers, tailors, masons, day laborers, and all variety of workingmen. Many still belonged to viable crafts, but most were becoming permanent wage laborers with little chance of attaining autonomy through the dying apprenticeship system. Members of ethnic groups—Irishman, blacks, and Jews—were especially drawn to the ring because of their lowly social and economic status and because it offered a chance to compete against Englishmen on an equal footing.[25] Prize fighting was thus part of a hybrid culture that appealed to the highest and the lowest in the English social structure, combined some of the ancient recreations brought from the countryside with new sports and games, and fitted them all into emergent patterns of commercialization and industrial rhythms of work.

The ring was above all a focus for cultural conflict that arose from the new economic and social order. Evangelical religion and capitalist forms of business organization—and here I refer not simply to the rise of factories but to the specialization of labor, concentrating productive resources in ever fewer hands—militated against the free-and-easy cultural style that prize fighting represented. For the prosperous bourgeois and the dissenting preacher, the ascendant ethos of productivity, humanitarian reform, steady habits, sober self-control, accumulation of property, and devotion to the domestic family seemed as inevitable as sunrise. But the values and power of such new men were a direct threat to the gentry, old aristocrats, wealthy young dandies, professional gamblers, the urban underworld, and a large segment of the working class.[26]

The flowering of pugilism was a cultural statement opposing efforts by the middle class to reshape the world in its own image. Every prize fight addressed this conflict, asserting the importance of grand display and passional excess over the more restrained new mores. With a shared dramatization of values, the ring momentarily unified great men and small. "There is something peculiarly exhilarating in a boxing match," wrote the editor of a journal entitled *The Fancy.* "The rich man forgets his pride, the poor his modesty before his betters,—equality reigns triumphant for the day, and with perfect good nature, 'Lords hustle with jockeys,' and exchange jokes, and laugh at the rude, yet often witty remarks of the lowly train.'' Such a leveling was only temporary, of course, and by keeping the lines of patron and patronized clear, the rites of the ring ultimately reinforced hierarchy. Still, for an instant, the mighty and the humble spoke each other's language, shared each other's joys. Every match defied the law of 1750 banning boxing and gave testimony, however tenuous, to the influence of the old ruling class, to the loyalty of those who received their largesse, and to the unity of great men and small in quest of the pleasures of the fancy life. It was precisely because the aristocracy legitimated prize fighting with their support that Lord Byron and John Keats, William Hogarth and George Cruikshank, could risk offending the middle class by giving to boxing an artistic expression.[27]

Even champions of labor, who often appropriated abstemious values as tools of working-class pride, were attracted to the culture of the ring. William Cobbett, perhaps labor's greatest spokesman, penned his ''Defense of Pugilism'' in 1805. Cobbett declared that boxing was the safest way for men to settle differences while upholding their honor. More important, he grounded his case in republican ideology, a set of beliefs quite compatible with defense of workingmen's rights. Cobbett, like so many other English writers, feared that his nation might slide from liberty into slavery, that prosperity would degenerate into opulence, then luxury, effeminacy, cowardice, and finally foreign domination. Thus the supreme republican ideal—productive labor for free and autonomous men—contained seeds of its own destruction. England had already reached the stage of effeminacy, but such sports as boxing might help stop the decline. Prize fights dramatized manliness and self-esteem, traits essential to the advance of workers. Decades after Cobbett wrote his article, militant labor newspapers still carried news of the ring. Despite some misgivings that wild sports were a kind of opiate to oppressed workers, many radicals maintained both their political ideals and their love of old leisure traditions.[28]

Support from diverse social groups notwithstanding, bare-knuckle fighting's golden age lasted little more than a generation. Just when boxing was being hailed as the national sport whose lessons helped English armies prevail, it began to decline. Great matches continued to occur in coming decades, and many men still found in the ring an expression of their sensibility. But after about 1825 purses grew smaller and crowds more furtive. Prize fighting was driven underground, never again to enjoy the open support of influential men which had protected it in earlier years.[29]

The reasons were many and complex. In 1824 John Jackson, who did so much to set a gentlemanly tone and encourage aristocratic patronage, closed the doors of his academy. Shortly after the ''Commander in Chief'' retired, the Pugilistic Club disbanded, forcing individual fighters once again to secure their own patrons. This became increasingly difficult to do because suspicion had been building that many boxers were throwing matches. The doubts raised by fixed fights not only undermined men's loyalties, they jeopardized gambling, one of the sport's main attractions. The very intimation that a boxer, bribed by professional gamblers, might throw a bout, subverted the fancy's confidence that fights truly represented the best efforts by the best men and that one could wager on a pugilist and be certain of his integrity.[30]

But these were superficial reasons for the ring's decline, symptoms as much as causes. Boxing was one of many sports altered or swept aside as English society evolved. A renewed evangelical crusade, obsessed with man's sinfulness and his ability to choose salvation, demanded strict piety and renounced all of the old pleasures of the flesh. The middle class in particular found confirmation of its outlook in militant Christianity's zeal to reform men and women. The bourgeoisie—owners of productive property, especially new businesses and industries based on capital investment, intensive division of labor, and expansion of markets—was coming into its own early in the nineteenth century, and as its assets and power grew, it sought to reshape the national culture in its own image. Compared to new, middle-class sources of wealth, the gentry's and aristocracy's material base in land and rents was steadily shrinking in importance. Of course, the middle class never completely imposed its views on the rest of society; indeed, there were important divisions within the bourgeoisie itself. Nevertheless, a new cultural ethos was emerging. A melange of middle-class goals and evangelical ideals—making war on disorderliness, enforcing labor discipline, safeguarding public morality, pursuing humanitarian reforms, and stamping out such irrational behavior as gambling, drinking, swearing, and public bloodletting—now headed the cultural agenda.[31]

The spirit of reform was at full tide by the early nineteenth century, which is another way of saying that middle-class and evangelical values were gaining the upper hand over more traditional views. Men formed organizations, petitioned government, passed laws, and enforced new behaviors. Piety, productivity, and moral earnestness did not square with Corinthian life. As the elite patrons of popular recreations saw their economic power, political control, and social prestige challenged by the bourgeoisie, they began to turn inward as a class and withdraw from public life. Now the old sports themselves were undercut, for where the gentry and aristocracy had seen manly fortitude, healthy paternalism, and a chance for some innocent slumming, the middle class found only depravity and the debasement of the poor. Faith in progress, in an ever brighter future for humankind, was the touchstone of bourgeois thought. Yet atavistic spectacles such as boxing matches symbolically denied the inevitability of progress, displaying instead man's penchant for evil. The old sports and leisure traditions were obstacles to the spirit of improvement because they seemed to encourage an ethos of pleasure for its own sake, of living for the thrill of the moment.[32]

The reformers' weapons included new anti-prize fight laws and strengthened police departments; officials began hounding the sporting fraternity as never before. A definitive sign of this crackdown came in 1824, when local magistrates stopped a fight between Ned Neale and Jem Burns outside London at Moulsey Hurst, long the favorite venue for great bouts. Moreover, the courts now prosecuted fighters, seconds, bottleholders, and even spectators to an unprecedented extent.[33] But it was more than a matter of force alone. The evangelicals and the bourgeoisie were in a position to begin shifting public opinion their way, to articulate their own ideology and have others adopt it. For growing numbers of Englishmen, the pious, benevolent, and liberal outlook became compelling, for it held out the promise of shaping one's own destiny in an era that increasingly subjected men to social forces beyond their control.

The old ruling classes retained considerable influence, but their ability to set the tone of cultural life grew ever weaker. Increasingly, the upper classes retreated into their own exclusive circles because they now lacked the secure superiority that had allowed them to mingle with the lower orders and because birth, not power, was becoming their only way of distinguishing themselves from wealthy parvenus. Many working men continued to enjoy the wild sports of old, but without upper-class support their activities were often stopped by police and local officials intent on enforcing morality, upholding labor discipline and breaking up all riotous gatherings in this era of working-class rebellion. The old recreations were not dead, but lacking protection by powerful men, they were forced underground. Important matches still occurred on occasion, yet no longer could it be claimed with accuracy that prize fighting was the national sport of England.[34]

Crib and Molineaux had squared off at a propitious moment. Their bouts would have been great ones in any era, but the social world in which they occurred made them singular. That world, however, was already crumbling. Although prize fighting would prosper again, it would never be quite the same.

1

Hats in the Ring

"The Tremendous Man of Colour"

If Englishmen were apprehensive as a foreigner attempted to seize their championship, Americans should have been overjoyed by the efforts of Tom Molineaux to humble the old Mother Country. Twisting the British lion's tail was always great sport for the young nation, and symbolic displays of prowess could have proved quite useful as relations between the two countries deteriorated on the eve of the War of 1812. Yet Molineaux's fellow citizens paid him little attention. Descriptions of his fights against Crib, excerpted from English journals, appeared sporadically in the American press. But these second-hand accounts generated a feeble response in America. Even the controversial end of the first match—when, it was alleged by friends of Molineaux, Crib's seconds used underhanded tactics to buy their man precious extra seconds of rest, allowing him to recover and reverse the tide of the fight—received little notice. While tens of thousands of Englishmen could recite Molineaux's exploits, relatively few Americans even knew his name.[1] No doubt word of his deeds circulated orally, but the sparseness of documentary evidence forces us to the conclusion that American interest was neither broad nor deep. Indeed, the most astonishing thing about Tom Molineaux is that we know so little about him.[2]

He was born in either Maryland or Virginia in 1784. According to legend, young Molineaux lived in bondage until he fought his way to freedom. Promising to manumit his servant in exchange for a victory against another slave, Molineaux's master bet heavily on Tom, won his wager, and freed his slave. Unfortunately, no evidence exists to back this charming story. That masters had slaves fight each other is a common motif in Afro-American and white southern folklore, and such fights probably did take place. William Faulkner included a variation on the theme in *Absalom! Absalom!* However, there is no substantial proof that the practice was widespread. Except for white rough-and-tumble fighting, boxing was known but not particularly popular in the pre–Civil War South.[3] Even brutal masters recognized the need to protect their investments, and in the name of productivity slaveowners generally discouraged violence among their bondsmen. Promoting fights would have undermined the very discipline they sought to bolster. Perhaps, as the legend goes, Tom Molineaux came from a line of fighting Molineaux men, a family of slaves who battled their way to freedom. But the evidence fails to uphold these claims.[4]

Whether born a slave or not, Molineaux was a free man by the opening years of the nineteenth century. Like many other free blacks, he decided that the city offered life's best opportunities, and as he reached his twentieth year, he migrated to New York. There Tom hauled and lifted as a porter and dock worker, earning a living while adding muscle to his solid frame. He probably engaged in informal, surreptitious boxing matches with fellow laborers and British seamen. By 1809 Molineaux was sufficiently confident of his abilities that he sailed for England with hopes of attaining pugilistic fame.[5]

Shortly after arriving, Molineaux sought out Bill Richmond, another ambitious and talented free black American. Richmond, born on Staten Island in 1763, had somehow come to the attention of General the Earl Percy, later the duke of Northumberland, who made him his servant. At the beginning of the American Revolution, both returned to England, where Percy secured for his charge an apprenticeship to a cabinetmaker. Richmond eventually worked as a journeyman in his trade, but along the way he learned to box and soon began displaying his skills in regular ring battles. He was quite successful as a prize fighter, winning numerous bouts with a unique style of quick blows followed by defensive retreat. With his earnings from the ring, Richmond opened a tavern in London, the Horse and Dolphin, where he served the fancy and trained hundreds of young men in pugilistic science. A quiet, dignified individual, Richmond gained from boxing a status and security not readily available to free blacks in America.[6]

Although almost fifty years old, he was still an active prize fighter when young Tom set foot in the Horse and Dolphin. The two men were temperamentally dissimilar, but the veteran saw in Molineaux the strength and skill necessary to challenge for the title. They formed an alliance: Richmond became Tom's manager, trainer, patron, and second. He also tried to shield young Molineaux from the dangers of the sporting life.

With his size and speed, the novice easily defeated his first two opponents, setting up the battles with Crib. But his fall, as we have seen, was as meteoric as his rise. The two black Americans drifted apart as Molineaux failed to learn his mentor's steady ways and business acumen. Richmond could only watch as the fancy life of the English ring leached his protégé's magnificent physique. The "tremendous man of colour," as Egan called Molineaux, fought a few more battles and gave sparring exhibitions, until the dissipations of the sporting underworld destroyed his health. He died penniless in Dublin at the age of thirty-eight.[7]

Virtually all we know about Molineaux comes from English sources. Either because of hostility, or more likely because of indifference, the American press paid little attention to the young hero. Even the first history of prize fighting published in the United States, the *American Fistiana* of 1849, failed to mention Molineaux's name.[8] His fame in England and obscurity at home give testimony to the state of American prize fighting during the early years of the century. Transplanting the manly art to American soil was no simple matter. Until the proper conditions developed, boxing was socially and culturally meaningless on these shores, and so it went largely ignored. Only very slowly would Americans infuse the ring with significance.

First Blood

Scattered references to boxing appeared in America during the eighteenth century. In 1733 the *Boston Gazette* reprinted a few matter-of-fact lines about an English fight, perhaps the first and certainly one of very few references to the ring across the entire colonial era: "On Monday last a Boxing Match was fought on the Bowling Green at Harrow on the Hill, between John Faulconer of Brentford, Carpenter, and Bob Russell, who keeps an Alehouse at Paddington. . . ." No comment appeared with this item.[9] A generation later two English soldiers garrisoned at Castle William in Massachusetts engaged in a bout to settle an alleged affront. One of the men died from the beating, and a jury of inquest decided that his opponent must be committed for trial. No doubt similar matches occurred without so tragic a result. Perhaps some Americans even began to emulate English soldiers and sailors. But such incidents remained uncommon.[10]

Years, even decades, still separated news stories on pugilism, and little evidence suggests that boxing existed as part of an underground culture. English fighters were prospering and had every reason to remain at home. International turbulence disrupted migration to America from the Revolution through the War of 1812, and even when the flow resumed, the former colonials deprecated all things English, envying the old Mother Country's power while despising her social life. Brutal, riotous, patronized by effete aristocrats and debased urban rabble, boxing symbolized the corruptions that a virtuous republic must avoid. Moreover, material conditions were not yet ripe for transplanting pugilism. Labor remained scarce and well-compensated in America, and prize fighting depended on an underclass of unattached men who had little to lose by entering the ring.[11]

As the eighteenth century became the nineteenth, however, the pace of pugilistic events quickened. A French émigré, Moreau de St. Méry, fled his country's Revolution and settled in Philadelphia, where he recorded his observations of American life. St. Méry included the following description of a bout from the 1790s:

> Boxing has its rules and regulations. The two athletes settle on a site for the fight. They strip to their shirts, and roll up their sleeves to the elbows. Then at a given signal they run at each other and swing on chest, head, face and bellies, blows whose noise can only be realized by those who have been present at such spectacles.
>
> At each new clash, they draw back, and start again from the mark. If one of the two has fallen in one of these attacks, his adversary cannot touch him as long as he is on the ground; but if he makes the slightest movement to get up, the other has the right to hit him again and force him to remain on the ground. Nobody interferes to separate the combatants: a ring is made around them, and the spectators urge on their favorites.

Clearly the fighters recognized some rules, but the apparent absence of rounds, seconds, and defensive techniques makes it equally obvious that the Philadelphians' battles did not faithfully replicate the English ring under Broughton's code. St. Méry concluded his remarks with a graphic description of the bout's outcome:

> At the end of the fight the boxers are bruised, disfigured, and covered with blood, which they spit out, vomit out, or drip from the nose. Teeth are broken, eyes are swollen and shut, and sometimes sight is completely obliterated. Boxing matches are always held in the later evening, by the light of the moon, unless the participants belong to the lowest orders, or are drunk, in which case they fight in broad daylight where any one can see.[12]

St. Méry's observations are important for several reasons. Although he attributed these bouts to quarrelsomeness, it is clear that the fights were staged for the enjoyment of spectators as much as for the honor of the combatants. There was a strong element of ceremony here. The men agreed where they would fight ahead of time, stripped in a certain way, came up to the scratch, began with an agreed signal, refrained from hitting each other while down. They fought without interference, and the spectators formed a human ring from which to cheer and wager. If not exactly models of pugilistic decorum (hitting a man trying to rise was a clear violation of Broughton's rules) the battles were structured affairs. They occurred often enough for St. Méry to generalize about their timing. No doubt most bouts were held at night because boxing already had an unsavory reputation, and perhaps the cover of darkness protected participants from the constabulary. Nevertheless, St. Méry's cryptic remark about drunks and the lowest social orders indicates that some respectable people were also involved, although just how respectable— artisans, laborers, perhaps the gentry—is impossible to say. Above all, St. Méry's account is the most substantial early evidence of boxing taking root on American soil. He described not simply brawls occasioned by inebriation or quarrelsomeness but the beginning of fistfighting as ritualized, rule-bound, repeatable spectacles.[13]

Two decades later an 1816 fight between Jacob Hyer and Tom Beasley marked a new watershed. With the War of 1812 settled, English merchant seamen were again welcome in American ports. Their pugnacious example apparently inspired Americans Beasley and Hyer— respectively a mariner and a butcher—to settle a quarrel with a stand-up fight. The encounter was not a regular prize battle since no stake money was involved, but the two men did attempt to observe Broughton's rules. Unfortunately, the bout degenerated into a brawl. Hyer broke his arm, Beasley was badly beaten, and mutual friends intervened, declaring the contest a draw. The Hyer-Beasley match was not the first ring fight in this country, as *American Fistiana* would claim, nor was it the first match at which spectators were welcome. Rather, its significance lay in the *perception* that it was a historic event worth recording, in its being the earliest American fight kept alive as living memory of a heroic past. When men gathered at New York's Empire Club decades later, they recounted this battle time and again. By sharing memories of early fights, boxing aficionados established standards for comparison across generations; Hyer and Beasley were important precisely because they were remembered as founding fathers. Indeed, the sense of historical continuity transcended mere memory, for Jacob Hyer passed his pugilistic talents on to his son Tom, who became one of the great champions of the nineteenth century, setting an American precedent for fistic families.[14]

Another milestone was reached in 1823 when the first full newspaper coverage of an American fight appeared in the *New York Evening Post*:

> On Tuesday the 8th July, at half past 6 P.M. being near the Ferry at Grand Street, I observed a large number of men, women and children collecting, and like others, I followed to Gardner's wharf, at the upper end of Cherry Street, where I saw a large ring forming, and on enquiry found a lad about 18 years old, a butcher, and a man whom they called the champion of Hickory Street, both stripped, and each had a second. After the proper arrangements, the seconds drew back a little, and the word was given for battle.

A round-by-round description followed. The fight lasted forty minutes, during which the young butcher showed the "boldness and courage of a bulldog," "strutting around the ring like a game-cock," until he finished his opponent in the eighth round.[15]

Here was the beginning of a literary convention, the assertion by the reporter that he chanced upon the bout; already boxing was held in such low regard that editors apologized for covering it. The *Post*'s article confirmed the presence of formal trappings: umpires, a roped ring, prearranged signals for commencing hostilities. The fighters and seconds adhered to rules limiting the violence against an injured man, while spectators backed their favorites with loud cheers and new wagers as the odds changed with the ebb and flow of the fight. Although previous American battles must have involved monetary stakes, the $200 purse provides the first incontrovertible evidence of a regular American "prize" fight.[16]

But much more than just money was at risk here. The reference to the "champion of Hickory Street" indicates that boxers were already becoming neighborhood heroes. There were nationalistic overtones as well. On Independence Day, just before the match, the butcher had quarreled with a foreigner and beat him severely. Accused of foul play by his antagonist's countrymen—probably Irish immigrants—the butcher challenged any one of them to a regular prize fight, and the bout described by the *Post* was the result. The ethnic community raised the money, chose a representative, and brought the match off inside four days, making the fight a comparatively spontaneous affair. The principals engaged in no extensive prefight training, while convenient times, locations, and rules were settled on quickly. Above all, this and similar battles grew out of particular, local circumstances, and the motives behind them were a melange of financial incentives, personal honor, neighborhood pride, and ethnic antagonisms.[17]

Unfortunately, crucial information is missing from the *Post*'s account. We will never know how the two hundred dollars were raised (in 1823 the amount approached the average man's income for one year). Perhaps some well-to-do patrons helped stake the fighters, but such men of means were more likely gamblers than bankers. The money probably came from a broadly based subscription collected in neighborhood taverns and shops. In addition, the social identities of the "men, women, and children" attending the fight, the frequency of such encounters, even the names of the principals and seconds, all remain lost to history.[18]

Nevertheless, the manly art acquired its own practitioners, traditions, and fans. No doubt more ring activities took place than the surviving record indicates; some editors probably censored boxing news as morally corrupting. Yet the sketchiness of documentation also reflects the nature of early pugilism, for fights remained local and sporadic, arising spontaneously from real conflicts. Boxing was becoming part of an oral culture based on powerful community ties, and it was slowly being woven into the texture of lower-class male street life. But all of these trends were embryonic. Through the first quarter of the nineteenth century most Americans were unaware that boxing matches even took place in their country.[19]

The most important fights of the 1820s were the two battles between Ned Hammond, formerly of Dublin, and George Kensett, an immigrant from Liverpool. Neither was a big man, each standing about five feet, six inches tall and weighing one hundred fifty pounds. Their first fight took place on October 14, 1824. The participants pitched the ring on Coney Island, only to be chased away at bayonet point by infantry under the sheriff of Kings County. They reconvened at Jamaica, Queens:

> Round 1—the men came up cautiously and in good style. A hit from Hammond which drew the claret from Kensett's mug. After some counter-hitting they closed. Kensett down. . . .
> Round 11—Kensett quite groggy—a jaw-cracker from Hammond. Hits, "like angel visits, few and far between"—a close; both down—quite tame. . . .
> Round 27—Kensett still weaker, and still obstinate. Much hitting: a struggle at the ropes, and Kensett down. A blow from Hammond being adjudged foul, concluded the fight, most unexpectedly in favor of Kensett.

The breezy style of the newspaper coverage offered at least a pale reflection of English sporting life, and the author clearly knew the work of Pierce Egan. Nonetheless, the fight proved disappointing, for Kensett was a good hitter yet a poor defensive boxer while Hammond's "nerve, hardiness, and bottom" failed to compensate for his lack of aggressiveness.[20]

Hammond's backers fumed over the outcome believing that the fight had been fixed. Bickering lasted two years, and friends of the principals arranged the first known rematch in American prize fight history to clear up accusations of foul play. They drew up regular articles of agreement, a custom borrowed from the English ring. Despite the fact that magistrates and judges prosecuted boxers under laws against assault, mayhem, and riot, and that prize fighting was universally regarded as an illegal activity, these articles were contracts, signed by the principals, seconds, and witnesses, setting forth in legalistic detail the terms of the bout. In this particular case, the parties agreed to fight for five hundred dollars a side, to pitch their ring within fifty miles of New York, and to allow the usual half-minute rest between rounds. The articles also specified a date for the contest, named a stakeholder, and directed each party to charter a steamboat. On fight day all went smoothly, with careful regard to proper forms. The sporting crowd arrived safely, umpires were appointed, and the seconds placed side bets. The fighters toed the scratch, shook hands, and awaited the call of "Time." Thousands of dollars in wagers, it appeared, would be settled within an established framework of customs, rules, and conventions.[21]

Yet the forms that men established for a fair fight failed to contain their passions. According to the report, Hammond could barely rise from his bottleholder's knee for the seventh round, but his opponent appeared fresh as when the fight began. While Hammond reeled, his second, James Sanford—who fought under the ring name "The American Phenomenon"—ran to referee Patrick Burns claiming that Kensett had defaulted by falling without a blow in the previous round. Although it was a specious charge, Burns agreed and awarded the fight to Hammond. Supporters of the winner then broke into the ring and "set up a yell equal to the most savage tribe of Indians—bearing Hammond away from the ground, calling him victor, and this outrageous turbulence was continued into the very streets of New York."[22]

Despite the breakdown of pugilistic etiquette, the Hammond-Kensett battles were archetypes for bouts of the next two decades. Coverage of these contests was unusually detailed, revealing the rituals and ceremonies that now clustered around the ring. By the 1830s round-by-round newspaper reports, combining disclaimers of support for the prize ring with detailed accounts written in the slang of insiders, became common-place, especially with the publication of gentlemen's sporting magazines such as *Porter's Spirit of the Times* and penny dailies for the urban working class, chiefly the *New York Herald*. New customs appeared, such as the taking of battle colors—painted handkerchiefs tied around the fighters' waists and on the post in each man's corner, the winner seizing the loser's colors as a trophy. Flipping a coin for choice of side quickly became the rule, as did the fighters' habit of throwing their hats into the ring as they approached. Articles of Agreement, specifying stakes, forfeits, dates, locations, seconds, and other details now governed most bouts. And the amount of time separating the signing of articles from the fights themselves lengthened to accommodate larger crowds, higher stakes, and stricter training.[23]

Perhaps most significant, the Hammond-Kensett fights replicated in microcosm the long-standing enmity between Irish and English. "Ould Ireland forever," cheered one hackney coachman. "Down with the English . . . Hurrah for the Irish," his comrades chimed in. But when Kensett delivered some good blows, it was "Well done Liverpool" from the Anglophiles. Once the Napoleonic period and the War of 1812 ended, thousands of immigrants poured into American cities. Fights like Hammond and Kensett's re-created a familiar cultural pattern for the new arrivals, as many of Britain's most intense prize battles pitted Englishmen against Irishmen. Ethnic conflict sometimes became so hot, however, that ring violence spilled over into the crowd. The inability of Hammond and Kensett to finish a fight without charges of fraud being raised set an enduring American precedent.[24]

English and Irish pugilists migrated to the United States in part because growing immigrant communities provided ready-made bases of support. More important, boxers were pushed out of the Old World as much as pulled to the New. As we have seen, from the late 1820s onward England's climate was inhospitable to prize fighting, causing a few first-rate boxers, among them James "Deaf" Burke, to journey to America. Burke succeeded Jem Ward as champion of England in 1832 and defended his title against Harry Macone and Simon Byrne of Ireland. Unfortunately, Byrne died as a result of their ninety-eight-round, three-hour-and-sixteen-minute battle. Burke was acquitted of homicide, and other fighters had weathered similar troubles in the past, but England's chilling moral climate made things difficult for him. Over the next three years he was unable to find an acceptable match; his backers gone, the "Deaf Un's" fighting skills found no outlet. Rather than give up the ring, he came to the United States in 1836.[25]

James "Deaf" Burke, champion of England, 1832–39. When Simon Byrne died at his hands in 1833, the champion sailed for America, where he prolonged his career and helped transplant the ring.

The trip to America added a few years to Burke's career. His broad provincial dialect and colorful phrasings—he referred to America as "Yankeeshire"—made him a curiosity. In sparring exhibitions the champion's quickness and strength allowed him easily to dispose of such American pugilists as Jim Phelan and Abe Vanderzee. For a while Burke toured with Sam O'Rourke, who had migrated from Ireland to America earlier. In 1837 the two agreed to transfer their talents from the sparring stage to the prize ring.[26]

For their battle they chose New Orleans, a town whose large Irish population adopted O'Rourke as a hero. Handbills posted in taverns and on street corners helped whip up excitement. By one o'clock on May 9 a large crowd had gathered at the forks of the Bayou Road to witness the contest. The fight went well until the middle of the third round, when O'Rourke's second approached Burke, and suspecting foul play, the Deaf 'Un struck him. At this the crowd broke the ring, and a free-for-all began. Some claimed that the O'Rourke party intended to give Burke a thrashing all along, by fair means or by foul. Crowds of Irishmen armed with whips, sticks, shillelaghs, and dray pins, pursued Burke, who escaped with a horse and Bowie knife. But his flight did not end matters. O'Rourke's friends returned to New Orleans, drawing their champion through the streets in a wagon. Enflamed by ethnic hatreds, frustrated by hard economic times, and drunk on cheap liquor, partisans of the two men battled throughout the afternoon. The mobs beat several individuals, numerous arrests failed to quell the "wild spirit of anarchy and confusion," and the mayor finally called out the militia to restore order.[27]

Burke made his way back to New York, where friends honored him with appearances in theaters and clubs. Before returning to England in 1838, he engaged in one more prize fight, and in contrast to the New Orleans debacle, the Burke-O'Connell battle of August 21, 1837 was an orderly affair. Backed by local sporting men, the fighters signed articles and went into training. Exercise, beef, and brown bread made up their daily regimen, and according to the *New York Herald,* both men joined voluntary temperance societies. Three hundred members of the fancy came from as far away as Albany and Baltimore, paid five dollars each for steamboat tickets, packed the vessel at the Catherine Street dock, and headed for Hart's Island, a few miles up Long Island Sound.[28]

Once on the ground the participants went through the traditional pugilistic customs. Sentries and scouts watched for the constabulary, a twenty-four-foot ring was formed, and outside it another ring kept spectators at bay. As challenger, O'Connell threw in his hat first, then entered the magic circle with printer Abraham Vanderzee and distiller Alexander Hamilton. Burke followed with his seconds, butcher Jake Somerendyke and carpenter Bill Hatfield. Each side then selected an umpire, and the umpires chose a referee. As the rules specified during the bare-knuckle era, all three stood outside the ropes, the umpires pled their cause when they believed a foul had been committed, and the referee rendered a final decision. Next the principals stripped and revealed themselves to the crowd. Finally the two shook hands and began.

From the very beginning the fight belonged to Burke. He punched and wrestled O'Connell down for ten bloody rounds. Finally Burke declared to O'Connell's seconds: "I wish to fight honorable—I will not strike him—Does your man fight any more?" With this the battle ended. Aside from the one-sidedness of the contest, everything went remarkably smoothly. The umpires asked for and received order from the crowd during the fight, and, concluded the *Spirit of the Times,* "those who conducted the affair deserve all the praise. Not the slightest disturbances of any kind took place. It was what the prize ring ought to be—an exhibition of manly and courageous contest."[29]

The Burke-O'Rourke and Burke-O'Connell fights were the extremes of pugilistic behavior. Unfortunately, the disorderliness of the former was more the rule than the exception. According to *American Fistiana,* many, probably most fights of this era ended with the ring broken and spectators fighting one another. Matches were informal, paying haphazard attention to rules and customs. The modern practice of strictly dividing audience from performer applied only tenuously, while a combination of drink, wagers, and ethnic loyalties caused men to defend their opinions passionately, often making participants of spectators.[30]

Early bare-knuckle fighting was very much a folk recreation. Hammond, Kensett, Burke, and O'Rourke—all immigrants—were probably the only boxers in America during the 1820s and 1830s who attempted to make a living mainly through prize battles and sparring matches. Most men who entered the ring never fought more than one or two bouts, and city directories reveal that pugilists engaged in a variety of preindustrial trades. Bill Harrington was a butcher, Bill Hatfield a carpenter, John McLain a driver, Robert Flannagan a blacksmith, Thomas Hooper a shoemaker, Abe Venderzee a printer, Jim Phelan a grocer, Jim Bevins a carter, Bill Madden a porter. Even those who participated as seconds, umpires, and promoters were intimately tied to local communities and markets: filer Patrick Burns, for example, grocer Peter G. Hart, and tavern keepers Manny Kelly, Jack Benjamin, Randall Smith, and Andrew McLean.[31]

But a large group of early fighters cannot be traced in city directories at all. More often of Irish than English or American ancestry, these individuals were part of a growing urban population cast adrift by increasing labor specialization and the rise of national markets, unskilled laborers who moved frequently in search of work. Compounding its fugitive nature, prize fighting, along with several other popular recreations, was supported by an underground economy of gamblers, hustlers, sportsmen, and most important, saloon owners, who took the lead in sponsoring matches. If men of higher status—whether from the old gentry, urban professions, or the budding manufacturing elite—patronized the ring, I find no record of it.[32]

What cannot be emphasized too strongly is that into the 1840s American prize fighting remained a local phenomenon, largely ethnic, decidedly working-class and traditional in origins. Because Irish and English ancestries were so important—that is, *boxing* did not immigrate, *boxers* did—pugilism thrived where ethnic communities were largest, in New York and Philadelphia and, to a lesser degree, Boston, Baltimore, and New Orleans. Matches were more structured and rule-bound than street fights, but both grew out of genuine personal enmities; public spectacles and private quarrels became indistinguishable.[33] Placing bets and contributing stake money were not merely profit-and-loss decisions, moreover, but expressions of individual, neighborhood, and ethnic loyalties. Commercialization was not yet pervasive, and the boundary separating daily life from sport—a special realm set off from mundane concerns, containing its own unique goals and rules of conduct—remained ambiguous. Our sharp contemporary distinctions between leisure and work, participant and spectator, the "real world" and the realm of play are socially constructed ideas, products of a highly rationalized society, modern ideas alien to other times and places.[34]

Early heroes battled for stakes ranging from a few dollars to five hundred dollars a side, and their individual animosities readily merged with local conflicts. After James Sanford lost to Andrew McLane in 1832, for example, he enlisted Bill "Liverhead" Harrington to take on his conqueror. Philadelphian McLane and New Yorker Harrington were each heroes in their respective towns, and although their fight originated in a personal dispute, some interpreted it as a contest for urban superiority. Passions ran so high that the fight ended in a free-for-all. Again and again social divisions cut too deep to allow fair stand-up battles. Pat O'Donnell and Jim O'Hagan fought outside Newark, New Jersey, in 1832 for one hundred dollars a side, "but the excitement was so great that all the rules of the ring were ignored and a general row ensued, lasting the entire afternoon." Jem Reed and "Long Tom" Burrett fought at Hart's Island in 1835, and their battle quickly became an excuse for universal mayhem. By the late thirties, even sparring matches were occasionally ending in melees, because boxing was infused with the larger social antagonisms of the urban lower class.[35]

In tracing early prize-fighting history with such detail, I do not mean to overemphasize the place of the ring in the national consciousness. American boxer Andrew McLane wrote a letter in 1832 to former English champion Jack Langan, the "Brave Irish Lad." McLane assured his colleague that "in the Eastern States boxing is now in much practice," that a man like Langan could "make a good thing of it in America," that English fighters "would be received with great respect in our Yankee towns." McLane listed America's "pugilistic corps," all of whom were residents of Baltimore, Philadelphia, and New York. No doubt he missed some, but McLane mentioned only fifteen names, a rather small figure given the fact that hundreds, perhaps thousands of Englishmen had boxed for prize money during the past decade. "Our early missionaries and converts," *American Fistiana* concluded about these early years, "might almost be considered as members of some secret society, and had to meet in 'caves,' or some such 'back slums' of society."[36]

But a foundation had been laid. Men in key cities were familiar with boxing customs, knew the special slang of the English ring, and were acquainted with rules of a fair, stand-up fight. A small pugilistic fraternity had been born within America's urban working class. Boxers exhibited together and seconded each other, while ring promoters— mostly tavern keepers and gamblers—arranged matches, officiated, and nurtured oral traditions centered on heroic encounters of the past. And in a separate auspicious development, sparring masters began teaching the manly art of self-defense to fashionable men of American cities.

Professors of Pugilism

Prize fighting was not the only incarnation of American boxing at this early date. Sparring—in which combatants wore gloves, endeavored to show their mastery of pugilistic "science," but did not attempt to win a purse or to hurt each other—grew up alongside the prize ring. Sparring masters exhibited their skills on stage and gave boxing lessons in private gymnasiums. Although the same men who taught "scientific" pugilism sometimes fought professional battles, participants in these two forms of boxing were not precisely the same. Unlike prize fighters, "professors of pugilism" gained a toehold of respectability.[37]

As it had done in the England of Fig and Broughton, sparring entered America cloaked in the mantle of swordsmanship. Under the title "Fencing," the following advertisement appeared in the elite *Columbian Sentinel* on February 10, 1798: "G. L. Barrett informs the gentlemen of Boston, that he proposes teaching the elegant accomplishment of FENC-ING, on the following terms: Entrance, 3 dolls, every 8 lessons 5 dolls. . . . Mr. Barrett likewise teaches the Scientific and manly art of BOXING, on the above terms. Exactly according to the attitudes of either Humphries or Mendoza." Here boxing clearly took a back seat to fencing. By early in the new century, advertisements for schools such as Barrett's appeared more frequently. In 1815 an English immigrant offered his services:

SELF-DEFENSE
At the request of several gentleman of Philadelphia, Mr. GRAY will for a short time teach the following arts scientifically, viz:
PUGILISTIC SCIENCE; SWORD AND CANE EXERCISES,
And all the other exercises necessary to the defence of gentlemen who may at times accidentally be subjected to the consequences resulting from the ungovernable passions of man.

Gray's notice contained two significant departures: he placed boxing ahead of sword exercise, and he was less concerned with "elegant accomplishment," in Barrett's aristocratic phrase, than with self-defense.[38]

Soon fencing was subordinate to boxing throughout northern cities, and the need for gentlemen to defend themselves from unprovoked attacks was sounded again and again. Some sparring masters explicitly sought an elite clientele. Boxing lessons were healthful for individuals in sedentary—respectable—occupations, "opening the chest, strengthening the arms, and adding strength to the valetudinarians." Moreover, pugilistic skills obviated dueling: "Every generous heart must acknowledge the art of self-defense as a necessary branch of useful education," the *National Intelligencer* of Washington declared, because "it must greatly tend to lessen the frequency of duelling." Pugilistic arms were a humane alternative to firearms.[39]

By the second quarter of the century several sparring masters offered their services in major East Coast cities. Their efforts coincided with an embryonic health-and-fitness gymnasium movement, allowing the manly art of self-defense to take on some of the dignity of purposeful exercise. Thus James Roper kept two gymnasiums in Philadelphia, and although he taught boxing along with other exercises for many years, he apparently never entered the prize ring. J. Hudson itinerated between Boston and New York to exhibit and give lessons. "Hudson is a capital teacher," the *Spirit of the Times* declared, "entirely respectable in all relations of life, and of gentlemanly manners." John Sheridan kept sparring rooms and ran Boston's "pugilistic club," where in 1836 he taught the manly art to "forty or fifty of the finest" young men in the city. Sheridan's pupils were so pleased with their master that they presented him with a silver pitcher. Sparring with gloves, the *Boston Evening Transcript* declared, offered Sheridan's students an invigorating exercise for mind and body after long sedentary hours of work. All of this represented a major change: "We remember that some few years since, a gentleman who possessed any skill in pugilism or was known to be the pupil of an instructor in the science, was noted down as a turbulent fellow, fit only for low tavern rows, or drunken encounters. But times have changed, or at least public sentiment has. It is now admitted, that a gentleman may 'know how to use his fists,' and not be less a gentleman. . . ." The editor concluded that, thanks to Sheridan, "pugilist" and "ruffian" were no longer synonymous.[40]

Others disagreed. Although professors of pugilism endeavored to keep their profession honorable, many Americans still regarded any form of boxing as a debased activity. The *Telescope,* a nonsectarian evangelical newspaper, rejected the distinction between sparring and fighting pitched battles. The former led to the latter, because amateurs either became prize fighters or patronized the ring. "Is it not evident that such shameful and inhuman practices lay the foundation of vice, licentiousness and murder?" All involved were "guilty equally in the eye of the law and reason, and should be held in disgrace by all honest and moral men." Similarly, "An Old Citizen" praised the editor of the *New York Evening Post* for refusing to cover an 1826 fight, taking the side of "truth, morality and virtue" over that of "the interested, the ignorant and the profligate." He saw an inherent connection between teaching sparring, giving glove exhibitions, and fighting for a prize:

I certainly hope that the corporation of this city will interpose to take their licenses from those houses where this brutal art is nightly taught. A taste for the practice threatens, if not speedily discouraged, to gain ground among us, and stages may ere long be erected in our city, where the eyes of our citizens may be regaled by the spectacle of men murdering each other according to art. The boxing match of which you refused to publish the account, took place on Thanksgiving day; the next step will probably be to introduce this refined and humane amusement on Sundays.

Sparring schools taught the rabble new forms of brutality, and "gentlemen" who wasted their time on such activities reinforced republican fears of an English-style aristocratic class eating away at the substance of a virtuous and Christian nation.[41]

The connection was not just in the minds of critics. Despite the efforts of such men as Sheridan, Hudson, and Roper to dissociate scientific sparring from prize fighting, other pugilists practiced all facets of the manly art. Ring fighters—George Kensett, Ned Hammond, James Sanford— itinerated from city to city, exhibiting and giving lessons. Among the very first men in this country to try making a living with nothing but their fists, they earned their money wherever they could. In 1824, for example, Sanford fought a prize battle against Bill Hatfield at Elizabeth Point, New York; a year later he kept a sparring school with George Kensett in Baltimore; in 1826 Sanford gave lessons in Boston with Hammond's assistance; then he moved south again for a new round of exhibitions.[42]

Sparring matches on the urban stage bridged boxing lessons and regular prize fighting. While not all-out battles, exhibitions contained important elements of display and competition. For fifty cents—about half the daily wage of a laborer—individuals witnessed a few three-round bouts, ostensibly insulated from the prize ring's worst excesses: "G. Kensett begs leave to inform the gentlemen of Georgetown and Washington that he intends giving a display of the art of SELF DE-FENCE. . . ." Despite the genteel tone of advertisements like Kensett's, however, prize fighting's image of brutality and riotousness always threatened the tenuous status of both sparring lessons and exhibitions.[43]

This tension was best revealed in the career of William Fuller, the most prominent sparring master of his era. Born and raised in Norfolk, England, young Fuller was apprenticed as a copperplate printer. His pugilistic genealogy drew him toward the ring, for men on both sides of his family boxed, refereed, and seconded bouts. He grew intimate with several heroes of the English fancy, including Jack Slack, Tom Crib, and Bill Richmond, who was one of the Norfolkman's teachers. Fuller developed into a good prize fighter, never champion but always well respected. In 1814, after Molineaux's second defeat at the hands of Crib, Fuller fought a two-round battle against the American black that lasted over an hour. Molineaux won, but it was the intensity and duration of the fight which attracted attention. As a display of skill and stamina, Pierce Egan believed, this battle was "without parallel."[44]

Within a few years Fuller moved to France, where he became clerk of the race course, keeper of a billiard room, and master of an elegant sparring school at Valenciennes. Egan attributed Fuller's success not only to his business acumen and fluency in French but to his demeanor as well: "From his appropriate deportment, his hotel is much frequented both by French and English gentlemen; and many of the former, it appears, have been induced to have a trial (*à la Anglaise*) with the gloves." It remains unclear why Fuller, with his apparent success in England and France, emigrated to America in 1824. What can be said with certainty is that he arrived with credentials as a fine prize fighter, a master of scientific sparring, a successful businessman, and a gentleman in the style of the English ring.[45]

That Fuller attempted to maintain his stature is indicated by his posing twice in 1824 for the eminent Dublin-born artist Charles Cromwell Ingham. Such luminaries as the marquis de Lafayette and New York governor DeWitt Clinton sat for Ingham, and certainly no equally distinguished artist in America before Thomas Eakins and George Bellows, nearly three-quarters of a century later, deigned to do images of pugilists. In contrast, Old World artists often took boxers as their subjects, and even Tom Molineaux was reproduced in paintings, engravings, and statuary by men as well known as George Cruikshank, Douglass Guest, and Théodore Géricault. No doubt Ingham's roots in Ireland, where fighters were renowned heroes, influenced his decision to paint a boxer. But Fuller's image as a gentleman—some called him the "Jackson of America," a reference to "Gentleman" John Jackson, former champion of England, friend of Lord Byron, and sparring master of the aristocracy—no doubt attracted Ingham's attention.[46]

For a few years during the late 1820s Fuller traveled from city to city between Charleston and Montreal, staying long enough in each to give lessons, exhibit his skills on stage, and appear in the theater. His thespian efforts were confined to Pierce Egan's popular *Life in London*, described by the newspapers as "The Extravaganza Burletta of Fun, Frolic, Fashion and Flash." Fuller played the roles of both John Jackson and Tom Crib, exhibiting the manly art of self-defense to large and appreciative audiences. Though tame by modern standards, *Life in London* was risqué in its day, a Regency Era panorama of fashionable young men slumming in the dives and back alleys of London. Individuals who identified with the characters of Tom and Jerry—the well-to-do

Sparring master William Fuller, 1824. Artist Charles Cromwell Ingham here portrayed the "professor of pugilism" in the ring, but Fuller soon renounced prize fighting for gentlemanly sparring. Courtesy of the Print Collection, The New York Public Library, Astor, Lenox and Tilden Foundations.

gentry, not strict moralists but young gentlemen with ragged edges who came from the old upper class rather than the rising bourgeoisie—were likely candidates to drop in at Fuller's sparring rooms.[47]

After his first half-dozen years in America, Fuller settled into a stable routine. He published a primer on gymnastics, built a gymnasium, and for his remaining two decades made New York City his home. He continued to advertise himself in the most gentlemanly tones and added fencing, gymnastics, quoits, and bowling to the activities taught at his establishment. The sparring master's status reached its peak when the son of former mayor Philip Hone allegedly saved his own life by fending off a gang of toughs with techniques he had learned at Fuller's gym. Significantly, the elder Hone staunchly opposed prize fighting yet allowed his son to take sparring lessons. Here Fuller also drew the line. He fought only one ring battle in America, shortly after he emigrated. Once he opened his New York sparring rooms, however, Fuller avoided such encounters and was careful to declare that he had no intention of introducing prize fighting to America.[48]

Fuller's efforts to distance himself from the ring paid off. Even editors who refused to publish bare-knuckle news noted his "careful demeanor" and "modest conduct," and pointed out the "respectability" of his pupils. Thus the *Charleston Mercury* condemned prize fighting for brutalizing men but recommended Fuller's sparring lessons: "We hope that the young gentlemen of this city will avail themselves of the present opportunity to acquire a knowledge of Pugilism, and afford that encouragement to Mr. Fuller which his conduct, since he has been amongst us, so much deserves."[49] Similarly, Gabriel Furman, a Brooklyn lawyer, municipal court judge, state senator, and Whig candidate for lieutenant governor, condemned prize fighting as "barbarous" and "sanguinary" but praised Fuller's gym for being "conducted in such a manner as to give the public no reason to complain of its existence as an evil." He noted that Fuller refused to make a public spectacle of his establishment, discreetly covering all of the windows facing the street. Here was boxing in its most refined state, taking its place beside other health-giving gymnastic exercises.[50]

Pugilism under Fuller's auspices could even alleviate violence. In an open letter to a New York newspaper a visitor from Virginia praised the sparring master's "gentlemanly deportment and agreeable manners." Fuller had converted a skeptic:

The writer entertained strong prejudices against Pugilism, and believed, like many others, it had a tendency not only to foment quarrels, but to create a turbulent disposition. Since visiting Mr. Fuller's school, and witnessing the good humour and urbanity of the pupils, and the polite attention of their teacher, he cheerfully recants his former opinions; and feels no hesitation in saying that the science, if encouraged, will have a strong tendency to eradicate a disgusting system of fighting, unfortunately very prevalent in this state.

Dueling, no doubt, was that "disgusting system of fighting," yet the author of this letter appealed to precisely those values which undergirded the code duello: proper manners, gentlemanly deportment, a sense of honor, and antipathy to personal affronts. Boxing lessons allowed a man to "support his dignity, repel insult, resist attack, and defend his rights from aggression." Some individuals could therefore imagine pugilism— once purged of bloodlust, filthy lucre, and the unwashed rabble—as the moral equivalent of dueling, the ring as a new field of honor.[51]

More than anyone else, Fuller was able to maneuver around the stigma that confined boxing to society's least privileged groups. He deliberately appealed to the urban elite, advertising that his New York gymnasium would preserve the health of sportsmen returning from the country. He offered to show letters written by doctors endorsing his regimen of sparring and gymnastics. He claimed that leading citizens, including clergymen, enrolled in his program. Above all Fuller, along with his partisans and colleagues, argued that a scientific knowledge of boxing techniques allowed a gentleman to chastise the "insolent," repel the assaults of "ruffians," and defend himself from "blackguards."[52]

These, of course, were code words of class prejudice; *insolent* and *ruffian* referred to social inferiors who did not know their place. The growing notion that gentlemen must now prepare to protect themselves was based on fear of the burgeoning urban masses. It is uncertain whether crime actually spread as the household economy, with its paternal system of rights and obligations between master and apprentice, declined. What is clear, however, is that individuals were increasingly cast as independent agents—employees—into urban markets. As the old artisan system broke down and men exchanged their labor for cash wages in an impersonal national economy, at least the perception that crime and violence threatened respectable citizens grew in intensity.[53]

Robert Waln, a self-styled Philadelphia aristocrat, made these points clear. Waln rejoiced in 1820 that the "savage pleasures of public pugilism" did not yet disgrace Philadelphia. He rejected arguments that bloodsports offered models of gallantry and courage, insisting that they merely indulged depraved tastes for violence. Worse, the ring "elevates the coal-heaver, the publican, the porter or the negro—who happens to possess muscular strength, large bones, and a thick skull—into the society of rank and fashion.'' Prize fighting broke down class barriers, allowing a tavern keeper or a black man, Crib or Molineaux, to mingle with the aristocracy. Sparring, on the other hand, helped maintain social distinctions. ''In all civilized societies,'' Waln reasoned, ''an aristocracy must and will exist, either founded on letters, family or fortune.'' American demagogues who denied this truth unleashed the insolence of the lower orders. Sparring lessons, however, would help the upper class keep hack drivers, wood sawyers, carters, and draymen in their place: ''Tobacco-smoke would not be puffed in the faces of our ladies at every corner, nor white silk stockings jostled into gutters, by every athletic and malicious porter. The aristocracy of fashion and gentility would be more clearly recognised, and the farce of relative republican equality cease to ornament every ragged vagabond with the same attributes as a gentleman.''[54]

Clearly, men like Waln dreaded the masses and, equally clearly, they sensed that political and social power were eluding their grasp. The success of Fuller and other sparring masters was due at least in part to fears that the social transformation of American cities was subtly changing class relationships, that inferiors no longer respected their betters, and that gentlemen must learn to protect themselves against ruffians. The rise of boxing schools signaled new anxieties that a dangerous underclass now threatened social order.

In sum, sparring's early associations with fencing, the appeal to individuals traveling abroad, the suggestion that the gloves replace dueling pistols, the genteel deportment of the professors of pugilism, the notion that gentlemen must develop their ability to chastise their inferiors all helped sparring teachers establish a tiny bastion of respectability within the world of boxing. But we must be precise about the nature of this respectability. Professors of pugilism were not wholly successful in convincing Americans of the utility or morality of their craft; there were never more than a handful of boxing schools in America at any time before the Civil War. And given sparring's ties to the English aristocracy, men like Fuller evoked fears of an effete upper class drawing men away from republican simplicity toward fashionable decadence.

For it was indeed fashionable young men—the kind who might enjoy seeing Pierce Egan's *Life in London*, frequent the country for field sports, read the *Spirit of the Times*, and worry about attacks on their honor—who were most likely to enroll at gymnasiums like Fuller's. In future decades boxing lessons and sparring matches attracted a growing working-class clientele, but for now several professors of pugilism catered to a self-declared elite that cultivated an aristocratic style. Unlike the English sporting crowd, however, few of America's gentry crossed the border into open slumming. Insecurities over the lack of fixed and entitled upper-class status—Robert Waln was a perfect example—made elite amusements insular and inward-looking, while republican, evangelical, and bourgeois ideologies tempered the gentry's ways. American sportsmen drew the line at particularly wild and violent amusements. Thus sparring exhibitions and boxing lessons offered a sanitized version of pugilism, retaining some of prize fighting's elemental excitement without the taint of lower-class life.[55]

The story of the early sparring masters provides an excellent example of how class divisions increasingly manifested themselves in nineteenth-century popular culture. Particular styles of entertainment appealed to distinct social groups.[56] More antiseptic than gory prize fights but not exactly a deacon's ideal of moral amusement, sparring was a fine compromise for an insecure gentry. Later, as the middle class grew more open to new forms of leisure, boxing lessons and exhibitions became a half-way house to prize fighting. Indeed, the restrained form of pugilism taught by Fuller and his kind, emphasizing blows with neatly gloved fists, eventually found its enthronement in the marquis of Queensberry rules. This code, adopted late in the century for amateur and then professional boxing, gloved prize fighting itself with newfound respectability.[57]

Ideology and the Ring

Because most partisans of the ring were not highly literate, they rarely penned justifications for their sport. Still, a few defenders of boxing came forth. The author of the only surviving description of the second Hammond-Kensett fight vented his rage against society's moral guardians:

In giving the history of a contest or combat between two men, I am aware of the risk I run of offending the feelings of many a canting, whining swindler and fastidious hypocrite, who will shake the head of disapprobation at the name of a fight, and fleece you at the same instant. I know I shall commit great violence upon these shadows of morality, who so much infest the world, who have the impudence to hold themselves up as our judges and superiors, entitling themselves to great respect—constantly assuming a solemn gravity before the world, to cover their own ignorance or crafty designs; who condemn in others what they practice without scruple.

Particularly striking is the vehemence of the attack, especially the charge that the moralists were at once impudent for holding themselves superior to others and hypocritical because solemnity masked their greed. That these "shadows of morality" were "swindlers"—men "without scruple" who would "fleece you" with their "crafty designs"—underscored the author's assumption that moral arrogance went hand-in-hand with sharp business practices, that lofty pretensions and crass money-getting were of a piece.[58]

Supporters of pugilism believed that their sport offered alternatives to petty acquisitiveness. In 1806 Englishman R. Payne Knight's "Eulogy of Boxing and Cock Fighting" appeared in the *Literary Magazine* and articulated the viewpoint of the British gentry for Americans. Knight denied that violence alone rendered bloodsports interesting. Lovers of cockfighting or bullbaiting took no pleasure in seeing livestock butchered in slaughterhouses, any more than men of the fancy enjoyed watching bloody mismatches. Only violence in the context of fair combat afforded genuine displays of fortitude and honor. The prize ring's scenes of valor were a credit to England, a source of pride, not shame, for all citizens.[59]

Knight argued that suppression of English matches by magistrates with the mistaken notion of preserving the peace threatened "an end to that sense of honour and spirit of gallantry, which distinguishes the common people of that country from that of all others; and which is not only the best guardian of their morals, but perhaps the only security now left either for their civil liberty or political independence." Boxing promoted patriotism as well as a national ethos of courage and fair play. If men were prevented from fighting for prizes or honorary distinctions, they would use daggers to settle quarrels. In the end, "the lower order will become a base rabble of cowards and assassins, ready at any time to sacrifice the higher to the avarice and ambition of a foreign tyrant."[60]

It is difficult to take seriously Knight's fear that boxing matches were all that stood between England and foreign domination. Nevertheless, his essay was one of the earliest published in America supporting pugilism. He rejected sharp distinctions between fighting for a prize and fighting to settle a disagreement; the two were bound together, each serving as a model for the other. Knight made no apology for the passions displayed in the ring, arguing that they were fundamental to man. Rather than deny these passions, boxing and similar sports taught individuals how to channel them. The ability to accept violence yet place limits on it, to order mayhem with rules and a spirit of gallantry, was the true measure of a civilization and the surest bulwark of freedom. Most important, the prize ring was not only a source of entertainment for the lowly, but also, in this age of revolutions, a school where they acquired the etiquette and decorum of their betters, where they imbibed the concept of fair play, and where they learned to identify with rather than reject the upper class. Thus both paternalism and self-interest compelled the elite to promote sports among the lower orders. Sharing the old aristocratic values of honor, gallantry, and courage did not erase social distinctions but maintained a spirit of mutuality among classes.[61]

Knight's aristocratic perspective was unusual in America, though gentlemen's publications occasionally reaffirmed his ideas. The *New York Sporting Magazine,* for example, reprinted a letter to the editor of *Bell's Life in London* which declared that the "noble art" set a "manly" tone both for rich boys in boarding schools and for the working class, combating effeminacy and preparing men to defend their country. An article reprinted in the *American Turf Register* declared that the ring had no room for bullies and braggarts, because the best boxers were the coolest, most self-possessed, least quarrelsome individuals. By the 1830s William T. Porter's *Spirit of the Times* could argue that prize fighting had redeeming virtues: "There is a feeling of courage—of proud, manly self-dependence, accompanying the champion of the ring, that otherwise would not be elicited. The manly stand-up fight is surely far preferable to the insidious knife—the ruffianly gang system—or the cowardly and brutal practice of biting, kicking or gouging now so prevalent." But such comments were rare, and editors reversed themselves at the first signs of criticism.[62]

In the early years of the American ring, then, only a hint of upper-class support appeared. A small coterie of men who identified with the cultural style of the English gentry defended popular recreations, occasionally even boxing. The *Spirit of the Times* was the most vocal organ of this group, which included landed gentlemen, north and south, as well as heirs to urban mercantile wealth. Editor William T. Porter tried to capture the ethos of English leisured gentlemen who pursued age-old recreations, especially field sports and horse racing. Such men embraced personal honor, competitive prowess, and conviviality as transcendent values. They rejected the perfectionism of reformers and assumed that strife was sown in man's nature. Though boxing was only a minor and controversial sport in their canon, at least a few individuals openly approved of prize fighting's rejection of piety and diligence. It would not be surprising to find that some of these gentlemen attended or even patronized the ring. But without an independent aristocracy, the American upper class was much more cautious than its English counterpart in partaking of raucous sporting life. Little evidence actually exists of gentry patronage for prize fighting, and most gentlemen, if they cared at all, were probably satisfied reading about English fights or slinking off to an occasional sparring match. The majority no doubt agreed with Robert Waln, that the ring was for the rabble and that the elite should keep its distance.[63]

Indeed, there was powerful opposition to prize fighting within the gentry. Republicanism's greatest champion, Thomas Jefferson, was one of the earliest critical voices. A young American who goes to England for his education, Jefferson declared, "learns drinking, horse racing and boxing." Worse, "he acquires a fondness for European luxury and dissipation, and a contempt for the simplicity of his own country. . . . He is led by the strongest of human passions, into a spirit of female intrigue . . . or a passion for whores, destructive of his health, and in both cases learns to consider fidelity to the marriage bed as an ungentlemanly practice." Here Jefferson placed sports in a broad ideological context. "Luxury,""dissipation," and "simplicity" were charged words in the lexicon of republicanism. Aristocratic societies bred self-indulgent practices such as drinking, gambling, and whoring; men of inherited wealth set an example of debauchery that corrupted the lower classes. A republic based upon the spirit of mutuality among informed and productive citizens could not survive such behavior. Farmers and mechanics, tempted by visions of luxury, abandoned simplicity to pursue personal aggrandizement. Once the waste and purposelessness of wild sports entered a republic, they grew like cancers, destroying that self-restrained virtue, that sense of communal welfare, which alone allowed freedom to prosper.[64]

Editors, reformers, and clergymen of the solid middle class concurred with Jefferson. Before prize fighting even became established in America, a few men were voicing their opposition to it. In 1790 the editor of the *Massachusetts Sentinel* revealed his mortification at finding a description of a prize fight rather than something truly important under the headline "By Express" in an English paper. That two noblemen acted as umpires and that 100,000 guineas were wagered on the contest particularly piqued him. Such incidents confirmed American accusations that aristocratic corruption rotted all of English society. Agreeing that such spectacles must never corrupt a republic of virtuous farmers and tradesmen, the influential *Gazette of the United States* reprinted the *Sentinel*'s editorial.[65]

Other American journals soon joined the chorus, reissuing antiboxing articles from English sources. An essay reprinted in the *New York Magazine,* for example, argued that human intelligence would inevitably obviate violence, including wars and revolutions. While the author acknowledged the need for martial courage to secure peace in a turbulent age, he denied that boxing bred valor. In good Enlightenment fashion he cited classical authors—Solon, Xenophon, Galen, Euripides—to show that ancient boxers came from the most vile social classes in Greece and made the worst soldiers. Brutality, cowardice, and greed were the fruits of pugilism:

> If we did not know some who are generous and courageous who through habit and carelessness of conduct attend these fights, we should pronounce against the possibility of such virtues enhabiting the bosoms of those who can be diverted by seeing two naked men hammering each other, till their faces and bodies are covered with blood and contusions: the pertinacity of the man who is knocked down as fast as he can rise, gives us rather a proof of his baseness than of his courage, and should disgust every reasonable man; for he is animated to act this brutal part, from a desire of satisfying the connoisseurs, of whom he is to receive the wages of sin.

The corrupting influence of money, the callousness of those who paid to witness such events, the debasement of men who accepted remuneration for brutalizing each other, the carelessness of good citizens who failed to put an end to such displays, all delayed the advance of human progress.[66]

Similarly, "On Pugilism," reprinted in the *Literary Magazine and American Register* in 1806, posited a hierarchy of recreations based on levels of civilization—art and music for the refined, bloodsports for the vulgar. Prize fighting elicited "nothing but brutality, ferociousness, and cowardess [*sic*]," tended to "debase the mind, deaden the feelings and extinguish every spark of benevolence." Boxing was only slightly less violent than daggers or dueling pistols, and this was not good enough: "The force of laws, as well as the persuasion, example, and influence of all the good should be vigorously exerted to outroot every kind of violence, all contests of brute force and lawless passions, among the members of human society." The belief that violence could be completely expunged represented a long stride toward romantic faith in human perfectibility. For these early critics, prize fighting's offense was its denial of mankind's moral progress. Even before boxing really existed in America, then, republican ideology, with its suspicions of all things licentious and immoderate, gave men a frame of reference with which to judge the ring.[67]

By the 1820s a new criticism appeared. Even worse than bloodlust, prize fighting had social consequences that continued long after bouts ended. According to the *New York Spectator,* boxing encouraged insubordination: "And what will become of the morals of the rising generation— our apprentices, youth from school, servants, male and female, if they have opportunity to mingle in these scenes of riot, brutality, and systematic violations of order and decency, where customs must be acquired which will not bear repetition?" Here was a crucial problem. Boxing not only destroyed republican simplicity and betrayed the nobility of human nature, it was socially disruptive. The early nineteenth century witnessed the beginnings of wrenching transformations in family roles and productive relationships. If the proliferation of urban working-class recreations such as prize fighting were not really causing social insubordination, they were a symptom of change. Apprentices, servants, youths—increasingly all were freed from customary obligations in the new wage-labor market, all grew ever less respectful of rank and title in this democratic age, and all turned to raucous sports and pastimes as the old moral economy broke down. Staging their own recreations offered working-class Americans an alternative source of values, one that the middle class feared because it encouraged pride and independence. Engaged in its own wild pleasures, the lower class seemed volatile, dangerous, and out of control.[68]

As ring traditions grew ritualized, so did press condemnations. The criticisms contained a strong element of hypocrisy: "In the name of decency let us not imitate the manners of the old world. . . ." This off his chest, the editor of the *New York Evening Post* published a round-by-round report of a bout.[69] Such disclaimers preceding eyewitness accounts became typical by the 1840s. But the antiboxing rhetoric was not all sham. Editors struggled with their consciences to lead the public toward virtue. That newspapers must be guardians of morality was axiomatic inside and outside publishing circles. Commenting on an 1832 fight that took place in Delaware, noting that thousands of spectators had attended, the editor of a Baltimore newspaper declared "the condemnation of such a breach of decency and morals, as in this brutal exhibition, should not be left to public opinion." Both legal authorities and molders of public sentiment had a responsibility to curb these outrages.[70]

Not only conscience, however, but profits shaped editorial decisions. By the 1830s many Americans desired news of prize fighting and were willing to purchase papers that carried it. Their dollars were powerful incentives to bend genteel morality, so that practicality and idealism fought each other for editorial attention. Here, in the very early stages of commercialized leisure, the markets' insistence on profitability conflicted with ideological strictures. The result was decades of indecision, some newspapers publishing fight news one year, righteously refusing to do so the next.[71]

Even the working-class press and the upper-class sporting magazines wavered. The *New York Herald,* for example, was the most successful penny daily of the era, appealing to the new urban masses by mocking bourgeois and evangelical tastes with lurid stories about disasters, atrocities, and corruption in high places. Although the *Herald* was one of the most reliable sources of boxing news before the Civil War, editor James Gordon Bennett still felt the need to issue disclaimers with boxing stories.[72] More revealing still, *Spirit of the Times* editor William T. Porter vacillated wildly. For its first half-year his journal contained a regular column giving scraps of news on English and American matches. Then Porter suddenly declared, "we have today evinced our respect to the 'public voice' by expunging the 'Sports of the Ring' from our columns. . . . The kind admonitions of our friends instruct us that we may have mistaken 'the taste of an American Public.' "[73]

The *Spirit of the Times* continued covering news of sports, fashion, and the theater, but Porter was persuaded that prize fighting was beyond the pale. A letter from the journal's Liverpool correspondent explained why pugilism endangered public morality:

> If you knew what a curse the prize ring has been; how low—how brutalizing—how dreadful in its effects, you would exult as I do, that this fashionable curse has abated in England, and that its taint is little known in America. Had I an enemy whom I wished to ruin, body and soul, I would ask no more than to turn him out into the company of pugilists and their clique, and the matter would be effected without delay. . . . Ten years ago, the pugilistic corps, in London, amounted to as many as 500 to 1000. Of these, there was scarcely one who was not a depraved character: scarcely one who was not "cock of the walk" in some public house. There he ruled the roost, and bragging of the delights of "The Fancy," innoculated callous apprentices and journeyman artisans with a thirst for such polite accomplishments. Ten to one that the pugilist was also a pickpocket or a burglar; if so, the ruffian could and did make converts, when and how he pleased, to his more secret and more nefarious calling.

The ring brutalized taste, bred crime, demoralized laborers, and corrupted youth. More pernicious than horse racing or the theater, it had no place in a virtuous nation.

The very next year, however, the *Spirit of the Times* published a full account of the Burke-O'Connell fight, with a long apologia explaining the value of pugilistic science. Although Porter continued to issue exculpations, his journal regularly carried boxing stories in succeeding decades. Yet because American prize fighting was so totally associated with the urban lower class, and because Porter's readership identified with the English landed gentry, the *Spirit of the Times* gave much more attention to British bouts, with their clinging if faded bits of aristocratic glory, than to American ones.[74]

Soon short stories appeared with the anti-prize fight message. In 1838 the *New Yorker* carried a fictional account of a young country lad taking on a celebrated pugilist in order to save his mother's home from foreclosure. "Nothing is more disgusting," the narrator assured his readers, "than the description of a prize fight, where the most dreadful disfigurement and injuries done by man to man in a cool deliberate manner for the sake of lucre, are if possible, made worse by being recounted in a slang phrase and systematic form to minister to the worst appetite of the depraved." Through sheer tenacity, the lad knocked his opponent insensible, but not before receiving mortal blows. With dying breath, he urged the onlookers to bring the prize money to his mother. The woman lost her mind when she learned her son's fate.[75]

Similarly, "The Boxer," which appeared in the *Spirit of the Times* and *Atkinson's Casket,* depicted prize fighters as barbarians. Here a rough-neck broke his ankle when lightning frightened his horse. The drunken bully cursed, threatened his wife, and browbeat the physicians attending him. "Such a foul mouthed ruffian I never encountered anywhere," his doctor declared. "It seemed as though he was possessed of a devil. What a contrast to the sweet speechless sufferer who I had left at home! and to whom my heart yearned to return." The glimpse of domestic bliss underscored the frenzied violence of the boxer's drunken oaths:

... a flash of lightning gleamed ruddily over him. "There it is!—Curse it—just the sort of flash that frightened my horse—d—— it!"—and the impious wretch shook his fist and grinned horribly a ghastly smile!

"Be silent sir! be silent! or we will both leave you instantly. Your behavior is impious! It is frightful to witness! Forbear, lest the vengeance of God descend upon you!"

"Come, come: none of your d—— methodism here! Go on with your business! Stick to your shop."

With that, another bolt of lightning—the "wrathful fire of Heaven" —filled the room and blinded the sinner.[76]

In so many ways, then, prize fighting threatened deeply held ideals. Why would responsible individuals punch each other senseless and, equally important, why would anyone watch such spectacle? Raucous sports violated central tenets of republican ideology, that world view of the revolutionary era which still moved nineteenth-century Americans. Prize fighting confirmed republican fears that idleness and indulgence had tempted men from the path of selflessness. Rather than acting as autonomous producers who contributed to the general welfare, the sporting crowd threw off all sense of personal restraint, substituting hedonism and luxury for virtue. Indeed, debauched pleasure-seeking seemed symptomatic of the larger social declension afflicting American cities, where greed and opulence now supplanted the old communal spirit of mutuality and simplicity. Boxing matches disgraced all citizens, including otherwise good men who looked away rather than stop these bloody spectacles.[77]

Prize fighting not only fed republican fears, it mocked the more optimistic ideologies ascendant in the early nineteenth century. The ring contradicted romantic assumptions of man's reason triumphing over his passions, of the moral progress of humankind, of a "benevolence empire" spreading over the world. Just when reformers glowed over the perfectibility of human nature and institutions, here was evidence of man's ineradicable rascality; just when evangelicals urged men to choose salvation, the growing sporting fraternity chose sin; just when the middle class saw visions of material progress for all, the fancy was wasting its best energies on crime and brutality. Especially galling was the fact that men fought for money—the "wages of sin"—while others bet on the outcome of bouts. Such behavior perverted the very meaning of wealth. It was bad enough that men gambled away their family's futures and went into debt. But winning money was equally pernicious because instead of denoting virtue, prosperity flowed to those most lucky, treacherous, or brutal. Far from being a reward for hard work, a tool of material progress, or a sign of godliness, money became a symbol of depravity.[78]

Above all, there was a strong class bias in the antiboxing rhetoric. The American middle class might scorn effete English aristocrats but, with or without noble sponsors, the lower class was staging its own sports. The references to the vileness of Greek and Roman boxers, to the baseness of men who fought for lucre, to the vulgarity of the mobs attending fights, all point to a sense of unease with urban masses that remained culturally unconverted in an era which demanded that men stand up and be counted. Members of the fancy were "ignorant and profligate," wasting time and treasure on immediate gratifications rather than channeling their energies toward rational self-improvement. Impulsive, violent men, prize fighters and their ilk scorned sober discourse and productive behavior; they lived to drink and carouse. Worst of all, the ring corrupted the young, turning them away from steady labor and destroying their respect for masters and elders.

In all of these charges the critics were partly right. The prize ring *was* a "magic circle," a "sacred circle." Here a loosening of conventional morality was sanctioned, indeed expected, as men indulged in the irrationality of violence, drink, and gambling. If boxing partisans failed to write extensively about their sport, they spoke a symbolic language through prize-fight rituals which revealed their core values. In a social world grown prosaic with materialist desires and evangelical rigidity, a good fight was a grand display filled with excitement, high drama, and ceremony. The wagering, special slang, tying of colors, appointment of a referee, prefight speeches, and other ritualized practices, all denoted entrance into a unique realm with its own rules and customs.

Most striking was the enjoyment of sheer masculine beauty found in the ring:

> Burke presented an iron frame, in which all superfluous flesh seemed excluded. His broad and extended chest, his outward turned knees, that take off from beauty to add so much to muscular power, his muscular and well knit lower limbs left no doubt in the minds of the spectators that no common skill or bodily strength would be sufficient to overpower or vanquish the possessor. O'Connell stripped to greater advantage than expected. His upper frame is large and muscular, but it wants compactness and tension. His sinews hang loose, and his frame is far from being well banded together.

This description was typical, and it was followed, again typically, by details of the positions each man took in the ring, their thrusts, parries, and wrestling throws. Such loving word portraits of muscles and sinews are particularly surprising in light of the era's renowned delicacy of language.[79]

While their contemporaries sought to deny human animality, ring partisans gloried in man as an aggressive, natural being. Yet love of physicality was counterbalanced by admiration for the cool self-control of the scientific boxer. Of course, the pugilistic world was neither a model of Victorian propriety nor, as critics charged, a locus of pure anarchy. Neither self-restraint nor untrammeled aggressiveness but razor-edged balance beween rules of decorum and violence, a poetic tension between fair play and bloodletting, lay at the heart of boxing's aesthetic appeal.

Ideally, the ring was also a true democracy, in which men succeeded or failed under conditions of perfect equality of opportunity. But as a market place of violence, boxing symbolically mocked the liberal belief that atomistic competition led to social good. After all, bloodied bodies were what the ring "produced." Spectators identified with those boxers who best represented their ethnic group, neighborhood, or trade. Personal toughness, local honor, drunken conviviality, violent display—every bout upheld these powerfully antibourgeois values. Bare-knuckle fighting was thus a transitional phenomenon, incorporating old values and new. The prize ring's form was "modern"—achievement-oriented, meritocratic, egalitarian—but its content "premodern"—ascriptive, nonrational, hierarchical. For men in passage between ways of life, boxing was a symbolic way station.[80]

But if the ring offered brilliant drama and vivid ritual, working-class men still had little power in the dawning Victorian world. From the beginning, prize fighters were prosecuted under laws against riot, mayhem, and assault. By the mid-1830s the influx of New York pugilists into New Jersey prompted the nation's first anti-prize fight legislation. Newark, Hoboken, and Belville had already witnessed battles, and in 1835 Jim Reed and Andrew McLane chose Elizabethtown Point for their encounter. The sheriff appeared and read the Riot Act, but he was powerless to stop the battle.[81] The "brutal and demoralizing exhibition," as the *New Jersey Emporium and True American* called it, incensed the local citizens, and at a public meeting they demanded legislation. One week later another hundred New Yorkers crossed the Hoboken ferry for a new match. Ferry superintendent Van Buskirk ordered the interlopers off the Elysian Fields, so the crowd moved to Weehawken Hill. Just as they were getting ready for the battle, another peace officer arrived and ordered the crowd to disperse. Partisans of both fighters turned on him, and were it not for the arrival of Van Buskirk and his deputies, they might have killed him. Nearly a dozen participants in this "pugilistic riot" were incarcerated in the Hackensack jail.[82]

The incident was too much for the New Jersey legislature. In little more than a month it drafted, debated, and passed laws against the "degrading practice of prize fighting." To aid, abet, or participate in a regular ring contest or even a "test of pugilistic skill"—a sparring match—was now a high misdemeanor, punishable by up to two years' imprisonment and a one-thousand-dollar fine. Steamship owners and captains who allowed their vessels to convey passengers to fights hazarded similar penalties, and even spectators risked a year's incarceration and a two-hundred-dollar fine. "This is a wholesome law," the *New Jersey State Gazette* concluded, "and there is no doubt that the morality of East Jersey will carry it rigidly into execution."[83]

In future years other states would follow New Jersey's lead. But it would be a mistake to read a sudden shift of attitude into these laws. Animosity toward the prize ring developed early and remained strong throughout the era. The new laws were more a culmination than a break with the past, one benchmark among countless others of the ascendance of such values as piety, diligence, and progress in a nation where evangelical religion and the market place were becoming the fonts of ideology. The emergent Victorian ethos, profoundly shaped by Protestant Christianity and capitalism, had a sharper edge, a more brittle quality than the old republican ideals; heady faith in human perfectibility gave reformers little tolerance for moral backsliding. The anti-prize fight laws made amorphous attitudes toward the ring explicit, bolstered magistrates who otherwise resorted to less specific statutes, codified existing attitudes. The laws were never very successful in bringing down the ropes, yet they reflected middle-class faith in clear-cut moral precepts and Victorian impatience with the haphazard ways of the old order.[84]

But laws or no laws, American prize fighting failed to claim a solid base of support among influential men until nearly the end of the century. For this reason, the ring could not have attained the heights that English pugilism reached during the Regency Era. Simply put, America never had a powerful aristocracy to counter the opposition of the middle class. Boxers in the United Kingdom received patronage from great men, and in return the exploits of fighters confirmed the love of the old upper class for valor. The lower and higher orders of society remained sharply divided, but through events like prize fights they momentarily shared a cultural style that cherished pageantry, camaraderie, and masculine feats of daring. The old elite not only enjoyed a little good-natured slumming, it secured the loyalty of the masses with great displays of largesse. For their part, the commoners got support for their sports, protection against evangelical and middle-class meddlers, and flattering attention from the high and mighty.

Yet America had no hereditary aristocracy, no Prince Regent to patronize her champions, no dukes and earls to form a pugilistic club, no lords and peers to frequent the sporting houses and attend matches. Rich American merchants and landed gentlemen might take sparring lessons or read the *Spirit of the Times,* race thoroughbreds or practice field sports, but there they drew the line. Even a rich young frontier hell-raiser like Andrew Jackson—known for his breeding stock of horses and fighting cocks—took care to disavow his wild past once he became a national political figure. Wealthy men of leisure such as John Cox Stevens of New York, Colonel Ransom Johnson of North Carolina, and William Henry Herbert of New Jersey, all of whom loved the conviviality of popular recreations, stopped short of embracing the full panoply of English sports. In other words, the group to which boxing primarily appealed—the new urban working class—was socially isolated.[85]

Not only boxing but all pastimes suffered under these circumstances, so that before 1840 American sports were rather anemic. Occasional horse races, running meets, and sailing regattas attracted considerable attention, but such events were sporadic and crudely organized. The American work ethic, with its roots in republican producer culture, evangelical Christianity, and new capitalist imperatives of growth and profit, impeded the development of all recreations. In his advice manual, William Alcott warned young men to improve every moment of every day, for "he who loses an hour or a minute is the price of that hour debtor to the community." Similarly, the editor of *Nile's Weekly Register* mused after the great 1832 horse race pitting Eclipse against Sir Henry that "few have gained much by it—but many have lost what should have went to the payment of their just debts. . . . The money expended or lost and time wasted . . . is not far short in its value of half the cost of cutting the Erie Canal."[86]

Men who burn for the heavenly city, or the community of virtue, or worldly treasure do not waste their carefully husbanded energy on frivolous pastimes. Sports like boxing would eventually be accommodated to both capitalism and Christianity, but for now the most powerful ideologies in American life barely tolerated "innocent" amusements, let alone the wild ways of the sporting fraternity. After all, half-naked men skillfully pounding each other for cash hardly squared with the spirit of human progress, universal benevolence, and social improvement.

2

The First American Champions

The Rise of "Yankee" Sullivan

Prize fighting continued to carve out its own urban niche, despite the negative social, ideological, and legal climate. Boxing has always brought forth charismatic figures because it places the lone individual at the center of attention. Fighters such as Crib and Molineaux, Hickman and Neate, transformed mere fisticuffs into epic drama. The ring elevates heroes and antiheroes who take their destinies in their own hands, who succeed through sheer will and ability, and whose struggles dramatize the humbler conflicts of us all.

Such a man slipped little noticed into America in 1840. The facts of his early life are fragmentary and contradictory; even his true name is uncertain. Variously called Frank Murray, Francis Murray, Francis Martin, and James Ambrose (probably his true name), to the American public he was always "Yankee" Sullivan. He was born in Banden, near Cork, Ireland, on April 12, 1813; all we know of his youth is that he managed to get into a variety of scrapes, and some of these resulted in the issuing of challenges and the raising of stake money by friends. As his skills became apparent, Ambrose sought sparring matches and regular ring encounters. The young fighter met and defeated journeymen pugilists such as George Sharpless and Tom Brady. He lived at the fringes of Britain's criminal underworld and before his twenty-fifth year was arrested—some accounts say for murder, some say for burglary—and sent to the penal colony at Botany Bay, Australia. Here Ambrose was hired out as a farm laborer, which allowed him to fight a few regular battles with other convicts. He soon stowed away on a ship bound for America, landed in New York, but stayed less than a year.[1]

Seeking a reputation in the London prize ring, Ambrose slipped back into England under the assumed name of Yankee Sullivan. In a characteristic show of nerve the escaped convict published a note in *Bell's Life in London,* challenging any man weighing eleven stone (154 pounds) to meet him for £50 a side. A fine English fighter named Hammer Lane picked up the gauntlet. Sullivan was overmatched in this fight, but by a stroke of luck Lane fractured his right arm in the third round. Nevertheless, Lane came up to scratch sixteen more times, and before his seconds "threw up the sponge"—capitulated—the one-armed fighter severely punished Sullivan. In contrast to Lane's "extraordinary display of British bravery," Sullivan fostered much ill will by deliberately attacking his opponent's injured right limb. Probably fearing rearrest, he returned to America.[2]

Though Sullivan was hardly a shining light in the English ring, his fame as conqueror of Hammer Lane served him well in America. Guided by another immigrant boxer, George Overs, the "Manchester Pet," Sullivan held a few successful sparring benefits and before long was running a saloon in the Bowery. His Sawdust House quickly became a clearinghouse for all pugilistic activities and a resort for working-class men interested in sporting life. Irish immigrants, whose numbers grew steadily during the 1840s were especially attracted to his establishment. According to an anonymous biographer, they "would get together of a Saturday night, in a back room of the Sawdust House, and over their well-filled glasses, would sing and talk of the exploits of the daring Sullivan, who couldn't be beat." Of course, Sullivan's Irish friends hoped that he would duplicate his victory over the English in the United States, and in an era of growing nativism, tests of prowess with American fighters were also eagerly anticipated. Sullivan obliged his friends with a series of bouts.[3]

He fought Englishman Vincent Hammond near Philadelphia on September 7, 1841. Each side put up one hundred dollars, and Sullivan advised his chums to wager all they could on his winning "first blood." But in the early moments of the fight Hammond caught Sullivan with a quick blow, cutting the inside of his mouth. Yankee clinched his lips, sucked in the blood, and delivered a tremendous punch that split Hammond's cheek and sent him reeling to the ground. Sullivan clapped his hands with delight, shouted "first bood," and retired to his corner for the customary thirty seconds' rest. The entire fight lasted eight rounds in ten minutes, and Sullivan's friends left more certain than ever of their man's prowess and cunning.[4]

His victory set off what *American Fistiana* called an explosion of

"Hibernian crowing": "Sullivan was hailed by all sorts of endearing epithets, such as 'Yankee,' 'Sully,' 'Bully,' etc. The largest cities and the largest states seemed not large enough for expressing the delight of Sullivan's enthusiastic admirers." For days fight talk raged like an epidemic. Drunk with excitement and ale, Yankee's friend John McCleester rushed out of Sullivan's saloon, found Tom Hyer—the son of Jacob Hyer and a well-known native-born bruiser in his own right—and challenged him on the spot. They took the Albany steamer north the next day, got off just above New York City, and held an informal battle. McCleester's enthusiasm could not overcome Hyer's three-inch, sixteen-pound advantage; after 101 rounds and almost three exhausting hours of combat, McCleester was convinced by his friend Sullivan to give up and avoid further injury.[5]

The native-born sporting crowd was elated, and now Hyer was seen as the man to humble Yankee Sullivan. But the American refused to fight for less than three thousand dollars a side, far more than Sullivan's backers could raise. Another native with prize-ring pretensions, Tom Secor, was willing to challenge Sullivan for one-tenth of that amount, so on January 24, 1842, five steamers carried about two thousand interested spectators to the New York Narrows. Yankee easily pummeled Secor into submission, though the job took sixty-five rounds spread over one hour. Sullivan not only won the fight, he humiliated his opponent. He peppered Secor's face, then fell to the ground at the slightest blow, ending round after round. Sully taunted and unnerved his antagonist, pointed to his bloody features, made faces, and laughed at him.[6]

The more invincible Sullivan appeared, the more his enemies wanted him beaten. As *American Fistiana* put it, "they cast their eyes round about the pugilistic circle to find a man capable of holding up the honor of the Stars and Stripes against the encroachments of the Green Flag of the Emerald Isle."[7] They settled on William Bell, an English immigrant and sparring master who had been "teaching the good people of Brooklyn how to defend themselves against the 'wily influence'" of foreigners. Each side staked three hundred dollars for a fight to be held on Monday, August 29, 1842.[8]

Heated discussions, heavy wagering, and street fights preceded the bout as the sporting crowd weighed the merits of the two men. Ten steamboats transported at least six thousand spectators to Hart's Island, a favorite pugilistic hideaway about twenty miles north of New York City in Long Island Sound. All proper forms were observed, including the fighters' dress and colors, the presence of seconds, bottleholders, umpires and a referee, the choice of corners, and the roping off of inner and outer rings. In its extensive coverage of the match the *Spirit of the Times* revealed its mixed fascination with the lower class and contempt for the crowd. The steamboats, "with their heaped up masses, rocking to and fro in the stream, looked like some infernal cortege seeking the waters of the Styx, or a savage eruption bursting forth for ravage and for plunder." On the ground, the massive crowd surged forward in anticipation of the battle:

> Four times was a large outer circle made, and as often did the wild and insane savages break it in. For ourselves, in the first struggle, we were fortunate enough to obtain a hold of the rope. . . . At last, with our knees forced devotionally two or three inches in the soil, our shoulders bearing the weight and press of three or four sweaty proximitants [*sic*], with the sun pouring down his fiercest vertical rays upon our uncovered caput, and boiling the effluvia thrown off from the neighboring bodies into a floating lava of most execrable odor, we saw the gladiators enter the ring.[9]

Despite advantages of an inch-and-a-half in height and ten pounds in weight, the courtly Professor Bell lacked prize-ring experience and was no match for the clever Sullivan. Yankee feigned fatigue in the third round, then caught Bell off guard with a sharp blow to the eye. His countrymen shrieked their delight. In the sixth round, Bell had Sullivan in trouble on the ropes. " 'Let me go, Belly' said Sullivan, faintly, as he stood with Bell's arm around his neck . . . 'let me go, Belly; I can stand it no longer; I'm a going to give in.' " When Bell relinquished his grip, Yankee punched him in the ear then threw him heavily. Bell quit after twenty-four rounds lasting thirty-eight minutes. Concluded one reporter, the sparring master fought defensively, but Sullivan controlled the battle because he had an "instinctive love for strife," went in sure of victory, and above all was an "intellectual fighter" who calculated every move.[10]

Yankee was now at the peak of his fighting form, and his Irish supporters spared no efforts to remind the English and native-born sporting crowd of his dominance. Boxing enthusiasm reached unprecedented heights. A new saloon, the Arena, opened on Park Row, and the fancy packed it nightly. The prize ring attracted growing attention from the urban lower class, and Sullivan's prowess gave him the central role in boxing's development. His courage and guile in the face of larger opponents evoked grudging admiration in some, adoration in others, while his unfailing shrewdness was deeply admired by working-class men. A Yankee and a Sullivan, an American and an Irishman, he personified the possibility of acquiring new identities and opportunities without giving up old allegiances. Sullivan was the first in a long line of fighters who symbolically mediated the conflict between American nationalism and immigrant pride. In this sense, fighting style, ethnic affiliation, and personal bravado all reinforced each other.[11]

Of course, the growing popularity of the ring, as evidenced by the Sullivan-Bell fight, elicited renewed criticism. The editor of the *New World* wondered aloud if New York City still had any laws in force and called on magistrates to arrest not only the principals but also newspaper editors who covered the ring. The *New York Morning Express* marveled at the numbers of "loafers and rowdies" who boarded boats for Hart's Island, the even larger crowds that assembled at the landing places when the vessels returned, and the huge public exhibitions honoring the boxers after the battle. Under the headline "Demoralization in New York," the evening edition of the same paper condemned the steamship owners who aided and abetted the band of "ruthless vagabonds" in violating the law. The only good to come of the fight was that most other crime ceased for a day; felons, allegedly, were preoccupied with Sullivan and Bell. For this editor, at least, popular recreation could be explained simply enough as the work of thugs.[12]

But the sporting fraternity was little disturbed by such moralizing. Just two weeks after his fight with Bell, Sullivan sailed north to assist at a fight in Westchester County. He arranged this battle from his saloon and would act as bottleholder for his friend Christopher Lilly against Thomas McCoy. No one guessed the grim result of their encounter.

The Battle of Hastings

Two thousand men came by coach and steamboat to Hastings to witness the fight between Lilly and McCoy. Most were New Yorkers out for a mid-week revel on Tuesday, September 13, 1842. No doubt many of them had attended the Sullivan-Bell fight or sat in at sparring matches, almost weekly affairs now in New York saloons. Indeed, the Lilly-McCoy contest grew out of a quarrel at an exhibition, heightening interest in the bout.[13]

The fight attracted a festive gathering of the fancy. Twelve vessels sailed twenty-five miles up the Hudson, the steamboat *Saratoga* bearing McCoy's party, the *Indiana* serving as Lilly's flagship. In addition to Sullivan acting as bottleholder for the young Englishman, pugilists William Ford and John "Country" McCleester seconded Lilly. McCoy, an Irish boatman, had the aid of two veterans, James Sanford and George Kensett, as well as actor Henry Shanfroid. All the ring regulars were on hand, and at least ten thousand dollars were "up," mostly at even odds. On board the Hastings-bound steamers, McCleester helped promote the festive spirit by tending bar, Kensett earned a few extra dollars making and selling ham sandwiches, and once on the battle-ground saloon keeper Manny Kelly lubricated the crowd with generous draughts of whiskey.[14]

The ring was pitched on a small plateau commanding a panoramic view of the Hudson Valley. Spectators sat or stood behind a second ring, thirty feet from the fighting square, while club-bearing friends of both parties kept them out of the intervening no man's land. Shortly before the battle began, a lone magistrate entered the ring. He was Jaspar J. Golden, resident of Dobbs Ferry and a teacher in the Hastings school district. Unable to raise a posse, he nonetheless left his classroom, walked to the fight scene, boldly strode up to Sullivan, McCleester, and Lilly, and stated his business. Sullivan politely told him to proclaim his desist-and-disperse order. Golden's little speech met with jeers, and the teacher decided, amidst shouts of "Hustle him out," and "Kick him out," that he had done his best and could leave the ring with a clear conscience. Golden stayed to watch the fight, however, not because he wanted to, he later told a jury, but because as a potential prosecution witness, he was compelled to.[15]

With the time approaching one o'clock, the officials tossed a coin for choice of sides. McCoy won. The men stripped—both were in their early twenties and weighed under one hundred-forty pounds—and their physiques revealed the fruits of a full month's training:

[Lilly's] skin was very clear and light in color, but firm in texture and healthy in tone. His form is round almost to perfection; his sides, instead of branching from the waist, gradually outwards to the armpits, circle concavely inwards like reversed crescents; his neck is strong and muscular in a high degree; his head—a fighting one, remarkably well set. . . .

If Lilly's appearance was fine, McCoy's was beautiful. His skin had a warmer glow than the former's; his form was more elegantly proportioned, and his air and style more graceful and manlike. His swelling breast curved out like a cuirass: his shoulders were deep, with a bold curved blade, and the muscular development of the arm large and finely brought out. His head was rather large and long, yet it indicated courage and a love for strife, and the manner in which it was set betokened strength.

The homoerotic quality of this passage, its emphasis on manly beauty, underscores the extent to which prize fighting appealed to a distinctly male sensibility, a masculine aesthetic shared by many working-class men.[16]

Like other recent American fights, this one was held under the new 1838 rules of the London prize ring, a code that explicitly forbade the hair-pulling, head-butting, eye-gouging, gut-kneeing, and neck-throttling tactics too often winked at under Broughton's rules. Equally important, the fight promised an important test of competing styles. McCoy represented the "old school" or body attack method, Lilly the "new school" that stressed punches aimed at the head and neck. Confident in his strategy and abilities, McCoy tied his colors to the ropes, a black handkerchief signifying "victory or death." He then pulled two one-hundred-dollar bank notes from his pocket, crossed over to his antagonist's corner, and wagered it with Lilly at even odds. Principals and seconds, bottleholders and umpires now shook hands all around, the parties returned to their corners, and with the call of "time!" the battle commenced.[17]

In a violent sport the Lilly-McCoy fight stands out. The Irish lad's strategy of going for the body paid off at first. By the fourteenth round his partisans shouted $100 to $60 on their man with no takers. In the fifteenth Lilly was accused of a low blow. The referee agreed, but McCoy's backers confidently waved off the awarded victory and let the fight proceed. They made a fatal mistake. Within another fifteen rounds it became clear that Lilly was the superior hitter, that McCoy was exhausting himself more quickly than his opponent. "Ain't Chris a portrait painter," one exuberant fan declared in the thirty-ninth round, referring to Lilly's work on McCoy's face. The battle was not totally one-sided, for each man landed heavily, and both came gamely up to scratch, but as the fight wore on the ultimate result grew unmistakable:

> Round 70th.—McCoy was now indeed a most unseemly object: both eyes were black—the left one nearly closed, and indeed that whole cheek presented a shocking appearance. His very forehead was black and blue; his lips were swollen to an incredible size, and the blood streamed profusely down his chest. My heart sickened at the sorry sight. When he came up he appeared very weak, and almost gasping for breath, and endeavored, while squaring away, to eject the clotting fluid from his throat.

The scene grew uglier:

> Round 76th.—The sun appeared now to have a painful effect on McCoy's nearly closed optics. The eyelids were so swollen and stiff, with extravasated blood, that he was obliged to throw his head back, and expose his neck to his enemy, to enable him to look through the slight crevice left. . . . It was now perfectly apparent to every one present that poor McCoy had not the slightest chance to worst his cunning and active adversary. Blow after blow came raining in upon him, drawing blood, or threatening death at every stroke, and when he would seek to return, his antagonist would step lightly away, and his blow, wasted upon the trenchant air, had no other effect but that of wasting his strength.[18]

Spectators called for a halt: "Take him away. Don't let him fight any more"; "For God's sake, save his life"; "It's a d——d shame to see a brave man used so." But McCoy came up for every round. Sullivan and Ford in Lilly's corner asked McCoy's seconds to concede and save their man. They refused. McCoy, choking on his own blood and spitting coagulated clots, insisted on continuing. Despite being knocked down eighty times, he told his seconds at the end of one hundred and eighteen rounds, "Nurse—nurse me and I'll whip him yet." He fought one more round, collapsed, and died. A coroner's inquest determined that McCoy's wounds had drained into his lungs, drowning him in his own blood. The battle at Hastings lasted two hours and forty-one minutes. Newspapers reported that a second fight was scheduled, and as McCoy's body was borne back to the river, one man allegedly called out. "Come, carry off your dead, and produce your next man."[19]

This first fatality in the American ring prompted an outburst of rage. Lilly fled to Canada and from there to England. Others were not so lucky. At Mayor Robert Morris's request, the Common Council of New York City authorized bounties for the apprehension of the responsible parties. Suspects were rounded up, and shortly thereafter the grand jury sitting in Westchester County indicted eighteen accessories—ringkeepers bottleholders, seconds, backers, and others—on charges ranging from riot to manslaughter. Most escaped with fines, but George Kensett, John McCleester, and Yankee Sullivan were dealt with more severely. The trial of these three created a sensation. The courthouse and inns at White Plains overflowed daily. The rough urban street fighters and flashily dressed gamblers attending the trial seemed not only incongruous but menacing in this tidy rural township. Wrote one observer, "the appearance of the prisoners, and indeed some of their associates, lurking in the courtroom, or loafing about the village, is strongly marked with ruffianism and the grossest passions." New York dailies sent special reporters to the trial, dispatched their stories by express rider, and kept the public informed with detailed extra editions.[20]

Sullivan, McCleester, and Kensett were tried before five circuit court judges—Justice Charles R. Ruggles presiding—and a jury consisting of eight Westchester farmers, two innkeepers, one carpenter, and a merchant. For a full week the court heard eyewitness testimony by reporters, spectators, and local officials. Defense attorneys minimized their clients' role in the fight, attested to their good characters, and noted their efforts to stop the bout before McCoy's death. But the evidence was overwhelming given Judge Ruggles' charge to the jury.

He pointed out that a homicide resulting from any felony or misdemeanor constituted manslaughter, that a prize fight was an illegal assembly, and that all present at the match, especially participants, were therefore culpable. The tone of his instructions was as important as the substance:

> A prize fight brings together a vast concourse of people; and I believe it is not speaking improperly of such assemblages, to say that the gamblers, and the bullies, and the swearers, and the blacklegs, and the pickpockets and the thieves, and the burglars are there. It brings together a large assemblage of the idle, disorderly, vicious, dissolute people—people who live by violence—people who live by crime—their tastes run that way, and though some respectable people probably were there . . . you can readily perceive the influence which such assemblages are likely to exercise on the public peace, and morals, and taste; and you can therefore estimate correctly the propriety and necessity of that law which forbids their existence. Upon that spot, then, no one can hesitate to say—even had no fatal result ensued—there were collected a body ferocious and demoralized. The assemblage was in itself indictable as an unlawful one.[21]

Gamblers, bullies, pickpockets, and thieves; the idle, disorderly, and dissolute; all came together for a feast of blood which destroyed public peace and morality. "If these be acquitted," Judge Ruggles concluded, "who can be convicted hereafter?" In less than four hours the jury returned three guilty verdicts of fourth-degree manslaughter. Because he organized the fight, Sullivan received the maximum sentence, two years in Ossining prison, but within a few months he obtained a governor's pardon. McCleester was sentenced to eight months in the county jail and fined $500, while Kensett received a four-month, $200 sentence.[22]

McCoy's death confirmed all the old criticisms of boxing and gave new ammunition to prize-ring opponents. George Templeton Strong, scion of a leading New York family and a man devoted to civic betterment, fantasized about exterminating all who attended the fight as they returned to the city: "I only wish I'd had the old Fulton with seven Paixhan guns mounted, loaded with a bushel of grape each, one to rake each steamer as it came up and then one hollow shot for each gun, to sink them one after another. It would have been a great public benefit." Former New York mayor Philip Hone, a patrician man of leisure and no stranger to the racetrack or pedestrian matches, took the occasion of McCoy's death to condemn the ring: "The amusement of prize fighting, the disgrace of which was formerly confined to England . . . has become one of the fashionable abominations of our loafer-ridden city." In his diary Hone contrasted the good citizens who "wept for the shame which they could not prevent" with the "brutal gang of spectators" who relished the fight. The former mayor added that now Lilly would be all the fashion in decadent Old England, where he might associate with corrupt aristocrats and find his portrait engraved in their elegant boxing tomes.[23]

Hone accused the *New York Herald* of encouraging such spectacles, but even the *Herald* momentarily repented for supporting the ring. It circulated a petition of clemency for the convicts on the condition "that no more such scenes are enacted—and that Sullivan and all shall reform hereafter." The *Spirit of the Times* backpedaled faster. "It is well known," William T. Porter declared in the issue following McCoy's death, "that the Editor of this paper has ever discountenanced The Ring and its professors, as such—that he never has attended a Prize Fight; and he would add, moreover, that he had no acquaintance with nor knowledge of any of the individuals referred to, in the report which, with infinite regret, he now subjoins." A long and very detailed description of the fight followed.[24]

Beyond the sporting press, the attack on the ring became a minor crusade, and the reform-minded *New York Tribune* led the way. A contrived interview with McCoy's mother began the campaign: "Oh Sullivan! Sullivan! What have you done!" she sobbed. "You have robbed a poor widow of her darling boy. I told him not to go—I begged him—yes I got down upon my knees on Sunday night before him, and pleaded, 'My son! My son! Do not break the heart of your poor mother—do not go.' "[25] Tom gave his word that this was his last fight. When his coffin was brought home, Mrs. McCoy threw herself on it, frantic with grief: "Oh, Tommy—my son—my beautiful boy—where are you? But Sunday night you was before me so young and beautiful— and where are you now? In this coffin. Come here my children and see your lovely brother." The *Tribune* concluded that Mrs. McCoy held the rival *Herald* responsible for her woes, a happy blend of righteous indignation and good business.[26]

But the tragedy went beyond an old woman left desolate. The death of Tom McCoy was no chance event; it was inevitable, *Tribune* editor Horace Greeley implied, given the kinds of men responsible for the rise of the ring:

> How shall we speak of the getters up and encouragers of this fight?—the gamblers, brothel-masters and keepers of flash groggeries, who were ever the chief patrons of "the ring" and who were the choice spirits of this festival of fiends! They were in raptures as the well-aimed, deadly blows descended heavily upon the face and neck of the doomed victim, transforming the image of God into a livid and loathsome ruin; they yelled with delight as the combatants went down—often on their heads—with a force that made the earth tremble around them—as the blood spurted in rills from the fatal sacrifice. . . .

There is a powerful sense of Satanic evil here, of utter hellishness: a "festival of fiends" "yelled with delight" as the "image of God" was battered into a "loathsome ruin."[27]

Indeed, from a bourgeois or evangelical point of view the violence, revelry, and debauchery truly represented the world turned upside down. The *Tribune*'s rhetoric was filled with a sense of fear and loathing. Prize fighting was but a symbol of "the evils which now afflict and threaten our City. . . ." Civic institutions had failed as guardians of public morality; the press, the police, the steamship companies, all facilitated rather than discouraged such immoral activities. Neither spectators nor participants demonstrated any sense of internal restraint, any outward effort to stop the evil. Personal and social controls had all broken down. Grogshop owners, brothel keepers, "king gamblers"—operators of faro banks and roulette tables—the very dregs of society financed and organized the fight, defying law and morality.[28] A once well-ordered city, weakened by corruption, had fallen to barbarian invaders. Boxers and their hangers-on were not real Americans, according to the *Tribune*, but foreigners steeped in vice. Now, however, the contagion was starting to infect American youths, hardening them into idle, drunken, blood-thirsty ruffians. In a word, McCoy's death kindled new fears of a permanent lower class in the American Eden, of a corrupt, aggressive, and alien underworld poisoning the wellsprings of national virtue. The Lilly-McCoy fight became a metaphor for the degraded mob that threatened to destroy all that virtuous citizens held dear.[29]

The battle of Hastings capped the generation which began with Tom

Molineaux's spectacular rise in England. By the early 1840s substantial numbers of urban working-class men were familiar with boxing customs, read the newspaper coverage of upcoming battles, attended sparring exhibitions and prize fights, discussed the ring in neighborhood saloons, and idolized men like Yankee Sullivan. But boxing's young roots were shallow and easily severed, and the Hastings tragedy temporarily destroyed English-style pugilism in America. Tom McCoy's death made all of the old arguments against prize fighting palpable by highlighting the ring's brutality. Renewed constabulary efforts, stiffened public opinion, chastened newspaper editors, and perhaps feelings of remorse among the fancy effectively destroyed boxing for a few years.

The fate of Charles Freeman testified to pugilism's decline. The "American Giant"—Freeman was about six feet, six inches tall and weighed over two hundred and fifty pounds—had never entered the regular prize ring, yet in 1841 he challenged the English champion, Benjamin Caunt, then touring in Philadelphia, to a sparring match. Before long the two were exhibiting together in American cities, and by the spring of 1842 Caunt had persuaded Freeman to continue their tour in Britain. The English sporting crowd was fascinated with Freeman's size and strength. As the summer waned, Caunt arranged a regular ring fight for Freeman against the veteran pugilist William Perry, the "Tipton Slasher," for one hundred pounds a side.[30]

The nationalistic implications of the battle were lost on neither side. A correspondent for the *Spirit of the Times* reminded Freeman of his patriotic obligations: "Recollect that it is to vindicate her [America's] claims to, at least an equal standing in the sporting world with her great mother, that you have left your own fireside; recollect that every time you strike a blow, every time you take a position, it is to the credit or dishonor of your native land. Let this move your arm, and let every blow be emphatically the blow of a Freeman for free-men!" The English sporting press saw the pending struggle in equally nationalistic terms.[31] Unfortunately, the fight failed to live up to these lofty expectations. Freeman's awkwardness, inexperience, and disinclination to fight aggressively, Perry's constant falling without receiving a blow to compensate for his lack of scientific skills, produced an uninspired bout. Ringside thugs exacting tribute from the fancy did not help matters. In addition, arrangements were so poorly made that the two began fighting just moments before darkness, forcing them to stop then resume the following day. After thirty-seven sloppy rounds in thirty-nine minutes— fighting time averaged half a minute per round—the referee finally disqualified Perry for falling without a blow, giving Freeman the victory.[32]

The American ring community, though still small, had anticipated a good fight; as the *Spirit of the Times* put it, "a great degree of excitement pervades our sporting circles as to the result." Shortly after these words were written, however, Tom McCoy's body was interred in Potter's Field. As a result, Charles Freeman's exploits received little coverage in American newspapers, and prize fighting virtually ceased.[33] But even without the Hastings tragedy, Freeman's fame would have been limited. Boxing was still too new and too controversial to appeal much beyond a segment of the working class. Like Tom Molineaux, the American Giant remained largely unknown to his countrymen. Also like Molineaux, Freeman never returned to America, dying in England of tuberculosis in 1845.[34]

"The Great $10,000 Match between Sullivan and Hyer"

Five years passed before pugilism recovered from Tom McCoy's death. Only a handful of matches occurred, mainly around New Orleans and up the river in the notorious gambling town of Natchez, Mississippi. Many of those not imprisoned as accessories to McCoy's death left New York and stayed away for years.[35]

Still, there were countertrends. Yankee Sullivan opened a new Bowery saloon in 1845 where men could gather and reminisce. A year later Chris Lilly returned to the American ring. The *Spirit of the Times* showed some renewed interest, indexing fight stories for the first time in 1846 and offering its readers a five-volume edition of Pierce Egan's *Boxiana* for fifteen dollars. In 1847 Joe Winrow of Liverpool and Irishman Tom O'Donnell fought a spectacular battle in Natchez that lasted one hundred nineteen rounds, spread over two hours and forty-five minutes. Despite its brutality, readers of the *Spirit of the Times* were assured, the fight, which Winrow won, was greatly preferable to dueling, still in flower in the South: "I have been more shocked and disgusted," special correspondent "Yazoo" wrote, "at a meeting on the 'field of honor,' where gentlemen have shot down their man in the most gentlemanly manner possible. It would not be a bad change for our country, if the influence of these meetings should so diffuse itself as to forever supersede the bowie knife." We cannot know how often fists replaced more deadly weapons, but as the years passed, increasing numbers of men considered it honorable to settle their personal disputes with ring fighting for their model.[36]

As Tom McCoy's name receded from memory, as immigrants, especially the Irish, poured into American cities, and as economic hardships caused by the maturing capitalist economy merged with ethnic conflicts, pugilism found new life. Before the Hastings tragedy roughly half-a-dozen matches were reported each year. By the mid-1850s scores of fights were taking place annually. Moreover, the geographical base of boxing expanded. River men from the Ohio Valley to New Orleans, miners in California, Missouri, Pennsylvania, and Tennessee, and new immigrants in countless towns and cities, all grew familiar with boxing as a way to settle personal quarrels and as a form of entertainment. Above all, a series of spectacular championship fights—Tom Hyer vs. Yankee Sullivan, Yankee Sullivan vs. John Morrissey, John Morrissey vs. John C. Heenan, John C. Heenan vs. Tom Sayers—made boxing America's single most important spectator sport from the late 1840s through the Civil War.[37]

A few years after the Lilly-McCoy affair the resolve of New York State to keep Yankee Sullivan out of the ring weakened, and Sully's desire to fight grew commensurately. Eighteen forty-six found him behind the counter of his public house, assuring patrons in newspaper advertisements that he would be "happy to receive their calls and will endeavor to please and amuse them." Sullivan's saloon remained a gathering spot for those who enjoyed the fancy life: "The Bar is stocked with good liquors, Segars, etc. A Free-and-Easy will be held every Saturday Evening. The Art of Self-Defense taught in a few lessons." But Sullivan could not remain content with this life for long. By early 1847 he began sparring at Johnny Ling's "Sportsman's Hall" and other gathering places of the fancy. He itched to reenter the prize ring and finally found an opportunity.[38]

"Since my arrival in this country," Robert Caunt, brother of former English champion Benjamin Caunt, wrote in an open letter to the *Spirit of the Times*, "I have received numerous challenges from Yankee Sullivan, but have never been able to bring him up to the chalk. . . . If he means business I am already to fight him for one thousand dollars, and if he will not accept this challenge, I hope he will not annoy me anymore with his bounces." Sullivan's backers arranged the fight, and interest boomed in the struggle between Anglo-Saxon and Celt. Englishmen embraced Caunt as their national representative, so large sums of money were wagered overseas as well as in the United States. Native-born Americans had divided loyalties. For some, the very name "Yankee" Sullivan offered a nationalistic alternative to the hated English, but others longed for anyone to defeat the "Irish braggart."[39]

The two fought near Harper's Ferry, Virginia, before seven hundred men on May 11, 1847. Odds of 100 to 40 were offered on Sullivan, and by the second round these were down to 100 to 10. It was, in the slang of the day, a "jug handle fight," with Caunt unable to continue after twelve minutes. But if the match was disappointing it reintroduced large stakes, charismatic personalities, and symbolic ethnic conflict to the ring. James Gordon Bennett of the *Herald* felt public interest warranted the use of express riders between Virginia and New York. Citizens as far away as Milwaukee learned of the outcome in their local papers.[40]

Sullivan's reemergence gratified the sporting fraternity, but even the most ardent member of the fancy could not have predicted the coming explosion of boxing mania. "We do not remember," the *New York Herald* declared only a year and a half after the Sullivan-Caunt fight, "ever to have seen so great an excitement among certain classes of society, as has been developed during the last few days in relation to the approaching prize fight between Yankee Sullivan and Tom Hyer. It is similar in some respects to the agitation produced in the public mind by the first accounts of the Mexican War...." Each side raised five thousand dollars for the "winner take all" struggle. The *National Police Gazette* estimated that three hundred thousand dollars in wagers hinged on the outcome, and for half a year a man could scarcely enter a saloon without being asked his opinion of the two gladiators.[41] Moreover, the upcoming bout aroused interest beyond the usual sporting crowd. One New York paper declared, "all classes of society—the rich and the poor, the high and the low, the elegantly dressed denizens of Wall Street and Park Place—all shades of our heterogeneous society, were as desirous to know the result as the loafers of Chatham Square or the rowdies of the Bowery." The *Police Gazette* agreed that Hyer and Sullivan "occupied a large share of the attention of refined society." Both papers exaggerated, but an increasing number of well-off men did take vicarious pleasure in the fight.[42]

In a narrow sense the Hyer-Sullivan battle of 1849 merely picked up where boxing had ended in 1842, for even then the two were recognized as the best of their day. The social context of American cities, however, was considerably altered. Tensions between immigrants and natives grew with the unprecedented influx from abroad. Over one hundred thousand immigrants entered the country for the first time in 1845, two hundred thousand in 1847, three hundred thousand in 1850. Among these masses the poor of Ireland were overrepresented, for the potato famine and the brutal policies of landlords now squeezed them off the land and sent a wave of unskilled peasants toward America. During the 1830s, two hundred thousand Irish had landed in America; four times that number

James "Yankee" Sullivan and Tom
Hyer dressed as urban dandies.
Both were idols to working-class
men, leaders of political factions,
and heroes of street corner gangs.
Sullivan (left) was an Irish
immigrant, Hyer a native-born
American.

emigrated in each of the next two decades. Forty-five thousand Irish immigrants in 1845 grew to one hundred sixty-four thousand in 1850, and they settled mainly in large Northeastern cities. More than any group, the impoverished Irish bore the wrath of the native born. Terrifying images abounded of lazy peasants, idolatrous Catholic parishioners, and servile masses swearing allegiance to the pope. Worse, nightmarish visions of ignorant laborers providing business with a cheap alternative to American workers deepened the tensions between natives and immigrants.[43]

Even Hyer's occupation—he was a butcher, a task that demanded a powerful physique and a strong stomach—contributed to the intensity of his rivalry with Sullivan. Hyer's trade had been a proud native bastion, with its own symbols, rituals, and organizations. American butchers, Hyer's father Jacob and "Boss" William Harrington among them, had a tradition of entering the ring as upholders of native honor. But in recent years Tammany (for which Sullivan worked) had begun selling licenses to Irish butchers, threatening the native monopoly. Thus the clash between the two boxers was not just a test of physical superiority but a playing out of deep social, cultural, and economic conflicts.[44]

It took Sullivan's backers several weeks to raise the five thousand dollar stakes demanded by "Young America." In the meantime almost daily fights broke out between friends of the two men, as talk of their respective merits filled working-class saloons. Because of his experience and training, Sullivan felt he could defeat Hyer easily, despite large disadvantages in height, weight, and age. Indeed, half-drunk one April evening in 1848, he tried. Yankee entered an oyster bar on the corner of Park Place and Broadway. Whether he knew in advance that Hyer was inside is unclear, but instantly the two were at each other. A few minutes later Hyer had Sullivan in a headlock, and in leisurely fashion he punched the champion insensible.

Now officer George Walling, future New York City chief of police, entered the room:

> There stood Tom Hyer, whom I knew well by sight and reputation, placing a percussion-cap upon the nipple of a pistol which he held in his hand. In one of the boxes was Yankee Sullivan, who looked as if he had been roughly handled. I took in the situation at once.
>
> "Put up that pistol," I said to Hyer, who looked calm and collected enough and with no trace on his person of having been engaged in a fight.
>
> "Who the devil are you?" he asked, in a gruff voice.
>
> "I'm an officer," I replied, exhibiting my star.
>
> "They're going to bring the gang here," said Hyer, in a calm voice;

"and I'm not going to let them murder me without a pretty tough fight for my life."

"Come, get out of this. Come along with me," I said, and Hyer, taking hold of my arm, we left the saloon. Just as soon as we reached the street, Hyer said he thought he would go to the Empire Club, and bidding me good-night, crossed Broadway.

No sooner was he out of sight than a howling mob of Sullivan's friends came rushing toward me. They had heard of Sullivan's discomfiture, and were in search of Hyer, who, if they had caught him, would most assuredly have been murdered. Some of the crowd asked me where Sullivan was, and when I told them where I had last seen him, they made a rush for the oyster saloon. I could plainly hear their yells of rage when they found their friend. Hyer had not left the place a moment too early.

For nearly a week little else was spoken of in Bowery taverns. Newspapers teemed with the story of Sullivan's humiliation, and crowds roamed the streets hoping to catch a glimpse of his conqueror.[45]

Still, a match had not been made. Newspapers reported that Sullivan's and Hyer's partisans began arming themselves and that gang warfare between the two sides threatened. Although the papers exaggerated, street conflicts had intensified. To avoid bloodshed, some claimed, Sullivan finally issued a personal challenge in the *New York Herald* on June 1, 1848:

A CARD

About six weeks since, while in the saloon on the corner of Park Place and Broadway, in a condition rendering me unable to defend myself against any attack, I was assailed in a most cowardly manner, by a man of the name Hyer. . . . If I knew I had been worsted in a fair fight, and by a person who knew anything at all about fighting, or had the courage to fight as a man, I should have taken no notice of it; but I consider it due to my friends, to inform them in this way of the real character of the occurrence. I am no "Irish braggart" or "bully," although I am an Irishman and believe I can show myself worthy of my country whenever I am required. If there are any who think they can make me "cry enough like a whipped child," if No. 9 Chatham Street is not too far out of the way, I will be happy to have them call and make the experiment. As for Hyer, I can "flax him out" without any exertion.

JAMES SULLIVAN.[46]

The tone of this challenge, no doubt ghostwritten, contrasted sharply with its content. Even though he expressed his thoughts in moderate, subdued language, Sullivan accused Hyer of lying, cowardice, and attacking a defenseless man, not to mention fistic incompetence. The next day, Hyer responded with a public advertisement declaring that he had chastised Sullivan for an unprovoked assault and that he would meet his enemy anywhere to prove again that he was Sullivan's master.[47]

On August 7, 1848, at Ford's Tavern, friends of the fighters initialed a formal document detailing the terms of the match:

> *ARTICLES OF AGREEMENT* entered into this seventh day of August, 1848, between James Sullivan and Thomas Hyer.... The said James Sullivan agrees to fight the said Thomas Hyer a fair stand up fight, half minute time, in a twenty-four feet roped ring, according to the new rules as laid down in the *Fistiana* for 1848, by which rules the said Sullivan and Hyer hereby mutually agree to be bound.... The said fight shall be for the sum of Five Thousand Dollars a side. The said fight shall take place within the states of Virginia or Maryland, or some other place, if the parties can mutually agree upon such other place....

The articles stipulated that the men fight within six months, that the referee arrange a rematch should legal authorities intervene during the battle, and that each fighter be properly attired for fair ring combat. Both sides agreed jointly to charter steamboats and split the proceeds from ticket sales. Backers of the men would put up the five thousand dollars in seven monthly installments, alternately at Sullivan's and Ford's taverns. Each side was to choose an umpire and the umpires a referee, whose decisions were final and binding.[48]

"Every transaction shall take place in a fair business-like manner," a contemporary observer declared, and without any taint of barroom brawling. Whether or not the articles' moderate tone actually calmed churning urban enmities, it is clear that ring rituals sought to channel working-class rivalries, giving them clear and coherent expression. "The public drew a long breath of relief," one commentator concluded, "at having escaped the danger of a street slaughter which had so long been threatened." The factional hatreds between neighborhood and ethnic cliques did not disappear, but a hiatus in the violence seemed possible as the gangs turned to a symbolic expression of their differences. For a moment, at least, two men in the ring would do the work for many in the streets.[49]

The fight rules were written in the same precise, legalistic language as the Articles of Agreement, further attempting to alleviate angry passions. These regulations codified practices already acknowledged though not always honored. Falling without receiving a blow, kicking, butting, gouging, hitting below the belt, striking a fallen man, using foreign substances, leaving the ring, all were grounds for forfeiture at the referee's discretion. Yet the rules were designed not just for safety's sake but with an eye to custom and protocol. Rule number one, for example, lavished great care on the construction of the "sacred inclosure": "That the ring shall be made on turf, and shall be four and twenty feet square, formed of eight stakes and ropes, the latter extending in double lines, the uppermost one being four feet from the ground, and the lower two feet from the ground. That in the centre of the ring a mark be formed, to be termed a scratch; and that at two opposite corners . . . spaces be inclosed by other marks sufficiently large for the reception of the seconds and bottle-holders, to be entitled 'the corners.' "[50]

The rules further specified that principals and seconds all shake hands; that the seconds tie fighting colors to the corners, where these banners remained until the winner claimed the loser's as a victory trophy; that each umpire protect his party's interest but defer to all decisions rendered by the referee; and that no one except principals, seconds, and bottle-holders enter the ring. Finally, the participants must refrain from irritating or offensive remarks, "in all respects conducting themselves with order and decorum," confining themselves "to the diligent and careful discharge of their duties." The rules were concerned, in sum, not only with safety and fairness but with ritual. They prescribed stylized actions, demanded patterned behavior, emphasized ordered procedures. In this way they made a fight into a special expressive event, a dramatization of larger social conflicts.[51]

The half-year build-up to the bout was filled with sparring exhibitions, saloon speculation, and hard training. Sullivan gave his first benefit on September 30, 1848, at the Shakespeare Hotel in New York. Patrick Timony of the *Police Gazette* estimated that eight hundred people, including "editors, doctors, lawyers, brokers, clerks, exquisites, philosophers (no clergymen who were identified as such), and swarms of the boys and 'hitters out,' " paid fifty cents each to watch the heroes of the pugilistic fraternity don the gloves and battle on stage. John McCleester acted as master of ceremonies, genially introducing each pair of sparrers. In the final set-to, Yankee Sullivan "exhibited his quality" against George Thompson, Hyer's trainer. Emotions were close to the surface. Thompson landed several clean blows on his antagonist, but in the third round Sullivan suddenly closed and threw his opponent hard. Yankee's friends rushed the stage, tossed up their hats, and cheered their man. Order was restored, but exchanges between the two fighters grew increasingly sharp until Thompson threw Sullivan among the spectators.

Now the friends of both rushed forward, each side menacing the other. A brawl was narrowly averted.[52]

For enemies of the ring, here was proof that boxing encouraged violence, but partisans of pugilism drew the opposite conclusion. "We are well convinced," the *Police Gazette* concluded, "that had not the present match been made, the large bands of resolute men who adhere to each, would have met, Philadelphia fashion, before now, and cost the census records some half a dozen lives. In this view, the present fight may be considered the safety valve of a much greater danger." Prize fighting was a tool of peace:

> The pugilistic spirit has let off the fever of assassination, and the six-barrelled pistols and the murderous bowie knives which a few weeks ago were the pet weapons [sic] of every rake-hell and swash buckler in town, have given place to the doctrine of the knuckles and hitting from the "shoulder." A peaceful man may, therefore, now walk the street where the fighting crowds perambulate, without fear of being sped to his account by a whiff from some deadly muzzle, or by a slivering stroke from some sweeping blade.

The claim was not only dubious but, for a newspaper trying to justify its coverage of illegal events, self-serving. Nevertheless, during the coming decade the borderline between symbolic prize fights and real personal violence would often be ambiguous. More and more men retired to secluded spots with nothing save fists to settle their quarrels, while others came along for the sport of it. Boxing according to prize ring rules was becoming a useful, if not strictly legal, means of regulating relations between men.[53]

With two months left before the battle Hyer and Sullivan went into intensive training. Their regimens were surprisingly strenuous and in some respects seem very modern. Sullivan and his trainers, "Country" McCleester and Tom O'Donnell, took up residence at Shaw's Tavern near the Union raceway, Jamaica, Long Island, while Hyer, supervised by George Thompson and Joe Winrow, retired to Dodge's Public House, north of New York City. Their training techniques differed slightly in detail, but they followed essentially similar programs.

Sullivan rose at dawn, ran five to seven miles on the Union course, and returned to awaken his friends. Next he worked out with a pair of light dumbbells to improve his aim, reach, and strength. Then he sparred with one of his trainers—striking, dodging, feinting, wrestling—to sharpen his fighting skills, followed by punching the heavy bag to improve his hitting power. Washing his upper body with cold water after these exertions, Sullivan and friends retired to breakfast. Fine rare beef or, occasionally, boiled chicken was the order of the day. Small amounts of ale and water were permitted, although dietary lore demanded strict avoidance of vegetables and starches for men in strenuous training. After breakfast Sullivan reposed for an hour with Pierce Egan's *Boxiana*, immersing himself in the great ring strategies of the past. He and his trainers then set out on an eight-to-ten-mile cross-country circuit, along the way performing such exercises as picking up large stones at a dead run. This over, McCleester and O'Donnell again doused Sullivan with cold water, then toweled him off until his skin glowed cranberry red. Dressed in fresh flannel, Sullivan and company partook of their second and last meal of the day, a duplicate of the first. Following an hour-long evening break of more reading or fight talk, Sullivan concluded with another session of sparring, dumbbells and bag punching, a five-mile moonlight walk, and bed by nine o'clock. With the exception of a glass of wine instead of ale, mutton rather than beef, and mountain climbing in lieu of running, Tom Hyer pursued a similar regimen.[54]

There is a peculiar irony in all of this. As men stripped off their clothes for a prize fight, symbolically they also stripped off layers of civilization. Violence, prowess, the quest for physical domination, all have a barbarous quality. Boxing was part of culture, a man-made product, but it evoked images of instinctual life, of animals battling over food, mates, and territory. It was precisely this primitive atavism, this lack of restraint and self-control, that critics condemned in boxing and bloodsports. Yankee Sullivan, whose "bull dog courage" made him "cock of the walk," reaffirmed the animality of prize fighting by raising a bull terrier and a main of fighting birds while he trained.[55]

But in the accounts of preparation for the ring, opposite images predominate. Training required hard, above all regular, work to expunge "all the refuse of a long period of ease." Sullivan's and Hyer's regimens taught lessons on "the privations, the hardships, and the self-denial which a man must practice before he can arrive at his physical climax, and stand as nature intended him, free from all vitiation of perverted habits." Temperance, chasteness, self-restraint were the keys to physical and mental perfection:

> Mr. Sullivan lives in all respects, a virtuous and abstemious life. He will not touch liquor; he will not smoke a cigar; nay, he will not stay in a room where one is smoked, and above all, he does not see Mrs. Sullivan at all—except in a Pickwickian sense. One dereliction of the latter kind

would throw him back whole weeks in his training, and put him very low down in the betting. The result is, he is as strong as a lion, as gay as a lark, with a free conscience and a cheerful spirit, and in all respects in that high condition of animal perfection which enables a man to set at naught all manner of disease or ailment. . . .

Hyer equaled Sullivan in rectitude, leading a "perfectly chaste and abstemious life," offering "a pattern to many who claim to lead up middle aisles, and to sound the key note in sacred psalmistry."[56]

The steady habits of the contenders made them paragons of Victorian rectitude; self-indulgence, whether in tobacco, liquor, or sex, they shunned as the font of corruption. The controlled little world of the training camp countered all forms of immoderation with lessons in disciplining one's impulses for the sake of future rewards. Such behavior, however, was upheld not for the sake of Christian morality or capitalist productivity but in the name of violent sport, successful wagers, and barroom camaraderie. Here again the ring reconciled seemingly contradictory norms. Just as prize fights created a meritocracy of violence, so the boxers' training regimens turned bourgeois and evangelical ideals on their heads, enlisting abstemiousness in the cause of wild pleasures.

As 1849 dawned, the combatants were well on the way to physical perfection. In mid-January, Sullivan left New York to select a location for the fight. He chose Poole's Island, a deserted bit of land in the Chesapeake Bay, claimed by both the federal government and the state of Maryland. The *Spirit of the Times* directed fans to be in Baltimore on Tuesday, February 6, where they could catch steamers for the secret battleground.[57]

As thousands made their way to Maryland, however, local officials obtained writs against the vessels. On the eve of the fight they impressed one ship, the *Boston,* and used it to pursue the others. At the same time a posse under High Constable Gifford of Baltimore County hunted Hyer and Sullivan, who were already billeted on Poole's Island. Aware of the danger, the fighters' friends chartered two craft and headed for the island, hoping to pick up the principals before the magistrates arrived. They succeeded by convincing Gifford that George Thompson and Tom O'Donnell were really Hyer and Sullivan. The two were arrested, allowing the real combatants to escape. But the chase was not over. Early the next day the *Boston* sighted the boxer's vessel, bore down on them, and prepared to arrest the whole party. By a final stroke of pure luck, however, the magistrates' boat ran aground. Hyer and Sullivan, with about a hundred friends each, glided past the *Boston,* gesturing their contempt to the Maryland officials. All itched for a fight, and they were ready to anchor at the first convenient spot, "whether it was in Maryland, or Delaware, or Virginia, or hell."[58]

They landed at Still Pond Heights, Kent County, Maryland. A ring was hastily constructed of local pine and the topgallant halyards of one of the boats. A light blanket of snow covered the ground. At about ten minutes past four Yankee Sullivan threw his hat in the ring; Tom Hyer's followed a few minutes later. Both wore their locks cut close, because long hair gave one's opponent a convenient handle. Following custom, each man sat on his seconds' knee, Sullivan's feet warmed by some hot bricks procured from a nearby home. The seconds—Tom Burns and John McCleester, substituting for the arrested George Thompson and Tom O'Donnell—tossed a coin for the choice of ground. Sullivan won and gave Hyer the corner facing the glaring afternoon sun. Onlookers considered this a significant victory for bare-knuckle boxers often fought from set positions. The men tied their colors to the ropes, the stars and stripes for Hyer, emerald green with white spots for Sully. Finally, the two stripped for battle. The disparity in size was striking, Sullivan giving away four inches and thirty pounds. But both looked impressive, as they exposed their bodies to the cold February air:

> They were as finely developed in every muscle as their physical capacity could reach, and the bounding confidence which sparkled fiercely in their eyes, showed that their spirits and courage were at their highest mark. Sullivan, with his round compact chest, formidable head, shelving flinty brows, fierce glaring eyes, and clean turned shoulders, looked the very incarnation of the spirit of mischievous genius; while Hyer, with his broad, formidable chest, and long muscular limbs, seemed as if he could almost trample him out of life, at will.

One newspaper account claimed that the spectators were so absorbed by the sight of the heroes that only a few dollars were bet on the ground, and this at even money. The odds gave no indication of what was in store.[59]

They began at twenty minutes after four, and the first rounds told the story. The two exchanged cautious blows, but neither man did any damage. Suddenly, Sullivan rushed in and clinched Hyer with an underhold. This was a crucial moment, for Yankee's friends counted on his wrestling ability to counter Hyer's reach and strength advantages. A few hard throws would weaken Young America for the later rounds, so Sullivan must take charge early. The spectators watched with rapt

The great $10,000 match, February 7, 1849, at Still Pond Heights, Maryland. After dodging legal authorities all night, Hyer and Sullivan fought sixteen short but dramatic rounds. *New York Illustrated Times,* February 1849.

attention as Sully knotted his muscles to throw his man—but all in vain. Hyer now grabbed Sullivan with an upperhold and wrenched him to the ground. The betting swung in the Chief's favor.

For seventeen minutes, eighteen seconds, they fought a bitter, unremitting battle, their efforts spurred by the desire for glory and revenge. The sporting press described the scene: "Both men came up bloody to the scratch; Sullivan being literally clotted with gore, while the clear crimson smoked on Hyer's chest, from a lance wound which had been made under his right eye to prevent it from closing out his sight." By the sixteenth round, Yankee's fighting star had set:

> Hyer . . . let fly both right and left in Sullivan's face, who, though he could not return it, took it without wincing in the least. Hyer then rushed him to the ropes again, and after a short struggle there, threw him and fell heavily upon him. . . . When he was taken off, Sullivan was found to be entirely

exhausted, and when lifted up reeled half round and staggered backward towards the ropes. The fight was done. He could not come in again, and one of his seconds took him from the ring. . . .

The "Great $10,000 Match" took less than ten minutes of actual fighting time.[60]

At most a few hundred men witnessed the hastily arranged battle, but tens of thousands awaited news back home. Even many who considered the ring brutal and degraded were curious about the outcome. Like men anticipating the fluctuations of grain and cotton markets, they wore their anxiety on their faces, for more money had been wagered on this battle than on any other recent sporting event. The *New York Sun* claimed that bets as large as forty thousand dollars hinged on the outcome. Newsboys hawked tons of papers, lithographers sold pictures of the combatants as fast as they could print them, and saloonkeepers worked overtime filling the glasses of men who gathered to share the word from Maryland. In one of the very earliest uses of the new technology, telegraph lines flashed the fight's result to the multitudes gathered at newspaper offices in northeastern cities.[61]

When Hyer reached Philadelphia the day after the bout, crowds frantic with excitement mobbed him. Chestnut Street was packed solid as ecstatic friends paraded the champion on their shoulders. "One would not have believed," a local paper complained, "that the city contained so many persons that would debase themselves, by following in the wake of such a hero." A Philadelphia prosecutor agreed, declaring that the fight excited "the worst passions of the community." Hyer was temporarily taken into custody, then released when Maryland authorities failed to have him bound over for trial. Meanwhile, downtown New York swarmed with men eager to hear the latest. As newsboys rapidly sold out their editions, they set to in pairs and demonstrated Hyer's and Sullivan's battle for their patrons. "Throughout this vast community," one New York paper concluded, "nothing has been heard or talked of for several days past but the fight between Hyer and Sullivan. . . . The only exceptions to the general prevalence of this excitement were the rigidly righteous, the pious, the saints, the puritans, or those who had no time to spare from their private rogueries or pious prayers, to public matters."[62]

Hundreds gathered at Yankee Sullivan's public house late on Wednesday and Thursday nights, but save for occasional cheers for their man, the crowd was quiet. Hyer's favorite haunt, in contrast, the Fountain House in Park Row, witnessed a "grand illumination" of fireworks Wednesday night, culminating with the hanging of a brilliantly lighted transparency displaying the words "Tom Hyer, the Champion of America." The phrase signified something new, a single, unified title owned by the one man who unequivocally could best all others. As befits heroes, men celebrated the gladiators' exploits with poetry and song. A *Spirit of the Times* column reported the battle, round by round, in mock heroic verse:

> The men both looked well, in excellent training,
> In capital order for cutting and maiming,
> The "Yankee' 'tis true, was a great deal the smaller,
> Tom Hyer being heavier, stouter and taller,
> But still it was thought, and asserted by many,
> The odds were in favor of "Yankee"—if any;
> That what with his dodging and practical tricks,
> His cunning and funning, the terrible "licks,"
> That he'd soon whip the Gothamite hero "like bricks."
> But—they enter the ring—from "the boys" came a burst,
> The men then shook daddles, and then—
> ROUND THE FIRST. . . .[63]

In saloons men harmonized "The Pleasant Ballad of Tomme Hyer and Ye Sullivan":

> Ho, all ye fancy gentlemen,
>   And patrons of the ring,
> Give ear unto the pleasant song,
>   I am about to sing.
>
> Tis not of merry revellings,
>   Nor love and ladies' charms,
> But of two doughty champions,
>   And fearful feats of arms.[64]

New chronicles of the ring recounted the pugilistic genealogy of the fight, while the *New York Sunday Mercury* compared the bout with the great battle between Tom Hickman and Bill Neate which William Hazlitt had immortalized almost thirty years earlier. Such historical allusions lent prestige to contemporary boxing, linking it to a glorious past. For weeks, even months after the stake money had been given up and wagers settled, the sporting fraternity still celebrated the great event. Hyer's popularity made him a favorite among politicians, actors, and show people, and all eyes followed him as he strolled along the Bowery.[65]

Others reacted with less enthusiasm. Former mayor Phillip Hone, patron of the arts, a leader of New York social life, now enjoying an elegant and cultivated retirement, noted with revulsion that James Gordon Bennett's *Herald* lavished attention on the fight: "The appropriate organ of such disgraceful recitals, is filled this morning with the disgusting details." The *Christian Advocate* considered the mob scenes on the streets of New York to be "painful and humiliating," juxtaposing them with the simultaneous gathering of a thousand children—all "neatly and uniformly attired"—in the Broadway Tabernacle to sing hymns for their families. Here was a telling contrast, Bowery depravity versus uptown righteousness.[66]

On the other hand, a few editors stopped apologizing for their coverage of the ring. The *New York Evening Mirror* declared that "the laws forbid prize fighting, but in spite of the mawkish twaddle which we daily see in the newspapers about the affair, we are inclined to believe from other manifestations, that public feeling is decidedly favorable to the fight. There are certainly much worse vices tolerated and encouraged by society than prize fighting...." The editor attacked the "squeamishness of those effeminate minds," horrified by "a set-to between two shirtless champions, who ... meet together, face to face and hand to hand in a trial of personal strength." What changed most radically, however, was not editorial attitudes but simply the willingness of journals to mention the prize ring at all. The Sullivan-Hyer battle generated far more comment in the popular press than any previous fight, and we therefore know more about it than any other match.[67]

The "Great $10,000 Fight" opened the floodgates. "From the time of the Hyer and Sullivan match," one sporting editor declared with a backward glance, "may be dated the actual rise of pugilism in America, into anything like importance." As a grudge fight, barely sublimating profound economic and ethnic tensions between rival urban factions— some observers had even predicted murders at ringside—the contest focused amorphous social conflicts into the crystal-clear image of two great fighters battling for an enormous amount of money. In noting the schisms that divided men, however, we must not lose sight of the larger unities of the sporting fraternity. Boxing was primarily a working-class preserve, the property, as the *Herald* so elegantly put it, of "the low and the vulgar." True, a small but growing number of more-or-less respectable men now attended an occasional sparring exhibition, and a greater number read accounts of prize battles even as they condemned the ring. But boxing really belonged to working-class males who rejected bourgeois standards of value, laborers dispossessed by new economic alignments, and men who lived in the netherworld of gambling, bootlegging, and petty crime. It was to these men—deeply divided by cultural and religious conflicts, by competition for status and power, and above all by a wrenching transformation of America's economy—that the great championship fight spoke so eloquently.[68]

With the Sullivan-Hyer match paving the way, prize fighting became one of the most important expressive forms of a flourishing plebeian culture. Indeed, half a century after their epic struggle Hyer and Sullivan continued to square off in lithographs that hung from the walls of working-class taverns.[69]

The Age of Heroes

"The Good Time Coming"

"Sparring became the fashionable amusement, the ladies complained of the negligence of their admirers, everyone who made any pretensions of being a 'knowing one' carried *Fistiana* in his pocket, and from that wonderful book recounted to the green 'uns the heroic exploits of Tom Spring, Bendigo and a host of others." The excitement generated by the Sullivan-Hyer match continued through the 1850s: Professor Mann, New York's most eminent sparring master, had more pupils than he could handle; talk of "lightweights," "uppercuts," "claret," "peepers," and "fibbing" filled the air; and Pierce Egan's *Life in London* enjoyed a successful revival at the Wall Street Theater.[1] The sheer number of bouts increased markedly, with dozens reported (and no doubt many more unreported) each year in the late 1850s. Moreover, "off hand" or "turn up" affairs—informal matches merging such trappings of the prize ring as stakes, seconds, rules, spectators, and press coverage with the spontaneity and angry passions of street brawling—were only sporadically noted by the press but becoming quite common. Even sparring exhibitions increased in frequency, and New York City newspapers carried advertisements for three or four per week.[2]

Prize fighting news proliferated in an oral culture, partly because of the ring's outlaw status but also because working-class life centered on the spoken word. It was in the personalistic world of the saloon, where the merits of boxers were discussed, their exploits sung, and their chances in upcoming battles assessed, that heroes of the ring acquired legendary status. Fight connoisseurs, retired pugs, and active boxers opened many new taverns and sporting houses during the 1850s. The

New York fancy patronized Jim Giddings's Old Crib, Harry Jennings's Sporting Museum, and James Regan's Clipper Shades. Similarly, Jimmy Hart in Boston, Jack Smith in Albany, Matt Rusk and Dominick Bradley in Philadelphia, Harry Gribben in Brooklyn, Izzy Lazarus in Buffalo, Dick Hewit in Newark, Johnny MacKey and Jem Parker in Chicago, all established new public houses that gave focus to boxing activities. These publicans offered men a place to raise a glass and discuss the ring. They arranged bouts, gave odds, took bets, chartered steamboats, and sold railroad tickets; they backed fighters, sponsored exhibitions, and offered sparring lessons; they served as stakeholders, seconds, referees, umpires, and bottleholders; they even entered the ring themselves.[3]

Saloonkeepers also engendered a sense of continuity across generations. George Kensett, for example, retired from the ring in 1829 after his second battle with Ned Hammond. For thirty-seven years thereafter he kept a New York tavern, first on Walker Street, than at Fordham, where men came to arrange, train for, and discuss fights. When Kensett died in 1856, William Fuller, Tom Hyer, William Tovee, James Sanford, and other members of the pugilistic fraternity mourned at his funeral. Similarly, boxer and publican Jimmy Hart passed away in Boston in 1859, and local fighters Ed Price, Barney Ford, Johnny Cosgrove, and Harry Finnegas served as pallbearers for their old friend. Saloonkeepers, then, were at the center of an informal, community-based network of prize ring activities.[4]

Although face-to-face meetings within the drinking culture were the primary means of spreading fistic news, the printed word became increasingly influential. Oral and written traditions are not necessarily antagonistic; indeed, here the two forms reinforced each other. Reporters gathered intelligence at the sporting fraternities' watering holes, while saloonkeepers kept press files for their patrons to read aloud and discuss. Boxers used the newspapers, as we have seen, to challenge each other through printed advertisements, "cards" as they were called. This custom apparently was borrowed from dueling's code of honor, where an aggrieved man was expected to control his anger and write a dispassionate note expressing his feelings. An exchange of private messages led either to "satisfaction"—an explanation or apology—or to a challenge, and if the offending party refused to fight, his opponent "posted" him, that is, publicly impugned his courage in printed advertisements. By 1850 dueling had died out in the north, but vestiges of its etiquette lived on in the ring. Of course, cards were not simply private expressions of wounded honor but public declarations, ghostwritten in most cases, intended to promote interest in upcoming battles. Here was a hint of an important transformation. Published challenges were an early indication of honor becoming marketable goods, a symptom of the commercialization of American leisure, a sign that the profit motive now mixed with desires for personal vindication. Fights still grew out of genuine grudges, but editors and promoters in this age of Barnum knew how to whip up excitement, and boxers recognized the value of publicity.

Newspaper challenges also signified the printed media's growing proficiency at conveying sporting information, especially as the telegraph connected editors' offices with distant athletic activities and as new technologies facilitated the mass distribution of news. Old workhorses, the *New York Herald* and the *Spirit of the Times,* continued their efforts. After mid-century, however, the gentleman's weeklies and workingman's dailies were joined by some of the respectable press, the *New York Times* and the *New York Tribune,* far-flung papers such as the *New Orleans Daily Picayune,* and more obscure local publications like the *Milwaukee Sentinel and Gazette* and the *Springfield Weekly Illinois State Journal.* The middle class was not yet attending fights, but its newspapers were gratifying a budding taste for sporting news.[5]

American publishers also began supplementing English books with native ones. In 1829 William Sharples of Philadelphia brought out a thirty-page training manual, *The Complete Art of Boxing,* America's first pugilism text. The trickle of instructional works continued with Samuel O'Rourke's *The Art of Pugilism* (1837), the anonymous *Whole Art of Boxing with Instructions in the Manly Art of Self-Defense* (1850), and Owen Swift's *Boxing without a Master,* which went through five editions in the 1840s and 1850s. Prize ring history also received attention in such pamphlets as the *American Fistiana* (1849, 1860, and 1873) and *The Life and Battles of Yankee Sullivan* (1854). Significantly, these were all cheap editions designed for working-class budgets, not the elegant and substantial volumes that English presses produced for the rich.[6]

Most important, the proliferation of print produced the first clear and unequivocal voices in support of the ring. Of these, editor Frank Queen's was the loudest. Born of working-class parents in Philadelphia, Queen worked his way up from a printer's devil to managing editor, then established his own newspaper in 1853. The *New York Clipper* specialized in covering the theater, horse and yacht races, pedestrianism, cricket, baseball, and rowing, as well as contests of skill between rival militia units and volunteer fire companies. Elevating pugilism, however, was Queen's special concern. Queen not only covered the latest ring news, he made his offices a clearinghouse for arranging matches. Because sparring taught the "grammar" of prize fighting, he publicized upcoming exhibitions, called for a New York sparring association to schedule and regulate matches, and urged the building of a large "sportsman's hall" with ring, animal pit, saloon, and a clubhouse for the fancy. In addition to regular news reports, the *Clipper* offered its readers a sense of pugilistic history, printing articles on early heroes and excerpting chapters from Pierce Egan's *Boxiana*. By stimulating the sporting man's interest in battles past, the *Clipper* created a context of meaning for current news, engendered a powerful consciousness of folk history, and thereby dignified each bout as part of a tradition. Like genealogy, accounts of early fights—of old champions begetting new champions—put working-class men in touch with a glorious past.[7]

Queen considered pugilism above all a "profession to be kept manly and honorable by its friends and practitioners." He frequently quoted the duke of Wellington's celebrated letter of 1845 to General Burgoyne:

> I regret to observe the decay of the good old English practice of boxing, as I believe that it tends to produce and keep up that national spirit of undaunted bravery and intrepidity which has enabled our armies to conquer in many a hard-fought battle. I think that if the physical standing and personal courage of the British soldier have degenerated during the long interval of peace which we have enjoyed, such a result may be fairly and justly attributed to desuetude and gradual extinction of this noble and truly natural art of boxing.

The ring was an exemplar of heroism, a teacher of manliness, a school for patriotism.[8]

Although Queen stood to profit by the expansion of sport, his advocacy of boxing was neither cynical nor insincere; the *Clipper*'s editor simply filled the vessels of Victorian culture with his own elixir. Like his contemporary, P. T. Barnum, whose museum was as much an educational institution as a freak show, Queen offered moral justifications for his actions, claiming that boxing taught useful lessons in health, discipline, and self-defense. Surrounded by advertisements for contraceptives, venereal disease cures, even a "marriage guide" illustrated with seventy-five color engravings of human genitals, *Clipper* editorials argued that manly sports "improved" American society: "A knowledge of the science of boxing is calculated to develop and encourage feelings of manliness, confidence, courage, and love of fair-play, and to discourage and check those appeals to the knife and the revolver which are so common in cases of personal quarrels in this country." Queen promulgated the rules of the ring because they curbed the "wild passions" of men. He advocated boxers' training regimens as a way to build health and courage. In a word, he believed that pugilism offered both entertainment and moral education.[9]

In defending not only boxing but the theater, cockfighting, and other suspect pastimes, Queen rowed against a still powerful current. Declared the Congregationalist *New Englander* in 1851, "Let our readers, one and all, remember that we were sent into the world, not for sport and amusement, but for labor; not to enjoy and please ourselves, but to serve and glorify God, and be useful to our fellow men. That is the great object and end of life." By the late antebellum era, reformers, intellectuals, clergymen, doctors, and journalists were growing more amenable to wholesome and innocent recreations that refreshed both mind and body. Rational exercise such as calisthenics found adherents, and baseball, cricket, and trotting had their advocates. Although the boundaries of propriety were expanding, however, they never grew to include activities that encouraged violence, revelry, or displays of man's "baser" passions.[10]

While liberals advocated participatory sports for the sake of health and refreshment, Queen covered staged events, titillating commercial spectacles that gave purely vicarious thrills. Most good Victorians still believed that such wasteful activities corrupted the lower classes. Reformer Junius Henri Browne singled out the *Clipper* as an "obscene" journal, part of a cycle of degradation for young urban thugs:

> They are fed tobacco and gin from childhood. Ribald songs and the roar of swinish carousals, in place of maternal lullabies, echo in their infant ears. Living much in the open air, and fond of rude physical sports, they grow up stout and hardy, in spite of bad habits and pernicious natures. . . . In their early teens, they find themselves lewd and lusty, thoroughly selfish and sensual, principled against work, predetermined to dishonesty and tyranny. . . . To bar-rooms and brothels they tend by a natural law and soon come to regard ruffians, thieves and prizefighters worthy examples of imitation and objects of envy. . . . Their first fight and first debauch are like the first honors of a college; and they mount higher and higher by sinking deeper and deeper into the slough of degradation. . . . They are water-rats and land-rats, river thieves and land thieves, pimps, confidence men, brawlers, burglers and assassins. . . .

Violent, lazy, impulsive, such men violated every principle of morality held dear by the middle class. And newspapers like the *Clipper,* Browne believed, nourished their depravity.[11]

Perhaps Frank Queen's greatest sin was inverting the Victorian belief that man played so that he might work. For the *Clipper* editor, sports gave not only strength and health but pleasure too, a value in its own right. Of course, pleasure came from dogfights and ratting contests, whose bone-crunching, carpet-drenching bloodiness were described in the *Clipper* with surrealistic intensity. But Queen also wrote in the idiom of the day, extolling American nationalism and the spirit of improvement. Pious middle-class Americans would hardly agree that boxing was a civilizing force. Still, in the Victorian view of things, manliness, confidence, and courage—in a word, self-reliance—were high values. Queen merged an earnest Victorian tone with a celebration of play, of release, of "The Good Time Coming," as he put it in a song dedicated to the New York fancy:

> There's a good time coming, boys,
>   A good time coming:
> Men who make a match to Fight,
> Will take good care that all is right
>   In the good time coming;
> Shun all tricks and crosses too,
>   For honesty is stronger,
> And holds all rascals up to view—
>   Wait a little longer...
>
> There's a good time coming, boys,
>   A good time coming:
> Henceforth all classes will resort
> Where they can see the best of sport
>   In the good time coming;
> Treat all alike—act "on the square,"
>   The cause will soon grow stronger,
> In view of this it is but fair—
>   To wait a little longer.

Queen's "Good Time Coming" was an adaptation of a popular lyric heralding millennial human progress; the editor simply appropriated the rhetoric of reform to the cause of sport. Pious saints and assiduous businessmen, needless to say, did not include prize fights in their visions of the good times to come.[12]

Though Queen articulated a defense of boxing and offered a forum for ring news, he could not reverse legal trends. As we have seen, statutes against riot, mayhem, disorderly conduct, assault, and even manslaughter were still used to prosecute prize fighters, and a few legislatures added new enactments in the wake of major bouts. Massachusetts formally outlawed prize fighting in March 1849, just a month after the Sullivan-Hyer affair. To arrange or engage in a fight brought a maximum ten-year prison term and five-thousand-dollar fine, while serving as a second, surgeon, or promoter carried a three-year, one-thousand-dollar sentence. Nevertheless, ring activity increased markedly in the Bay State during the next decade, and aside from a few arrests, most fights occurred without interference.[13]

Ten years after the Massachusetts law, an anti-prize bill emerged in Albany, New York. The legislation came in response to a series of major bouts, the Horrigan-Lazarus, Bradley-Ranking, and Morrissey-Heenan battles of 1857 and 1858, all of which drew thousands of sporting men to Buffalo, who then crossed en masse to Canada for the fights. The State Senate passed the bill without a dissenting vote, and the Assembly followed with overwhelming approval. The New York law was more comprehensive than the one from Massachusetts, providing milder misdemeanor penalties—six months to one year in jail, $200 to $1,000 fines—yet authorizing magistrates to prosecute not only participants and fighters but even spectators. Indeed, the legislation threatened sparring matches, previously considered distinct from prize fighting and perfectly legal.[14]

These laws grew out of the bourgeois and evangelical assumptions of Victorian culture. They indicated not a sudden hardening of previously tolerant attitudes toward the ring but specific legislative action in the face of more pugilistic "crimes." While the new laws stiffened the old anti-ring sentiment, they failed to stop prize fighting's spread. Most boxers simply conducted their business surreptitiously, in isolated rural areas or in saloon back rooms. As long as the belligerent parties were discreet, magistrates usually left them alone. When overzealous police did interfere, political influence and bribes often got fighters out of trouble.[15]

Laws or no laws, New York City remained America's undisputed boxing capital; meanwhile, other parts of the country enjoyed ring revivals. New Orleans was the site of several important matches, especially after Chris Lilly settled in the Crescent City. He not only fought, he promoted bouts, imported new talent to the region, and organized his muscular friends into a gang of Election Day enforcers. Later in the fifties, New Orleans–based Irish sportsmen raised stakes, arranged bouts, and passed the hat for the fighting men of the area.[16] Elsewhere, when gold was discovered in California, the violent boom-town psychology of the male mining camps offered fertile soil for raucous play. Lucre and adventure beckoned hordes of native laborers and immigrants, while the moral laxity, free-flowing money, and rough masculine camaraderie of the early years lured the likes of Tom Hyer,

Yankee Sullivan and less well-known fighters to the Golden State.[17]

Fed by the influx of talent from abroad, the ring prospered in other regions as well. Boston's enormous new Irish population generated a surge of pugilistic activity. Not only such residents as Jimmy Hart and Johnny Moneghan but boxers coming from outside the Bay State spread the fistic gospel. Thus, during the mid-1850s, Johnny Roberts of Chicago fought Boston locals Harry Finnegas and Johnny MacKey, as well as Jack Murphy of Liverpool and James Lafferty of St. Louis. Meanwhile, Ed Price of England and Joe Coburn of Ireland renewed age-old Anglo-Saxon versus Celtic antagonisms in Boston.[18] Similarly, St. Louis—a boom town with a large immigrant population including hundreds of rivermen, miners, and dock workers—provided another fine environment for the ring. During the 1850s, eastern publicans with ring connections, among them William J. Claxton of New York and Jimmy Hart of Boston, returned to the Gateway City and promoted several matches featuring native and immigrant talent. With purses ranging from about fifty to three hundred dollars—roughly the average yearly wages for a laborer—it is no wonder that working-class men were willing to risk their bodies. Smaller cities too witnessed a spate of battles, including Waterbury, Toledo, Pawtucket, Trenton, Leavenworth, and many others. Southern towns—Savannah, Lexington, Charleston, and Memphis also saw occasional battles. Even sailors aboard U.S. ships began setting up rings to settle questions of prowess and honor.[19]

With boxing's geographical spread, fighters began claiming new, informal titles: "champion of the prize ring in the Mississippi Valley," or "champion of the Gravois coal diggings in St. Louis," or "champion of Norfolk, Virginia," or "champion of Brooklyn's 4th ward." Folk characters fought under such colorful names as "Steel Ribs," "Saucy Aleck," "Young Duffy," Robert "Flying Dutchman" Rollins, "Shanghai" Connors, "Wild Irishman" Welch, "Awful" Gardner, "Chip-hat" Symms, "Red Nick" Lockwood, "Bulldog" Chapman, and "Chinky-Pin" Tom Jones. Ethnic affiliations were often expressed in monikers, such as "Wild Irishman" Welch, Young Molineaux the Black, and Lazarus the Jew, while other fighters adopted names revealing local identities: "Buckeye" Smith, "Liverpool Tom," William "Dublin Tricks" Hastings, "Mississippi" Bill Ramsey, "Utica" Jim Burns, and "Savannah Pet" Carlin.[20]

Paradoxically, even as boxers emphasized local and ethnic identities, they were entering a national market for commercialized leisure. Many fighters traveled widely, seeking always greener pastures. Johnny Moneghan, for example, emigrated from Liverpool in the early 1850s and settled in

Boston, where he first fought. Later he battled Londoner Barney Aaron in Providence, Rhode Island; within a year Moneghan was in Cincinnati, serving as a second in that city's very first prize fight; four months later he seconded Mike Trainor in a battle just outside St. Louis; another half a year found him in New Orleans, seconding Jack Tooney, and two months later, he aided Jim Phelan in a St. Louis fight. John Montgomery was equally well traveled, not as a fighter or second but as a "commissary," the man who pitched the ring and prepared the turf.[21]

Sparring exhibitions as well as prize battles were part of the growing variety of commercialized urban pastimes, of repeatable and profitable spectacles.[22] Ed Price, another Englishman with new roots in Boston, enjoyed great success staging exhibitions throughout New England. Late in 1859 he held a well-attended tour of one-night stands in Worcester, Springfield, Hartford, New Haven, and Bridgeport. As he moved from town to town, local sporting men, sparring masters, and their pupils smoothed Price's path. He described a typical reception in a letter to Frank Queen:

> Before you have left the cars half a minute you are taken in charge, and your shoulder nearly dislocated by shaking hands with men whom you have no recollection of ever having met before. One will say: "Are you going to give us an exhibition?" "Yes." "Good! Tom will get you a hall, Harry will give you a notice in our paper, George will post your bills, and I will sell for you 100 tickets;" and they all are as good as their words. Then you adjourn to a temple of Bacchus, where, through shaking hands, and receiving compliments, and being introduced to so many gentlemen, you get so confused in your ideas that you can hardly recollect anything till you find yourself in the cars, and ready to be set down at another city. Ah! Frank, you have a deal to answer for, to see what a change you have wrought in the steady, sober, Puritanical-minded people around here! Instead of pining themselves to a skeleton by fasting and prayer, and howling over their wickedness, as of yore, they now quietly meet in some sporting house, and discuss with their glass, the respective merits of their favorite milling coves; and the style in which each argues for his favorite would do justice to a Philadelphia lawyer.

Delighted with the success of his exhibitions, Price planned another northern tour at year's end, and included Bangor, Manchester, Quincy, Fitchburg, and Lowell on the itinerary. Here were early signs of boxing becoming businesslike. It was not upright shopkeepers and substantial entrepreneurs, however, but fighters, pool sellers, professional gamblers, saloon owners, and other sporting men who were finding ways to profit within the antibourgeois ethos of the fancy.[23]

During the 1850s, then, prize fighting experienced unprecedented growth. Steam power facilitated sparring tours, telegraph lines connected newspapers with matches, sporting houses multiplied, a few fighters became nationally known, and the *New York Clipper* offered a central location for arranging fights and disseminating reliable information. The exploding urban centers, with their vast numbers of immigrants, provided unparalleled markets for the consumption of recreation, new outlets for commercialized leisure. Boxing was one of many sports that benefited from these developments, as boating regattas, foot races, baseball, cricket, and horse racing all enjoyed newfound popularity. Though anti-prize ring legislation grew sterner, laws often were difficult to enforce, local magistrates bought off, and pugilists circumspect. Fighters, tavern keepers, gamblers, and sparring masters slowly created informal, underground promotional networks. These men were a blend of small entrepreneur and buccaneer, of social outcast and community leader.

The profit motive, the commercialization of leisure, and the growing importance of new transportation and communication networks, all point to the embryonic "modernization" of the ring—and all contributed to several spectacular matches during the 1850s. But though these trends helped prize fighting spread, they generally did not alter its character. Boxing remained locally based, loosely organized, in close touch with its working-class origins. The ring continued to be a stage for symbolically enacting particularistic tensions between neighborhoods, gangs, and ethnic groups. That many bouts still ended with foul blows, spectator interference, even attempted gougings, attests to deep schisms in the burgeoning cities which neither rules nor customs could fully contain. Boxing was primarily the property of young men of the urban streets, individuals victimized by an economy now consolidating its transition from the ancient apprenticeship system to sweated labor and modern capitalist production. These young men made the ring a centerpiece of male street life, for it celebrated an ethos of braggadocio, masculine prowess, and violent defense of honor, all in opposition to stable middle-class ways. Circumventing the law to stage a boxing match became an act of cultural independence. Prize fighting implicitly rejected the humanitarian, universalistic, and progressive Victorian world view.[24]

Here, then, was a battle for cultural legitimacy. When sportingmen spoke of the "magic circle" or the "sacred enclosure," they implied that the ring embodied the core of their cultural sensibility. They needed the neutral space denied by the law in order to resolve their own competing claims to achievement through tests of virility. The pious and productive ethic rejected their right to neighborhood, class, or ethnic honor based on success within the ropes. Thus the legal and ideological battle over the ring was a fight for cultural space, a contest over social legitimation. The story of the most famous and controversial prize fighter of the 1850s helps bring these issues into sharp focus.

The Era of John Morrissey

Dreams of the poor turned rich and the weak grown mighty are as old as folklore itself. In the American nineteenth century, however, such dreams were converted into expectations. More specifically, the bourgeois ethic taught that hard work, determination, and a little luck transformed any poor boy into a successful man. But the Victorian measure of achievement included far more than mere material wealth. Prosperity was a sign of success, but equally important, men had to cultivate character while making money. Good business and good morals went hand in hand, and truly virtuous citizens discovered that each reinforced the other. Comparatively few actually made the leap from rags to riches, and most men died in roughly the same social class as they were born. Moreover, many individuals selectively adapted the success ethic, accepting the importance of wealth but rejecting the strict moral imperatives dictated by the cult of respectability. In John Morrissey we have a distinctly working-class version of the American dream.[25]

John was born to Timothy and Julia Morrissey in Templemore, county Tipperary, Ireland, on February 12, 1831. Three years later the family moved to Troy, New York, where Timothy made a meager living as a day laborer. Poverty forced young John, like so many other immigrant youths, onto the labor market before he reached his teens. He went through a series of jobs, building his physique with manual labor in a rolling mill, a cannonball molding foundry, a wallpaper factory, and on river steamers. Work left Morrissey little time for education, though his wife later taught him the rudiments of reading and writing. Anyway, young Morrissey's temperament was far more pugnacious than contemplative. During his teens ferocity and grit won him several neighborhood brawls and the leadership of a Troy gang. By the time he reached his twenties, Morrissey had acquired a checkered work record, a reputation for viciousness, and sundry indictments for burglary and assault.[26]

There was a legendary quality to the stories that circulated about Morrissey. He was employed as a bartender for Alexander Hamilton, owner of a Troy saloon and a backer of the ring. Visiting New York at the end of the 1840s, Hamilton entered Isaiah Rynders's Empire Club. He got into an argument with "Dutch" Charlie Duane, a boxer and friend of Tom Hyer (it was Duane who hoisted Hyer onto his shoulders and carried him into the ring for the Yankee Sullivan fight). Hamilton boasted that he had a barkeeper back in Troy who could "take the Dutch courage" out of Charlie, and he offered to arrange a match. When Morrissey learned that Duane had scorned his boss's offer, he headed for New York. With characteristic bravado he strode into Rynders's saloon and, when he found Dutch Charlie was absent, offered to fight anyone in the house. Several men pounced on Morrissey and beat him senseless. Rynders, a riverboat gambler, gang leader, Tammany Hall chieftain, and Democratic politician in New York's Sixth Ward, admired the lad's courage. He allegedly nursed him back to health, though the Troy youth retained a longstanding hatred of the Empire Club. Morrissey stayed in New York after he had recovered, working as an emigrant runner (one who helped immigrants settle, obtained their political loyalty, and often fleeced them) and political shoulder hitter (one who broke up opponent's rallies, bullied their partisans out of voting, and secured a high turnout of loyal repeaters at the polls). Morrissey's temperament served him well in both jobs.

Brutal street fights enhanced his reputation. In a battle over turf on the New York docks, Morrissey defeated two other emigrant runners, one of whom had had a hand in his beating at the Empire Club. The combatants fought with belaying pins—heavy bars used to secure a ship's riggings— instead of fists. In another fight a brawler named Tom McCann chal- lenged Morrissey when he suspected the Troy youth of making advances toward his mistress. They fought inside a saloon, McCann quickly gaining the advantage. He threw Morrissey, knocked over a coal stove, then pinned the young man's back to the burning embers. Friends doused the coals, and Morrissey finally beat McCann into submission, but the fire, steam, and burning flesh earned Morrissey his life-long moniker, "Old Smoke."[27]

The wanderlust so common to the American working class struck Morrissey in 1851. In search of gold and adventure, he stowed away on a California-bound ship. The Sierra foothills did not yield their ore to him, but he quickly found other ways to make money. Before leaving New York, Morrissey had learned how to run a faro game, then an immensely popular form of gambling in America. Bankrolled by San

Francisco friends, Morrissey and his partner "Dad" Cunningham enjoyed moderate prosperity. But always ambitious, he was not content. George Thompson, Tom Hyer's trainer for the Sullivan match, had just won the "Championship of California." Morrissey challenged him, and the Western press hyped the fight as an ethnic contest, Irish-American versus Anglo-American. They fought for two thousand dollars a side on August 31, 1852, at Mare Island, California. Morrissey's main asset was an incredible ability to take punishment, but Thompson was a highly skilled fighter, and for several rounds the Englishman gave the novice a boxing lesson. Rather than see their man lose, however, Morrissey's partisans so menaced Thompson with a show of weapons that he deliberately fouled his opponent after eleven rounds. Forfeiting the match and two thousand dollars probably seemed a small price compared to losing his life.[28]

Old Smoke returned to New York, his reputation enhanced and his pockets full. Several fighters were willing to give the newcomer a try. Most important, Tom Hyer wanted revenge for the wrong done to his friend. Hyer openly identified himself with nativist factions in New York City politics, so personal ambition once again merged with deep social tensions. Offended at remarks made by "Young America," Morrissey challenged him; each man put up a one-hundred-dollar deposit to arrange a match. Hyer, however, insisted on fighting for no less than ten thousand dollars a side. Whether because of lack of funds or lack of confidence, Morrissey's friends found the amount too high, so they forfeited their hundred dollars, a serious loss of face.[29] The Troy man and his backers itched for a big fight, and the next logical opponent in terms of fame and ability was Yankee Sullivan, who by this time had reconciled with Hyer. Although both Morrissey and Sullivan were Irish-American champions, the ethnic motif was again played up by the newspapers. Old Smoke's arrogance, youthful virility, and enmity with Thompson and Hyer made him seem the more active threat to native Americanism, so Sullivan became by default the Anglo-American favorite.[30]

After an angry meeting in a New York saloon they signed articles of agreement on September 1, 1853, pledging to fight for one thousand dollars a side six weeks later. Morrissey selected the battleground: Boston Corners, a tiny town one hundred miles north of New York City where Massachusetts, Connecticut, and the Empire State met. He chose this spot because state jurisdiction was unclear, confounding local magistrates who might want to interfere. Moreover, the Harlem Railroad connected New York City with Boston Corners, and the village was also near Albany and Troy, assuring Morrissey of a large number of supporters. The fight was scheduled for a Wednesday afternoon, men began trickling into Boston Corners on Monday, and by the morning of the bout extra cars had to be added to the seven o'clock train out of New York. At least three thousand, perhaps as many as six thousand people, including rural folk from the surrounding countryside, came to witness the great event. Many carried their own food and slept outdoors. By fight time, acres of spectators crowded the ring.[31]

The *Clipper* estimated that two hundred thousand dollars rested on the outcome. At ringside the betting was lively, with Morrissey the heavy favorite. Never one to miss an opportunity for bravado, he strutted around the ring, offering $1,000 to $800, or $500 to $400 on himself. He found no takers, for not only was Sullivan three inches shorter and thirty pounds lighter, but at age forty-one he looked old enough to be Morrissey's father. Appearances proved deceiving. Through thirty-seven rounds Sullivan pummeled his opponent at will. As early as the fourth round, "Morrissey's face exhibited the most revolting appearance imaginable—his eye was dreadfully swollen, and the blood was flowing in a perfect stream from each nostril." By the thirty-second round Morrissey was a "sickening sight," with "blood gushing in streams from nose, mouth and half a dozen gashes on his face." Even Morrissey's endurance had its limits.[32]

But five rounds later, just when Sullivan's science and speed seemed about to carry the day, chaos broke loose. Precisely what happened is unclear. Some reports declared that Morrissey was choking Sullivan on the ropes and that Sully's seconds interfered to save their man. Friends of Sullivan claimed that Old Smoke's seconds broke the ring to spare Morrissey further humiliation. In any case, partisans of both men were instantly in the ring, engaged in a free-for-all brawl. Meanwhile, the timekeeper ordered the thirty-eighth round to begin. Morrissey came up to the scratch, but Sullivan, busy punching it out with Morrissey's second, Orville "Awful" Gardner, failed to answer the call. Old Smoke's umpire asked for a judgment, and the referee decided in his favor, awarding him the match and the stake money in clear violation of the rule specifying that a fight be halted until the ring was cleared. A war of words raged in the newspapers for weeks. Yankee Sullivan demanded a rematch and advised his followers not to pay their wagers. But by custom and regulation the referee's decision was final.[33]

While sporting men sang the heroes' praise, others responded with predictable scorn. The *New York Tribune* declared that such infernal scenes degraded all of humankind; the *Evening Post* suggested that

Sullivan and Morrissey would have accomplished much good by killing each other; the *New York Times* covered the event but editorialized against its barbarity:

> With the benefits of a diffused education; with a press strong in upholding the moral amenities of life; with a clergy devout, sincere and energetic in the discharge of their duties, and a public sentiment opposed to animal brutality in any shape; with these and similar influences at work, it is inexplicable, deplorable, humiliating that an exhibition such as the contest between MORRISSEY and SULLIVAN could have occurred. In any other light, from any other point of view, it must be a subject of profound and enduring degradation that the authorities permitted it to occur.

Still, the *Times* editor took heart that at the sight of blood, the "assembled ruffians" turned on each other like hungry beasts of prey. Next time, he hoped, the sporting fraternity would eradicate itself completely.[34]

Two weeks after the fight, warrants were issued by Massachusetts officials against the principals. New York City authorities captured the luckless Sullivan and bound him over to the Bay State, where he was jailed for a week in Lenox, Berkshire County. In a display of fraternal solidarity, Tom Hyer came forth and raised fifteen hundred dollars bail from prize-ring supporters to secure the release of his old antagonist. Eight months after the fight Morrissey too stood before a Berkshire County grand jury and paid a twelve-hundred-dollar fine rather than serve sixteen months in jail. Sullivan never entered the ring again, but Old Smoke rode the crest of his newfound prestige. He prospered during the early fifties as a keeper of a taproom, proprietor of a faro parlor, and promoter of cockfights. More important, his charisma and organizational abilities gave him a leading role among grass roots Tammany loyalists.[35]

Morrissey had found an environment that rewarded his talents. Still, his impulsiveness continued to get him in trouble. For years he had taunted Tom Hyer, and on various occasions they were about to face each other with fists or dueling pistols, only to be prevented by friends or the authorities. But Morrissey's violent temperament was not confined to his fellow prize fighters, and the assault indictments begun in Troy continued. One night in 1856 he pulled a pistol and shot at two waiters during a drunken spree in a New York saloon. Political influence kept him out of prison. In 1857 he faced three different charges of assault with intent to kill, but again he served no time because of the intervention of well-placed friends. His most notorious brush with the law came in 1855, with the assassination of William Poole. Poole was a butcher by trade, as well as an infamous thug, gambler, and rakehell. A local political leader who used his muscle to gain grass roots support, he was a native-born American, a ward leader for the Know Nothing party, and a friend of Tom Hyer.[36]

The two bruisers had previously fought a street battle on Poole's turf, among the New York docks, and Old Smoke got the worst of it. While the butcher gouged and bit Morrissey's face, Poole's gang kicked him insensible. They met again on February 24 in Stanwix Hall, a Bowery saloon. Their shouting match culminated with both men drawing pistols, but police separated the two before any damage was done. Later that night Morrissey met with several friends, then went home to bed. A few hours later his companions returned to Stanwix Hall, where Poole stood drinking. Words quickly led to gun shots, and in a few seconds four men lay wounded, Poole mortally. Morrissey was afterward implicated as the "mastermind" of the murder, but no evidence was ever produced and charges were quickly dropped. Still, the incident lived in public memory. Poole's funeral was one of the grandest the nation ever witnessed, and his killing was interpreted by nativist Americans as an illustration of their victimization at the hands of the bloodthirsty Irish.[37]

Despite Morrissey's personal problems, prize fighting continued to prosper. The summer of 1857, for example, witnessed three major bouts. Izzy Lazarus—a Jew, an English immigrant, a former boxer, and the father of two fine lightweights—made his saloon in Buffalo the headquarters for these battles. The first pitted Dominick Bradley against S. S. Rankin, both Irishmen, both Philadelphians, and both saloonkeepers. Bradley, however, was Catholic and Rankin Protestant, a fact that created intense interest in the Irish community and caused Philadelphia's Irish Protestant Association to help raise the Orangeman's thousand-dollar stake. Neither fighter was very experienced, yet six thousand members of the fancy came from Baltimore, New York, Boston, Albany, Cleveland, Montreal, and Philadelphia for the battle. Even a few men of status quietly made their way to ringside. "In the event of an arrest," the *Buffalo Commercial Advertiser* declared, "some names of gentlemen who would not restrain their curiosity to 'see this sort of thing just once' would be likely to figure to the astonishment of those outside the circle of excitement." Names were never revealed.[38]

The Buffalo wharves on fight day offered a colorful spectacle as a flotilla of steamers and small craft headed into Lake Erie, bound for Point Albino, Canada West. Ringside presented an equally striking sight. Spectators perched in trees or on carriages, and others walked around the ring calling out wagers, as a motley crew of urban sports drank, argued, and jostled one another before the call of "time." The appearance of Hyer and Morrissey at ringside sent waves of excitement through the crowd. In contrast to the American constabulary, the local Canadian sheriff, a Yorkshireman, eased logistical problems and made sure the proceedings went smoothly.[39]

Bradley and Rankin battled for nearly three hours through one hundred fifty-two grueling, if not very artful, rounds. Passions ran so high during the contest that fights broke out among the spectators. Eventually, however, Bradley's edge in experience paid off. "Rankin has lost," the *Clipper* declared, "but we know that he has gained many a friend by the gallantry and indomitable endurance so well displayed." Men at ringside contributed to a consolation purse for the fallen warrior. When results reached Philadelphia, the sports packed into Bradley's tavern danced with joy, toasted their man, and counted their winnings. Outside, the overflow crowd that had kept a vigil for days in the sweltering summer heat held their own victory celebrations through the night. In the Moyamensing district Rankin's house was also packed, but here the patrons shared mixed feelings: sorrow, suspicion of foul play, pride in their man's pluck, and chagrin at the loss of wagers.

Twice more in the next few months the Eastern sporting crowd took the "specials" to Buffalo. Those who could not afford eight-dollar tickets—the usual fare from New York City was five dollars, but railroad companies and promoters knew a good thing when they saw it—gathered at wharves, newspaper offices, telegraph terminals, train stations, and taverns awaiting news from Canada. Though not quite of the magnitude of the Bradley-Rankin affair, the "game and manly" rematch between lightweights Denny Horrigan and Harry Lazarus, and the "gallant contest" between Irish immigrants Joe Coburn and Harry Gribben, kept the sporting pot boiling."[40]

Many Philadelphians believed that Bradley's victory made him champion of America, but most men felt that the honor still belonged to Morrissey by virtue of his victory over Sullivan and Hyer's refusal to fight. The 1857 matches whetted appetites for Old Smoke's return. His opponent was John C. Heenan, twenty-three years old, born of Irish immigrant parents in Morrissey's hometown of Troy. Heenan's background was working-class, but his family seemed a bit more respectable and prosperous than the champion's. Timothy Heenan, John's father, was a machinist and foreman in the ordnance department of the Watervleit Arsenal near Troy. John, however, had spent his early years as an unskilled laborer. In 1852, at the age of seventeen, he headed west to

John Morrissey and John C. Heenan.
The two most celebrated fighters
of the 1850s were both born of Irish
immigrant parents, grew up in
Troy, New York, and were leaders in
the rough masculine subcultures
of San Francisco and New York City.

California, where he swung a hammer in the Pacific Mail Steamship Company's workshops in Benicia. He took the nickname "Benicia Boy," filled out his six-foot, two-inch frame with two hundred pounds of muscle, and acquired a word-of-mouth reputation for toughness. Heenan soon quit his job to try his luck at mining, and that failing, he became a political enforcer in San Francisco. His electioneering activities got him in trouble, so he left the Golden State before being thrown out.[41]

He returned to New York where his muscular support of Tammany was rewarded with a sinecure in the customs house. Like many other strong and ambitious men with limited career horizons, Heenan's thoughts turned to the ring. He paid a call at the *New York Clipper* office and met Frank Queen. Whether as a result of genuine enmity, instigation by friends, or deliberate promotion by the press—most likely it was a combination of all three—heated charges and countercharges between Old Smoke and the Benicia Boy began appearing in the *Clipper* and the *Herald*. Morrissey, forever taunting his rivals, questioned Heenan's courage, belittled his fighting ability, and told him to "put up or shut up." The youth published a card on July 3 challenging the champion to fight. Suddenly, heated words gave way to the cool language of articles of agreement: "The said John Morrissey agrees to fight the said John C. Hennan a fair stand up fight according to the new rules of the London Prize Ring, by which the said John Morrissey and John C. Heenan agree to be bound. . . ." It is testimony to the folk nature of prize fighting, its rootedness in street reputation, that Heenan was about to contend for the championship without ever having entered the regular prize ring.[42]

The fighters went through several weeks of rigorous training, including purgative taking, induced vomiting, and the usual regimen of exercise and diet. They also held several sparring exhibitions. These benefits not only stirred public excitement, they were also quite lucrative. Morrissey gave one in Buffalo, three in Boston, and several in New York, one of which yielded $2,500. Although both men were of Irish descent, ethnic rivalry was projected onto the fight as in the Boston Corners battle. This was in part a journalistic device to whip up interest, but the ploy was grounded in a larger divergence of the two boxers' public images.[43] Morrissey was always the outlaw figure, a strutting braggart associated with corrupt politics, gang violence, and urban vice, while Heenan's persona was a little more compatible with the ideals of the "respectable" working class. In coming years the Benicia Boy would marry the notorious "naked lady," Adah Isaacs Mencken, infamous for her seminaked stage performances and open love affairs; he would also be identified more closely with urban bullies and political strong-arm men. But for now he seemed not so closely tied as Old Smoke did to gangs, groggeries, and gambling dens. A bit less threatening than the swaggering Morrissey, Heenan was tentatively adopted as the representative of native-born Americans battling a vicious foreign foe.[44]

Like other recent bouts, this one came off in Canada to avoid police interference. What began as necessity ended in pleasure, for the excursion to Buffalo, the hospitality of Izzy Lazarus, the exciting crossing to Canada, all helped expand the fight from a brief event into a pageant lasting several days. Gamblers and saloonkeepers worked out profitable arrangements with rail and steamship companies. By mid-October sporting men were once again pouring into Buffalo, many from as far away as New Orleans. The *New York Tribune*'s special correspondent called the gathering, "the most vicious congregation of roughs that was ever witnessed in a Christian City." *Frank Leslie's Illustrated Newspaper* offered engravings of these "different varieties of American ruffians," noting that many were "always ready with the pistol or the knife, which they do not scruple to use against any opponent who refuses to be converted to their own way of thinking." William Poole's murderer, Lew Baker, and Morrissey's old gambling partner, Dad Cunningham (who had killed Paudeen MacLaughlin in a saloon brawl), were among the more notorious characters in attendance. For all the righteous fears expressed in the press, however, a little cursing, drinking, and scuffling at Izzy Lazarus's saloon was about all the trouble that occurred.[45]

After dodging arrest by the legal authorities, both principals made it to Buffalo. The stakes were five thousand dollars a side; Morrissey backed himself with earnings from his faro business, while gamblers, emigrant runners, grogshop owners, and sporting men supplied the rest of the money. Thousands purchased tickets marked "excursion" or "pic-nic," boarded steamers docked on the Buffalo wharves, and set out for Canada at 11:30 P.M. on Tuesday, October 19. By 8:00 A.M. the following morning, the vessels dropped anchor three-quarters of a mile from Long Point, a peninsula of sand jutting into Lake Erie. Three more hours were consumed landing the passengers, who waded, rowed, or were carried ashore on the backs of sailors. Long Point was so barren that to satisfy the rule that the ring be pitched on turf, a few stray tufts of grass had to be found then transplanted within the ropes.[46]

Finally, at nineteen minutes past one, Heenan threw his hat in the ring and it was followed moments later by Morrissey's. Each party appointed twenty-five ring keepers, bruisers armed with large clubs who stood outside the ropes and maintained order by keeping spectators beyond a large outer ring. Reporters estimated that in New York State alone a quarter of a million dollars rested on the outcome, and betting in far-off towns, St. Louis, Chicago, and New Orleans, was also quite heavy. Morrissey's friends offered last-minute wagers, walking around the ring calling out $100 to $75 on Morrissey, then $100 to $70 and $100 to $60, $50 on first blood, $50 on first knockdown, $50 on first fall, all with few takers. Morrissey himself offered Heenan a $1,000-to-$600 side bet, but the Benicia Boy declined, pleading lack of funds. All of this was designed as much to intimidate the smaller, poorer Heenan party as to secure real wagers. In the meantime the seconds prepared their men, helping them strip to their fighting drawers and lace up their spiked shoes. By the time the colors were tied to the stakes—the stars and stripes for Heenan, blue with white spots for Morrissey—gamblers were shouting $100 to $50 on Morrissey with little luck, and Old Smoke himself found no takers at $500 to $300 for first knockdown. Morrissey's friends were so sure of themselves and Heenan's so diffident not only because of the champion's prowess but also because the Boy had developed a serious abscess on his leg. Unable to train for a week as a result of his painfully swollen limb, feverish and bedridden the whole time, Heenan looked to have slim chances despite his three-inch, twenty-pound advantage.[47]

After two hours of wrangling over choice of referee, an important question given the power of that position, the parties compromised by appointing two men. Finally, sixteen hours after leaving Buffalo, the crowd's patience worn thin, the men came up to the scratch at the first call of "Time!" Round one lasted four-and-one-half minutes and astonished even Heenan's most loyal friends. Following some cautious sparring, feinting, and parrying, the Boy caught Morrissey with a vicious right to the eye and a left to the nose (first blood), then pinned Old Smoke against the ropes and pummeled him at will. Science, speed, and power were all with Benicia. Some observers later claimed that only when Heenan smashed his hand against a corner stake, damaging two knuckles, was Morrissey saved from elimination in the first round. As in previous fights, however, Old Smoke's endurance—"bottom" as the fancy called it, borrowing a racetrack term—amazed everyone. "John never seemed to know when he was licked," a contemporary observed, "and just as you got tired of thumping him, he kind o' got his second wind, and then you might as well tackle the devil as try to make any headway against him." For several rounds Heenan dominated the fight, punching and throwing Morrissey at leisure. However, the Boy's illness finally sapped

Morrissey battles Heenan, October 20, 1858, at Long Point, Canada West. *Frank Leslie's Illustrated Newspaper,* October 30, 1858, railed against the "depraved" sports at ringside and then printed several engravings of the action.

his strength. By the eleventh round both men had to be led to the scratch, but Morrissey could still stand and hit, while Heenan was defenseless. The Boy finished ingloriously, swinging wildly, overreaching himself, and collapsing insensible.[48]

Old Smoke's friends were beside themselves with joy. When Heenan recovered his strength, the sporting fraternity procured a carriage, seated the two heroes side by side, and paraded them around the ground. After copious drinking, backslapping, whooping and hollering, the ring keeper pulled up stakes, and the multitude headed back to Buffalo. They steamed in at 2:30 A.M., Morrissey's boat firing rockets to announce their arrival as crowds cheered at the wharves. Back in New York City, taverns and newspaper and telegraph offices were in a virtual state of siege. Thousands clamored for news of the results, and street fights threatened the public peace.[49]

"Probably no human eye," the *New York Tribune* declared solemnly,

> will ever look upon so much rowdyism, villainy, scoundrelism, and
> boiled-down viciousness, concentrated upon so small a space. . . . Scoundrels
> of every imaginable genus, every variety of every species, were there
> assembled; the characteristic rascalities of each were developed and dis-
> played in all their devilish perfection. The talk of establishing the Prize
> Ring in America, under an orderly supervision, is simply nonsense,
> judging from the people present at Long Point on Wednesday last. At
> present its patrons seem to be men who seek not to encourage a perfect
> development of physical strength and beauty, and an occasional good-
> tempered contest for mastery, but who only desire to gamble on the result
> of a fight between two fine animals.

The *Tribune* correspondent concluded that manliness and fair play were
nowhere to be seen amidst the barbarism at Long Point. *Frank Leslie's
Illustrated Newspaper* concurred: "a worse set of scapegalloweses . . . could
scarcely be collected; low, filthy, brutal, bludgeon bearing scoundrels—
the very class of men who have built up the Tammany Hall party in New
York. . . ."[50]

However, it was left to *Harper's New Monthly Magazine* to best
capture the contrast between genteel ideals and the latest pugilistic
outrage. Sentimental verse, packed with romantic clichés, described the
undefiled northern landscape on the day of the fight:

> . . . Grandly the autumn forests shine,
> Red as the gold in an Indian mine!
> A dreamy mist, a vapory smoke
> Hangs round the patches of evergreen oak. . . .
> Nature is tracing with languid hand
> Lessons of Peace over lake and land. . . .

But the most brutal, dregs of society polluted God's tabernacle:

> . . . Round about is a bestial crowd,
> Heavily-jawed and beetle-browed;
> Concave faces trampled in,
> As if with the iron hoof of Sin!
> Blasphemies dripping from off their lips,
> Pistols bulging behind their hips;
> Hands accustomed to deal the cards,
> Or strike with the cowardly knuckle-guards. . . .

Criminal, foul-mouthed, sin-stained, the fancy lived on blood, and all of humankind was degraded by their acts. Fine young specimens of God's highest creation, Morrissey and Heenan betrayed their Maker's work:

> ... It is a pleasure their limbs to scan,
> Splendid types of animal man;
> Splendid types of that human grace,
> The noblest that God has willed to trace.
> Brought to this by science and art,
> Trained, and nourished, and kept apart;
> Cunningly fed on the wholesomest food,
> Carefully watched in every mood;
> Brought to this state, so noble and proud,
> To savagely tussle before a crowd—
> To dim the light of the eyes so clear,
> To mash the face to a bloody smear,
> To maim, deface, and kill, if they can,
> The glory of all creation—Man! ...

Once again the ring inverted pious, humanitarian ways and upheld the impulsive values of the urban underworld. More than merely brutal, the fight overturned the cherished Victorian ideal of universal benevolence suffusing the natural world. Unreasoning, savage, depraved, the sporting fraternity implicitly denied the optimistic faith of reformers in the perfectability of man and society.[51]

Worse still, the cancer was spreading. Daily papers were filled with news of the fight because, *Harper's* editors admitted, growing numbers of people wanted it. Twenty-five years earlier the concern among journalists for public morals and the "good sense and feeling of the readers" had prevented such shameless reporting. Now, however, America slid down a moral spiral, pushed along by unscrupulous men who lined their pockets by gratifying depraved tastes. One expected the ring to attract attention in New York's Five Points, where "all the haunts of Dead Rabbits, gamblers, and thieves were crowded with the scum of a festering metropolis, eagerly gaping at every rumor, and as promptly consoling their disappointment with cheap whiskey." But it was surprising that Heenan's autograph had become a valuable commodity on Wall Street.[52]

Declared the *Troy Evening Times*, "the mania created in anticipation of this fight exceeds any before ever known." The arrangements were more open, the press coverage more detailed, and excitement deeper than for any previous battle. Local politicians and officials freely curried

the fighters' favor. "Southern planters and dry goods merchants bet on
the results of the conflict," the *New York Times* lamented; "a mighty,
populous and refined metropolis waits with hushed anxiety to know
which of the two ruffians had his pate first broken, or his chest stove in
by the other." *Harper's Weekly* declared that Morrissey and Heenan
preempted discussion of all other public issues: "On Thursday, especially there was nothing heard of—uptown, downtown and in the country—
but the great prize fight. . . . [It] was, we venture to assert, the only topic
discussed that morning in bank parlors, counting rooms and offices
generally throughout the city—to say nothing of barrooms and places of
like character." Prize fighting might remain indelibly corrupt, but
increasingly it was being "countenanced by a kind and indulgent
public."[53]

The celebrations in New York City topped all before. Morrissey's
friends rejoiced in victory, while the Benicia Boy's partisans consoled
themselves that their man must soon be champion. Heenan was ready to
sign new articles immediately, but Old Smoke refused, declaring that
win or lose, he had intended the Long Point fight to be his last. The two
men publicly boasted, goaded, and belittled each other during the next
several months, yet no rematch was arranged, and Old Smoke never
fought in the ring again. He engaged in a few sparring exhibitions during
the 1860s, but as Morrissey entered his thirties, he spent more of his
time with his family, his gambling establishments, and politics. The
burning young Irish brawler had settled into a comparatively quiet and
prosperous manhood.[54] Decades later, however, taverns still resounded
with his praise. Before long, the sporting crowd sang of "Johnny
Morrissey" or "Jack Morrisy," the hero of a traditional broadside ballad
that combined real and fictive events. Challenged by a Russian sailor in
Tierra Del Fuego, the champion defiantly picked up the gauntlet:

> Then up spoke Jack Morrisy, with a heart so stout and true,
> Saying, "I am a gallant Irishman that never was subdued;
> Oh I can whale a Yankee, a Saxon Bull or Bear,
> And in honor of old Paddy's land I'll still those laurels wear."

Morrissey of course, defeated the Russian, and the song closed triumphantly,
recalling the champion's victories:

> Our hero conquered Thompson, the Yankee Clipper too,
> The Benicia Boy and Sheppard he nobly did subdue;
> So let us fill a flowing bowl and drink a health galore
> To brave Jack Morrisy and Paddies evermore.

A century after his fighting career ended, Irish pubs still rang with the saga of bold John Morrissey.[55]

The Fate of Champions

The three great champions of the antebellum era—Sullivan, Hyer, and Morrissey—revealed in exaggerated terms the opportunities and limitations of their social background. After losing to Morrissey, Sullivan sought greener pastures in California. Well-versed in unorthodox methods of securing political majorities, he put his skills to work in the Golden State. New York's ethnic factions, street gangs, and grass roots political organizations had equivalents, writ small, in California. By the mid-fifties Sullivan was allegedly one of the West's most successful ballot box stuffers, selling majorities for a few hundred dollars each.

In 1856, however, a group of "the most respected merchants in San Francisco," as some newspapers called them, decided that men like Sullivan were destroying good order in their city. Imbued with a brittle sense of morality, a strict work ethic, and a strong streak of anti-Irish nativism, the vigilantes moved against their political and cultural enemies with Draconian zeal. In the name of democratic government they deposed elected officials and suspended the rule of law. Chris Lilly, still remembered for the fatal battle with Tom McCoy, Dutch Charlie Duane, a bruiser with long-standing ties to both pugilism and politics, and James Cusick, who helped arrange and promote fights back East, along with dozens of others, were rounded up and deported for various crimes.

The "popular tribunal" of businessmen next charged two citizens with murder and hanged them. Sullivan's name appeared on their black list of May 25, 1856. He was captured on the twenty-sixth and immediately tried with two others as "disturbers of the peace of our city, destroyers of the purity of our elections, active members and leaders of the organized gang who have invaded the sanctity of our ballot-boxes, and perfect pests to society." All were convicted within twenty-four hours. Four days after sentencing the former champion to deportation, members of the committee found him dead in his cell, the blood drained out of a gash in his right forearm. The California vigilantes claimed that Sullivan committed suicide, but the *Clipper* and other newspapers believed that he was either murdered or deliberately driven to take his own life.[56]

Tom Hyer's end was more prosaic. After defeating Sullivan, he operated a New York saloon and cultivated ties to the Bowery B'hoys and nativist politics. Though he never entered the prize ring again, he was involved in several vicious brawls. Always associated with the netherworld of gangs and violence, he and William Poole had stood at the gallows in the early fifties to shake hands with two young harbor thieves about to be hanged for murder. Fighting was Hyer's only real talent, and his postchampionship business efforts in gambling and saloonkeeping ended in failure. Like so many other boxers, his health broke down early. By the early 1860s this paragon of manly perfection could be seen crossing Broadway, "leaning on crutches, almost doubled up, as helpless as a child, ragged, ill-clad, and never free from pain." In October 1863 friends gave a benefit to aid the destitute ex-champion. Nine months later he expired from heart failure, his once magnificent frame broken by a diseased liver and an enlarged spleen. Like Yankee Sullivan, the Chief was forty-five years old when he died, the average lifespan for men who became bare-knuckle fighters. Only a handful of people attended Hyer's funeral, after which John Morrissey contributed two hundred and fifty dollars to his widow and mother. For a generation, sporting journalists and barroom raconteurs, especially native-born ones, remembered Hyer as America's greatest champion.[57]

John Morrissey's fate was much less grim, and it is illustrated by an event he organized just six months after the Heenan fight. "Boss" William Harrington had fallen on hard times, and Old Smoke came forth to aid his family. Harrington was a butcher, pugilist, nativist gang leader, and political organizer during the 1830s. "What a flutter his presence used to create around New York about the old time election days," *American Fistiana* recalled. The boss was so successful in business that he purchased the premium stall in the new Washington Market, and some estimates claimed that his trade generated $25,000 per year. As time passed, however, Harrington's business, health, and sanity all failed him. Early in 1859, at age fifty-five, he simply disappeared, and for the family he left behind, Morrissey arranged a benefit. Tom Hyer helped promote the affair, John C. Heenan put on the gloves and sparred with Old Smoke, and other famous ring men exhibited their skills. Over two thousand tickets were sold, and the fancy packed Hoyim's Hall to aid the widow Harrington.[58]

In vintage Victorian prose, doubtless ghostwritten for the *Clipper,* Morrissey offered his thanks for the "manly and self sacrificing spirit" demonstrated by the fighters who volunteered their services, adding that "next to the satisfaction attending the fruition of a protracted and somewhat delicate transaction, is the pleasure of being aided by such noble and disinterested coadjutors. . . . But, above all is the consciousness that we have done our duty, while able to congratulate the public that 'the heart of the widow has been made glad.' " Frank Queen never missed an opportunity to point out such displays of generosity, but with the Harrington benefit his praise soared: "There is no class of men who are more prompt and willing to assist others than the pugilistic profession, and none who are more grossly misrepresented. The admirable manner in which the proceedings of this entertainment were conducted, and the great decorum and propriety of conduct manifested, was a source of satisfaction and gratification to the promoters of this noble work of charity."[59]

For once, some of the New York dailies agreed. The *Times*, referring to the recent caning of Massachusetts senator Charles Sumner by Congressman Preston Brooks of South Carolina, advised politicians to learn from the pugilists. The benefit for Harrington's widow revealed that in addition to "mere bruising and battering, hard drinking and swearing," the boxing fraternity could also display generosity, good manners, and brotherhood. The *Herald* agreed, praising the fact that Morrissey and his fellow prize fighters—men with "sinful hearts and bloodstained hands"—joined in the spirit of friendship for a charitable cause. Unlike the "Wall Street or Fifth Avenue Christian, who gives alms as an advertisement here and an investment in the world to come," these rough pugilists ennobled their effort with sincere, unselfish generosity. Here, in sum, was a spirit of mutuality momentarily transcending the deep schisms of the streets.[60]

The Harrington benefit was the sort of act that secured Morrissey's role as a community leader, a symbolic gesture that helped ingratiate him with a broad base of working-class people. Even before Old Smoke retired from the ring, he employed his influence as an Irish-American hero and leader of political gangs to help Fernando Wood win election as mayor of New York. Gradually Morrissey rose through the machine ranks, cultivating ties to Tammany Hall and becoming one of New York City's most powerful politicians.[61]

Old Smoke used his clout to expand and protect his gambling interests. He was one of a small group of Irish-Americans who took gaming out of the hands of footloose confidence men and reorganized it into a complex, stable business. The new gambler-businessmen maintained close ties to respectable backers for investment capital, to local politicians for protection, and to saloons, brothels, hotels, and restaurants for support services. By 1870 roughly three thousand New Yorkers were employed in gaming, and their efforts brought seventy-five thousand dollars into the local economy every week. With most avenues of social mobility closed to the Irish, organized gambling offered unusual financial opportunities, protected by other ethnic enclaves in politics, the courts, and police departments. A cultural tradition more forgiving of the sins of the flesh merged with the American success ethic, making "vice"—especially drinking, prostitution, and gambling, three of the most heinous activities in the Victorian canon—into lucrative businesses for at least a few Irishmen.

By the mid-1860s Morrissey was perhaps America's wealthiest gambler-businessman. Political connections helped him expand his interests from a single faro partnership in 1859 to sixteen just five years later. He also became the largest shareholder in a million-dollar company that monopolized "policy," a very popular and lucrative form of lottery. But the former pugilist sought prestige as well as wealth. After the Civil War horse racing entered a golden age; rich patrons sponsored great new tracks at Saratoga (1864), Jerome Park (1866), Monmouth Park (1870), Pimlico (1870), and Churchill Downs (1875). Soon an umbrella organization, the American Jockey Club, led by men such as August Belmont, was helping regulate schedules and rules of entry. Morrissey recognized an opportunity. In 1861 he opened a gambling house in Saratoga Springs, New York. Impressed with the potential of the locale, he began cultivating local elites and wealthy visitors. By 1864 he had built Saratoga race track but, more important, behind the scenes he organized and financed a prestigious sponsoring society. Incorporated in 1865, the Saratoga Association for the Improvement of the Breed of Horses had socially prominent men, William R. Travers, John R. Hunter, and Leonard W. Jerome among them, on its board. Morrissey was the largest, albeit anonymous, stockholder. In the next decade he helped substitute the cumbersome, face-to-face system of pool-selling for more rationalized forms of gambling, including pari-mutuel ticket sales, English-style bookmaking, and off-track betting. Simultaneously he and his partners opened the greatest gambling parlor of its day, a magnificent house run on strict business principles. Morrissey's financial acumen, then, helped make Saratoga into one of America's most elegant resorts.[62]

As a politician, Morrissey maintained arms-length contact with the gangs, brothels, and saloons of his youth, though his personal manner had become quiet, even genteel. Seeking not only power but respectability, he merged honor with expediency: Old Smoke opposed Boss William Tweed in 1868, and his testimony on corruption within Tammany contributed to the downfall of the machine. Morrissey rode the roller coaster of New York politics until he died in 1878, serving two terms in the U.S. Congress and two in the State Senate. More important, his popularity with working men and his organizational skills made him a power broker in New York City politics. Fifteen thousand mourners, including the lieutenant governor of New York and most of the state legislature, came to Troy to pay their last respects to the ex-champion.[63]

Little more than a decade separated Morrissey's alleged complicity in the murder of William Poole and his election to Congress. Amidst the ethical laxity of Gilded Age business and politics, the elevation of a former bruiser seemed to guardians of propriety an especially telling sign of moral decline. "Ideas of respectability differ," the *New York Tribune* editorialized on his death:

> Mr. Morrissey's scheme consisted in wearing a good coat. It implied no particular change in his morals, and only a little variation in his manners. Prize-fighting would not do any longer; so he reformed himself into a gambler, and set up a first-class hell; and inasmuch as his patrons spent a great deal of money, and did not cut one another's throats for the sake of the stakes, he made no doubt that he was now entitled to the consideration of an honest hard-working citizen. . . . Having opened a gilded and alluring pest house for the corruption of good society, he asked the applause of the virtuous on the ground that he no longer made it a business to exchange blows with a half naked ruffian for the amusement of the mob.

The righteous dismissed him as an ex-pugilist, a gambler, and a political street fighter; the pious could not forgive his sins.[64]

But this was an extreme view. By the 1870s the anti-Irish sentiment had abated somewhat, a full generation had passed since the great migration, and the children of immigrants were finding a little more acceptance in America. Besides, Victorian moral strictures were slowly loosening, and as a politician Morrissey had been by Gilded Age standards honest and conscientious. Indeed, compared to such businessmen and public servants as Jay Gould and Boss Tweed, Morrissey seemed a model of probity. Thus most newspapers praised the former pugilist on his death, observing that he had transcended his rowdy youth to become a useful citizen, a man of shrewdness, rectitude, and generosity.[65]

The fate of these mid-nineteenth-century champions helps illuminate prize fighting's social and cultural environment. Sullivan's violent end in the face of a strident assertion of nativist morality, Hyer's pathetic lapse into impoverishment and disease, Morrissey's giddy rise to wealth and power through ward politics and organized gambling—all reveal the potentials, the dangers, and the turbulence of urban street life. The three men were far from "typical," but their lives were structured by the opportunities and limitations of working-class experience. It is to the larger questions of culture and society in antebellum cities that we must now turn in order to understand the golden age of bare-knuckle fighting.

4

The Meanings of Prize Fighting

Working-Class Culture in Antebellum Cities

The rise of the ring was a complex phenomenon, an integral part of American social and cultural development. On one level, the great champions were not just heroes but celebrities in the sense that their fame depended at least partly on commercialized media. Newspaper stories, cheap biographies, lithographs, and photographs all helped raise public interest and disseminate the names and deeds of fistic heroes. The public personas of the champions were now marketable goods, giving them fame beyond their class and community. However, commercialized cultural production was in its embryonic stages. Even the great champions, Sullivan, Hyer, and Morrissey, were not alienated from their origins; they remained well-known figures on the urban streets, influential yet approachable men with whom one might share a bottle or play a hand of cards. Fame was not merely a product of impersonal media but was based on intimate knowledge of local customs and institutions. Heroic deeds of prowess and bravado were known at first hand.[1]

By the 1850s boxing was arguably America's preeminent sport—certainly the championship fights were among the greatest spectacles of the decade—but its popularity was not uniformly spread throughout the population. Despite the efforts of Frank Queen and his likes to argue the utility of the ring in Victorian terms, respectable native-born Americans rejected such claims. Pugilism in other words, did not simply "mirror" American culture. Although it could be argued that boxing reflected such mainstream values as individualism, the will to succeed, and materialism, the ring remained primarily a working-class preserve and conveyed a working-class sensibility.

The ring's social isolation occurred during a period when Americans' interest in sports was expanding. Certainly influential citizens were more accepting of leisure and recreation on the eve of the Civil War than they had been twenty years earlier. The hard shell of Victorian morality remained intact, but by the late antebellum era small cracks were appearing on its brittle surface. Reformers such as Thomas Wentworth Higginson, William Ellery Channing, and even Henry Ward Beecher believed that man could improve himself in body as well as spirit, so they advocated fresh air and exercise as antidotes to the ills of cramped urban life. Spectator sports enjoyed newfound popularity as rowing regattas, trotting matches, and pedestrian races became very popular among diverse Americans. A few well-off men displayed their status in baseball, cricket, and yachting clubs, pastimes that required large amounts of leisure time. An occasional young rakehell, for instance Frederick Van Wyck, son of a wealthy mercantile family, even showed up at urban dives such as Tommy Norris's Livery Stable: "When you start with a dog fight as a curtain raiser," Van Wyck reminisced, "continue with a cock fight, then rat baiting, next a prize fight, then a battle of billy goats, and then a boxing match between two ladies, with nothing but trunks on—after that I think you have a night's entertainment that has enough spice—not to say tabasco sauce—to fill the most rapacious needs."[2]

Perhaps experiences like those of the young Van Wyck were more common than the surviving evidence indicates. But for most of the middle and upper classes, Victorian propriety still hedged recreations onto narrow ground, and even leisured bons vivants usually shunned the more raucous pastimes of the English sporting gentry, confining themselves to such activities as yachting and horse racing. Much of the liberalization that occurred before the Civil War gained impetus from a handful of reformers who argued for rational amusements to develop character and refresh men for labor. Parks, reading rooms, and gymnasiums, it was said, led workers away from such riotous activities as prize fighting. A few bold individuals, among them Oliver Wendell Holmes, Sr., might openly attend sparring matches, write in praise of champions' physical excellence, even speculate on the outcome of a bout. Judging by the coverage in the "respectable" press, growing numbers of men were at least willing to view the ring from afar. No doubt many in the bourgeoisie envied what they perceived as the uninhibitedness of the working class and itched to break out of their own cultural confinement. But in public, at least, Victorian strictures were still too strong and the desire openly to violate them too weak to allow much deviation. The ring remained a symbol of urban depravity, proof that the lower classes wallowed in dissipation.[3]

Despite bourgeois injunctions, working-class men—including ones in old-established trades, unskilled laborers, the chronically underemployed, and those in the shadows of urban vice such as gamblers, pimps, and unlicensed liquor dealers—continued to stage their own recreations. Urban growth helped provide potential audiences for commercial spectacles. In 1820 only New York City and Philadelphia contained one hundred thousand people; by mid-century, Boston, Baltimore, Cincinnati, and New Orleans were over the mark. New York's 1830 population of two hundred thousand would increase fourfold in a mere thirty years as rural migrants and foreign immigrants came in search of work. By 1855 over half of all New Yorkers had been born abroad, and three out of ten had drawn their first breath in Ireland. This large and heterogeneous population needed leisure as well as jobs and, Victorian repressions notwithstanding, the urban working class pursued boisterous amusements.[4]

But the mere growth of cities and influx of immigrants do not wholly explain boxing's appeal. Between roughly 1820 and 1860 the economic life of urban areas was transformed. Certainly by mid-century the old apprenticeship system, in which a boy learned a trade, then worked as a journeyman and acquired the skills, property, and independence of a master, was moribund. Under the old order, shopkeepers and apprentices held mutual rights and obligations; they worked and even lived under the same roof, and their relationship was in the nature of a patriarchal family. But now the venerable ideal inherent in small-scale shops—that a craftsman was as much a father to his workers as a businessman—had dissolved. Gone too was the household economy, where labor was often performed in the home by all family members. This old social organization of work had not been without tensions; apprentices, wives, and children had often chafed under domineering masters. But it offered an ideal of mutuality, faith in the honorability of labor, and a path toward modest mobility for young men.[5]

Replacing artisan traditions in many trades was a modern system of capitalist production which tended to reduce relationships between employers and employees to questions of wages or piece rates. Most young workers no longer lived in surrogate families based on craft but in boardinghouses, seedbeds of "immoral" influences. Although many native-born tradesmen still called themselves journeymen and clung to craft traditions, most had in fact become employees, "wage slaves" in the parlance of the day. Moreover, new immigrants were filling unskilled positions in such volume that by 1850, half of all Irish males were either day laborers or cartmen. Women too, both native and immigrant, now occupied large numbers of unskilled jobs, as did the masses of native-born rural migrants pouring into the cities.[6]

This new social organization of work asked both employers and employees to exercise internalized self-restraint, to subdue their impulses and discipline their passions, if they were to accumulate wealth in increasingly competitive markets. The old republican ideology had demanded similar behavior, but the heightened importance of profit and the fear of financial failure now elevated assertive individualism over communal welfare, giving the emergent capitalist ethos an unmistakable harshness. The increasing emphasis on productivity brought employers to demand rigid self-control from themselves and their workers; industriousness and frugality become litmus tests of personal worth.[7]

Workers responded in a variety of ways, but it is probably best to think of their reactions as points along a continuum. At one extreme were those who accepted totally the stiffened ethic of abstemiousness. Like their bosses, many joined evangelical sects and temperance societies, merging piety and strict morality with industrial values. As their employers had promised, some rose through hard work to bourgeois prosperity and independence. On the opposite end of the continuum were those who rejected the safe and sober ethic, working so that they might play. For such lovers of street life, leisure more than labor formed the core of personal identity and cultural values. Raucous play offered these men a temporary escape from an oppressive working environment. In the middle were workers who adopted self-control as an implement of radical reform, a tool for building a revitalized producers' culture centered on the values of mutuality and communal improvement. Such men were the spiritual heirs of William Cobbett, and their assiduousness was aimed at collective improvement rather than purely individual gain.[8]

These categories are ideal types, of course, and few individuals matched them perfectly. The radical editor Mike Walsh, for example, wrote in the workingman's language, mixing admonitions for labor unity with endorsements of Yankee Sullivan's saloon, praise for jovial "Boss" Harrington, with announcements of rat-killing contests. Similarly, one as impulsive as John Morrissey offered his name and money to shipbuilders striking for an eight-hour work day. But on balance, activities such as prize fighting appealed to those in the working class inclined more toward self-indulgence than toward constant diligence, conviviality rather than abstemiousness, "the good time coming" instead of sober self-control.[9]

The decline of the old apprenticeship system and the new emphasis on wages gave workers reason to value wild recreations and scope to indulge their tastes. The capitalist economy created a sharp separation of work time from leisure time, freeing at least a few discretionary hours and dollars. Moreover, most laborers were not becoming bosses and few journeymen would ever be masters. For many men, the realm of play more than work now held out the best chance for finding a sense of challenge and fulfillment. Places such as New York's Bowery offered a kaleidoscope of plebeian pleasures. Working-class males revitalized such ancient pastimes as theater going, drinking, gambling, and bloodsports. They also frequented houses of prostitution, dance halls, oyster bars, minstrel shows, and circuses. Men reasserted mutuality among their compatriots in countless cliques and barrooms; they upheld a masculine honor that brooked no slighting of one's status among peers; and they demonstrated physical prowess in acts of strength and daring.[10] If not on the job, then in their free time individuals took control over their lives, found refuge from bosses, and inverted the bourgeois ethos with an antithetical assertion of rough male conviviality. Away from the impersonal workplace, where their power was ebbing, journeymen, mechanics, and laborers found alternative sources of value and esteem.[11]

Within this blossoming street culture, the new working class created a plethora of voluntary associations that engendered a sense of group autonomy. Labor unions, craft organizations, and mutual aid societies offered hope for real social and economic change. But less respectable institutions also embodied the sensibilities of many men. Saloons, fire companies, street gangs, and political organizations all had overlapping memberships, all were deeply rooted in the social structure of mid-nineteenth-century cities, and all had ties to the prize ring.[12]

Saloons were at the heart of working-class life. Cliques of men created informal but stable brotherhoods in particular bars, where politics were argued, grievances aired, heroes toasted, sports discussed, legends told, songs sung, and friendships cemented. The tavern keeper was a businessman, but he was also the caretaker of a cultural style that emphasized camaraderie and reciprocity among peers. The line separating bars from billiard halls, gambling houses, even brothels was not always clear, because in all of these establishments, entertainment was the order of the day. Saloonkeepers promoted various recreations, including dogfights, rat-baiting contests, and boxing matches, partly to sell more liquor and arrange profitable betting pools, but also to fulfill their role as leaders of working-class culture. Foot on the rail and glass in hand, a man could momentarily feel in control of his life, for here amidst friends the harshness of labor and the moral arrogance of the middle class were left behind. From the 1840s on countless boxers made particular bars their headquarters, and the saloons that prize fighters owned, managed, or frequented were made doubly popular by their presence, because boxers symbolized the successful flaunting of oppressive social and cultural norms.[13]

Volunteer fire brigades also became focal institutions of the working class. Men spent their leisure hours in the pump houses playing cards, drinking, and maintaining the equipment. Once the call for a fire went out, they rushed from their homes or shops, gathered at the station house, then dragged their gear to the blaze. For men whose working lives were prosaic and unchallenging, fighting fires offered a chance for heroic community service, a real sense of adventure, and an outlet for competitive self-assertion. Because neighborhood and ethnic conflicts often made rivals of different companies, all sought tough men who were willing to battle it out with opposing brigades, sometimes while a building burned to the ground. Boxers' fighting skills and courage were real assets to the fire companies, so Yankee Sullivan was recruited as a member of the Spartan band company, named for Mike Walsh's clique of radical workers, while Tom Hyer, Jim Jerolomon, William Poole, and John McCleester joined other brigades. Similar chances for heroics and display were offered by ubiquitous volunteer militia companies.[14]

Urban street gangs such as New York's mostly Irish "Dead Rabbits" and their arch rivals, the nativist "Bowery B'hoys"—made up mainly of journeymen and apprentices—overlapped the fire companies' constituencies, and again boxers were prominent members. Middle-class commentators feared that New York, Philadelphia, and Baltimore were now overrun with gangs that were committing heinous attacks on the innocent.[15] But though some of the gangs attracted social misfits who reveled in violence, most members were workers ranging in age from their teens through their thirties. The gangs were surrogate families, based on neighborhood, occupational, and ethnic affiliation. Here, as in the volunteer fire companies, laborers and apprentices turned loose after work sought adventure with their comrades. Drinking, fighting, gambling, playing sports, attending the theater, and especially promenading in distinctive dress filled their leisure hours. Because the gangs were intent on settling scores and intimidating rivals, prize fighters often became their leaders, and the Bowery B'hoys even wore "Tom Hyer hats" as part of their garb. Undomesticated by women, loving drink, and seeking distinction among peers, members valued strength, independence, and devil-may-care audacity. Though their violence was directed mainly against one another and was much less socially disruptive than the middle-class press feared, the gangs were perceived as deeply threatening to urban peace.[16]

Politics was also a crucial part of working-class life, and political organizations often blended almost imperceptibly into gangs, fire companies, and saloons. In New York and other burgeoning cities a fierce competition for place and power characterized the antebellum era. Lacking the stability of the modern two-party system, factions came and went, and no group dominated for long. For the working class in general and ethnic Americans in particular, political life had little to do with reformers' dreams of clean and efficient government. Jobs for the unemployed, power to the ambitious, protection for those involved in vice, licensing of trades, and naturalization for the immigrant—these were the lifeblood of urban politics. With so much at stake, unorthodox electioneering methods thrived. Nominations for city office were held in open meetings, often taverns, and anyone who could pack the hall with loyal supporters and menacing toughs might carry the day. Men as diverse as Mike Walsh, the radical leader of "subterranean" laborites, and Isaiah Rynders, head of the Empire Club, which bent with any political wind, pioneered such methods, and before mid-century the regular parties retained the services of political "shoulder hitters." On election day, repeaters at the polls, ballot-box stuffers, and strong-arm boys all had their usefulness, especially in hotly contested wards.[17]

These conditions allowed politicians and pugilists to form shifting but mutually beneficial alliances. At various times John Morrissey worked for Mayor Fernando Wood, William Poole and Tom Hyer for the Know Nothings, John C. Heenan for regular Tammany, Yankee Sullivan for the Empire Club. Countless lesser fighters were employed by various parties and factions. Mike Walsh made political hay with his ties to Hyer and the Bowery B'hoys, while Poole and Morrissey used their charisma and organizational ability to raise gangs of shoulder hitters whose motives were usually a mixture of ethnic pride and self-interest. The usefulness of prize fighters to urban politicians gave the ring protection it had not enjoyed since the days of Regency England, for in case of arrest, boxers knew that men in positions of power could get them out of trouble. In New York, pugilism's mecca, aldermen regularly had their friends released from police custody, especially muscular supporters who could be counted on next election day.[18]

Political factions, youth gangs, volunteer fire companies, saloons, ethnic brotherhoods, and nativist clubs added up to more than just a handful of adhoc organizations. These were interlocking institutions with shared memberships, focal points of a distinct working-class culture.

Changes in the nature of daily labor and in the relationships between employers and employees elicited creative cultural responses. It is only in this full context of work and leisure, economics and politics, that we can begin to understand what prize fighting meant to the tens of thousands of working-class men who followed the careers of the champions or even entered the ring themselves.

Meaning in Mayhem

On the simplest level, boxing gave elemental expression to deep social conflicts, to the pervasive parochialism dividing the working class. Intense devotion to one's neighbors, shopmates, and drinking partners engendered suspicion of outsiders and the need to defend turf. Ethnic rivalries, of course, caused the deepest divisions. Boxers, saloonkeeper-promoters, pool sellers, and editors all recognized that a battle between an Irish and an American fighter was good for business. But the enmity of the native-born and the Irish for each other was grounded in more than the mere manipulation of ethnic hatreds. Cultural and religious schisms ran deep, and they were exacerbated by parallel fissures in the social structure.

American-born workers bore the brunt of economic changes that destroyed old skills and crushed their autonomy. Many seized on the presence of foreigners as an explanation for their plight and accused the Irish of immiserating all laborers. Simply put, it was easier to blame one's problems on a rapacious and ruthless foreign enemy than on impersonal market forces over which one had no control. Lending credibility to nativist fears was the fact that in the competition for political power, the Irish were not passive victims but active organizers who used bloc voting as a way to secure offices and patronage. The suspicions, naturally, were reciprocal, and the Irish interpreted nativist prejudice as the source of their own special plight. Prize fighting was a means for both sides to dramatize and thereby understand these very real tensions over wealth and power. A good match focused their conflicts through the transparent symbolism of two heroes meeting under equal terms and orderly conditions. Whereas the divisions of the streets were shifting and chaotic, the ring created meaning from the chaos of existence, and the outcome of a fight offered cathartic if temporary resolution of deep social problems.[19]

Below the surface of ethnic turbulence was a less obvious battle over the nature of labor, for workplace affiliations also entered into ring loyalties. It was said of Harry Gribben, a sawyer, for example, that he had "many friends among the working classes, more especially those of his craft." Numerous native-born boxers practiced skilled trades, especially butchering. Tom Hyer, Bill Harrington, and William Poole were all members of this, one of the last bastions of the old artisan system. For young apprentice and journeymen butchers, boxing and other traditional recreations evoked the freer morality and less structured working rhythms of the preindustrial city. Better than most other tradesmen, the butchers retained their old cultural patterns centered around drinking and carousing after the markets closed.[20] But even the native monopoly on butchering was threatened in the 1840s, when Tammany politicians began selling licenses to Irish-born tradesmen. In this and other crafts the Irish were accused not simply of taking natives' jobs but of selling their labor for a pittance, aiding the extreme specialization of task which was destroying the artisan system. And indeed, impoverished, reviled, and largely unskilled, the Irish were providing cheap manpower for capitalist expansion. In this sense a fight between an American butcher and an Irish day laborer dramatized not only ethnic conflict but tensions over the nature of work as well, especially the artisan's fear of losing his trade and the laborer's envy of the craftsman's privileges.[21]

But we must not dwell exclusively on these schisms, for the ring also unified men in an expression of their lives' contradictions, momentarily resolving through a shared set of symbols the intractable conflicts of daily life. Even as it gave voice to tensions between skilled and unskilled labor, for example, prize fighting upheld the ideal of craft as a transcendent value, for pugilists demonstrated superb skill in a world that threatened labor's competence. Here, at the very beginnings of commercialized leisure, sports offered a chance for cartmen, dock workers, miners, coal stokers, and other men engaged in exhausting and dangerous jobs to supplement their meager incomes.

Equally important, spectatorship provided vicarious compensation for the destruction of traditional skills in the workplace. This can be seen in the very language of the ring. Boxing was a "profession," and pugilists were "trained" in various "schools" of fighting. Newspaper reports regularly used such phrases as "they went to work," or "he did good work," in their round-by-round coverage. "Art," "science," "craft," such words were constantly invoked to describe boxers' abilities. Symbolically, the ring was a surrogate workplace. In an environment that rapidly eroded the skills of many laborers, prize fighters retained their autonomy and traditions, their sense of craftsmanship. Sullivan, Hyer, Heenan, and Morrissey did not submit to the rigid regularity of industrial working rhythms; they might train diligently for a fight, but once it was over, they returned to their old, free-and-easy ways. In other words, prize fighters controlled the rhythms of their "work," enjoying precisely that independence which was sorely lacking in most men's lives. And even for less-than-famous boxers, the ring offered not only a chance to make a few extra dollars but a compensatory sense of accomplishment, of pride in one's own courage, grace, and skill which the work world denied.[22]

This shared sense of craft highlights the fact that even while prize fighting dramatized the parochial social conflicts of the streets, it also bound men together with their own cultural style. Despite political, ethnic, and occupational schisms, despite the intense rivalries of urban cliques, boxers and their fans shared values and behaviors. Tom Hyer helping raise Yankee Sullivan's bail, John Morrissey giving a benefit for Bill Harrington's widow, pugilists acting as pallbearers at their comrades' funerals, all reveal that a sense of unity often transcended the volatility of working-class culture. Boarding the trains or steamboats for a fight, the sporting crowd sought a neutral space where its social divisions could be dramatized even as the rites of the ring brought it together into a larger whole.[23]

The overarching unities of pugilism derived from the shared ethos of a large segment of the working class, and boxing's symbolism, in turn, reinforced that ethos. Prize fighting inverted Victorian norms, not necessarily rejecting them but adapting, transforming even parodying them. Boxers and their backers were all ambitious men, seeking to make money with their skills. Saloonkeeper-promoters prospered when new patrons flocked to their drinking establishments, and gamblers thrived when fans bought into their betting pools. Pugilists not only profited from taking a share of the stakes plus side bets, but the glory they gained in the ring also opened up new opportunities. Like John Morrissey, Irish-born Mike Norton parlayed his prize ring fame into local political power, becoming a Tammany district leader, state assemblyman and senator, and municipal court judge. When he died in 1889 he left twenty thousand dollars' worth of real estate to his family, property purchased with profits from his liquor and hotel businesses. Men such as Norton attained wealth and respect, but they did so on terms acceptable to the culture they came from. By their example they proved that bourgeois propriety and evangelical piety were not the only routes to success.[24]

Boxers, then, embodied a distinctly working-class version of the American dream, providing models of upward mobility within bounds acceptable to the street culture. Alone in the ring with only his own skills, the prize fighter refracted the American cult of individualism through the norms of his peers. As we have seen, training regimens, with their temperance, chastity, and self-discipline, read like Victorian manuals on upright behavior. Boxers who underwent such preparation temporarily accepted a kind of middle-class, goal-oriented behavior, a version of the delayed gratification that is the hallmark of the modern personality in industrial society. In this narrow sense, plebeian culture incorporated elements of bourgeois culture.[25]

But no one claimed, as observers would in the twentieth century, that the success of oppressed peoples in sports was evidence that social mobility was available to all who sought it, proof that any poor boy might "make it" in America. Quite the contrary, the very word "sport" implied social deviance. The gambler's bold wager, the drinker's revelry, the gang leader's profane boast, these were central to ring culture, and they offended middle-class sensibilities profoundly. A boxer who trained assiduously in order to mutilate another man mocked the goals of a society that deemed itself earnest, productive, and humane. Large crowds who set off on riotous excursions in the middle of the week implicitly denied the sanctity of the work ethic. Sinful excess, vulgar conviviality, open dissipation, fanciful pageantry, and unvarnished violence all sharply contradicted the ways good men were supposed to behave. And the fact that steamboats and railroads—charged symbols of social progress—carried the rowdies to their destinations stoked higher the flames of middle-class resentment.[26]

The centrality of money to prize fighting gives further evidence of the ring's inversion of evangelical and bourgeois ways. When a prize fighter or gambler flaunted his earnings, he was inherently attacking the cherished hope of the middle class that prosperity, piety, and hard work flowed together. Working-class men who marveled at the ten thousand dollars Tom Hyer and his backers won against Yankee Sullivan accepted the importance of wealth as a sign of success. But they valued money as a means to conviviality more than as a reward for sober self-control, or a sign of God's grace, or a vehicle of progress. Liquor sellers, gamblers, politicians, and boxers were not just petty entrepreneurs who, given the chance, would have chosen more respectable occupations. These men were successful by the standards of their communities, and they were leaders and heroes because their lives expressed the values of a large segment of the working class.[27]

Indeed, the revenues from liquor sales and gambling were the engines driving the sports boom of the 1850s. It would be an exaggeration to say that prize fighting existed solely so men could gamble, but without betting the ring would have stirred far less excitement. When a man wagered on a boxer—perhaps in a seemingly irrational amount—he risked not only his money but also his self-esteem. Choosing to bet on a particular fighter was a statement of ethnic, neighborhood, or occupational pride. Gambling brought excitement to a prosaic world, and shrewd wagering offered an alternative display of skill for men whose working lives too often denied them a sense of craft.[28]

Above all, both the small bettor and the professional gambler reversed the Victorian meaning of money. Rather than sanctifying wealth by putting it to prudent use, those who risked a high-stakes loss found in the risk itself what made gambling attractive. A man who put his money on a fighter gained status among his peers because he revealed his willingness to lose all in an effort to win big; gambling was a mark of courage. Of course, men wagering on a prize fight did not want to lose. Businessmen and gamblers both sought to increase their resources, and both assumed that agreements must be binding. But while the businessman argued that personal enrichment went hand-in-glove with material betterment for all, the gambler made no claim that his deeds brought social improvement. He was content to enjoy the thrill of the moment, thereby mocking middle-class ideals of thrift and progress. In this way the successful bettor was more dangerous than the failed one, for the latter merely jeopardized his own and his family's security, where the former was rewarded, encouraging him and others to continue their immoral behavior. As a stimulant to gambling, then, prize fighting undermined the Victorian meaning of wealth, transforming it from a sign of virtue into a source of corruption.[29]

Within the magic circle of the ring, not only were concepts of wealth altered, but gender too became inverted. With the breakdown of the household-based artisan economy, sexual identity grew increasingly bifurcated. Moreover, men and women were encouraged to moderate their passions and keep them from interfering with the goal of economic success. In the bourgeois canon, masculinity meant, above all, taking responsibility, controlling one's impulses, and working hard in order to support a family. Being a good provider was the touchstone of being a man, so probity, dependability, and resistance to temptation defined a middle-class male ideal. The very word manly was usually conjoined with "independence" or "self-reliance," thus linking the bourgeois concept of masculinity with autonomy and self-possession, key elements of Victorian character which flowed from diligent labor. Not all Victorian men fulfilled the role; many slid back into less morally rigid ways. The sporting underworld could stir the envy of those who felt themselves deprived of the freedom and openness they perceived in working-class culture. Despite these deep feelings of ambivalence, however, the bourgeois male ideal remained compelling, and it was reinforced by a new female role. For middle-class women, the home became a separate sphere, not a place of production but a haven where their superior morality refined men, nurtured children, and inculcated tender emotions. This domestic ideal placed women at the center of moral life, freeing men to go out into the corrupting world, then return to a purifying sanctuary.[30]

If the fundamental test of masculinity was, by Victorian lights, being a good breadwinner, if work was a man's primary source of self-definition, the measure of his worth, and proof of his manhood, then many working-class men in industrializing cities were doomed to failure. Of course, those who performed heavy or dangerous tasks could take pride in their strength and stamina. But fathers now had diminishing legacies of wealth or skill to pass on to sons, and for most men, earnings were small and opportunities limited. Put simply, daily labor undermined rather than buttressed masculinity. It made sense, then, that many workers turned to a more elemental concept of manhood, one they could demonstrate during leisure hours. Toughness, ferocity, prowess, honor, these became the touchstones of maleness, and boxing along with other sports upheld this alternative definition of manhood. The *manly* art defined masculinity not by how responsible or upright an individual was but by his sensitivity to insult, his coolness in the face of danger, and his ability to give and take punishment.[31]

Sociologists have talked of a "bachelor subculture" to capture a phenomenon so common to nineteenth- and early twentieth-century cities: large numbers of unmarried males finding their primary human contact in one another's company. In some large cities unweddedness was so common that at mid-century, 40 percent of the men between twenty-five and thirty-five years of age were single. Irish immigrants contributed to this tendency, bringing a tradition of late marriage and high rates of bachelorhood to America, but even among the native-born, working men in the nineteenth century tended not to marry until their late twenties. The bachelor subculture, however, included betrothed men as well as unattached ones. Sullivan, Hyer, and Morrissey, for example, were all married, but their wives seemed almost tangential to their lives as the champions passed their nights drinking and carousing among friends. With the breakdown of the household economy, men and women spent diminishing amounts of their work time together, and many chose to take their leisure too in gender-segregated realms. In saloons, pool halls, and lodges as well as in gangs, firehouses, and political clubs, men gathered to seek companionship, garner one another's esteem, and compete for status.[32]

Here, implicitly, was a rejection of the cult of domesticity so characteristic of bourgeois Victorian life. Members of the bachelor subculture expected women to be submissive; they also tended to view them as either pure and virginal or exciting and whorish. Women were both exploitable and less than central to men's affective lives. Rather than spend their nonworking hours within the confines of the family circle— where women's allegedly superior moral nature and "instinctive" sense of self-sacrifice tamed men and elevated children—members of the sporting fraternity chose to seek rough male companionship. It was not only men, however, who felt stifled by the domestic ideal. The Victorian home emotionally suffocated many middle-class women as well, and to compensate for the deprivations caused by their gender-based role, they sought one another's company. The homoerotic tone of letters women wrote to each other and the sensual descriptions of their meetings at spas where they went for physical and emotional therapy had less to do with simple homosexuality (though no doubt homosexual acts and relationships occurred) than with women reaching out for the warmth, love, and emotional contact that homelife denied.[33]

There was a parallel in the bachelor subculture that supported the ring. Of course heterosexual prowess was an important element of masculinity; fathering a family, picking up unattached women, and frequenting prostitutes all demonstrated virility. But maleness seemed most emphatically confirmed in the company not of women, but of other men. The loving descriptions of boxers' bodies so common in antebellum fight reports grew less from narrowly defined homosexuality than from a common male aesthetic. Men perceived men as creatures of beauty because they focused so much emotional attention on one another. In the saloon, the firehouse, or the gang, many working-class males found their deepest sense of companionship and human connectedness. The boxer's physique was a palpable expression of such masculine values as strength, power, and stamina. With his body alone the prize fighter attained financial autonomy. Conversely, women were associated with those family responsibilities made so onerous by low pay and lack of economic opportunity. Rather than accept domesticity as the highest good—and domesticity, after all, was a bourgeois luxury; working-class women often toiled in factories or as laundresses or maids—many laboring men sought refuge from the family in all-male peer groups where heroic prize fighters symbolized independence through physical prowess.[34]

Here the concept of male honor helps us understand the culture of the ring. Honor, as historians have recently applied the term, is distinct from the more modern ideals of conscience and dignity. The Victorian man of character possessed a particularly well-developed conscience (an internalized sense of morality stressing strict self-control) and a profound belief in human dignity (especially faith in the fundamental equality of all men). Thus each Christian faced God alone, businessmen were responsible for the fulfillment of their contracts, and good citizens acted on inviolable principles to perfect society. Although the approbation of others was gratifying for such men, good deeds brought their own internal satisfactions and immoral acts evoked a sense of guilt.[35]

But honor more than conscience or dignity depended on external ratification. It was conferred when men acknowledged one another as peers, often in symbolic acts such as buying drinks, spending money lavishly, or toasting one another's accomplishments. Honor had no existence outside group life, for only reputation and the esteem of others conferred it. Honorific societies have tended to be tightly knit and nonbureaucratic, placing special emphasis not on inward virtues but on outward signs that must be approved or rejected by one's status equals. The objects of honor have varied across time and cultures. They have included the protection of the chastity of wives and daughters, grand displays of hospitality, and tests of male prowess. But regardless of the specifics, an individual had honor only when his kin or his fellows said he did. Honor was denied him when his peers refused to acknowledge his status as an equal, and no amount of arguing could restore it. Only acts of valor, especially violent retribution, expunged the sense of shame, proved one's mettle, and reasserted one's claim to honor.[36]

The fights between boxers and the collectivities they belonged to—fire brigades, gangs, political factions, saloon cliques, militia companies, and so forth—were often animated by a sense of lost honor, of having had one's status impugned. Stake money for fighters, turf between gangs, and elected office for political parties, these were tangible objects to contend over, but the real battle was for peer recognition, for a sense of distinction that made a man first among equals in the small male cliques of working-class society. Saloons were so central to the culture of the ring in part because here, with alcohol lowering inhibitions, men affirmed their right to drink together or, alternatively, to cast aspersions that only blood could redeem. The ethic of honor had roots in the Old World, but it continued to thrive where individuals were concerned less with morality or piety, more with flaunting their status among peers through acts of masculine prowess. In mid-nineteenth-century America, then, character, conscience, and dignity were hallmarks of middle-class culture, while honor remained central to the lives of the poor and marginal, the acid test of personal worth in the male peer society.

The Rites of Violence

Perhaps most important, the bloodiness displayed in the ring was symptomatic of the violence endemic to urban working-class life. Unemployment and poverty were constant threats, and a cycle of alternating depression and inflation made the antebellum years particularly unstable. New York City's per capita wages fell by roughly 25 percent in the decade before mid-century. Moreover, the *New York Times* estimated in the middle of the 1850s that a family of four needed a minimum yearly income of six hundred dollars, double the salary of many laborers and well over what the majority of working-class men earned. In the impersonal market economy, lack of job security and inequalities of wealth and power were becoming intractable problems. And it was not only underemployment, poverty, and powerlessness, but occupational hazards that hit the working class with unrelieved force. Staggering numbers of men were killed or maimed on the job. Indeed, by 1860 there were four Irishwomen for every three Irishmen in New York City, partly because of desertions, partly because of breadwinners' need to travel in search of work, but also as a result of brutally high job-related mortality rates. In addition, poor diet, overcrowding, and lack of modern sanitation contributed to waves of deadly epidemics. Between 1840 and 1855 the city's mortality rates rose from one in forty to one in twenty-seven, and nearly half of all New York children died before reaching age six.[37]

The death sounds of livestock slaughtered in public markets, the smell of open sewers, the feverish cries of children during cholera season, the sight of countless men maimed on the job, all were part of day-to-day street life. The poor lived as their ancestors had, in a world that did little to shield them from pain. Men tolerated violence—created violence— because high death rates, horrible accidents, and senseless acts of brutality were a psychological burden that only stoicism or bravado helped lighten.[38]

This context makes sense of the ring's violence. Boxing, as well as cockfighting, bullbaiting, and ratting, did not just reflect the bloodiness of life. Rather, these and similar sports shaped violence into art, pared away its maddening arbitrariness, and thereby gave it order and meaning.

Here, ideally, was true equality of opportunity, a pure meritocracy free of favoritism and special influence. At their best, the ring and the pit rendered mayhem rule-bound instead of anarchic, voluntary rather than random. Boxers, like fighting cocks and trained bulldogs, made bloodshed comprehensible and thus offered models of honorable conduct. They taught men to face danger with courage, to be impervious to pain, and to return violence rather than passively accept it.[39]

As members of male peer societies steeped in the conflicts of their day, prize fighters embodied community values, giving them concentrated symbolic expression. Often harsh and brutal, working-class life required a dramatic form to express its reality. Boxing acknowledged, rather than denied life's cruelty, even celebrated it. In the midst of nagging hatreds and festering rivalries, often unleashed by flowing alcohol and blustering attacks on masculine honor, the cool restraint needed to sign articles, train, organize excursions, and bring off matches made bloodletting comprehensible. A properly carried out fight was a performance, a pageant, a ritual, that momentarily imposed meaning on the savage irrationalities of life. Out of chaos the ring created an aesthetic of violence based on bodily development, fighting skills, and controlled brutality.

This is not to argue that boxing and similar sports supplanted real with vicarious brutality. On the contrary, as recent research reveals, symbolic displays of violence tend to promote further violence.[40] Even as pugilism brought order to bloodiness, made it comprehensible by confining it to two men who represented larger collectivities and fought by rules, the ring also upheld, indeed gloried in the fact that brutishness was part of man's fate. Not the pious homilies of evangelicals, the sentimental humanitarianism of reformers, nor the optimistic progressivism of the middle class, prize fighting as a metaphor declared that there was limited good in this world, that every man's victory implied another's loss, that the way was harsh and bloody for all, and that hardship, even death, were the soulmates of life. The ring thus expressed an outlook in which pain and defeat were ineluctable parts of living, a notion almost heretical in this rationalistic age.[41]

Despite the divisions among sportingmen, then, all were united by disruptive change in their patterns of work, alienation from bourgeois or evangelical ways, and shared attitudes toward wealth, labor, leisure, masculinity, and honor. Working-class men adopted their own forms of expressive culture, and prize fighting symbolically affirmed their distinct ethos. If not a political threat to new alignments of social and economic power, the ring at least offered cultural opposition; if not a challenge to evangelical or bourgeois authority, here at least was a denial of the values that undergirded oppressive social relationships.

Above all, the manly art gave men a way to get a symbolic grip on the contradictions in their lives, to see these conflicts neatly arranged and played out. It offered an alternative to the Victorian vision of an ever-improving world, stressing instead a constant balance between victory and defeat. As drama, the prize fight depicted pain as the portion for both winner and loser, violence as a necessary means to human ends, and loyalty to one's communal group along with honor in defending one's good name as the very highest human ideals. The ring celebrated the high-stakes gamble, the outrageous boast, the love of strife. Prize fighting made Old World virtues such as prowess, courage, and virility the essence of manhood, while loving descriptions of muscles and sinews gave palpable expression to naked physical beauty as a source of masculine pride.

Of course the culture of the ring had an ugly, disturbing side. Bare-knuckle fighting attracted some social misfits who reveled in brutality. Boxing could become an outlet for bully boys who enjoyed inflicting pain, sociopaths who responded only to their own pleasure at other's suffering. The special order of the ring, moreover, sometimes broke down under the tensions it symbolically reconciled, unleashing further violence. Prize fighting also defined masculinity in a narrow way that encouraged male exploitation of women and alienated men from a whole range of softer emotions within themselves. But at its best the ring dramatized a world of victory for the socially downtrodden, realistically counterposed to defeat and bloodshed. It offered colorful, satisfying rituals that embodied the most profound human strivings but always presented them in mercilessly unsentimental terms. Boxers responded to a violent world by embracing violence, by accepting brutality and returning it with interest, by being as tough and savage as life itself.

In all of these ways bare-knuckle prize fighting was woven into the texture of working-class culture during the antebellum era. A plethora of urban street institutions supported the ring, as boxing helped crystallize the ethos of laboring men. Pugilism gave controlled expression to the schisms of working-class life, not in order to drain away violent passions but to make those divisions comprehensible and thereby transform chaos into meaning. Divided by neighborhood, ethnic, and workplace tensions, large segments of the lower classes were nonetheless united in opposition to key Victorian values, values on which an onerous new social system was built. Every bout inverted bourgeois and evangelical assumptions about such fundamental social phenomena as money, gender, and violence. More, the prize ring conveyed its own alternative outlook. Pugilism was an autonomous expressive form that symbolically opposed the drift of modern society. In crucial ways, then, boxing during the age of heroes captured the values, the ethos, the distinct culture of countless working men who felt dispossessed amidst the Victorian era's heady optimism.

Triumph and Decline

"The Great Contest for the Championship of the World"

"I, John C. Heenan, of the City of West Troy, United States of America, hereby challenge Thomas Sayers, the Champion of England, to fight me in six months from the time of his reception of this challenge, or from the date of the first deposit under it, for £200 a side and the champion's belt; the fight to take place near London (England), and to be governed by the rules of the London Prize Ring." Thus the Benicia Boy, now self-styled champion of America, sought to become king of all pugilism with one bold stroke.[1]

For the third time in half a century an American crossed the Atlantic seeking supremacy of the boxing world. This time not apathy but an explosion of excitement accompanied the event. Staying one step ahead of authorities, who sought his arrest for seconding a recent fight, Heenan and his trainer, James Cusick—a sometime prize fighter expelled from California by the vigilantes—boarded the Liverpool-bound steamer *Asia* on January 4, 1860, protected by a multitude of burly friends. After countless farewell exhibitions, benefits, and toasts in his honor, the Benicia Boy left with songs of praise ringing in his ears:

> Come friends, a drink, and let no fear
> For me yours hearts annoy,
> But let your bets and hopes be buoyed
> By your Benicia Boy.

I go to strive in honest fight
For dear Columbia's pride;
Nor shall, I swear, my courage ebb,
Whatever may betide.

So grasp again by bunch of fives,
My shoulder-hitting hearties,
Of all the arts, the manly art
The highest style of Art is . . .

I'll wind our colors round my loins—
The blue and crimson bars,
And if Tom does not feel the stripes,
I'll make him see the stars! . . .

So here's one toast before I go,
The Yankee land, God bless it,
And for her sake, the Champion's belt
I hope I may possess it.[2]

For the sporting fraternity, the upcoming battle overshadowed all other issues, including the crisis over slavery. The Sayers-Heenan bout infected countless new fans with fistic fever, for the fight seemed a genuine test of national supremacy. Thus, Oliver Wendell Holmes, Sr., one of America's most distinguished medical researchers, men of letters, and essayists, openly attended Heenan's prefight exhibitions and visited the Boy to measure his muscles.[3]

Popular interest in the ring surpassed the peak attained at Long Point, Canada West, two years before when Heenan fought Morrissey; indeed, the upcoming contest drew more public attention than any other athletic event during the fifty years straddling mid-century.[4] Journals sent special correspondents overseas to write about everything from the training of the champions to the sentiments of the English public. The *Clipper* even published a series of letters, allegedly written by Heenan, detailing the drama as it unfolded. In New York, Adah Isaacs Mencken, the estranged wife of the Benicia Boy, became an instant hit in Broadway melodramas. Night after night she brought down the house, testimony both to her name, Mrs. John C. Heenan, and to her scantily clad body.[5]

The iconography of the ring also grew more prominent. *Harper's Weekly* condemned the "bloody, brutal and blackguard prize fight" but reproduced a full-page etching of the ringside scene. *Vanity Fair* published a satirical engraving, "The Two Champions," depicting George Washington on the left, leading his men against the English, and the Benicia Boy on the right, gripping Sayers in a headlock, while Liberty stands aside, sighing for her country. Miniature statuary froze the two fighters as they toed the scratch, on drinking mugs Heenan drove Sayers to the turf, and Currier and Ives—that bastion of Victorian taste, a firm that helped make the middle-class ethos palpable to millions of Americans with countless mass-produced images of idealized bourgeois life—rushed to press with cheap lithographs of both heroes.[6]

No matter how much they published on the preliminaries, editors found the public thirst insatiable. The standard sources, especially the *Herald* and the *Clipper,* were crammed with news, and countless dailies throughout the country kept their columns full of second- and third-hand stories. George Wilkes, who acquired the *Spirit of the Times* in 1856, went even further. He sailed to London, negotiated on Heenan's behalf, and, along with editor Francis Dowling of *Bell's Life in London,* helped organize the match. Small-town newspapers might rail against the coverage, upholding rural virtue in the face of urban depravity, but more than ever the ring generated excitement beyond its traditional constituency. "All classes of people," the *New York Times* observed, "share this anxiety to hear the results—not all in the same degree or the same extent, but with the masses of the people it is just now the great topic of speculation . . . throwing completely into shade all political themes and everything else which can afford to wait."[7] Interest in the bout so overwhelmed the usual expressions of outrage that, *Harper's Weekly* complained, "moralists must be writing and clergymen must be preaching to very little purpose, since the bulk of the people in England and America are heart and soul engrossed in a fight compared to which a Spanish bull-bait is a mild and diverting pastime."[8]

Editors were caught between morals and balance sheets. Shortly before Heenan sailed for England, *Frank Leslie's Illustrated Newspaper* condemned the ring for encouraging "all the coarsest, lowest vice of our cities." Boxing, *Leslie's* declared, "is so mingled with the associations of the groggery, we are so accustomed to hear of its heroes as habitues and bullies of low gambling houses and brothels, that rightly or wrongly, and despite the many exceptions which may be urged, no one pretends to deny that 'the ring' is the very last subject which should be mentioned in a paper which finds its way into decent families." The editor concluded that pandering to public taste by reporting the upcoming contest was not only immoral but, from a business point of view, short-sighted. Yet as the day of battle drew near, *Leslie's* engaged in fierce competition for sales with the *New York Illustrated News*. Each promised the fullest coverage, each made celebrities of its artists and correspondents in London, and each ballyhooed the importance of this fight for the "CHAMPIONSHIP OF THE WORLD."[9] If the editors at *Leslie's* felt morally compromised, they buried their qualms under the revenues that accrued from selling tens of thousands of extra editions in England and America. A little short-sighted profit taking, even at the risk of offending public decency, was not so bad after all.[10]

Excitement also raged in Great Britain, following decades of hard times for the ring. The generation after the Regency Era produced notable men, among them "Deaf" Burke, William "Bold Bendigo" Thompson, and Ben Caunt. English newspapers regularly pronounced prize fighting's final demise, only to report the corpse's revival a few years later. Nevertheless, though working-class interest kept boxing and other fancy sports alive, the old culture of the Regency Era had been shattered. The day was long passed when pugilists had served as ushers at royal coronations, when gay young gentlemen drank with their favorite pugs, or when the likes of Lord Byron and Sir Robert Peel sparred together. Bourgeois earnestness gave no quarter to the aristocratic love of pageantry. Gentlemen and nobles remained interested in "manly" sports, and they even attended an occasional match, but they kept a low profile and newspapers respected their wish for anonymity. And although great champions still toed the scratch, their exploits were tainted by declining purses, crossed matches, and increased rowdyism at ringside.[11]

Under these less than optimal conditions, Tom Sayers—a London bricklayer and the son of a Brighton cobbler—began supplementing his income with ring combat. Sayers stood five feet, eight inches tall, usually fighting at a mere eleven stone (one hundred fifty-four pounds). Yet by 1859 he had beaten every conceivable opponent, including Aaron Jones, William Perry, Tom Paddock, and Bill Benjamin. A dozen fights behind him and the championship belt round his waist, Sayers lacked a worthy opponent until Heenan's challenge arrived.[12]

As a contrast in styles, the two boxers embodied qualities that today still arouse the deepest interest of the fans: experience versus youth, cunning against strength, ring science opposing brute power. Although Heenan was five inches taller, two stone heavier, and eight years younger, ringside odds favored Sayers by as much as three to one, partly because of English chauvinism but mainly because the Boy lacked experience. After all, his career consisted of only one regular ring fight, a battle he had lost. A final factor weighing in Sayers's favor was the presence of John Morrissey in London. Allegedly, Old Smoke was so angry with Heenan's presumptuousness in claiming the title that he counseled the London bricklayer on how to fight the young upstart, predicted Sayers's victory, and backed his opinion with a thousand pounds in wagers.[13]

Long odds notwithstanding, it had been decades since a prize fight so aroused Britons. Parliament debated the morality of the match, lords and peers made surreptitious plans to attend, and as much as a hundred thousand pounds were wagered on the contest. On fight day, rumors circulated that Prime Minister Palmerston stood at ringside and that Queen Victoria demanded immediate notification of the outcome.[14]

Chauvinism, of course, contributed to the trans-Atlantic interest in the contest. Fighting colors made the battle's larger meaning clear—red and buff with the British lion and seal for Sayers, red, white, and blue with an American eagle and the motto "May the Best Man Win" for Heenan. "Thus, you will perceive," the Benicia Boy wrote in a letter to the *New York Clipper,* "Sayers has for his emblem the King Beast of the forest, while mine is the King Bird of the air; and if he does not clip my wings, I will cut his tail." Mock warfare under conditions of perfect equality, boxing was an ideal vehicle for exploiting such nationalistic symbolism. In the sharp-focused imagery of the ring, Sayers and Heenan, wearing their countries' colors round their waists, stood for England and America toe-to-toe. "The ordinary objections to vulgar pugilism" *Wilkes' Spirit of the Times* solemnly declared, "are waived in the real importance of this first-class struggle, and there is scarcely a mind that is amenable to the national pride, which does not for once lay aside its prejudice against fighting in the hope to see the American champion win."[15]

Sayers and Heenan's battle resonated with American charges of John Bull's effete decadence and English contentions that Anglo-Saxon stock degenerated in the Yankee Republic. Because the symbolic stakes were so high, men talked obsessively about the impending conflict: "If you go to the market, the odds are your butcher asks you which man you fancy, and if you want to bet on it. Your newsman smiles as he hands you your daily paper, and informs you that 'there is something new about the great fight in it this morning.' If you drop into Bryant's or Christy's in an evening, you are certain to hear some allusion to the Benicia Boy or Sir Thomas de Sayers that never fails to bring down the house." Even as the clouds of civil war gathered, George Templeton Strong confided to his diary that the fight totally absorbed men's attention, that the symbolic ring combat eclipsed all interest in the painful realities of sectional conflict.[16]

The fight proved worthy of the build-up, momentarily bringing back

John C. Heenan and Tom Sayers square off, April 17, 1860. Currier and Ives produced this popular lithograph, which glossed the ringside scene in England with a thick coat of gentility. Courtesy of the the Print Collection, The New York Public Library, Astor, Lenox and Tilden Foundations.

the glory that William Hazlitt and Pierce Egan had so brilliantly captured decades earlier. Railroad tickets went on sale just hours before chartered trains rumbled out of London at dawn on April 17, 1860. Waiting to board the cars at first light were "statesmen, peers of every grade, legislators, judges, great physicians and surgeons, royal academicians, famous novelists, dramatists and professors of literature of every kind, journalists, draughtsmen, engineers, soldiers and sailors of every grade, . . . publicans, pugilists, bookmakers, masters of foxhounds; in short, every class of society. . . ." The fancy had been up all night, carousing and reveling into the wee hours. Bleary-eyed, they jammed themselves into luxury coaches, cattle cars, and all variety of rolling stock, bound for the tiny hamlet of Farnborough on the heaths of Hampshire. The South Eastern Railroad and the publicans who sold tickets grossed four to five thousand pounds for their night's labor.[17]

Farnborough awoke to find town toughs, laborers, sporting gentlemen, and a scattering of noblemen making their way from the railroad station

Climax of the Heenan-Sayers fight, which lasted forty-two rounds spread over two hours and twenty minutes. *Frank Leslie's Illustrated Newspaper* of May 12, 1860, captured the chaotic finish—constables pushed forward to stop the fight, driving fans into the ring.

to an open field with a roped ring in the middle. By 7:30 Sayers and Heenan threw their hats into the sacred circle. After the usual ring rituals—introductions of the supporting cast, referee selection, stripping, handshaking, and final wagering—the men toed the scratch and began.[18]

For over two hours Sayers and Heenan mutilated each other. Probably the American had a slight edge in the fighting, winning the majority of rounds by knocking or throwing his opponent down. But Sayers's indomitable will, his ability to endure punishment and finish strong, made Heenan's advantage dubious. The tempo of the fight shifted back and forth, Heenan using his power to maul his opponent, Sayers returning with quick but debilitating blows to the body, neck, and head. In the sixth round the bricklayer deflected a Heenan punch with his right arm, sustaining a fracture that grew worse with repeated pounding. In exchange for his nearly useless limb, Sayers slowly beat Heenan's handsome face into an ugly mask, and the swelling caused by well-placed blows to the eyes left the Benicia Boy nearly blind. After two hours the only question was who would give out first. The issue was never decided.

In the thirty-seventh round a contingent of Hampshire constables battled their way through the crowd to stop the fight, and as they pushed forward, spectators were forced into the ring. Now Heenan groped for Sayer's neck, allegedly forcing the Englishman's throat against the ropes. Here the record becomes murky. Some sources claim that the cords were cut to end the bout and prevent an American victory; others report that Sayers's seconds legally lowered them to save their man from strangulation. One rumor even had John Morrissey himself slashing the ropes. With outsiders now pouring into the ring, referee Francis Dowling declared the fight drawn, but an uncomprehending timekeeper called the men back for five more short and confused rounds. Finally, after two hours and twenty minutes, spread over forty-two rounds, the chaos in the ring made more fighting impossible. With the battle terminated, the constables fell back to lick their wounds and the crowd returned to the railroad cars, thence to London.

At the end of May, Hancock Silversmiths completed duplicate championship belts that were presented to the fighters by editors Francis Dowling and George Wilkes at a grand benefit. The joint champions then toured the land together, giving exhibitions throughout the summer. Sayers was the toast of all England: "Never in the annals of the ring," Frederick Locker-Lampson declared, "were courage, science, temper, judgement and staying qualities combined and displayed in such marvellous measure as by Tom Sayers on this memorable day."[19] William Makepeace Thackeray witnessed the fight first-hand and, assuming the persona of an ancient pugilist, memorialized it in verse:

> Two hours and more the fight had sped,
> Near unto ten it drew,
> But still opposed one-armed to blind,
> They stood those dauntless two.
> Ah, me! that I have lived to hear
> Such men as ruffians scorned,
> Such deeds of valour "brutal" called,
> Canted, preached down and mourned!
> Ah! that these old eyes ne'er again
> A gallant mill shall see!
> No more behold the ropes and stakes
> With colours flying free . . .

To his young heirs the old fighter laments that Sayers and Heenan were the last of a dying breed;

> And now my fists are feeble,
> And my blood is thin and cold,
> But 'tis better than Old Tom to me,
> To recall those days of old.
> And may you, my great grandchildren,
> That gather round my knee,
> Ne'er see worse men nor iller times
> Than I and mine might be,
> Though England then had prize-fighters—
> Even reprobates like me.[20]

While Sayers's skill and grit won the hearts of his countrymen, many in Ireland remembered Heenan's ancestry and embraced him as their representative against the English oppressors. For decades after the battle at Farnborough, pubs throughout the United Kingdom rang with songs of praise for the two champions.[21]

America's enthusiasm for its young hero reached equal heights. There were, of course, the usual street ballads, with Irish-Americans singing loudest:

> Attend you sons of Erin, and listen with delight,
> To a ditty, 'tis concerning the great and glorious fight,
> On the seventeenth of April, when thousands went with joy,
> To see the English Champion and the bold Benicia boy. . . .
>
> When Heenan came to England, far from a distant land,
> They said he was a fool to come to face an Englishman,
> But they were all mistaken when they saw the glorious battle,
> Heenan cooked the Champion's bacon, and made his daylights rattle.

As many as fifty thousand people came to Jones Wood, a New York City park, to greet the returning conqueror and witness a benefit exhibition in his honor. Later, twelve thousand Bostonians feted the Boy, and other cities arranged similar greetings.[22]

After the initial euphoria had worn off, many Americans began to grumble about the joint championship, and some editors suggested that the English cheated the Boy out of his rightful title. That Sayers trained unmolested while constables chased Heenan from camp to camp—a fact publicly deplored by Sayers—was now reinterpreted as the first signs of a larger pattern. The *Herald* insisted on Heenan's superiority, claiming that men broke the ring to save their wagers. The *New York Times* agreed, adding that England's declining international prestige caused it to stoop so low. *Wilkes' Spirit of the Times,* which originally assured its readers that Heenan would be treated with even-handedness, now implicated Her Majesty's government in the conspiracy, agreeing with the other papers that the Boy had been swindled because the British feared humiliation in the eyes of the European community. All felt that England's vaunted sense of fair play stood revealed as a sham. The issue faded in intensity as the sectional conflict galvanized the nation's attention, but when Anglo-American relations deteriorated during the Civil War, many would recall the Farnborough fight as an early sign of English treachery.[23]

In sporting house legend, on the popular stage, and in barroom song, however, members of the fancy made right the wrong done to America. A ballad entitled "Heenan and Sayers" conflated each boxer with a cherished national symbol.

It was in merry England, the home of Johnnie Bull,
Where Britons fill their glasses, they fill them brimming full,
And of the toast they drank, it was to Britons brave,
And it is long may our champion bring victories o'er the waves.

Then up jumps Uncle Sammy, and he looks across the main,
Saying, "Is that your English bully I hear bellowing again?
Oh, has he not forgotten the giant o'er the pond,
Who used to juggle cannon balls when his day's work was done?

"Remember, Uncle Johnnie, the giant stronger grows,
He is always on his muscle and ready for his foes;
When but a boy at Yorktown I caused you for to sigh,
So when e'er you boast of fighting, Johnnie Bull, mind your eye" . . .

Come, all you sporting Americans, wherever you have strayed,
Look on this glorious eagle and never be afraid;
May our Union last forever and our flag the world defy,
So whenever you boast of fighting, Johnnie Bull, mind your eye.

The identification of the champion boxer with national virility could not have been clearer. Momentarily, pugilism dropped the distinctive garb of working-class street gangs, donned the stars and stripes, and paraded boldly up Main Street.[24]

Twice before Americans had ventured to England seeking the championship, and hardly anyone had noticed. Now, however, increasing

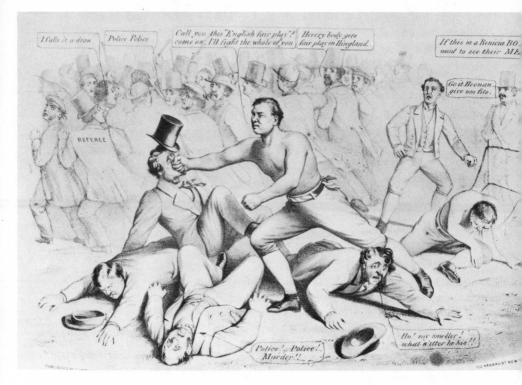

" 'Yankee Doodle' on his muscle." A Currier and Ives lithograph reveals Americans' belief that Heenan had been swindled. Here the Benicia Boy takes on the crowd after disposing of Sayers. Courtesy of the Print Collection, The New York Public Library, Astor, Lenox and Tilden Foundations.

numbers of men could imagine prize fighters as representative Americans, symbols of national prowess, defenders of the Union against foreign foes. Boxing matches hardly offered a model of Victorian decorum, but Heenan seemed a comparatively respectable champion. Although the Benicia Boy loved the free-and-easy life of saloons, so far he had avoided the public association with gang violence and political corruption—"open ruffianism," as the *Times* put it—which made Sullivan, Hyer, and Morrissey notorious.[25] The timing of the Sayers-Heenan fight was also important, for a subtle shift was just beginning in the bourgeois view of the world. That view still insisted upon morally rigid and self-controlled behavior, but latent values, competitiveness, the will to win, and masculine toughness, also were beginning to emerge. These ideals took on new meaning as class tensions deepened and capitalist competition grew ever more intense. Boxing and other violent sports would be embraced in coming years by many respectable Americans as confirmation of personal and national virility, metaphors for the rough-and-tumble struggles of business, politics, and diplomacy. But this shift, as we shall see, was primarily a development of the late nineteenth century.

The most obvious and most important reason why the Sayers-Heenan fight attracted such broad-based attention was its nationalistic overtones. Ambivalent as some men might be about the ring, here was a chance to twist the British lion's tail at a time when symbolic international contests at pedestrian tracks, cricket fields, racecourses, and boating regattas were an established phenomenon. By 1860 sports and chauvinism were intertwined tightly, and John C. Heenan, born in America of Irish parents, united natives and immigrants and thereby became a symbol of opposition to a common enemy.

Above all, the fight occurred when American nationhood was disturbingly tenuous. With the sectional conflict openly threatening the Union, cravings for emblems of solidarity were particularly acute. England, a traditional antagonist made doubly menacing by its need for Southern cotton, proved a convenient foil. Deflecting internal divisions onto an outside enemy, the fight allowed men to experience a rush of patriotic fervor precisely when things were falling apart. Just as Secretary of State William Seward later predicted that a war against England would patch up sectional divisions, so the Farnborough fight temporarily drowned American differences in a wave of national unity. All of these factors came together to make the Sayers-Heenan fight one of the most dramatic sporting events of the nineteenth century.

Civil Wars

One need only visualize English soldiers during World War I kicking a soccer ball as they charged the enemy trenches to appreciate the ties between sport and modern warfare, especially during the twentieth century. Gene Tunney, for example, received his ring training as a member of the American Expeditionary Force, fighting his way to the light heavyweight championship of the armed services. During World War II the aging Jack Dempsey and champion Joe Louis each staged countless exhibitions to entertain troops; both were therefore hailed as model fighting men. Images of warfare and the prize ring have grown so close that many Americans saw only hypocrisy in Muhammad Ali's courageous and costly decision to resist the draft during the Vietnam war era.[26]

During the Civil War, however, there was nothing automatic about the association of boxing with warfare. John C. Heenan was criticized for returning to England and failing to serve in the Union Army, but few people seemed surprised by his action, and he received little of the opprobrium heaped on Ali a century later (or, for that matter, on Dempsey, who avoided service in World War I). After all, boxing and warfare both demanded brutal behavior, but laying down one's life for love of country was fundamentally different from thumping another man for money. As we have seen, some of the earliest criticisms of prize fighting in America asserted that ancient Greek boxers made the least reliable soldiers because they came from the "vilest classes" of society. Union General Thomas Wentworth Higginson revived this notion, declaring that the bookish young scholar might possess selfless idealism while the barroom brawler's courage extended no further than his egotistical interests.[27]

Still, a tenuous logic connects boxing and warfare. On the simplest level, the good boxer, like the good soldier, is a violent man, doling out more punishment than he receives. Both live in a world where physical conflict is the norm. During the Mexican War, for example, it was assumed that John McCleester's pugnaciousness transferred to the field of battle; he boasted that he killed twelve Mexicans one day before breakfast. More important, boxing and modern warfare shared a preoccupation with the techniques of violence. Boxers did not simply pound each other any more than generals simply overwhelmed opposing armies. Discipline and science were central to both occupations. Not mere destructiveness but destructive techniques—bringing skill, finesse, and intellect to the cause of violence—were hallmarks of both boxing and warfare. Even the language of the ring and that of the battlefield began to interpenetrate. Thus officers alluded to boxing when they spoke of "feinting" and "parrying" with the enemy—terms borrowed from fencing—while prize fighters began receiving praise for their "generalship" on the "field of battle."[28]

Americans had just started to make these connections during the Civil War, and the process was more haphazard than planned, more unconscious than deliberate. A few individuals argued, as Englishmen had two generations earlier, that boxing taught courage by example. More important, the Civil War duplicated on a massive scale some of the cultural qualities on which the ring thrived, especially the all-male peer groups. Camp and field rewarded toughness, punished squeamishness, and created "working" conditions that freed up distinct periods of leisure time. Also significant, American men rushed to war in 1861 and 1862 with Sayers and Heenan still fresh in their memories.[29]

The efflorescence of sports in the 1850s offered ready-made models of recreation for the soldiers of the 1860s. Baseball, running and leaping contests, wrestling, horse racing, and football, obstacle-course runs, sharpshooting, and even cockfighting became standard entertainments in camp and field. The war spread knowledge of new styles of play to individuals from every corner of the country. Soldiers organized their own games for entertainment and to alleviate boredom, but athletics were also encouraged by officers. Some battalions held gala sports days, erecting grandstands, inviting local ladies and politicians, and awarding prizes. Leaders of a few regiments, Berdan's Sharpshooters, for example, deliberately promoted sports, believing that they enhanced endurance and combat readiness while fostering esprit de corps. Thus boxing proliferated as, increasingly, tests of physical skill became a part of army routine.[30]

The Civil War not only encouraged sports, it left unusually detailed evidence about them. The conflict was life's single greatest event for many men, so officers and soldiers alike felt compelled to write their memoirs. In so doing, they recorded some of the best evidence of boxing's penetration into American culture by the 1860s. The ring's unsavory and short history in America makes its familiarity to soldiers seem surprising. But it was mostly the poor and the working class, often from immigrant backgrounds, who served in combat, so the conflict brought together in massive numbers precisely those sorts of men who had contributed to pugilism's recent popularity.

Several Union and Confederate soldiers recalled sparring matches as part of their regular camp entertainments. Members of the 37th Massachusetts Volunteers, for example, warmed their blood on cold days with brisk exhibitions. Philip Creek, of Wisconsin's Sauk County Riflemen, noted that boxing was in great vogue in his camp. Alonso F. Hill, of Pennsylvania's 8th Regiment, remembered crowds gathering around gloved soldiers who were "batting away at each other's heads most delightfully." Virginians N. W. Wood and W. M. Dame described regimental bouts, and Delavan S. Miller, who served in New York's Second Heavy Artillery, wrote years after the war of Bowery newsboy Pete Boyle enlivening the camp with his sparring exhibitions.[31]

The Army of the Potomac's Sixth Corps was especially renowned for its pugnacity, a trait encouraged by commanders and relished by the men. Just before the Battle of Fredericksburg, officers set up sparring matches as regular exercise, and a dozen accomplished pugilists helped teach the novices. The Irish regiments were particularly noted for their skill with the gloves, in part because many professional boxers of Irish extraction were drafted into the service. Occasionally the men even staged regular prize fights, at which officers were "unofficially" present.[32]

The "Bloody Old Sixth" also contained plenty of raw-boned Green Mountain bruisers, Lackawanna miners, Allegheny ironworkers, and strapping lumbermen from Wisconsin and Maine. In one of their prize fights, soldiers subscribed a purse of five hundred dollars, made a ring from spare picket rope, and bet heavily on a Vermont whaleman and a Pittsburgh ironmolder. A sergeant refereed the battle, some corporals acted as seconds, and a thousand Union soldiers—including officers ranking as high as brigadier general—watched the two heroes strip to their drawers on a blistering Sunday morning in July 1864. Augustus Buell's description of the battle reads like the sporting journalism of his day. The iron-headed Pennsylvanian, his face resembling "a badly-carved joint of roast beef," kept coming back smiling for more, unnerving the clever Vermonter who expected to win on his "cat-like activity and sailor tricks." Endurance triumphed over craft in this fight, and everyone was delighted with the battle. New matches were arranged, but they failed to come off when the Sixth Corps moved down the valley of Virginia and back into the real battle.[33]

The draft reduced the numbers of regular matches in the big cities during the war, but boxers-turned-soldiers carried on the manly art. On New Year's Day 1862, for example, Jimmie Laville and M. O'Rourke, both of Company A, First Fire Zouaves, repaired to the beach at Newport News, Virginia, to settle a dispute. Ring veterans Denny Horrigan and Mike Trainor served as seconds, and lightweight Harry Lazarus acted as referee. Yet the most surprising manifestations of boxing during the war were not regimental sparring matches or regular prize fights, but the personal quarrels settled according to prize fight rules. Pugilistic customs were sufficiently well known that many men resorted to them to resolve their differences. One soldier insulted another, army and cavalry men disagreed over who had priority access to a road, two men argued about which should fill his mess pail first—all offered potential reasons for fisticuffs.[34]

These and the countless other grievances that arose among men trying to cope with unfamiliar and uncomfortable surroundings, living cheek-by-jowl, eating bad food, sleeping on the ground, suffering through heat and cold, sharing intense boredom punctuated by profound danger and sickening brutality, led to countless informal but rule-bound matches.

Colonel Warren of the Fifth New York Volunteers preferred ring combat to festering quarrels, so he had his men retire to a secluded spot where they engaged "in a fair stand-up fight, to settle some rivalry or grudge that had been engendered in camp." Among the 27th Indiana Volunteer Infantry, fistfights often grew out of personal quarrels, and proper etiquette demanded that the combatants fight until one cried "enough." "In fact," Edmund Randolph Brown recalled, "it was not safe to quarrel unless one wanted to fight. A ring was often formed with the two quarreling fellows inside, and they were almost compelled to knock it out or cease quarreling."[35]

The close-knit life of the camp and the dependence of men in war on one another required that disputes be resolved expeditiously and with finality. Individuals released their rancors in the ring and left the magic circle with social equilibrium restored. In this sense, boxing provided for foot soldiers a safe equivalent to the duels that military officers had favored a few decades earlier. Both forms of combat were highly public dramas, merging violence with restraint. Boxing matches were not set off sharply from "real life," moreover, because one man's personal battle was another's entertainment, and the roles of pugilist and spectator shifted with daily circumstances. Each match, then, was a model for future conduct. The lack of rigid barriers between observers and participants underscored the necessity of fair play and demonstrated how emotions must be released under conditions that were rule-bound and even-handed, so that life in camp and field could return quickly to normal.[36]

Most important, amid the most brutal and deadly conflict between the Napoleonic Era and World War I, pugilism offered a glimmer of idealized, restrained combat. During the Battle of the Wilderness, a singularly hideous episode in a war of unprecedented ugliness, a Union and a Confederate soldier found themselves trapped in a deep gully midway between opposing lines. Each claimed the other as prisoner of war, and they decided to settle the issue with a regular fistfight. As the two arose and stripped off their coats, a yell went up from the lines. Troops on both sides ceased fire and surged forward to watch the battle. Before long the Rebel bested the Yank. They both rolled back into the gully and shooting resumed until nightfall, when captive and prisoner emerged.[37]

In a similar incident near Fredericksburg, in 1862, the 24th Michigan Regiment relieved the Second Wisconsin on picket duty but was not told of an informal truce with the enemy. When the Michigan men shot down several unwary Confederates, a bitter skirmish ensued. Late in the day, however, a rebel soldier shouted a challenge to a Yankee, and the two walked to a turnpike and began exchanging punches. The boxers drew the attention of both picket lines, and before long Union and Confederate troops stopped shooting and gathered to watch the mill. After a long battle the spectators intervened and called the fight a draw, ratifying their decision by shaking hands all around, trading coffee and tobacco, and agreeing to reinstate the truce.[38]

In the midst of intense and bitter struggle, then, the ideals of fair stand-up combat momentarily overshadowed the surrounding carnage. Guns and bayonets were available to the two men in the gully—indeed, to all soldiers who poured out their enmities in the ring—but the opponents rejected them and chose instead a culturally sanctioned method of settling disputes. For a brief moment the limited, rule-bound, and less lethal techniques of boxing were sufficiently compelling that men stopped killing one another to watch the symbolic drama. Here was an archetypical example of the play element in culture, of man's need for ordered, regulated competition, often deadly serious yet circumscribed by tacitly agreed upon rules.[39]

It is significant that such incidents occurred not in the midst of regular battles but during the chaos of outpost skirmishes, where the enemy was often hidden and death lurked near but unseen. Just as the ring brought momentary symbolic order to the chaos of working-class streets, so the drama of fistfighting between equals presented a poignant if fleeting alternative to the ghastliness of battle. Sport became much more than the moral equivalent of war. It supplanted war because, under the circumstances, it was an authentic expression of men's needs. The finitude and limited violence of a fistfight were more compelling, more understandable than the daily carnage. In the crush of war's moral horror, here was limited combat filled with significance, a palpable example both of human aggression and of human ability to control it. For the men who temporarily laid down their arms and swapped tobacco, the symbolic violence of play offered meaning denied by the anarchy of war.

"...The Gangs Who Rage and Howl at the Ropes"

By the early 1860s prize fighting had reached a highwater mark. Sports in general were gaining acceptance, the Sayers-Heenan battle identified the ring with American patriotism, the Civil War helped familiarize countless men with pugilism, and even the middle and upper classes showed signs of interest. The sheer volume of ring activities continued to increase. Large northern cities saw numerous exhibitions, some of which resembled prize fights more than ever before. The spirit of mutuality also continued when, in the spring of 1862, several ring men staged a benefit for Yankee Sullivan's destitute mother. A year later John Morrissey and Bill "Dublin Tricks" Hastings organized a grand sparring benefit for the starving poor of Ireland.[40]

Boxing's center of gravity began shifting west during these years. Con Orem, an excellent fighter from the Colorado Territory, became the unofficial "Champion of the West" and displayed his talents before as many as twenty-five hundred spectators in the new mecca of frontier pugilism, the mining town of Virginia City, Nevada Territory. Here the speculative scramble for wealth within an all-male work culture encouraged a relatively free moral atmosphere. Saloonkeeper J. A. Nelson built Leviathan Hall—an arena attached to his tavern with graded seats descending toward a ring—and openly arranged, promoted, and refereed bouts. Virginia City's finest hour came in January 1865, when Orem fought Hugh O'Neal to a one-hundred-eighty-five round draw for a purse of one thousand dollars in gold plus the gate receipts. Other western promoters followed Nelson's lead, building amphitheaters, charging admission, distributing the gate receipts among the principals, and selling liquor and gambling pools to entertainment-starved men.[41]

For the next two decades saloonkeepers in the western mining territories of Nevada, Idaho, Montana, Dakota, and Colorado were prize fighting's primary commercial innovators. Even in the land of gun fights and six-shooters, boxing made headway as a means of settling disputes. On several occasions the young marshal Wyatt Earp of Dodge City took off his gun belt and fought outlaws with "nature's weapons." Cowboys with a grudge against Earp often believed they had a better chance with fists than pistols, though the marshal usually proved them wrong. Taking no chances, however, Earp's friend Bat Masterson came to these contests armed, to assure fair play. Late in the century the lawmen officiated at regular prize fights, and Masterson finished his days as a New York City boxing reporter.[42]

Far from satiating the country's taste for violence, the Civil War seemed to whet appetites for ring combat. Several prize fights attracted national attention, though none proved as spectacular as the great championship bouts of the previous decade. Late in 1863 Heenan, who now lived overseas, ended his pugilistic career against British champion Tom King. They fought in Wadhurst, Sussex, for two thousand dollars a side, and the battle stirred great excitement in the American press. Convinced that the English had cheated the Boy in 1860 and angry over surreptitious British aid to the Confederacy, Americans saw a chance for vindication. Unfortunately, Heenan was not the fighter of three years earlier, and although he did well at first, King finally knocked him out of time after twenty-five rounds lasting thirty-five minutes. Like the Farnborough battle, the Heenan-King fight remained a controversial topic for decades. The London *Sportsman* claimed that the Benicia Boy's second, Jack MacDonald, accepted a pay-off to drug his man, but MacDonald charged in return that Heenan himself sold the fight. American writers later claimed that the Boy had the battle in hand and knocked his opponent unconscious in the nineteenth round, but that King's "mob" broke the ring, giving the Englishman fully two minutes to clear his head. Thoroughly dispirited, Heenan and his backers lost their will to continue.[43]

All of these charges and countercharges were symptoms of the lowest decline yet of the English ring. By the end of the decade a rash of fixed matches, riots at ringside, and magistrates' interference discouraged men from attending or wagering on fights. Late in the decade, at the urging of a few key boxers and noblemen, the marquis of Queensberry rules—a modified version of the code governing amateur sparring among gentlemen—were adopted for professional prize fighting, in the hope that they would help give the ring a more respectable image. In the meantime England's finest fighters began a new exodus to the United States. As for Heenan, America's most celebrated pugilist (though a man who never won a major fight) finished his career sprawled in his corner, vomiting uncontrollably. He returned home, did some political strong-arm work, gave a few exhibitions, failed as a faro parlor operator, and headed back west to California. He died on the way and was buried in Green River, Wyoming Territory. Like his old antagonist Tom Sayers, he failed to reach the age of forty.[44]

Despite Heenan's pathetic collapse, important fights were staged on American soil during this era. Con Fitzgerald and Ed Wilson fought an excellent ten-rounder at Port Penn, Delaware, in 1863, a fight remarkable because both men eschewed clinches and wrestling holds, preferring to stand and slug out the entire match. But most spectacular was the May 5, 1863, battle between Joseph Coburn and Mike McCoole for one thousand dollars each and a side bet of seven hundred dollars. With Morrissey's retirement and Heenan's absence in England, newspapers declared this a championship fight.[45]

Both combatants were naturalized Americans, sons of the Emerald Isle, yet the match was portrayed as a microcosm of the Civil War. A New York stonemason, small, muscular, about Yankee Sullivan's size

American Fistiana, cover of the 1873 edition. First published in 1849 and enlarged in 1860 and 1873, this work claimed to be the definitive history of the American ring. Much of its text reprinted old fight stories from the sporting press.

and very scientific, Coburn was still remembered for his three hour, twenty minute battle with Ed Price near Boston over a decade earlier. McCoole, in contrast, was a St. Louis deckhand who roughed it up among that "hard and quarrelsome set of fellows manning the steamers, flatboats, and floating palaces from St. Louis to New Orleans." The press evoked the rough-and-tumble heritage of the Southwest to describe his fighting style: "Ropes and stakes are not always to be found in the valley of the Southwest, and gentlemen who extract each others' eyes and mutually masticate noses can scarcely be expected to discriminate between what *Bell's Life in London* calls 'fair' and 'foul' blows." If not exactly Billy Yank and Johnny Reb, Coburn and McCoole would do.[46]

The North versus South symbolism, however, was a mixed blessing, as some journalists took the opportunity to contrast the selflessness of young soldiers dying for a noble cause with the low cunning of the gamblers who arranged the prize fight. Still the battle came off true to form, with articles of agreement, stake money deposited in Frank Queen's hands, regular training, and plenty of wagering. The press sized up the fighters with the usual loving care: "There was not an ounce of superfluous flesh on any part [of Coburn]; the muscles of his arms and shoulders . . . showed like bundles of cord under his fair, almost transparent skin. His loins, also, and legs were strong, firm and muscular, and his entire appearance that of a man of the highest form of physical development and in the perfection of condition. Nothing could be more beautifully artistic than his position, equally ready for offensive or defensive operations."[47]

At least three thousand people, including sporting men from major East Coast cities and river towns such as Cincinnati and St. Louis, boarded trains for the tiny station at Charlestown, Maryland. Many New Yorkers left two days before the fight, stopping to enjoy the hospitality of Philadelphia's saloons and brothels. By 6:00 A.M. on May 5 the ropes were pitched in an open field, and ring keepers began charging spectators one dollar each—a crude commercial innovation. Local townsfolk rented out their carts to those who wanted an elevated view, enterprising housewives did a brisk business in coffee, pancakes, and fried pork, and one man set up an impromptu bar with a barrel of whiskey, two bottles, and a glass. Around noon the principals appeared, and the usual formalities followed. Last-minute wagers at about 100 to 90 for Coburn were laid and deposited in the hands of referee Ed Price. Finally, the men came up for the first call of time.[48]

As many had predicted, the fight was comparable to the Sullivan-Morrissey affair of a decade before, cool judgment, experience, and science dominating youth, power, and grit. After sixty-seven rounds lasting one hour and ten minutes—an average fighting time of half a minute per round, not unusual during the bare-knuckle era—McCoole's corner threw up the sponge, their man terribly punished and Coburn showing barely a scratch. The loser returned to St. Louis to nurse his wounds, while the new champion staged several lucrative benefits. For weeks after the fight the *New York Mercury* and *Wilkes' Spirit of the Times* fought a protracted war of words over who best covered the match, until the battles of Gettysburg and Vicksburg overshadowed the skirmish at Charlestown.

For the fancy, the Coburn-McCoole fight was a homecoming. Putting up the final stakes evoked memories of old times, and the presence of such venerable ring men and gamblers as Izzy Lazarus and Jake Somerendyke served as "a reminder of the time when men like Hyer and Sullivan and Sullivan and Morrissey, were on the road to a fight, and the money newly up." No sooner was the champion crowned than rumors spread of a new international bout, pitting Coburn against Jem Mace, the English titleholder.[49]

At first glance, then, prize fighting seemed to prosper like other postbellum sports. Skillful fighters migrated to America, Tom Allen, Jem Mace, Joe Goss, Ned O'Baldwin, Joe Wormald, and Bob Brettle among them. The infusion of new talent led to some fine matches, such as the 1870 bout between Mace and Allen for $2,500 a side in New Orleans. "As they stood there, on guard," the *Clipper* observed, "their flesh glowing in the warm sunlight like polished bronze, as yet unspoiled and undefiled, an almost unconscious murmur of admiration ran through the anxiously awaiting crowd." After ten intense rounds lasting forty-four minutes, Mace emerged as the unquestioned victor.[50] Fighters at lighter weights also had their day, the most noteworthy match being the five-thousand-dollar "middle weight" championship bout between Tommy Chandler and Dooney Harris, held at Point Isabel, California, in April 1867. Because of his experience and ring skills, London-born Harris was the betting favorite by 100 to 75. But as the *Clipper* said of Chandler, "no finer specimen of a man has ever figured in the prize ring on the Pacific Coast. His appearance and expression are eminently pleasing and gentlemanly. No one seeing him on Montgomery Street (the Broadway of San Francisco) would dream that he was a professional pugilist." Chandler won, and such clean-cut new champions seemed to fulfill the ring's promise as envisioned by Frank Queen.[51]

Boxing's healthy exterior, however, belied internal corruption. Amidst the complexities of daily life, sports create an idealized world in which men bind themselves to special rules and rituals. Players and spectators must believe that sporting codes of conduct are consistent, not capricious. Far from being the cesspool of disorder critics charged, the ring demanded equality of opportunity and fair play for all. But how could men have faith in the "sacred circle" if violence, police interference, and dishonesty grew so common that no match was immune? Why should they risk being arrested, cheated out of their wagers, or roughed up to see a fight that might be fixed? Despite the fine bouts of the sixties, these problems began to overwhelm the ring's tenuous order, and the accumulation of offenses nearly destroyed prize fighting.[52]

With the moral zeal of the war as a backdrop, local officials redoubled their efforts to break up meetings of the fancy, especially in East Coast cities. Their efforts accounted in part for the rise to pugilistic preeminence of St. Louis, New Orleans, and the western territories. Billy Donnelly, for example, had two fights prevented by New York City police. In 1863 a well-publicized bout on Staten Island between Jimmy Elliott and Jim Dunn was stopped by harbor police. Backers of Dunn and Elliott decided to reconvene the fight two days later, on the Jersey shore. When the sheriff of Hudson County arrived just before the battle and ordered an end to the festivities, the crowd hustled him away. He later had his revenge: police arrested seventy-five spectators and held them on five hundred dollars bail apiece.[53]

This pattern of legal interference continued after 1865, indicating that more was involved than the moral strenuosity engendered by war. One major reason for prize fighting's legal difficulties was the changing nature of urban politics, especially in New York City. Before the Civil War a welter of shifting factions and tenuous alliances had placed a premium on extralegal electoral methods. But party realignments and the rise of the urban machine centralized power, tempered local conflicts, and rationalized the distribution of patronage. The countless factions that had fought each other so bitterly lost influence. With such men as Boss Tweed in control, the need was diminished for the old shoulder hitters to pack nominating conventions and secure the polling places. Urban politicians grew less dependent on the gangs that Hyer, Sullivan, Poole, Heenan, and Morrissey had led, so boxers lost their shield from the law. Without protection, increasing numbers of bouts were broken up, and more and more fighters landed in jail.[54] In 1868 Joe Coburn and Mike McCoole spent forty days behind bars for their renewed attempt to settle the championship of America, at Cold Springs Station, Indiana. That same year Ned O'Baldwin and Joe Wormald were prevented from consummating their championship fight three times, O'Baldwin eventually fleeing to Canada and Wormald finding himself incarcerated. Although police broke up only a small fraction of the era's matches, they were effective enough to make staging fights difficult, putting a damper on all pugilistic activities.[55]

The ring's internal problems, however, were much more debilitating than its external ones. Boxing's appeal always rested on a creative dualism between violence and order, impulsiveness and self-control, brutality and restraint. As far back as the legendary Hyer-Beasley fight, in 1816, emotions broke through the rituals of the ring. Sometimes the rules of stand-up prize fighting were no match for the hatreds of the streets, as the Deaf Burke–Sam O'Rourke bout and the John Morrissey–William Poole affair illustrated. Because the ring was a symbolic method of dealing with larger schisms between individuals, ethnic groups, and gangs, controlling violence always presented problems. After the war, however, the balance tipped toward the ring's anarchic qualities. As in so many other corners of Gilded Age America—politics, business, personal life—corruption became the rule.[56]

As early as 1859 a fight between Jim "New Orleans" Burns and Michael "Shanghai" Connors for the "Championship of the Mississippi Valley" had ended in a near-riot. All went well enough at first, with everyone enjoying the prefight revelry and the first few rounds. Yet it soon became apparent that Connors intended to drop rather than fight, and referee Sandy Moreland refused to do anything about it. In his frustration, Burns hit his opponent after he had fallen in the fourteenth round; Moreland immediately awarded the fight to Connors, giving Burns's friends the distinct impression that the fight had been fixed. Burns turned and struck Moreland, and with this, spectators broke the ring, brandishing knives, clubs, and revolvers. Frank Queen's *Clipper* commented on how such incidents violated prize fighting's "fair and manly" ethos: "several men were shot, one or two fatally, a few nearly drowned, and quite a number wounded. And this too among men calling themselves pugilists and lovers of boxing, etc. Out upon such creatures —they are *not* pugilists, but assassins in disguise and the law should punish every one of them that engaged in the murderous affray." In coming years Queen would have plenty of occasions to condemn such "mob fights."[57]

The precarious order established during the days of Sullivan, Hyer, and Morrissey, the poetic tension between bloodlust and self-restraint, lasted barely a decade. Boxing's outlaw status exacerbated the situation. Unlike horse racing, with its new jockey clubs arranging and handicapping heats, or early baseball, with leagues that worked out uniform rules of competition, prize fighting was allowed no associations that might assure adherence to fixed rules. The ring's illegality made it possible for the most violent and unscrupulous individuals to infiltrate a sport already flirting with underworld corruption. In an institutional sense, each prize fight was an isolated event, for no club or regulatory body had the power to standardize procedures and enforce rules; greed, ethnic hatreds, or gang rivalries could overwhelm ring customs and rituals without restraint.

These tensions had always existed, and it is not possible to say precisely why boxing was so vulnerable in the postbellum era. Perhaps the ring's success during the fifties attracted too many unscrupulous men who cared more for the opportunity to make money than for tests of personal and group honor. Surely the stock swindles, election frauds, and personal scandals of the Gilded Age offered object lessons in corruption by social elites. Also, the industrial-capitalist social order had by now brought in its wake a permanent underclass, men with no memories of artisan life and little prospect for decent employment, a true lumpenproletariat at the mercy of wild fluctuations in the business cycle. By the postwar era, all of these factors began to take their toll on the ring. "Things wasn't as they used to be," the 1873 edition of *American Fistiana* declared, "and the days of pugilism seemed to be drawing to a close."[58]

Charges that matches were fixed, fighters bought off, and referees dishonest became epidemic. In 1863, for example, a San Francisco battle between Johnny Lazarus and Pete Dailey ended in chaos. Dailey refused to fight because Lazarus fell without a blow, after which the crowd broke the ring and the referee declared Dailey the winner. The umpires and second rejected this decision and ordered a rematch, but it never occurred. That same year referee Michael Norton rendered a very dubious judgment in the Dunn-Elliot fight, and the fancy grumbled that the match had been fixed. In 1865 a referee deprived Mike Ford of his victory over Johnny Hickey; in 1867 a hostile mob on Fishers' Island, New York, forced a decision in favor of a badly beaten Charlie Collins; and in 1868, near St. Louis, crowd intimidation cheated Tom Allen of victory over Charles Gallagher. Joe Wormald and Ned O'Baldwin's three aborted attempts at championship fights in the late sixties were widely regarded as swindles, designed to cheat fans out of ticket money and gamblers out of their wagers.[59] By 1870 ring patrons were so suspicious of fixed battles that even the Mace-Allen fight, the best contest of the era, was not immune to charges of fraud. In Allen's adopted home town of St. Louis, some observers alleged that the fight was a "sham," that Mace's victory was a "put up job," that Allen had "sold out."[60]

One year later Mace's two championship fights with Joe Coburn appeared full of chicanery. Both men were renowned fighters, both had been champions, and Anglo-Irish rivalry promised vintage pugilism. Their first fight, on May 11, 1871, was well promoted with sparring tours, printed attacks on both fighters' courage, even an alleged assault by Coburn in Mace's New York saloon. All of this and a four-thousand-dollar stake notwithstanding, when the two finally entered the ring, they simply refused to fight. For one hour and seventeen minutes the champions circled, feinted, rested, drank water, and eyed each other, striking not a single blow before the sheriff and militia of Port Dover, Canada West, intervened. For the "rematch" in Bay St. Louis, Mississippi, each side raised the ante by fifteen hundred dollars, but because of exorbitant excursion prices and declining interest in the ring, not many people came. According to one observer, everyone tried to profiteer from the fight. The railroad company received $600 for a day trip, local police demanded $300 before they would let the train depart, various officials and journalists used threats to obtain free tickets. Fewer than a thousand men saw the contest, and only about three hundred and fifty of them paid their way. Coburn got the better of Mace for eleven mediocre rounds, then both reverted to stalling, which brought jeers from the crowd. The referee finally entered the ring and declared the fight a draw, though some claimed he did so only after a prearranged signal from Mace's second, Tom Allen. Coburn's refusal to follow up an early advantage elicited the charge of fraud, and the sporting crowd left thoroughly disgusted.[61]

By the seventies, then, the ideal of a fair fight to the finish had given way to a presumption of corruption. How many men could repeat without hesitation the boast of Yankee Sullivan's old partisans, that their man always gave his best and never sold out? Not just greed but violence threatened the ring. Beneath the humor in the oft-repeated phrase "the referee failed to be killed" lay the expectation of bloodshed before, during, or after a match. Many prize fighters died violently in the 1860s and 1870s. Dan Bendigo Smith was killed in a knife fight in St. Louis in 1862, and Barney Ford, who fought Ed Price and John Taylor, was stabbed to death in his own bar by his brother-in-law. Three years later Harry Lazarus met the same fate at the hands of Barney Friery, his next-door neighbor. Early one morning Friery entered Lazarus's tavern with some friends, ostensibly to reconcile an old feud. He offered his hand in friendship and, when Lazarus took it. Friery pulled a knife and stabbed him in the throat. The young lightweight bled to death where he fell. In 1875 Ned O'Baldwin's business partner shot him in their saloon, and in 1879, nine toughs set upon Paddy Ryan and stabbed him, apparently for failing to perform at a scheduled sparring exhibition. Fighters were perpetrators as well as victims. Joe Coburn was sentenced to ten years in prison for assault with intent to kill a New York City police officer, while Jimmy Elliott received a sixteen-year term after he robbed and mercilessly beat the well-known minstrel singer Hugh Dougherty.[62]

Such incidents darkened pugilism's already tarnished image, but it was the increased violence around the ring itself that most harmed the sport. In an 1863 fight between Con Orem and Owney Geoghegan, partisans of the latter made it clear they intended their man to win. Surrounded by toughs, Orem's seconds deserted, but he remained game, fearlessly carrying the fight to his opponent. When Orem hit Geoghegan as he was going down in the eighteenth, the latter's gang broke the ring and demanded a forfeit. A pistol pointed at the referee's head secured Geoghegan's victory on a call of "foul" against Orem. Toughs at an 1873 fight between Jack Conway and Billy Costello near Scranton, Pennsylvania, anticipating a call unfavorable to Conway, simply beat the referee senseless. Harry Hicken and his seconds were luckier, outrunning an enraged mob after only three rounds. Even when the crowds stayed calm, boxers and their seconds turned against each other, kicking, biting, gouging, blinding with chemicals, even pistol whipping, in their efforts to carry the day.[63]

In 1863, five men were shot, one fatally, during a match on the Washoe Track at Virginia City, Nevada Territory. A thousand individuals, mostly local miners, paid two dollars and fifty cents each to watch Thomas Daly battle William McGrath. In the fourteenth round a disputed call of "foul" occurred. Harry Lazarus, who bet heavily on McGrath, claimed no foul had been given, while Epitacis "Muchach" Muldonado, wagering on Daly, insisted his man had been wronged. Lazarus called Muchach a liar, pistols flashed, the crowd panicked, and in a few seconds five men lay wounded. Muchach died of his injuries that day, and Harry Lazarus survived only to meet a violent end two years later. Displays of pistols and knives to intimidate the opposition and win bets happened with alarming frequency even when no killings occurred. Tom Allen was victimized this way in three championship matches, against Mike McCoole in 1870, Ben Hogan in 1873, and Joe Goss in 1876.[64]

Fixed bouts, gratuitous violence, the unwillingness of boxers to fight hard, matches that failed to come off, disruption by local officials,

"The Sluggers of Nebraska: A prize fight brought to an end at Nebraska City after one round by a general resort to deadly weapons." The *National Police Gazette* of February 1883 here parodied the corruption of prize fighting after the Civil War.

. *175* .

attempts to defraud bettors, all slowly stripped support from the ring. Before long, well-behaved audiences were so rare as to be worthy of comment. In 1865 the *American Fistiana* noted the "disgust beginning to be felt by those who formerly were warm advocates and defenders of the institution." By 1868 *Wilkes' Spirit of the Times* opened a prize-fight report by referring to "the ring, or rather what is left of it." Later that same year *Porter's Spirit of the Times* sadly observed,

> That portion of the public which delights in manly sports had seen the ring fall under the control of notorious thieves, and forthwith sportsmen ceased to care anything about it. . . . There is now a thorough determination to put down prize-fighting in this country. . . . The fighting men have themselves been much to blame, but they are not to be held individually responsible for these assemblages, and the various communities have decided that it shall cease. Hence the proceedings in Indiana and Ohio [new anti-ring laws], the arrests in New York, New Jersey and Massachusetts.

The editor went on to imply that the Irish were behind the rise of mob rule.[65]

Although the *New York Clipper* refrained from ethnic aspersions, Queen's weekly agreed with the others' assessments. The very same boxers accused of crosses and double crosses in Britain now plied their trade in America, and gangs drove away honest friends of the ring. Queen was probably referring to himself when he declared, "exponents of the manly art can no longer find the influential backers and patrons who formerly took an interest in this sport, for they have become disgusted with mob rule, and leave the pugs to get along as best they can; and until this mob spirit is eradicated root and branch, 'manly artists' can expect to meet with little encouragement or favor." The "mob spirit" grew worse. With a dwindling number of legitimate battles to report, *American Fistiana* unceremoniously ended its history of pugilism with the "put up job" between Harry Hicken and Bryan Campbell in 1873, a bout that saw Hicken's second beaten, kicked, and pistol whipped by Campbell's corner men. The report concluded that this fight simply "drove another nail in the coffin of pugilism."[66]

Perhaps journalists exaggerated. After all, the ring had always been plagued by violence and corruption. It is certainly possible that prize fighting just *seemed* more troubled alongside comparatively clean sports. As bourgeois participation in leisure expanded, all pastimes were measured against middle-class standards of value. The growing interest of polite society in athletic news must have made editors acutely aware of boxing's unsavory associations, and perhaps a potential new readership rendered them more willing than ever to criticize and jettison pugilism rather than jeopardize sales.

But prize fighting's troubles were not merely matters of perception. Threats, suspicions, and recriminations kept mounting. New technologies exacerbated problems. Colt's revolvers began to appear in the antebellum era, and by the Civil War's end had grown ubiquitous on city streets. Concealed weapons and cheap alcohol were a volatile combination. No longer was a burly physique and a willingness to use one's fists the only way to display prowess. Still, the increased incidence of gunplay at ringside, in street fights, and in gang brawls was a sign of change as much as a cause. The great champions of the past were all tough men, but there was a pervasive tone of ruthlessness in the postbellum era, a willingness to go to new extremes. Boxers were more disposed to sell out their peers, gangs refused to abide by the old rules. The corrosive assumption that winning was more important than honor—boxing's own version of Gilded Age corruption—now overwhelmed the prize ring's ability to express deep social schisms in symbolic terms, to create meaning out of mayhem. One detects a note of desperation in the urban underworld and a sense of mercilessness born of debasement. The most violent characters at ringside were no longer displaced journeymen and immigrants of the bachelor subculture, who had seized on boxing as a dramatization of their enmities, but something closer to the "dangerous classes," the truly dispossessed masses, that reformers feared. In this environment the implicit code of sporting conduct, always delicate, broke down.[67]

Symptomatic of pugilism's condition was a new type of boxing literature which emerged around 1880. Backward-looking and nostalgic, it emphasized the battles and deeds of early fistic heroes. Ed James, long a writer for the *Clipper,* and William Edgar Harding, the new sporting editor of the *National Police Gazette,* led the way. They published over a dozen boxing biographies between 1879 and 1882. Both writers lamented the trickery and dishonesty that had caused the ring's decay and made great fights rare occurrences. For now, their solution was to turn back to the pre–Civil War days, exalt the old heroes with almost childlike adulation, and await the restoration of faded glory.[68]

Ironically, the very act of rejecting the present and looking to the past—of reinforcing the fancy's recollections of a golden age a generation back—helped lay the ground for a new heroic era. When young lions emerged, they would be seen as part of a grand historical tradition.

New men were canonized alongside their spiritual ancestors, the Yankee Sullivans, Tom Hyers, John Morrisseys, and John C. Heenans of old. Meanwhile, larger developments in Gilded Age culture and society were preparing the way for the ring's revival.

6

"Fight Like a Gentleman, You Son of a Bitch, If You Can"

The Rise of Sports

While the prize ring lapsed into corruption, other American sports enjoyed an unprecedented boom. As we have seen, the Civil War gave general impetus to athletics, and postbellum society encouraged a leisure explosion that touched all social classes. The war expanded markets, unleashed productive capacity, promoted urbanization, and stimulated the expansion of communications and transportation networks, while creating massive concentrations of corporate and bureaucratic power. These changes, in turn, altered values and ideologies. Before the century was over, sports and recreations flowed in the mainstream of American life. Even that old social outlaw, prize fighting, found itself becoming part of a national culture.[1]

The rise of sports to a prominent place in American consciousness was an exceedingly complex process. A growing faith in science and technology during the last third of the nineteenth century turned doctors into prominent advice givers, and increasingly they recommended healthful exercise to their flabby and overwrought patients. Ministers too advocated vigorous play. The Victorian preoccupation with hard work and steady habits did not evaporate, but many who previously had opposed popular recreations—and clergymen had been among the loudest critics—now embraced sports as a means of teaching "Christian" principles. Conducted under wholesome auspices, athletics built character. Thus, in a book pithily entitled *Sports That Kill,* the Reverend T. DeWitt Talmage condemned pastimes that distracted men from God or work; but he also bemoaned the fact that theology students did not spend enough time in gymnasiums or bowling alleys, and he pointed out that Christians too often confused sickliness with sanctity. Talmage was merely one of the more prominent reformers to join the health-and-fitness chorus. Supervised leisure, they argued, expunged wild old recreations such as animal fighting, discouraged drunk and disorderly conduct, and inculcated the lessons of leadership, cooperation, and fair play.[2]

Some reformers almost equated athletic development with godliness and good character. "Muscular Christianity" became a catchall for the association of piety not only with sports, but with active participation in the affairs of the world, including social reform, foreign adventurism, and urban settlement work. The most prominent institutional embodiment of Muscular Christianity was the Young Men's Christian Association. Founded in England around mid-century, the YMCA established gymnasiums, reading rooms, and lecture halls in scores of American cities during the Gilded Age. For many evangelical liberals, then, self-culture on the one hand and social consciousness on the other became more important than strictly theological issues. Religious mission was now defined in broadly secular terms, and this shift opened the way for a new emphasis on sports and leisure.[3]

But with or without the blessings of reformers, organized athletics grew at an unprecedented rate. By the 1880s football was a college mania; professional baseball teams played in every major city and hundreds of amateur nines gave workingmen a chance to show their skills; athletic associations ranging from exclusive gentlemen's organizations to neighborhood and ethnic clubs proliferated as never before; racing, rowing, golf, tennis, croquet, and a variety of other activities flourished. Despite chronic depressions that ravaged incomes, in the long run most families made modest financial progress. Not only did many workers have a few more disposable dollars and hours by late in the century, but the final destruction of the old artisan economy underscored the disjunction between worktime and leisure time. Indeed, there were few displaced artisans still in the labor force, so most workers knew nothing but wage employment. For this modern working class, leisure to a degree became a matter of selecting, purchasing, and consuming goods and services; commercialized amusements filled more and more free time.[4]

At the top of the organized sports pyramid, baseball and football were being integrated into the American business structure. They developed their own organizational hierarchies, promotional techniques, and national rules. Such sports reflected important modernizing tendencies in American life. As a small but growing part of the business world, sports were developing regulatory bureaucracies, marketing strategies, a managerial ethos, profit orientation, an obsession with victory, specialization of function, an emphasis on statistics, and an insistence on meritocratic values.[5]

Working-class recreations nevertheless still had room for backward-looking tendencies. Saloon-centered bloodsports continued to thrive, for example, and with them the old values of mutuality, reciprocity, loyalty to kin and community, bloodlust, prowess, and honor. For many men, the saloon-based bachelor subculture, with its drinking, gambling, and easy camaraderie, remained at the center of life. Working-class people were not merely passive consumers of commercialized leisure. They were highly selective about their pastimes, often resisting the efforts of businessmen to sell entertainment and of reformers to impose "wholesome" forms of leisure. Many poor and middling people stuck by their old, participatory folk recreations, their ethnic and neighborhood-centered traditions, preferring them to glittering spectacles.[6]

The mixture of "modern" and "premodern" elements in this transitional era is clearly visible in the development of sports journalism. Richard Kyle Fox's *National Police Gazette* was the most important sporting newspaper of the late nineteenth century. Fox's weekly contained plenty of records and statistics, it was produced with the most advanced printing techniques, and it was marketed aggressively all over the country. Yet the *Police Gazette* often seemed a throwback to the old fancy life of theaters, sporting houses, and bordellos. The paper was filled with engravings of scantily clad show girls, accounts of recent scandals and atrocities, advertisements for contraceptives, reports of bloody animal fights, and promotions of such bizarre "sports" as water-drinking contests and hair-cutting championships. The *Gazette*'s success was testimony to the public's growing appetite for amusement. More important, large metropolitan dailies in New York, Chicago, San Francisco, and other cities learned from Fox's success, incorporating sensational reporting into the mainstream press and bringing regular sports coverage—in special sections with their own unique reportorial styles—to the newspapers. Ironically, then, Richard Kyle Fox, promoter of dogfights and rat-killing contests, was as responsible as any man for the development of the modern sports page.[7]

New stadiums, more and more teams, and lengthening columns of newsprint were symptoms, not underlying causes, of the recreational boom in the Gilded Age. The reasons for the rise of sports were many and complex. By the late 1800s America's economic capacity had grown so rapidly that surplus production became a problem. As output expanded, a growing segment of the work force produced luxury items or labored in white-collar jobs, performing services rather than creating products. To keep the economy growing and to mitigate the volatile boom-and-bust gyrations of the economy, demand for new goods and services—not necessities but "the good things in life"—had to keep expanding. The ancient assumption of chronic scarcity was challenged by the revolutionary possibility of ever-growing abundance. Stimulated by advertising and new marketing techniques, a cycle of mass production and consumption had begun. Desires to spend freely and have fun ran up against Victorian austerity, but the grip of the old values was already loosening. The two great bulwarks of bourgeois character no longer held firm: God seemed ever more distant in an era of technology and scientific rationalism, and economic autonomy was threatened by large new corporations. As the consumer age dawned, old Victorian ideals and new, pleasure-centered ones coexisted uneasily, often being split into separate realms of work and leisure. But, slowly, the consumer ethic encompassed increasing numbers of Americans.[8]

New York City nightlife at the turn of the century offers a fine case study of this process. Before and soon after the Civil War cabaret entertainments, including variety and burlesque shows, were considered lower-class dissipations, inextricably tied to saloons and whorehouses. In the last few decades of the century, however, several owners of night clubs began to tidy up their raucous, crudely sexual establishments in order to tap the market of bored bourgeois Americans. Their efforts coincided with the desire of many Victorians to break out of old cultural constraints. Under the cover of darkness, night clubs offered a sanitized version of the "lascivious" pleasure-seeking that the middle class both feared and envied in its "inferiors."[9]

Urban sporting life now had a growing appeal among otherwise respectable people. Jacob Riis, Anthony Comstock, T. DeWitt Talmage, and their like entered dark alleys to reveal filth and sin, yet the middle class read the reformers' exposés with mixed feelings of moral outrage and vicarious excitement. On this voyeurism a cottage industry was built, devoted to condemning haunts of dissipation. A handful of tracts appeared in the 1850s, but by the Gilded Age scores of works were being published to titillate Victorians. The urban underground, with its rough men and loose women, at once fascinated and appalled solid bourgeois citizens. Increasing numbers of Americans longed to be where the prize fighters, gangsters, and harlots were on display. For many otherwise proper individuals, not merely reading about urban dives but actual slumming offered a chance to break through suffocating restraints.[10]

Probably the best-known establishment was Harry Hill's saloon, called by reformers "the most dangerous and demoralizing" place in New York, "the resort of a low class of prostitutes, and of the ruffians and idlers who support the prize ring." There were other famous hangouts. Billy McGlory's Armory Hall allegedly catered to a variety of criminals, streetwalkers, transvestites, and homosexuals; former prize fighter Owney Geogheghan's Bastille on the Bowery acquired a reputation for toughness from its pugnacious owner; and "The" Allen's Bal Mabelle attracted throngs of dissipated young men and women with its gawdy decorations, flowing drink, and cancan dancing. But Hill's establishment was the prototype. It was both deliciously deviant and relatively safe, attracting a clientele that cut across class lines and included judges, editors, and lawyers as well as laborers, sailors, and clerks.[11]

Painted chorus girls in tights, minstrel shows, sparring matches, female boxers, suggestive dancing, and the finest liquors, all could be enjoyed with little fear of assault or arrest. Hill and other proprietors worked to expand their clientele by cleaning up the most offensive instances of drunkenness, profanity, and prostitution. A combination of bribes and cooperation brought police protection, and as a result such men as James Gordon Bennett, Jr., Thomas A. Edison, Richard Kyle Fox, P. T. Barnum, and Oscar Wilde could be seen at Harry Hill's. During the 1870s and '80s, this was America's sporting center, where illicit events, especially prize fights, were arranged, stakes deposited, and wagers laid. Here one left behind moral restraints to choose from a variety of decadent activities and indulge in a little hedonism. The righteous still considered such places dens of iniquity, and the middle-class people who actually frequented them maintained a rigid barrier between daylight work values and nighttime leisure ones. But many Americans now saw acceptable entertainment where a few years earlier they would have seen only sin.[12]

If establishments like Harry Hill's were on the fringe of the leisure revolution, the concept of recreation had moved to the center of attention. Many advanced thinkers considered play as a positive good, not merely a counteractive to overwork but creative and therapeutic in its own right. Supervised recreation socialized children, taught lessons in cooperation, renewed people's vitality, and provided them with a sense of wholeness denied on the job. Youths were raised on books about athletic heroes such as *Frank Merriwell at Yale* (1896), which upheld the old moral verities of honesty, sobriety, and diligence but gave them their highest expression in play rather than in work. Put simply, austerity was not so compelling in this dawning age of abundance, especially because

Harry Hill's New York City Sporting House. By the last quarter of the nineteenth century, such establishments attracted not just the usual sporting crowd but also members of "polite" society. From the *National Police Gazette*, November 22, 1879.

both economic autonomy and intense stirrings of religious faith—the core of bourgeois Victorian ideology—seemed ever more fragile.[13]

Whole new groups of Americans, then, made play a central part of their lives. Therapeutic repose and, paradoxically, man's perceived need for exuberant recreation found powerful champions among professional advice givers. Doctors, ministers, and physical educators all advocated leisure to counter the killing pace of work. Both passive and strenuous activities became part of an arsenal of ``cures'' for social maladies. This therapeutic ethic, whereby pleasure and self-cultivation were prescribed as antidotes to the tensions of daily life, was especially strong among the middle and upper classes, which had the power and prestige to make their new outlook hegemonic. To understand the revival of the ring, we must explore more closely the reasons for the emergence of sports and sporting ideologies in respectable society.

The Strenuous Life

Although the entire postbellum generation participated more than ever before in leisure and recreations, the middle and upper classes especially were swept up by the athletic impulse. They were most influential in legitimating the new sporting boom. As the sons of America's newly wealthy industrialists and financiers began entering college, baseball, football, and rowing became central to student life. Athletics were part of the transformation of colleges from institutions devoted to educating teachers, ministers, and men of letters to training-grounds for future leaders of new corporate and governmental bureaucracies. As the old curriculum shifted away from its classical emphasis, an ``extra-curriculum'' also evolved, with sports at its center. Educators, alumni, and administrators became concerned less with imparting a particular body of knowledge, more with rendering profit making fit for gentlemen. Colleges sought ways to inculate the managerial ethic of efficiency and cooperation, and sports served this end well. Athletics not only kept the sons of the newly rich interested in college, they socialized young men into the values of teamwork and aggressive competition. In sporting contests old wealth and new, Brahmins and parvenus, mingled on terms of relative equality.[14]

Fathers of college boys also became infected with the sporting fever. New athletic clubs for the social elites upheld an amateur ideal to assure the purity of sportsmen's motives and to build high walls of exclusivity around yacht races, polo matches, track meets, and similar events. The

"Education: Is there no middle course?" A growing number of Victorians sought a path between airy intellection and worship of brute force; a sound mind in a sound body became the new ideal. From *Harper's Weekly,* November 30, 1879.

athletic club movement was part of a larger trend toward open displays of wealth by the upper class. Resorts, such as Newport, Rhode Island, lavish annual balls given by the Astors, the Vanderbilts, and other rich families, and cliquish urban organizations, prime among them the Union and Century clubs, allowed wealthy individuals to mingle and affirm one another's social status. The exclusive New York Athletic Club was the prototype for elite sporting organizations, setting an example by building elaborate facilities and sponsoring amateur championships in a variety of events.[15]

In addition to these institutional manifestations of upper-class sports, there was a powerful upsurge of interest in male physicality. As if in reaction to the new emphasis on the consumption of leisure and sensual pleasure, a cult of muscularity arose, emphasizing virility as a counter to sloth and ease. Young men especially became concerned with the shape of their bodies, and postbellum advice literature told them that physique and character were linked. Competitive athletics, it was said, developed the capacity for forceful action and were therefore instrumental to success in business. As a result, countless men and boys from good families began exercising as never before, measuring and recording their muscular development. Although elite interest in masculine strength and beauty arose out of social origins different from the old working-class bachelor subculture, both shared an aesthetic of hard male physicality. More than ever, images of bulging muscles and naked virility appealed across social chasms.[16]

Upper-class fascination with prowess was stimulated in part by fears that modern living rendered males intellectually and emotionally impotent; men emphasized the importance of vigor because, rather suddenly, they were terrified of losing it. It was not simply a matter of being cloyed with material goods. Large numbers of men, especially members of the old Eastern elite, dwelled on their own ineffectuality and "overcivilization" in the face of potent new captains of industrial wealth. Nervous breakdowns occurred with alarming frequency, and some doctors even argued that work-related stress gave rise to a new disease, "neurasthenia," the loss of vital "nerve force." Sports, however, offered a cure. The champion athlete had unusual reserves of magnetic energy, of will power, which allowed him to dominate other men. Physical exercise, therefore, was medicine for this epidemic now spreading through the managerial and professional ranks. Sports heroes became models of action because they seemed to tap limitless reserves of energy within themselves. As the sociologist Franklin Giddings observed at the turn of the century, the "struggle for existence" was "fraught with peril," giving men an "unusual adoration of power." Prize fighters, cowboys, and combat soldiers were heroes, according to Giddings, because they were paragons of virility who refused to give in to the forces that beset them.[17]

By the last decade of the nineteenth century power obsessed many American males. Half-naked strongmen such as Eugene Sandow, flexing his biceps at the 1893 Chicago World's Fair, beguiled them, because they now viewed physical strength as an emblem of force and energy in the larger social world. Not only athleticism but upbeat music, imperialist adventures, realistic literature, the allure of the wilderness, and a cult of Napoleon, all manifested the desire to break through genteel constraints and pursue, in Theodore Roosevelt's words, "the strenuous life." This new quest for vigor arose at least partly out of deep spiritual longings, because a thoroughly corporate, bureaucratized society was also a dull and soulless one. Countless men of means sought rugged action to compensate for their safe and overstuffed lives.[18]

Amateur sports were particularly well-suited to the task. In college stadiums and gentlemen's athletic clubs the ideal of stern self-testing for its own sake, of pure competition without corrupting materialism, reached its fullest expression. Indeed, many leaders of college athletics—for example, Dudley A. Sargent, director of Harvard's Hemenway Gymnasium—condemned professionalism and passive spectatorship as destroyers of the harmony between a healthy mind and a healthy body. Collegiate sports, Sargent argued, restored the balance. Amateur games were especially important to those coming of age after the Civil War, for violent contests on athletic "fields of battle" allowed young men to replicate the heroism of fathers who had sacrificed so much in their selfless commitment to saving the Union. Here the martial values of hardiness, courage, and endurance took their place beside the older Victorian ideals of piety and earnest hard work.[19]

Late nineteenth-century members of the Eastern Brahmin caste—the spiritual and lineal descendants of Thomas Wentworth Higginson and Oliver Wendell Holmes, Sr.—turned to violent sports as a moral equivalent of war, a symbolic field on which pain, sacrifice, duty, and glory were still attainable. Athletic strife grew especially important to a society that was rendering life soft with material comforts and empty with religious skepticism. Sports taught valuable lessons to young men from prosperous families, showing them how to suppress their social and spiritual doubts with bursts of vigorous energy. As Henry Cabot Lodge told a meeting of Harvard alumni, the injuries incurred at athletic contests were "part of the price which the English speaking race has paid for being world conquerors."[20]

Also contributing to the rise of elite sports was the fact that Americans had always worshiped success while fearing the corrupting effects of prosperity. As far back as the Puritan fathers, material wealth could signify either God's grace or the decline of true faith amidst worldly pleasures. Decades later, republican thinkers also viewed the piling up of luxuries as a threat to virtue, leading ultimately to decadence and tyranny. Shapers of Victorian culture too valued the *process* of wealth creation for its social usefulness and tests of characters, but feared the corrosive effects of inherited riches, money gotten by chance, not work.

Success thus contained the seeds of its own alienation. Once fortunes were amassed, corporations built, and frontiers closed, individuals were tempted to cease driving themselves and to lapse into slothful consumption of life's fruits. Violent sports and rugged stress seeking, however, allowed men such as Theodore Roosevelt to have it both ways, to enjoy their legacy of material comfort while denying that they had lost any of the masculine selflessness of pioneers and soldiers.[21]

Coexisting with the ethic of pleasure, then, were socially created anxieties that carried implications for the development of sports. Abundance had been purchased with brutal labor policies, cutthroat competition, and robber-baron disregard for human suffering. Indeed, one man's prosperity often seemed to spring from another's poverty. Bitter strikes hit major industries, and whole companies were gobbled up by competitors; the capriciousness of the economic cycle made a mockery of the old belief in self-help through hard work. In this era of corporate consolidation a new ideology emerged, one less concerned with character, autonomy, or control of the passions and more with power, money, and success. Life, it was said, was a jungle, and Charles Darwin's findings on natural selection provided a compelling metaphor for a society at war with itself. Survival of the fittest, killing competition, death to the weak—these phrases seemed to describe the real-life combat between social groups. Here again, sports fulfilled ideological assumptions. Hard and violent games not only toughened men for the battles of life, they rendered the Darwinian metaphor literal fact, making the dog-eat-dog, victory-or-death, give-the-enemy-no-quarter mentality appear inescapably real.[22]

Prominent men now declared that the entire Anglo-Saxon ``race'' was endangered, at home by radical workers and immigrant hordes and abroad by inferior but virile peoples. Moreover, many native- and well-born citizens saw America's future threatened by other imperialistic countries. The United States must gird itself to compete with belligerent nations or fall subject to them. In large measure, then, Darwinism became the ideology of a particular class, and sports helped give that ideology vivid expression. Military, political, and business leaders, especially those from old wealthy families, encouraged athletics in order to prepare men for the harsh struggles ahead, to foster combativeness and the habit of command. Sports taught manliness in a violent world. All that was feminine, sentimental, or romantic—and many late nineteenth-century writers worried aloud that America had become ``womanized''—was expunged on athletic fields of battle.[23]

The historian Jackson Lears has observed that as Victorian ideals began to dissolve in the acids of modernity, as creeping secularization

NEW YORK ATHLETIC CLUB,

104 WEST 55TH STREET.

SECOND AMATEUR BOXING CONTEST,

Saturday Evening, March 8, 1890.

Handsome and costly prizes will be given to First and Second in each of the following events.

110 pound Boxing.

120 pound Boxing.

130 pound Boxing.

135 pound Boxing.

140 pound Boxing.

145 pound Boxing.

160 pound Boxing.

A handsome Banner will be given to the Club scoring the greatest number of points.

A prize will be given to the winner of each bout in the 120 lb. class

Entrance Fee of $1.00 *must accompany all entries.*

Entries close March first, 1890, with

B. C. WILLIAMS,

104 WEST 55TH STREET,

NEW YORK.

Amateur boxing, New York Athletic Club, 1890. Some of America's wealthiest and most powerful men belonged to the N.Y.A.C. College sports and athletic clubs helped forge the social identity of corporate America's upper class.

undermined piety, relativism sapped moral certitude, and bureaucratization destroyed autonomy, Americans from old elite families responded in deeply personal ways. Their sense of being "weightless" and "over-civilized," even superfluous in an industrial society, gave rise to cravings for intense experience. Various forms of antimodernism, including orien-tal mysticism, a fascination with organic medieval communities, and the worship of military values, were all symptoms of their quest for a sense of purpose, for connectedness to "real life." Vigorous sports were another way out of the trap, not only offering models of action in a world of doubt but also serving as a rallying point for an entire class that sought its own revitalization. Through the metaphor of harsh competition on athletic playing fields, young gentlemen learned to throw off their uncertainties, charge into the fray, and take command.[24]

The result for the old Victorian ethos was not destruction but its reshaping. The ideal of character now took on a strenuous quality that rejected pious sermonizing or airy intellection and substituted a vigorous application of moral principles at home and abroad. As Francis Walker told the Cambridge Phi Beta Kappa Society in an 1893 address, "College Athletics," sports taught young men from good families that they must not withdraw as a leisure class but must participate in the nitty-gritty work of daily life: "Man is not a pilgrim but a citizen. He is going to tarry nights enough to make it worthwhile to patch up the tenement and even to look into the drainage. This world is a place to work in; activity and development, not suffering or self-repression its law." Participating in rough sports, Walker argued, gave courage to college youths and prepared them to see their lives as a struggle toward clearly defined goals. On athletic playing fields, young men learned that acts mattered more than words.[25]

Similarly, Oliver Wendell Holmes, Jr., believed that sports, like war, revealed strife to be the essence of life. Violent athletic encounters reminded Americans that prosperous commercial life was "merely a little space of calm in the midst of the tempestuous untamed streaming of the world." Sports trained leaders, and the occasional broken neck—no rarity in collegiate football—was "a price well paid for the breeding of a race fit for headship and command." Like war, athletic games caused men to strain every nerve and muscle, to feel "the passion of life at its top." Here, then, was Holmes's creed: "To ride boldly at what is in front of you, be it fence or enemy; to pray not for comfort but for combat; to keep the soldier's faith against the doubts of civil life, more besetting and harder to overcome than all the misgivings of the battlefields . . . to love glory more than the temptations of wallowing in

ease, but to know that one's final judge and only rival is oneself. . . ."
Through rugged self-testing, men beat back moral anarchy and found
renewed purpose.[26]

But it was not only the old Brahmin caste that became interested in
sports. The late nineteenth century witnessed the unprecedented growth
of a salaried white-collar class, including clerks, professionals, salespeo-
ple, engineers, and managers of new corporate bureaucracies. A product
of the extreme specialization of labor in an advanced economy, their
work was often sedentary and highly routinized, giving little inherent
sense of satisfaction. Indeed, such jobs violated important tenets of the
entrepreneurial ethic, for white-collar occupations offered neither autonomy nor ownership of productive property. Even those who earned large
salaries failed to attain the ultimate dream of independence. Like the old
artisans-turned-laborers earlier in the century, the new managers and
technicians were employees, dependent on the whims of others. Imbued
with the success ethic, with the belief that man makes his own fate, they
strove mightily for self-advancement only to be stymied by a social
system with little room for autonomous individualism.[27]

Here was a source of crisis for masculine identity: Where would a
sense of maleness come from for the worker who sat at a desk all day?
How could one be manly without independence? Where was virility to
be found in increasingly faceless bureaucracies? How might clerks or
salesmen feel masculine doing "women's work"? What became of
rugged individualism inside intensively rationalized corporations? How
could a man be a patriarch when his job kept him away from home for
most of his waking hours?[28]

It was precisely in this context that fears of feminized males and
domineering women emerged. In Henry James's *The Bostonians,* published
in 1886, Basil Ransom spoke for countless American men when he
condemned the "damnable feminization" pervading society. "The whole
generation is womanized," Ransom wailed. "The masculine tone is
passing out of the world; it's a feminine, a nervous, hysterical, chattering,
canting age, an age of hollow phrases and false delicacy and exaggerated
solicitudes and coddled sensibilities, which if we don't soon look out,
will usher in the reign of mediocrity. . . ." Ransom wished to restore
masculine character, which he defined as "the ability to dare and
endure, to know and yet not fear reality, to look the world in the face and
take it for what it is." Concerns that female sentimentality threatened to
overwhelm hard masculine realism pervaded the age; such phrases as
"over-civilization" and "over-refinement" conveyed male anxieties
about effeminization. Some men therefore began to wonder aloud if the

pious and gentle values that infused their mothers' homes had not unnerved them for the world of work. Thus Ernest Thompson Seton, founder of the Boy Scouts of America, feared for "the boy who had been coddled all his life and kept so carefully wrapped up on the 'pink cotton wool' of an over-indulgent home, till he is more effeminate than his sister, and his flabby muscles are less flabby than his character." Simply put, it was easier for many men to rail against emasculation than to come to terms with the profound social and cultural changes of their era.[29]

If mothers threatened to suffocate manliness, paradoxically, wives, sisters, and lovers assaulted it as the "new women" of the middle and upper classes attended college, sought work (sometimes in competition with men), campaigned for voting rights, and expected an equal share of America's opportunities. Women were also being more demanding sexually; some even rejected the cult of domesticity to seek sensual fulfillment at the expense of their own "purity." Where were men to turn as their gender-based dominance eroded? As well as seeking to keep women out of colleges, voting booths, and careers, many retreated to bastions of male exclusivity. Just as working-class men had learned earlier to find affirmation of their manliness outside the home and workplace in the saloon-centered bachelor subculture, now the middle and upper classes increasingly turned to leisure as a source of masculine identity. Sports for both participants and spectators became a realm of manly self-assertion, a closed male world that initiated them into the life of action, a place to escape from demanding women.[30]

"Sissy," "molly-coddle," "pussy-foot" now became popular terms of derision. Concern over feminized men and masculinized women could be seen also in more subtly altered language, as words were enlisted to shore up the sagging barriers between the sexes. The old bourgeois meaning of "manly"—to be adult, responsible, mature, self-possessed, independent, not childlike—was transformed into a negation of all that was soft, feminine, or sentimental. Being manly now meant being not womanly. Whether it involved fighting in a foreign jungle, battling in urban politics, or getting ahead on the job, the strenuous life taught men to purge longings for ease and to seek strife rather than comfort. To wage war, direct corporations, outsell competitors or manage other men required a bold assertion of self and a dominating physical presence. Virile, daring males—hunters, detectives, cowboys, adventurers—were now fantasy heroes because they projected hairy-chested images of manliness in a world that deeply threatened masculinity. Similarly, when men played rough sports or cheered their favorite athletes, they found temporary refuge from those forces which challenged their manhood, whether routinized work, soulless corporations, aggressive women, smothering mothers, rich new industrialists, radical laborers, or swarthy foreigners.[31]

Even as professional prize fighting languished and nearly died during the 1860s and 1870s, therefore, a social and ideological environment was developing which would encourage its rejuvenation. The commercialization of leisure, the beginnings of a consumer ethic, the development of middle- and upper-class interest in rugged sports, the increasing hollowness of Victorian ideals in a corporate age, changing gender relationships, and male fears of "feminization"—all provided a backdrop for the transformation of the prize ring, for the integration of the outlaw sport into a nationwide mass culture. Great championship fights of the past had transcended pugilism's provincial boundaries only temporarily; now the altered social and cultural climate would make prize fighting an acceptable spectator sport for whole new groups of Americans. Put simply, a burst of upper- and middle-class interest in boxing's elemental qualities, its glorification of male prowess, powered the ring's renewal. Equally important, prize fighting itself changed to meet the altered social conditions. These two factors, each reinforcing the other, became the basis for pugilism's dramatic revival in the last two decades of the century.

Fighting Clerks, Boxing Brahmins, Vigorous Victorians

Prize fighting has always spoken most eloquently to America's lower classes, especially to members of ethnic groups. Symbolically, the ring merged the American dream with Old World memories, the cult of success with ancestral ties, individual opportunity with group loyalties. Even today working-class and ethnic peoples tend to find special meaning in the sport and supply most of its practitioners and fans. No equivalent of the English aristocracy ever supported the American prize ring. But, slowly, boxing began to resonate for men outside the lower class.[32]

Just before the Civil War, Oliver Wendell Holmes, Sr., anticipated this trend. I know of no evidence that Holmes ever attended a prize fight, but he did appear at exhibitions and recommended friendly bouts to his peers. Holmes loved watching youths attack and defend themselves at sparring matches, and he was exhilarated when a gentleman displayed his "primitive nature." "Boxing is rough play," Holmes conceded, "but not too rough for a hearty young fellow. Anything is better than this white-blooded degeneration to which we all tend."[33]

Holmes gloried in the muscular development of boxers like John C. Heenan, attended the Benicia Boy at his training camp, and surveyed his remarkable physique. Indeed, Holmes openly fantasized about the ring:

> Here is a delicate young man now with an intellectual countenance, a slight figure, a sub-pallid complexion, a most unassuming deportment, a mild adolescent face, that any Hiram or Jonathan from between the ploughtails would of course expect to handle with perfect ease. Oh, he is taking off his gold-bowed spectacles! Ah, he is divesting himself of his cravat! Why, he is stripping off his coat. Well, here he is, sure enough, in a tight silk shirt, and with two things that look like batter puddings in the place of his fists. Now see that other fellow with another pair of batter puddings—the big one with the broad shoulders; he will certainly knock the little man's head off if he strikes him.

Yet the delicate intellectual proved his mettle:

> Feinting, dodging, stopping, hitting, countering—little man's head not off yet. You might as well try to jump upon your own shadow as to hit the little man's intellectual features. He needn't have taken off the gold-bowed spectacles at all. Quick, cautious, shifty, nimble, cool, he catches all the fierce lunges or gets out of their reach, till his turn comes, and then whack goes one of the batter puddings against the big one's ribs, and bang goes the other into the big one's face, and, staggering, shuffling, slipping, tripping, collapsing, sprawling, down goes the big one in a miscellaneous bundle.

Here was a perfect metaphor for a beleaguered social class seeking its own revitalization. Seizing the moment, the young man's courage and coolness overcame external threats and internal fears. He was in complete control.[34]

Pallid, scrawny, bespectacled, Holmes's little hero found his apotheosis less than a generation later when young Theodore Roosevelt began boxing at Harvard College. In 1890 Roosevelt looked back on his youth and saw in sports a necessary corrective to the soft life of turn-of-the-century America: "There is a certain tendency to underestimate or overlook the need of the virile, masterful qualities of the heart and mind. . . . There is no better way of counteracting this tendency than by encouraging bodily exercise and especially the sports which develop such qualities as courage, resolution and endurance." In Holmes's day the association of social elites with the strenuous life was half-formed and barely conscious. But the young man who stripped off the trappings of his comfortable bourgeois life and whipped the clumsy ploughboy was an archetype for Roosevelt's generation.[35]

As the nineteenth century began its last quarter, however, prize fighting remained mired in its own version of Gilded Age corruption. Not since the Lilly-McCoy affair had boxing been held in such low esteem. Of course, sporting houses in major cities still offered frequent exhibitions of the manly art of self-defense. But without much hope of good championship fights in the near future, sparring matches were flat affairs, arousing little passion. Seeds of revival, however, were about to germinate. If the seventies proved disastrous to the manly art, the eighties saw boxing become one of America's most popular spectator sports. Until the racism of the Progressive Era temporarily blighted boxing when the great black fighter Jack Johnson ascended the throne in 1908, interest in pugilism leaped the old barriers of class and ethnicity. Not coincidentally, boxing's triumph accompanied the end of bare-knuckle prize fighting.[36]

The Gilded Age, as we have seen, encouraged an enormous variety of recreations, encompassing new groups of people and fostering powerful institutions. The ring benefited from this general rise of sports, basking in the glow of baseball, rowing, and football while reflecting back a new luster of its own. But boxing's history was always distinctive, following only approximately the course taken by other athletic activities. After all, prize fighting languished during the 1870s while most sports prospered.

Theodore Roosevelt offers a fine example of the ambivalence many men felt about the ring. "A prize-fight," Civil Service Commissioner Roosevelt declared in 1890, "is simply brutal and degrading."

> The people who attend it and make a hero of the prize fighter, are, —excepting boys who go for fun and don't know any better—to a very great extent, men who hover on the borderlines of criminality; and those who are not are speedily brutalized, and are never rendered more manly. They form as ignoble a body as do the hundred frequenters of rat-pit and cock-pit. The prize fighters and his fellow professional athletes of the same ilk are, together with their patrons in every rank of life, the very worst foes with whom the cause of general athletic development has to contend.[37]

Yet Roosevelt loved boxing. From his early teens through his White House years, he regularly put on the gloves to battle an array of sparring masters and former professionals. As president, Roosevelt received former champion John L. Sullivan in the White House, and he visited

Jim Jeffries's training camp as the "Great White Hope" prepared to fight Jack Johnson. Mike Donovan, once bare-knuckle middleweight champion of the world, later boxing instructor for the exclusive New York Athletic Club, became good friends with Roosevelt, and the two enjoyed sparring during the latter's terms as governor of New York and president. Roosevelt even described affairs of state with boxing metaphors, and the near loss of an eye in one of his White House set-tos failed to dampen his enthusiasm for the manly art.[38]

Roosevelt's ambivalence was not uncommon. Prize fighting continued to elicit the old criticisms against immoral and rowdy behavior, but the fascination that had started to creep in during the antebellum era now became more open.[39] As early as mid-century, newspapers hinted that some surprisingly respectable people showed up at sparring matches, even prize fights. Although this may well have been true, the fact that names never came to light makes it seem unlikely that the practice was common. By the 1880s, however, names of individuals were appearing, some frequently. Editor Charles A. Dana, Senator Roscoe Conkling, Reverend Henry Ward Beecher, all allegedly were seen at one or more matches. Great tycoons such as William K. Vanderbilt, Lawrence Jerome, and Herman Oelricks also attended indoor bouts at Madison Square Garden, intensely fought glove contests for large stakes.[40]

Some men even wrote openly about their beguilement with the sporting underworld. G. Stanley Hall, a founder of the science of psychology in America, was captivated by the "raw side of human life," and unknown to his friends and colleagues, he ventured into urban backstreets whenever he got the chance. Hall's slumming led him to the fancy's pet sport: "I have never missed an opportunity to attend a prize fight," he confessed in his autobiography, "if I could do so unknown and away from home, so that I have seen most of the noted pugilists of my generation in action and felt the unique thrill at these encounters."[41]

The fine arts also reveled in the gutter. Aspiring young painters and writers were just beginning to discover previously taboo subjects as sources of art, and late in the nineteenth century boxing proved especially attractive. Frank Norris and Richard Harding Davis managed to varnish the ring with a coat of sentimentality, writing of their pugilists as noble heroes. The artist Thomas Eakins, on the other hand, cut through romantic conventions to paint anatomically impeccable forms, men of dignified strength in a violent and painful world. Eakins was familiar with boxing by the late 1860s, but a quarter century passed before he painted the passions—not to mention the seminudity—of the ring. He was the first American artist to use prize fighting as a symbol of rebellion against genteel conventions. Just after the turn of the century painter George Bellows and novelist Jack London interpreted the ring much more grimly than Eakins, depicting it as a microcosm of merciless competition where pain, loneliness, and betrayal were the order of the day. Violence was the means and survival the end of life, and often the best that men could hope for was to suffer defeat with their courage and integrity intact. For London and Bellows, the sheer physical beauty that Eakins saw in athletic competition was overshadowed by grim, work-manlike determination.[42]

Artists and writers implicitly rejected genteel propriety when they took prize fighting as their subject. The purpose of art or literature, as most bourgeois Victorians saw it, was to instruct, to elevate; American intellectuals must never use their talents to dignify wickedness. Even nineteenth-century England could tolerate an occasional boxing engraving by Cruikshank, a poem by Thackeray, a sketch by Dickens. New World canons, however, brooked no deviation. After Charles Cromwell Ingham painted William Fuller in 1824, I know of no distinguished American writer or artist depicting the ring until nearly the end of the century. But as Victorian absolutism crumbled, the social role of intellectual elites changed. They began viewing themselves less as upholders of high culture, more as adventurers on the frontiers of experience. For some of these new men and women, writing and the plastic arts became a forum for the expression of personal feeling and emotion rather than for declaring fixed public values. Others who felt stifled by old bourgeois verities turned outward instead of inward and embraced the teeming life of the streets, reveling in scenes of immigrants, the working class, and the urban underworld. Victorian restraint loosened slowly, but the impulse to test personal limits and explore uncharted realms of experience logically led to strenuous, or violent, or deviant activities. Prize fighting was all of these. The full flowering of artistic depictions of the ring came as the century turned, but the new intellectuals who painted and wrote about boxing often reached back to their own youthful sporting experiences during the eighteen sixties, seventies and eighties.[43]

Indeed, by late in the century countless American men of good families were personally familiar with boxing. The small numbers who had attended sparring classes given by the old professors of pugilism before the Civil War now became a multitude. Young men from the wealthiest backgrounds, such as Theodore Roosevelt at Harvard and William C. Whitney at Yale, fought with gloves in college during the 1870s. By the 1880s cabinet secretaries such as James G. Blaine and Zackary Chandler, former governor Flower and ex-senator Conkling of

New York, all took sparring lessons. Exclusive athletic clubs hired boxing coaches, YMCAs offered instruction, and self-defense manuals proliferated. The New York Athletic Club even sponsored the first national amateur boxing championship, in 1878. *Frank Leslie's Magazine* acknowledged pugilism's recent popularity when it bewailed the worship of brute force which filled New York City sparring rooms and urged that "prize-fighters be once more regarded as outlaws and not as public entertainers."[44]

Quite the opposite occurred, for amateur sparring's newfound popularity helped redeem professional ring fighting. The New York Athletic Club, for example, retained middleweight champion Mike Donovan to teach "gentlemen eminent in science, literature, art, social and commercial life." Unlike his professional ancestor, William Fuller, Donovan did not hesitate to assist at and arrange regular prize battles, apparently offending none of his elite clientele. Other cities followed New York's lead. The gentlemen of San Francisco's Olympic Club were so pleased with their sparring master, prize fighter James J. Corbett, that they paid him $2,500 per year. Boston elites also learned the fistic arts in their own private institutions. The Cribb Club, for example, where ring fighter Jake Kilrain gave lessons, had over one hundred enrollees by the mid-eighties, among them businessmen, lawyers, physicians, and journalists. Nomination by two members and the approval of an election committee were required for admission. Similarly, the Commercial Athletic Club charged an initiation fee and monthly dues to discourage all "unruly and turbulent spirits."[45]

Even an occasional Christian voice now spoke up for the prize ring. Reverend Brobst of Chicago's Westminster Presbyterian Church believed the Sullivan-Kilrain fight in 1889 contained important lessons for the faithful. Before going into training, the principals were "drinkers, sensual, beastly" men. But once articles had been signed, Brobst noted, the opponents resisted all temptation: "Talk about taking up your cross, Christians! You ought to be ashamed of yourselves. Take a lesson in hardship and denial from these pugilists!" The ends of prize fighting might be corrupt, but the means were divine, for hard training brought boxers to physical and mental perfection. Here was an important change from earlier decades. Although a few writers had praised the abstemiousness of boxers in training, no minister in the era of Heenan, Hyer, and Morrissey would have dared refer to prize fighters as paragons of Christian virtue. But Brobst argued that men in the ring offered models of will power, fortitude, and endurance to the faithful. Boxing was a metaphor for a grim world of stern competition, where toughness was

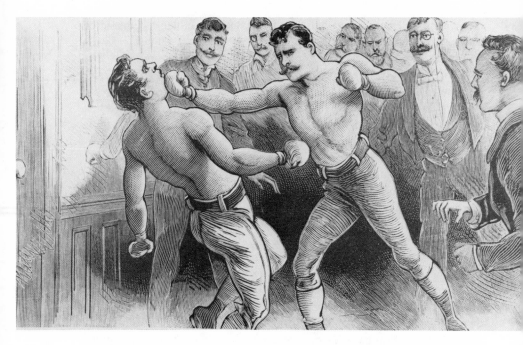

"Prize fight after a banquet: Society bloods of Rochester, New York enjoy a rattling six-round bout at a fashionable hotel." From the *National Police Gazette,* February 2, 1895.

both a religious and a secular duty. "Take a lesson," Brobst admonished his congregation, and no doubt many did, seeking spiritual enlightenment at the next convenient bout.[46]

In one form or another, then, boxing became familiar to men of solid social standing. Courage and confidence, self-command and graceful bearing, vigor and decisiveness, pugilism fostered all of these traits. The animal world, psychologist G. Stanley Hall declared, was filled with the struggle for survival. Man's aggressive "instinct" sometimes embroiled him in senseless combat, yet anger was a valuable trait and real men rejoiced in noble strife. Hall—who championed the concept of a distinct adolescent stage of life, with its own psychology—believed that boys must learn to fight, lest they grow up to be unmanly and craven milksops. Boxing lessons were the perfect means to channel aggression, tempering adolescent violence yet engendering courage, force of will, and self-assertion.[47]

Soon respectable journals advocated pugilism. Daniel L. Dawson, writing in *Lippincott's Monthly,* argued that sparring was among the very best forms of exercise, encouraging not only muscular development but also courage, temperance, and quickness of thought. *Outing,* which claimed to be *the* gentleman's magazine of sport, travel, and outdoor life, became a repository of information for genteel boxers. Essays not only discussed leverage, mechanics, and physiology; they upheld the moral worth of pugilism. Amateur bouts, A. Austin declared in "The Theory and Practice of Boxing," were tests of character, forcing men to confront their moral strengths and weaknesses.[48]

Some writers now called for the reform of prize fighting. Charles E. Clay, who wrote about yachting and exotic travel for *Outing,* did a series of articles based on his personal boxing experiences. The gentlemanly fighter, like Eakins's men in the ring, was beautiful: "His shoulders are broad, but graceful and sloping, and from them the arms, with full and rounded biceps, fall so easily and naturally to their proper position at the sides! . . . The chest expansive, and well filled out, shows plenty of room for the lungs to work. The deltoid and shoulder muscles are all thoroughly developed, and go to form a strong and shapely back." But the benefits were more than merely physical, for boxing taught pluck and endurance. Those who entered the ring developed the resourcefulness, the confidence, and the command to overcome life's daily obstacles and become leaders among men. However, Clay added, only the rules of glove fighting made boxing so excellent for moral and physical training; the old bare-knuckle ways must go.[49]

Duffield Osborn concurred. His "Defense of Pugilism," published in the *North American Review* in 1888, argued that as civilization grew overrefined, it degenerated into "mere womanishness." The rigorous self-denial of boxers in training, their unflinching courage in the face of pain and fatigue, helped counter these pernicious tendencies. Those who valued "high manly qualities" ought therefore to array themselves against the "mawkish sentimentality" that threatened to transform Americans into "a race of eminently respectable female saints." Boxing, Osborn concluded, must be reformed and supported.[50]

John Boyle O'Reilly, poet, editor of the *Boston Pilot,* and an acknowledged leader of the Irish-American middle class, became the ring's most articulate champion. Prize fighting was too valuable to be sullied by gangsters and criminals. "Let it stand alone," O'Reilly argued, "an athletic practice, on the same footing as boating or football." Sparring was the perfect recreation for businessmen whose nerves were frayed by competition and energies depleted by the frenetic pace of life. No other sport exercised the trunk, limbs, eyes, and mind so well. The intensity of sparring made it ideal training for the young: "The boxer in action has not a loose muscle or a sleepy brain cell. His mind is quicker and more watchful than a chess player's. He has to gather his impulses and hurl them, straight and purposeful, with every moment and motion." Watching honest professionals fight with gloves also taught valuable lessons in manly fortitude and confidence. "Where else in one compressed hour," O'Reilly asked, "can be witnessed the supreme test and tension of such precious living qualities as courage, temper, endurance, bodily strength, clear-mindedness in excited action, and above all, that heroic spirit that puts aside the cloak of defeat though it fall anew a hundred and a thousand times, and in the end, reaches out and grasps the silver mantle of success?" Ideal training for all citizens, boxing must be rescued from gamblers and thugs and restored to gentlemanly luster.[51]

Pugilism, then, was filled with meaning for turn-of-the-century America. Bloodletting, merciless competition, and stern self-testing in the ring addressed the newly perceived need of middle- and upper-class men for more active life. Alive in every nerve, the boxer was in complete control of his body, negating by example the pervasive fears of overcivilization, nervous breakdowns, and neurasthenia. The ring countered effeminizing tendencies, preparing men for the life of strife.[52]

The physical and mental acuteness of two fighters in combat offered an intriguing symbol for a society extolling "manly competition" in the market place and a culture beginning to substitute a cult of personal experience for tight self-control. Pugilists were models of poise and courage for an old upper class that felt threatened from above by new industrial wealth and below by immigrant hordes and labor radicals. Prize fighting upheld fantasies of untrammeled masculinity for a new white-collar class locked into distinctly unvirile, corporate jobs. As a spectator sport, boxing symbolically reconciled contradictory cultural imperatives. Pugilists were models of aggressiveness but also of self-discipline and self-control. Moreover, the fans, by passively imbibing images of ultramasculine action, by sitting back and watching others bleed, could have it both ways, extolling prowess while filling the role of consumer.

And here was the problem. Upper- and middle-class men were enthralled by the drama, the violence, the pageantry of the ring, but few were willing to accept prize fighting because of its associations with gangs, criminality, and the urban underworld. Change was needed, to purge the sport of its rowdy, even criminal elements yet retain the old vibrancy. For such men as Roosevelt and O'Reilly, the solution was to assimilate professional boxing to amateur rules.

Variations on the marquis of Queensberry code governed gentlemen's

"THE PRESIDENT HAS A GOOD RIGHT SAYS PROF DONOVAN AND WHEN IT LANDED ON MY EAR I THOUGHT JOHN L HAD ME BACK TO LIFE AND SWATTED ME"

President Theodore Roosevelt spars with former middleweight champion Mike Donovan. Young Roosevelt also boxed while a student at Harvard and later befriended such champions as John L. Sullivan. From Donovan, *The Roosevelt That I Know* (1909).

contests during the seventies and eighties. First compiled in England in 1866 by an old-style patron of pugilism, along with Lord Lonsdale and lightweight boxer Arthur Chambers, the Queensberry rules were designed to reform the ring. The new code borrowed freely from the conventions that regulated sparring; it disallowed all the old wrestling throws and holds and encouraged men to stand and slug it out. Punching with the fists was now the only legal way to attack an opponent. Combatants wore gloves, though usually these were much less heavily padded than the "pillows" used in sparring. Boxers faced each other for three-minute rounds alternating with one-minute rest periods, until one man was knocked down and unable to rise within ten seconds. Under the old rules, rounds averaged only half as long, sometimes much less, and a fallen man had thirty seconds to recover. Like the London Prize Ring rules and Broughton's code, the Queensberry rules set no limit on the number of rounds. Finally, the new regulations allowed the ring to be built indoors on a stage, supplanting the long-standing dictum that it be pitched on turf.[53]

The marquis of Queensberry rules drastically changed boxing's style and tempo. For decades popular histories have claimed that the new rules made the sport less dangerous, yet descriptions of bouts under the code reveal no diminution of violence. Consider, for example, the following account of the 1892 featherweight championship fight between George Dixon and Jack Skelly;

> What with bruises, lacerations, and coagulated blood, Skelly's nose, mouth and eye presented a horrible spectacle, and as the poor fellow staggered about almost helpless, even some of the most blase fans at the ringside were heard to shudder, and some even turned their heads in disgust as they saw Dixon savagely chopping away at that face already disfigured past recognition, and heard the ugly half-splashing sound as his blood-soaked glove again and again revisited the bleeding wounds that drenched them.[54]

Gloves protected fighters' hands more than their heads, added weight to each punch, and allowed men to throw innumerable blows to such hard-but-vulnerable spots as the temples and jaw. In bare-knuckle fighting, punches tended to be straight and cutting. A man who threw many hooks or roundhouse-style shots to the side or back of his opponent's head risked breaking his fingers. But with gloves, boxers could use these more dangerous punches with impunity. In addition, the new ten-second knockout rule further encouraged clubbing blows, because it was much easier to punch a man into ten seconds than into thirty seconds of unconsciousness. Unfortunately, gloved fists and an emphasis on knock-outs increased the likelihood that fighters would become brain-damaged over a long career, for the trauma of repeated concussions had a cumulative effect, producing lesions that resulted in the ''punch-drunk'' syndrome. In a word, boxing might look a bit less brutal but became more dangerous.[55]

Equally important, the Queensberry rules took control over the pace of action away from the fighters. Like factory whistles, boxing's new rhythms mandated regular periods of work and rest. With a referee now inside the ring urging them to fight, boxers could no longer steal a few minutes to glare at each other, tacitly agreeing to slow down, return to their corners for a drink, and regain their strength. Moreover, the new order banned wrestling, a skill on which many fighters depended. Above all, the Queensberry rules emphasized quick, dramatic blows. In important respects, boxing became simpler and faster-paced, essential qualities if it was to appeal to a wide if not particularly knowledgeable audience. The new regimentation and violent action were part of the larger pattern whereby players in various sports were losing day-to-day control over them. Increasingly, athletes were becoming subject to the dictates of owners and managers. Thus the most important result of the Queensberry rules was not to make the ring less violent but to make it more assimilable to the entertainment industry and to mass commercial spectacles.[56]

Perhaps the absence of grappling, the timed intervals of work and rest, and the muffled fists made boxing seem more scientific and antiseptic than it had before. As the new code derived from gentlemen's rules, some reasoned, boxing must now be gentlemanly. But the Queensberry rules merely pasted a thin veneer of respectability over the brutality; they did not obviate the bloody, confrontational nature of boxing. Equally important, the new fighting style itself did nothing to stop the gambling, drinking, and rowdiness that boxing's opponents condemned so vociferously. What changed was the relationship between commerce and the ring. By facilitating bouts on the indoor stage rather than turf, the Queensbury rules allowed promoter-entrepreneurs to charge admission, thereby opening the way for crowd control by police and private security officers. Prize fighting acquired a gloss of gentility that legitimated the violence and freed respectable men to enjoy previously forbidden fruits with safety and good conscience.

Thus the Queensberry code accommodated the larger social and cultural needs of well-off Americans. The new rules, however, were not simply imposed on boxing by the middle and upper class. Oldtimers might feel that championships should be won with bare knuckles, but boxers themselves and the new sports entrepreneurs had good reasons, both legal and financial, to favor the Queensberry rules. The expanding interest that respectable Americans showed in all forms of pugilism was an important factor in reviving the manly art. So long as important persons might be in attendance at Madison Square Garden for a match, police had to move cautiously. But even before bourgeois interest peaked, the ring's renewal under the Queensberry rules had begun. Change from within the pugilistic profession merged with interest in prize fighting by new and influential groups, transforming boxing into one of America's most important spectator sports. Breaking through old barriers of class and ethnicity, the ring became a central symbol for an energetic age. Pugilism, though still primarily a male passion, joined high-stepping dances, wild amusement parks, a rage for bicycling, and other intensely kinetic activities as manifestations of an expansive new tone in American culture. No individual better captured the spirit of the age or received wider acclaim than a strapping young Irish-American boxer from Boston. To him we must turn to understand the rebirth of the ring and its meaning for America.

7

The End of the Bare-Knuckle Era

"My Name's John L. Sullivan and I Can Lick Any Son-of-a-Bitch Alive"

"Sullivan is as fierce, relentless, tireless as a cataract. The fight is wholly to go in *his* way—not at all in the other man's. His opponent wants to spar; he leaps on him with a straight blow. He wants to breathe; he dashes him into the corner with a drive in the stomach. He does not waste ten seconds of the three minutes of each round." John Lawrence Sullivan's total mastery, his complete domination of the ring, captivated men's imaginations. He was more than just strong and skillful; he possessed "extraordinary nervous force," superhuman energy that overwhelmed other fighters. Having measured and evaluated every inch of Sullivan's body, described him in the most scientific prose, quantified his physique in an "anthropometrical" profile, and provided nude photographs (taken from the rear), Dr. Dudley Sargent of Harvard concluded that the champion was a model of "the brawn and sinew that conquers both opponents and environments and sustains the race."[1]

Sullivan was equally imposing outside the ring; everything about the man was larger-than-life. As champion of the world, he occupied center stage for a full decade, longer than any previous fighter. "Excepting General Grant," one newspaper reported, "no American has received such ovations as Sullivan." By the end of the nineteenth century he was certainly America's best-known sports celebrity, and perhaps the nation's most famous citizen.[2]

Sullivan was born in Roxbury, a suburb of Boston, on October 15, 1858. His father, Mike Sullivan, a short, wiry man, was a hod carrier from the county Kerry. Even after his son became champion, the fiery immigrant frequently reminded the lad that there were dozens of tougher men back in the old country. If feistiness came from his father, Sullivan inherited great size from his mother, Catherine, a five-foot ten-inch, one-hundred-eighty-pound woman from county Roscommon.[3] Young John was a product of Boston's Irish working-class culture. During his boyhood the family moved from one neighborhood to another, a common pattern for laboring families. Still, he completed grammar school then attended night classes. Sullivan claimed in his autobiography that his parents wanted him to become a priest, one of the few routes to social mobility open to Irish-Americans. His temperament, to put it gently, unsuited him for such work.[4]

Although life had improved for the Irish since the Great Migration, manual labor remained the lot of most. John watched his father work doggedly to keep the family barely above poverty. The first American-born generation had a few more opportunities than the immigrants, but the vast majority remained common laborers, working long hours in dangerous and tedious jobs for brutally low pay. Few fulfilled the rags-to-riches myth. As the life chances for Irish-Americans went, young Sullivan probably did better than most. He drifted through several trades before his teens were over. For about six months he worked as a plumber's apprentice, earning four dollars a week, but crawling into basements to thaw pipes frozen shut by the Boston winter made men short-tempered as their skin was alternately scalded and frost-bitten. John quarreled with a fellow worker one day, accusing his companion of not shouldering enough of the burden. He won their fight and lost his job. Next Sullivan apprenticed to a tinsmith, but his inability to get along with another journeyman sent him on his way again. He then entered his father's old occupation, masonry, where he spent two restless years. On balance, Sullivan's future looked hardly promising as he grew toward adulthood. Discrimination in Yankee Boston made skilled blue-collar and low-level white-collar work as high as most Irish could realistically aspire. Sullivan's fiery temperament jeopardized even these opportunities.[5]

Yet liabilities in the conventional work world were assets elsewhere; Sullivan's real talents needed only the proper social context. Like so many other young men of the working class, John drifted into the bachelor subculture during his leisure hours. Here drinking, prowess, and bravado were high virtues, and Sullivan excelled in them all. He loved the easy camaraderie of the saloons, as well as the admiration that his athletic talents brought. It was not a long step to earning some pocket money with his physical skills. As the market for commercialized entertainment expanded, he followed the lead of countless working-class men who supplemented their incomes by playing semiprofessional sports. His almost instinctive aggressiveness was backed by a powerful five-foot eleven-inch, near two-hundred-pound frame. Moreover, Sullivan's great strength was blended with unusual quickness and agility; he was a fine natural athlete. Late in the seventies, as his more mundane careers foundered, he joined various semiprofessional baseball teams, the Tremonts, the Etnas, Our Boys. The Eglestons paid him twenty-five dollars per game to play left field and first base. A substantial sum of money for a working-class youth at the time, the offer paled beside the $1,300 contract allegedly tendered by the Cincinnati Red Stockings in 1879.[6]

Sullivan never played in Cincinnati, for his athletic propensities already led him in another direction. "At the age of nineteen," he recalled, "I drifted into the occupation of a boxer." "Drifted" was precisely the right word. Despite the antebellum state law against prize fighting, Boston officials granted licenses for glove exhibitions. Sparring matches had taken on the intensity of regular ring fights, however, as men sought not just to demonstrate their skill but to knock each other out. Sullivan attended a variety show one night at the Dudley Street Opera House, and as part of the entertainment a young fighter named Scannel challenged anyone in the house to put on gloves and face him. Sullivan's aggressive temperament had previously embroiled him in several street fights, so he was far from a complete novice. Still, he had never taken a formal boxing lesson. He stripped off his coat, rolled up his sleeves, and walked to the front. A blow from Scannel to the back of Sullivan's head made the young man so angry that he knocked the professional over a piano sitting on stage.[7]

Sullivan now began fighting in Boston theaters and music halls. Johnny "Cockey" Woods, Dan Dwyer the "Champion of Massachu-setts," and Tommy Chandler all fell victim to the lad. Sullivan had trouble containing himself during these exhibitions, some of which were not supposed to include any hard hitting. In benefits given for ex-middleweight champion Mike Donovan and former English champion Joe Goss, friends had to restrain him from finishing each man inside the four-round limit. It took all of Donovan's skill to avoid Sullivan's rushes, and he left the stage convinced that the youth would soon be "boss of them all." These early fights kindled in young John a taste for fame and adulation that the workaday world could never satisfy. Few working-class men, their opportunities so limited by an oppressive social structure, could have resisted the glory, the money, and the peer approval that sports offered. Fewer still had the athletic skills to avoid the back-breaking labor of hod carrying, ditch digging, or carting and hauling. Earning a living in the ring was at best a dangerous business, but a disappointing past and an uncertain future made Sullivan willing to take risks.[8]

As he approached his twenty-first year, Sullivan decided to abandon more traditional occupations and support himself solely as a boxer. Known as the "Highland Boy," he won a handful of stage bouts in Boston and New York. Late in 1880 he left his hometown for Cincinnati to spar with John Donaldson, the "champion of the West." Donaldson's vaunted ring skills failed to intimidate the youth who punched the veteran around at will. Not satisfied, Donaldson challenged Sullivan to fight with hard gloves (under five ounces). Except for the gloves, this bout followed bare-knuckle rules, making it Sullivan's first prize fight. They battled in the back room of a beer hall for fifty-three dollars raised by the thirty sports in attendance. Donaldson lasted only ten rounds; after twenty-one minutes, he was unable to continue.[9]

The fight received considerable press attention, and the brash young Sullivan felt so confident of his powers that he now dared any fighter in America to meet him. His "defi," as such challenges were called, was widely reprinted:

Cincinnati, Dec. 9, 1880

To the Editor of the Enquirer:

I am prepared to make a match to fight any man breathing for any sum from one thousand dollars to ten thousand dollars at catch weights. This challenge is especially directed to Paddy Ryan and will remain open for a month if he should not see fit to accept it.

Respectfully Yours,
John L. Sullivan

Ryan was de facto champion, having defeated the aging English heavyweight Joe Goss six months earlier. Thus Sullivan early revealed his flair for self-promotion, challenging for the title though he was still but a novice.[10]

Ryan spurned the lad, advising him to "go and get a reputation." Sullivan did. He defeated several journeyman boxers in coming months and made his debut at Harry Hill's, mecca for all hungry young fighters. Here, during an exhibition given in his honor, Sullivan offered fifty dollars to any man who could stand in the ring with him for four full rounds under the marquis of Queensberry rules. This challenge created a sensation in sporting circles. Veteran Steve Taylor accepted the dare but lasted only two rounds. Legend has it that a few nights later, Richard Kyle Fox dined at Harry Hill's. Spotting Sullivan, he asked the proprietor to send the young man to his table. Sullivan—whose ego and ambitiousness equaled the editor's—allegedly barked that Fox could come to him if he had something to say. From that moment on the *Police Gazette* owner was determined to bring Sullivan down. Whether the story was true or not, the two commenced a long and profitable public antipathy. Indeed, one suspects that their well-publicized enmity quickly became less a personal affair than a business ploy.[11]

While Ryan remained inactive, Sullivan went on the road with his fifty-dollar challenge to knock out all comers. Managed by former boxer Billy Madden, who raised capital from Boston sporting men, Sullivan toured Buffalo, Pittsburgh, Cincinnati, Louisville, and Chicago. In Philadelphia he was paid $150 for a single week's work, roughly ten times an average laborer's wages. Whereas antebellum tours by such men as Ned Price had retained the pretext of teaching scientific boxing, Sullivan's appeal was more explicitly violent: men flocked to see him beat anyone who dared enter the ring.[12]

In addition to these stage bouts, he fought a prize battle against John Flood, "The Bullshead Terror," in May of 1881, a match that evoked all of the ring's old seaminess. They met on a moonlit barge towed a few miles up the Hudson, outside the jurisdiction of New York City police. Oldtimers Barney Aaron and Dooney Harris seconded Flood, while Joe Goss and Billy Madden stood behind Sullivan. The two fought with skintight gloves in front of the usual fancy crowd of working-class men, urban dandies, and professional gamblers. The "Boston Strong Boy," as he was now becoming known, easily took the winner's share of the thousand-dollar purse subscribed by the four hundred sports in attendance. The job lasted a quarter of an hour, and Sullivan knocked or threw Flood down in all eight rounds.

The lad's victories kept pressure on Ryan to make a match. Richard Kyle Fox offered to back the champion for up to ten thousand dollars and the *Police Gazette* bent all of its efforts to bringing the fight off. Sullivan suggested a glove battle for one thousand dollars a side. Fox's representatives retorted that gloves proved nothing and that the stakes were too paltry. Still, excitement mounted in anticipation of a championship bout. Finally Sullivan raised $2,500, agreed to a regular prize fight, and Ryan accepted. Stakes were deposited in Harry Hill's hands and articles signed.[13]

The men were to fight within a hundred miles of New Orleans, tacitly fixing on the Gulf Coast of Mississippi. Jem Mace, Joe Coburn, and

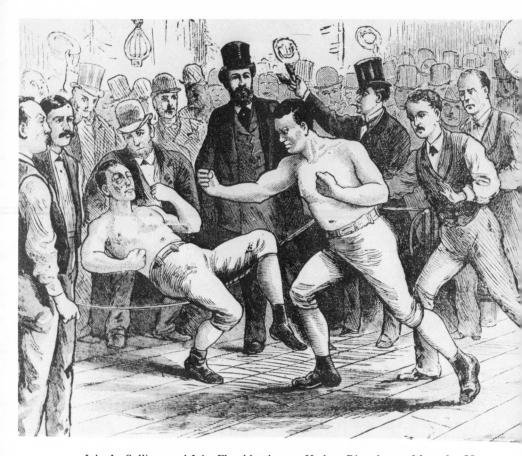

John L. Sullivan and John Flood battle on a Hudson River barge, May 16, 1881. Reports claimed that the combatants wore skintight gloves, but these are nowhere evident in this engraving. From William Edgar Harding, *John L. Sullivan: Champion Pugilist of the World* (1883).

Tom Allen had all based their championship matches in the Crescent City during the early 1870s, and the area's cosmopolitanism made it a natural choice for this battle. Sullivan began training in Bay St. Louis, Mississippi, in late December 1881, and Ryan quickly set up headquarters in Mississippi City. By mid-January, however, the state legislature mandated a thousand-dollar fine and five years' imprisonment for anyone engaging in a prize fight. Counterbalancing the Gulf Coast's traditions of moral freedom, the post-Reconstruction era, with its rapid modernization and capitalist development, brought new strictures to much of the South. Industrialization and renewed religious fervor in the region often made fugitive activities of wild pastimes, as the old ways and the new battled for legitimacy. Both fighters moved back to New Orleans.[14]

Week after week the *Police Gazette* filled its columns with news of the upcoming battle, and fear of being left behind caused metropolitan dailies to expand their coverage of the ring. A special correspondent for the *New York Sun,* José Martí—who would die in 1895 trying to help liberate his native Cuba from Spanish rule—described the scene in New Orleans: "Everywhere one heard the clink of glasses, boisterous talking, heated discussions in stores and on street corners of the respective merits of the fighters, and the rush of feet as droves of people hurried to satisfy their hungry eyes with a glimpse of the broad back, sloping shoulders and whipcord thighs of the athletes." By early February sporting men were pouring into the Crescent City from all over America. In response some prominent New Orleanians revived the old attack on the ring. The Reverend J. William Flynn, for example, condemned the boxing fraternity for corrupting local youth and leaving a "moral stain on their lives." With pressure building, officials resolved to keep the fight out of their parish. The principals decided to take a chance, and they secretly made plans to return to Mississippi.[15]

Arthur Chambers, a former English lightweight and coauthor of the Queensberry rules, now a Philadelphia saloonkeeper and backer of Sullivan, believed that more money was wagered on this contest than on any other in history. One estimate put the total betting at three hundred thousand dollars. Amidst the excitement, Governor Lowry of Mississippi issued a proclamation ordering the sheriffs of seacoast counties to summons their entire populations into posses—at gunpoint if necessary—to prevent the battle.[16]

Nevertheless, on February 5, 1882, ten-dollar excursion tickets went on sale at the Louisville & Nashville Railroad office in New Orleans. The following night Sullivan and Ryan boarded advance trains, accompanied by telegraph company employees who would connect the battleground to newspaper presses from coast to coast. A few hours later thousands of men packed railroad cars and headed for the battle site. José Martí described how they relived the ring's glory days en route to Mississippi:

> Now comes the drinking, the shouting, and the laying of bets. Now the agreement that a good fighter must be fearless, agile, and game. Now the reminiscing about the good old days in New York when electoral campaigns were bare-knuckle affairs in the alleys, the stories retold of how a certain McCoy killed Chris Lilly in the ring, and how the bonfires burned

along Park Row after Hyer defeated Sullivan "in a whirlwind fight," and how the huge sign hung for months on the famous old street where the post office now stands: "Tom Hyer, Champion of America." Between swigs of burning liquor, some recall how Morrissey left Heenan for dead; others remember the blow to the forehead with which McCool felled Jones, that left him vomiting as if his brain had been shaken from its moorings; others remember Mace as a great slugger, who threw punches like a windmill and broke Allen's neck with one good blow.

Dawn broke over the resort of Mississippi City with the multitudes streaming toward a ring pitched in front of the Barnes Hotel. The veranda provided the choicest views, priced accordingly. Mingling in the crowd were merchants, business and professional men, lawyers and judges as well as the usual gamblers and sports.[17]

Replicas of the fighters' colors sold well at ringside; *Police Gazette* employees charged ten dollars for reproductions of Ryan's. The champion chose a white handkerchief with red, white, and blue border, and in the corners an Irish harp, an American shield, the seal of New York, and the sunburst emblem of the Fenian Brotherhood. At the center an eagle straddled the globe, and in its mouth a scroll read "Police Gazette, New York, 1882." The challenger selected colors containing similar symbolism—a white silk handkerchief with green border, an American eagle in the center, and Irish and American flags crossed in each corner. Fighters' colors were coveted trophies, palpable relics of heroic deeds; just as faded duplicates of Sayers's and Heenan's emblems still hung on the walls of New York sporting houses, so Sullivan's and Ryan's soon would grace saloons across the country.[18]

The betting at fight time tilted slightly toward the challenger, but Ryan was heavily favored for first blood and first knockdown. Bets of $100, $500, even $1,000 were common, and one estimate put total ringside wagering at $60,000. Although Sullivan's youth and strength were evident enough, many of the cognoscenti still pointed to his inexperience. Knowledgeable sporting men noted that the Boston Boy had never before fought with bare knuckles, that Ryan was an inch taller and a few pounds heavier, and that the champion possessed excellent ring skills and the confidence to use them. If ovations were any measure, Ryan was the favorite. Even though he had recently sustained a rupture, for which he wore a truss under his fighting drawers, numerous members of the fancy considered the titleholder unbeatable.[19]

The challenger threw his hat in the ring first, then sat waiting for twenty minutes, wrapped in a blanket, until the champion arrived. Next the fighters' umpires haggled over the selection of a referee, finally compromising with two men. Ryan won the toss for choice of ground and made Sullivan face the sun. The champion then offered the Boston Boy a side bet of a thousand dollars, money given to Ryan by Richard Kyle Fox. Sullivan covered the wager. It was a little after noon when the men finally stripped, shook hands, and toed the scratch.[20]

"When Sullivan struck me," Ryan said after the fight, "I thought that a telegraph pole had been shoved against me endways." The battled lasted only nine rounds of about a half-minute each. From first to last Sullivan dominated his opponent. The pace exhausted both men, and neither escaped unscathed, but the challenger was always in control. Ryan's seconds counted on their man to outlast the lad, but when Sullivan knocked the champion senseless with blows to the temple and jaw in the ninth round, they threw up the sponge. "Among the sporting men and old ring goers that witnessed the mill," the *New Orleans Times-Democrat* concluded "it is generally conceded that the Boston Boy is a wonder. His hitting powers are terrific, and against his sledge-hammer fists the naked arms of a man are but poor defense. He forced the fighting from the start and knocked his opponent about as though he were a football." At age twenty-three, previously unable to keep a job, John Lawrence Sullivan was heavyweight champion.[21]

Given the ring's recent troubles, the *New York Times* marveled that the fight generated enormous interest in all parts of the country and "among all classes of men." The *Police Gazette* presses rolled for days with an eight-page illustrated special; Fox's man might have lost, but his paper profited handsomely. Indeed, all of the major dailies sent reporters, at once stimulating and fulfilling the demand for news. For the first time interviews with the fighters, obviously patched together by sports writers, began to appear. As much as any other single event, the Sullivan-Ryan fight fostered the development of modern sports coverage.[22]

In Boston men gathered outside newspaper offices and screamed their joy when word of Sullivan's victory came over the wires. Irish-Americans were especially delighted, for they still felt the sting of Yankee disdain, though not quite so harshly as in the antebellum era. Old Anglo-Saxon families continued to dominate Boston social life, so here was a source of group pride, of elemental virility, to counter the oppressor's haughtiness. Even the *Boston Pilot,* a newspaper of the middle class, "lace-curtain" Irish, embraced Sullivan as a hero. But it was not only the sons of the Emerald Isle who loved Sullivan; adulation for the new champion spread outward to new groups throughout the town. One wag saw irony in staid old Boston lionizing the burly Celt and suggested, tongue-in-cheek, that the Slugger could restore the city's past glory:

> Just fancy what mingled emotions
>   Would fill the Puritan heart
> To learn what renown was won for his town
>   By means of the manly art!
>
> Imagine a Winthrop or Adams
>   In front of a bulletin board,
> Each flinging his hat at the statement that
>   The first blood was by Sullivan scored.
>
> Thy bards, henceforth, O Boston!
>   Of this triumph of triumphs will sing,
> For a muscular stroke has added a spoke
>   To the Hub, which will strengthen the ring!
>
> Now Lowell will speak of the "ruby,"
>   And Aldrich of "closing a match,"
> And Longfellow rhyme of "coming to time,"
>   Of "bunches of fives" and "the scratch."

Doubtless many proper Bostonians were not amused.[23]

Sullivan's popularity was not confined to his native city, as the journey back North proved. At every railroad station, crowds surrounded the cars to catch a glimpse of the new champion. Appearing at leading saloons or sparring in local sporting houses, he was heralded in Chicago, Detroit, Cleveland, Pittsburgh, Philadelphia, and New York. The stakes in hand from Harry Hill, Sullivan returned to Boston for a thunderous reception at the Dudley Street Opera House, where just three years before he had sparred in his first exhibition. The adulation was just beginning. Over the next decade Sullivan became one of the best-known public figures in the world, and the most idolized athlete of the entire nineteenth century.[24]

The New Order

Just six weeks after he won the championship, the Boston Boy issued a new challenge:

The new champion, John Lawrence Sullivan. His reign lasted ten years, and he was easily the most popular sports hero of the nineteenth century. From William Edwards, *The Portrait Gallery of Pugilists of America* (1894).

There has been so much newspaper talk from parties who state that they are desirous of meeting me in the ring that I am disgusted. Nevertheless, I am willing to fight any man in this country, in four weeks from signing articles, for five thousand dollars a side; or, any man in the old country for the same amount at two months from signing articles, I to use gloves, and he, if he pleases, to fight with the bare knuckles. I will not fight again with the bare knuckles as I do not wish to put myself in a position amenable to the law. My money is always ready, so I want these fellows to put up or shut up.

John L. Sullivan

Boston, March 23, 1882

The tone was quintessentially Sullivan—brusque, blunt, and defiant. Here was the open pugnaciousness that endeared him to the public, especially the working class. The Boston Boy also renewed his challenge to any man who could stand four glove rounds of three minutes apiece against him, and raised the stakes to one thousand dollars. Except for drawing the color line—a phenomenon increasingly common in American social life as vicious new segregation practices emerged from the federal government's failure to enforce Reconstruction policies—Sullivan met all comers. He knocked out literally dozens of opponents in four-rounders governed by the Queensberry rules.[25]

In New York, Boston, and Rochester, Sullivan held a series of these "picnics," as he called them. In Brooklyn's Washington Park on July 4, 1882, veteran fighter Jimmy Elliott picked up the gauntlet. One hundred policemen kept order among the five thousand fans, all delighted by the prospect of a hard-fought battle. Outside the park nonpaying spectators watched from windows and rooftops. The crowd went wild as the champion forced the fighting, easily knocking Elliott out in less than three rounds with savage blows to the face and neck. As was his custom, Sullivan magnanimously tendered a small gift—in this case fifty dollars—to his fallen opponent.[26]

Just two weeks later the Boston Boy fought Joe Collins, alias Tug Wilson, in Madison Square Garden. Wilson claimed the championship of England, and Richard Kyle Fox financed his pilgrimage to America, hoping he now had the man to humble his nemesis. However, Sullivan insisted that before a title match, the Englishman must prove his mettle in a glove fight, and the champion offered one thousand dollars and half the gate receipts if Wilson survived four rounds. Five thousand fans, paying as much as five dollars each, packed Madison Square Garden, and five thousand more clamored for admission but were turned away. "Probably there had never been more excitement over a boxing contest before," one source reported; "the audience was composed of all classes, from the most intellectual to the lowest sport who could spring the price of admission."[27]

Betting was rampant before the match, much of it at two to one on Sullivan. Fans were in for a shock, however, because for the first time Sullivan failed to knock his man out. The Englishman was three inches shorter, thirty pounds lighter, and fifteen years older, and he went down nine times in the first round and eight in the second. But Wilson was never really hurt, and by the third round the odds shifted in his favor, as the out-of-shape Sullivan exhausted himself. Wilson sometimes danced out of the champion's reach, sometimes stayed too close for his devastating hooks, and often dropped without a blow. Yet he remained standing at the end of four rounds, thankfully accepted a draw, and took home seven thousand dollars for twelve minutes' work. No one doubted the Bostonian's superiority. Nevertheless, when Fox offered to back Wilson with five thousand dollars for a bare-knuckle bout Sullivan refused to sign articles, claiming he wanted a fight, not a footrace.

The champion received much criticism for holding Wilson too cheaply, not training hard, and refusing a rematch. But the twenty-four-year-old loved the good life. He discovered during the half-year after the Ryan bout a low-risk means to keep money and adulation flowing his way. The four-round Queensberry fights against all comers proved a goldmine, for the new rules greatly expanded a professional's opportunities. Gloves protected his hands, and the elimination of wrestling removed the danger of injury from a chance fall. So long as the rules were enforced and he fought men of only moderate skill, a good boxer like Sullivan could repel attacks and dispatch almost any opponent. Add to this the stage fright of a local hero or neighborhood bully going against the great Sullivan, and the result was a formula for easy victories. Americans gladly paid to see the king in action, and the new rules allowed him to oblige them.

Sullivan took his act on the road, starring in a traveling variety show put together by the sleight-of-hand artist Harry Sargent. In the midst of jugglers, wrestlers, and clowns, he came on stage, made his famous declaration that he could knock out any man, and challenged the house. If no one accepted (and by now there were few takers, despite growing purses), he sparred with another member of the troupe. Because a prize fight still meant a bare-knuckle bout on turf, these exhibitions were technically within the law, and as long as local officials looked the other way, the legal subterfuge held up. Occasionally, police intervened when a match grew particularly violent, or local opposition unusually vocal, but generally the crowds were orderly, even respectable. Under these circumstances, unprecedented numbers of Americans now had the opportunity to see ring heroes in action.[28]

Even more important than new rules circumventing old anti-prize-fight laws, the Victorian urge to stop every species of "immoral" amusement was weakening. As one spectator commented when Sullivan fought Charlie Mitchell in 1883, "men who doze in obligatory pews on Sunday to the soothing accompaniment of a clerical homily, struggled eagerly to see these Christians pound each other." Boxing's new trappings helped legitimate elite interest, so that now "men eminent in the higher walks of life lent the warrant of their presence to an exhibition of fistic skill which for once was stripped of the attributes which make such shows reprehensible." Thus Roscoe Conkling, Charles A. Dana, Lawrence Jerome, and William R. Travers, as well as members of the Knickerbocker Club and the Union League sat at ringside for one or more of Sullivan's exhibitions. Indeed, early in 1883 fifteen thousand Bostonians came to a benefit for the champion given by the prestigious Cribb Club. Harvard graduates, city councilmen, and members of the Somerset Society all attended the festivities.[29]

Sullivan made far more money from his "knocking-out tours" than from championship fights; in fact, bare-knuckle matches had become virtually a means to promote exhibitions rather than the other way around. The Boston Boy and his manager, Billy Madden, received five hundred dollars per night, usually six nights a week during one twenty-week road trip in 1882. A subsequent tour in 1883–84 yielded Sullivan around eighty-thousand dollars after expenses. In 1887 the champion formed a partnership with a circus impresario and earned sixty-two thousand dollars for sparring alongside acrobats, tumblers, and horseback riders. Late in the decade Sullivan toured England and Australia, grossing an estimated $168,000. Some of these figures are no doubt inflated, but the largest stake Sullivan ever won in a bare-knuckle fight was twenty thousand dollars, and he ended up spending most of it to stay out of prison. One can therefore understand his attachment to the Queensberry rules.[30]

Though extremely lucrative, the tours were grueling affairs. Managed by former boxers such as Billy Madden, Al Smith, and Pat Sheedy—all buccaneers by genteel Victorian standards, but all in the mainstream of Gilded Age hucksterism—the traveling shows required detailed planning to make sure the troupe made railroad connections, arrived on schedule, found accommodations, received plenty of advance billing, packed a local arena, and, above all, earned a profit.

The grand tour of 1883–84, organized by ex-prize fighter Al Smith, was the prototype. Sullivan traveled for eight months with several other professional boxers, including Herbert Slade, Jem Mace, and Steve Taylor, as well as Mike Donovan, Pete McCoy, and Mike Gillespie. Only about a dozen men accepted the champion's offer of one thousand dollars to stand in the ring with him for four rounds. They usually were knocked out in the first minute, but in most towns no one was foolhardy enough to try, so the professionals sparred with each other.[31] The tour started in Baltimore, where ten thousand fans attended a three-night stand. From there, the group went North, then into the Midwest, across the Plains States, through the Rockies, to the West Coast, north to British Columbia, then down to Los Angeles, across the Southwest and Texas into the Deep South, and finally back North, ending in Toledo, Ohio. Occasionally the troupe spent several days in one city, but more commonly they barnstormed a new town every night. Thus during the first full month of the tour, October 1883, they made twenty-four stops in six states and the District of Columbia, including such far-flung cities as Norfolk, Va., Scranton, Penn., Terre Haute, Ind., and Louisville, Ky. In small villages and big cities businessmen, politicians, and professional men got their first taste of the manly art, sitting beside local workers and sports. The national tour was on the road for 238 days and made 195 appearances in 26 states. The group cleared well over one hundred thousand dollars, as legions of men in obscure heartland towns paid their dollar each to see the champion in action, and countless more showed up at hotels and railroad stations just to catch a glimpse of him.[32]

Under Sullivan's reign, then, boxing borrowed promotional techniques and organizational structure from show business, especially vaudeville and the circus. Road managers, booking agents, and advertising men began replacing the old gambler-saloonkeeper promoters. In this sense the ring was leaving its folk roots behind and entering the modern realm of mass-produced, repeatable spectacles. And with its emphasis on maximum profit the new show business ethos put a premium on cleaning up pugilism in order to attract the widest possible audience.

The money-making possibilities did not end with boxing tours. Later in his career Sullivan joined several theatrical shows in which he acted, made speeches, or just plain posed with flexed muscles. He earned tens of thousands of dollars touring in the play *Honest Hearts and Willing Hands*, renewing the old connection between pugilism and the theater. All of this was part of the larger commercialization of sport, the growing trend toward rationalizing entertainment into repeatable spectacles. The profit motive opened new opportunities: a New York wax museum presented likenesses of Sullivan and Jake Kilrain, a circus advertised a boxing elephant named John L. Sullivan, and sheet music vendors hawked the popular song "Let Me Shake the Hand That Shook the Hand of Sullivan." In addition, Richard Kyle Fox offered the public numerous cheap biographies of prize ring heroes—many of whom were backed by *Police Gazette* money and wore *Police Gazette* belts—and these in turn were crammed with advertisements for training gear, pictures of the new stars, and more Fox publications, all available by mail from the *Gazette*'s offices. Sullivan himself endorsed everything from boxing gloves to beef broth. His very presence could attract a crowd. He earned more each year than presidents or business executives, and before his fighting career ended, he made nearly a million dollars. In a word, Sullivan had become a professional entertainer, a celebrity, a man whose livelihood depended on constant public adulation. Perhaps more than any American before him, Sullivan lived in the public spotlight.[33]

The commercialization of the ring opened unprecedented opportunities for other boxers, as growing numbers of working-class men fought bouts under the Queensberry rules. Contemporaries praised Sullivan for reha- bilitating boxing and giving pugilists an improved public standing. As the king of the ring, his courage and ferocity unquestioned, John L. made fighting with gloves acceptable to the sporting crowd. He prided himself on his scrupulous honesty and earned so much money from Queensberry four-rounders that he had no reason to engage in any of the ring's underhanded practices. Sullivan demonstrated by example how the new rules allowed fighters to circumvent the anti-prize-fight laws, engage in more frequent contests, and battle openly in public arenas. The lighter weight classifications particularly benefited because the new style rewarded footwork, defensive skills, and counterpunching. Great boxers such as heavyweights Joe Choynski (a Jew) and Peter Jackson (a black), middleweight Jack Dempsey the Nonpareil and Bob Fitzsimmons (before he became a heavyweight), welterweights Tommy Ryan and Joe Wolcott, lightweights Jack MacAuliffe and Joe Gans, and featherweights George Dixon and Terry McGovern, these and innumerable others all prospered under the new rules.[34]

Prize fighting failed to become as respectable as baseball or football, in part because it never developed a single, overarching regulatory agency to promulgate rules, award championships, and systematize challenges. Pugilism always retained some of its underworld flavor; a hint of corruption ever lingered. But by the 1880s boxing's tawdriness was an essential part of its appeal, especially as middle- and upper-class men flocked to the ring. A vestige of barbarism, the revitalized sport

"Modern consistency, thou art a (paste) jewel." Attacks on the ring continued, but they grew less frequent. This cartoon from *Harper's Weekly,* August 20, 1883, is testimony both to the criticism and to pugilism's new-found popularity under the Queensberry rules.

offered a vicarious thrill of violence. The Queensberry rules redrew the arbitrary yet essential border separating acceptable deviance from unpardonable vice; they sanitized prize fighting just enough to make it a legal spectator sport, yet not so much that gentlemen at ringside would lose the taste of "real life." The ring continued to call forth images of primitive brutality, of lower-class and ethnic peoples venting their violent passions. But gloves and new rules *appeared* to curb the animality sufficiently to allow a titillating sense of danger inside safe and civilized boundaries. With electrical lighting now available in grand new stadiums, going to a fight no longer seemed an illegal ritual of the underworld but a deliciously wicked after-work recreation.[35]

In his autobiography Sullivan himself argued for uplifting the ring. The old rules, he declared, permitted underhanded tricks, so the best men did not always win. Worse, spectators were subject to arrest, even muggings. Sullivan never claimed that the Queensberry rules made boxing less violent. They did, however, change the social composition of the crowd and the environment in which fights were held:

> Where such an audience assembles there will always be found a certain class of dishonest men practicing their nefarious work, whereas under the Marquis of Queensberry rules, the contest usually takes place in a hall of some description under police supervision, and the price of admission is put purposely high so as to exclude the rowdy element, and a gentleman can see the contest, feeling sure that he will not be robbed of any of his valuables or in any way be interfered with. Under the Marquis of Queensberry rules the manly art of self-defense, of which I am considered an authority, is conducted for the benefit of gentlemen, not rowdies. Fighting under the Marquis of Queensberry rules before gentlemen is a pleasure; to the other element it becomes a brawl.

Sullivan focused not on boxing itself but on the social background of the audience. Because the Queensberry rules were within the circle of the law, matches could be better governed. By eliminating the regulation that the ring be pitched on turf, the new code opened the way for electric lighting in indoor arenas, allowing promoters not only to profit through admission charges but to exercise crowd control as well. Evening bouts in urban stadiums obviated the need for the rowdy excursions that had encouraged men to abandon labor in the middle of the work week and underscored modern capitalism's sharp distinction between worktime and leisure time.[36]

Of course, the ring never became as pure as Sullivan claimed. The new rules helped rationalize boxing, took the sport away from the most disreputable gamblers, and allowed it to be run more like a business. But beneath the thin cloak of respectability, the old barbarism lingered. The very mixture of security and savagery, of safety and danger, made prize fights so exciting. Toward the end of the century men in evening dress and boutonnieres attended fights for the cathartic release of a little primitive violence. It was precisely this controlled atavism, experienced vicariously and at a distance, that gave boxing its new appeal.[37]

The dualism of impulsiveness and restraint accounts for much of Sullivan's own popularity. Under the new rules he transformed boxing from contests of endurance into dazzlingly quick and skillful performances, characterized by a new kinetic style in keeping with the up-tempo spirit of the age. But it was Sullivan the celebrity as much as Sullivan the fighter who electrified men. The Boston Boy's raw, spontaneous personality drew endless comment. He knew how to accumulate money, but he knew even better how to spend it. The champion's legendary conviviality, his embrace of the easy camaraderie of saloons and sporting houses, was at the heart of his public image. John L. loved the good life, including elegant clothes, expensive jewelry, the finest foods, the best cigars, and free-flowing champagne. Everyone knew of his drinking binges and his extramarital affairs. Everyone also knew of the gorgeous barroom he opened in Boston to treat and toast his friends. He embodied Gilded Age fascination with rich living and gaudy displays of wealth. In his reigning decade he strode into countless saloons, slapped a hundred-dollar bill on the counter, and treated the house. Like a padrone, Sullivan enjoyed the role of benefactor, meeting an endless stream of down-and-out men asking for a handout, widows without means, and religious missionaries in need of support. He always turned to his current manager—he changed them often—and barked a gruff demand for a five, or a ten, or a fifty to help the supplicant. The Boy's extravagance, his lack of bourgeois prudence, were an ingratiating part of his public persona in an era grown weary of stern self-control.[38]

Businessmen, politicians, entertainers, artists, and writers were fascinated by Sullivan, but he always retained special popularity with the working class. The champion spoke their language. He called one opponent "an awkward duck and the best foot racer in the country," another a cur, another a loafer, and each a son-of-a-bitch. Journalists marveled at his creative swearing, his clever epithets for opponents and prodigious boasts about himself. The Strong Boy claimed he could have beaten any previous champion, and any living man in class two, he alone being in class one.[39] Sullivan was a born democrat, a flag waver who mixed with all groups of people, but he always remained tied to his ethnic, working-class origins. He visited his old neighborhood often, helped out his brother and sister, and provided financial assistance to his parents. He also publicly supported striking coal miners on at least one occasion and maintained close friendships within the all-male saloon culture from which he came.[40]

The champion's bravado had special appeal for Irish-Americans, with whom he openly identified. His boast from a thousand stages, "My name's John L. Sullivan and I can lick any son-of-a-bitch alive," was a defiant cry for a downtrodden people who, in their first full postimmigrant generation, sought a fairer share of America's opportunities. Sullivan's giddy rise seemed to offer a model of success for self-assertive men. Under his reign, boxing and sparring became more prominent than ever in Irish-American communities. During the mid-eighties, for example,

Worcester, Massachusetts, witnessed grand fourth of July picnics sponsored by the Ancient Order of Hibernians. Three to four thousand people came to enjoy dancing, drinking, clambakes, and athletic events, but the center of attention was a series of sparring matches, often followed by impromptu fistfights. Thus working-class Irishmen celebrated the most sacred national holiday, not with uplifting oratory or solemn patriotic displays but with their own demonstrations of masculine prowess.[41]

Sullivan became an important symbol for other ethnic groups as well. The Jewish writer Abraham Cahan opened his 1896 novella *Yekl* with Jake, an immigrant desperately seeking to assimilate himself into American culture, demonstrating the fistic arts while boasting to his fellow sweatshop workers that he had a friend who personally knew the great Sullivan. Cahan here captured how sports celebrities such as John L. became standard-bearers of Americanization for countless new immigrants and their children. To play sports seemed an archetypically American act, because they were freighted with the values of success, meritocracy, and competition; to buy a ticket to an athletic event was to learn the new role of consumer; to root for a team or a champion gave one a sense of having freedom of choice; to acquire knowledge about baseball or football or boxing was to be informed about something distinctly American. One need not even understand English to sit among citizens, cheer the local heroes, and thereby feel at least partially integrated into an alien society. And when immigrants could applaud the deeds of one of their own countrymen, their sense of finding a place in America was doubly enhanced.[42]

But Sullivan's fame as a celebrity spread beyond working-class immigrant communities; he was much more in the public domain than previous fighters, much less an integral part of working-class street life than Hyer, Morrissey, or Heenan. Emblematic of an emerging mass culture that partially transcended the divisions of class and gender, of religion and ethnicity, Sullivan represented sensual fulfillment and consumption of leisure, both previously seen as working-class vices but now becoming national norms. The champion's monikers, "the Boston Strong Boy," "the Boston Boy," "the Strong Boy," or simply "the Boy," indicate that the public Sullivan was very much a child in a man's body. Above all, he seemed a creature of impulse. Editor Charles Dana of the *New York Sun* commented on Sullivan's enormous appetites; he dined like Gargantua, drank like Gambrinus, had the strength of Samson and the ferocity of Achilles. He moved with a child's ease but hit like a giant.[43]

Stories circulated about Sullivan protecting newsboys against bullies, aiding women in distress, and giving up liquor at his dying mother's request. More stories circulated that Sullivan kicked newsboys and chased waitresses, that he beat his wife and kept mistresses, and that he broke up saloons in drunken rages. One night in Philadelphia, for example, he allegedly became thoroughly inebriated at the Guard House Bar. He tore his room up, went outside to harass passersby for a while, returned at 5:00 A.M. for a breakfast of six dozen clams and whiskey, then had to be carried to bed. Belligerent when awakened at eleven o'clock, he calmed himself with another pint. Police avoided Sullivan during these drunken sprees, while newspapers editoralized that the immunity of the "hulking ruffian" encouraged his brutal lawlessness.[44]

Both images of Sullivan—the generous, good-natured boy and the brooding, destructive boy—contained much truth; both were united by themes of adolescent impulsiveness. He was a hero and a brute, a bon vivant and a drunk, a lover of life and a reckless barbarian. In the public mind, Sullivan the man and Sullivan the fighter were one. He cut through all restraints, acted rather than contemplated, and paid little regard to the morality or immorality of his behavior. He was totally self-indulgent, even in acts of generosity, totally a hedonist consuming the good things around him and beckoning others to do the same. For individuals deeply ambivalent about the transition from middle-class Protestant virtues of productivity to new values of consumption, he was a transcendent symbol. And for middle-class men terrified by the prospect of losing the vital "nerve force" that alone brought success, Sullivan seemed a glorious example of abundant human energy. He epitomized action in an age that feared inertia.

"...Nigh New Orleans upon an Emerald Plain..."

Between barnstorming tours Sullivan fought several major glove battles. Richard Kyle Fox kept importing boxers from abroad, backing them with thousands of dollars; Sullivan kept insisting that Queensberry fights precede London Prize Ring ones; the new heroes kept getting knocked out inside four rounds, obviating the need for bare-knuckle meetings. In the summer of 1883, for example, Fox bankrolled a gigantic New Zealander, Herbert Slade, "the Maori." Former champion Jem Mace, Slade's mentor and trainer, assured Fox of Sullivan's imminent demise. After months of *Police Gazette* hype, ten thousand excited fans packed the Garden to see the battle. John L. mutilated Slade for three anticlimactic rounds before knocking him out. The champion made as much money on such stage meetings as on bare-knuckle fights because the winner's share of gate receipts (in this case, 65 percent) often topped ten thousand dollars. He had no reason to risk his title.[45]

But circumstances eventually called Sullivan back to the old prize ring. On May 4, 1883, he fought an electric four-rounder with English champion Charlie Mitchell in New York. An overflow crowd paid sixteen thousand dollars to witness the bout, seats costing fans a dollar to five dollars each. Mitchell weighed forty pounds less than Sullivan, but rumors spread that dissipation had wrecked the old champion's constitution. Police stopped the fight before the Boston Boy finished Mitchell, but not before the acerbic Englishman had knocked him down, an embarrassing first. On May 30, 1884, Sullivan was scheduled to meet Mitchell in a rematch. Allegedly William K. Vanderbilt, Henry Ward Beecher, and assorted aldermen, judges, assemblymen, and police and fire commissioners all held tickets. According to Sullivan's account, Mitchell feigned illness just before the bout, and the battle was cancelled. The Strong Boy, of course, broke training and went on a drinking spree. Anticipating this, Mitchell had the match reinstated, but by then the champion was in no condition to fight. Sullivan staggered fully clothed onto the stage, mumbled that he was sick, and left the arena to a resounding chorus of boos. He blamed Mitchell for this humiliation and swore revenge.[46]

Mitchell was not Sullivan's only problem. Weary of the ring when he returned from a long road tour in mid-1884, he began to stagnate as a fighter. Over the next few years he fought only a handful of Queensberry battles, mostly against undistinguished pugilists. Certainly, Sullivan's success at dispatching opponents was making it difficult to find contenders. Equally important, because he really went for knockouts, politicians and judges in New York, Philadelphia, and even Boston sometimes ordered the police to break up Queensberry matches under the old anti-prize fight laws. Officials acted at the behest of such reformers as Henry Bergh who, despite threats against his life, crusaded to abolish the ring. Thus in 1885 citizens from civic and religious organizations such as the Philadelphia Law and Order Society persuaded a judge just hours before fight time to stop a sold-out match between Sullivan and Dominick McCaffrey. Disgusted, the champion broke up some furniture then left town muttering about going back to the wild West where there was not so much law and order. The two men finally met in Cincinnati later in the year, but when the battle ended without a clear victory for either side, suspicions that the champion was no longer the fighter of old seemed confirmed.[47]

Sullivan's difficulties kept piling up. His drinking was becoming serious, even life-threatening. His wife Annie, moreover, initiated divorce proceedings, and her charges of brutality and adultery against Sullivan became a public scandal. To make matters worse, the champion's avoidance of the regular prize ring caused many of his followers to desert him. Unreconstructed sporting men still believed that a real fight meant a bare-knuckle one. Richard Kyle Fox produced plenty of willing if mediocre contenders and Sullivan ducked them all, wanting only glove battles. To top off the Strong Boy's problems, early in 1887, five years after winning the championship, he broke his left arm during a cross-country tour.[48]

Nine months after this last calamity, his frustration mounting, Sullivan left his American problems behind and embarked on a tour of Great Britain. Crowds gave the champion a tumultuous welcome, presenting gifts, begging for speeches, following every move he made. In Cardiff a larger crowd greeted him than ex-prime minister Gladstone. In London a single-paragraph advertisement in the *Sportsman* drew thousands of admirers. The exclusive Pelican Club invited the champion to spar before peers and lords. Here Sullivan met the Prince of Wales and boxed for the future king of England. In Ireland he enjoyed an emotional homecoming, visited the sights he had heard so much about in Boston, and was cheered all the way as a hero of his people.[49]

But Sullivan's luck turned sour again. Partly for revenge, partly to accommodate the British people, and partly to truly earn the title "World's Champion," he signed articles to fight a bare-knuckle match with Charlie Mitchell. The champion trained down to a reasonable weight—one commentator noted that when Sullivan arrived in England, his ample waist would not have disgraced a city alderman—by scorning drink, rich foods, and cigars. "All his joys are gone," journalist William Edgar Harding observed. "When asked how he managed to stand it, he smiled not cheerfully, and said in his deepest tones: 'Somebody will have to pay me back for leading a Sunday school superintendent's life, and if I can't get at anyone else, Mitchell will have to foot the whole bill.' "[50]

Because of the vigilance of English authorities, the men crossed the Channel to France. They fought on a miserable March day, on the baron de Rothschild's estate, before a small crowd of sports and gentlemen. The Englishman was in fine trim, and he needed all of his quickness to stay away from the champion. Sullivan dominated the fight, but he never seriously hurt Mitchell. The challenger yanked the Bostonian's mustache and spiked him on the shins. "Fight like a gentlemen, you son of a bitch, if you can," the Slugger growled. But standing in the cold rain and grappling in the mud chilled Sullivan until he shook. Worst of all, in three hours of fighting spread over thirty-nine rounds he failed to catch the wily Englishman. Both sides finally agreed to a draw. Authorities arrested Sullivan and Mitchell on the way out of France, and the two men were forced to jump bail and flee to England. With the stakes drawn, the champion quietly sailed back to America.

His run of bad luck continued. He sparred at a few benefits and went on a short road-tour with a travelling circus, but within months his health broke down completely. Sullivan claimed to have typhoid fever, gastric fever, inflammation of the bowels, heart trouble, liver complaint, and incipient paralysis. Acute alcoholism was a more plausible diagnosis. He lay bedridden for weeks, finally rising on his thirtieth birthday against the advice of his doctors. It was time to cease being a victim, time to act. Within two months he posted five thousand dollars to fight a bare-knuckle championship battle, and a month later he signed articles. His claim to the title shaken by Mitchell, his health and age betraying him, his fans clamoring for vindication and his enemies out for blood, Sullivan staked his career on a single desperate battle.[51]

His opponent was Joseph Killion. The challenger told reporters that he learned to box because, as an awkward lad from the country, he had been victimized with cruel practical jokes by fellow workers at a Boston-area rolling mill. His efforts at self-defense paid off; he soon won several matches among his peers, making him "Champion of the Mill." A natural athlete, Killion also rowed in four-man crews during the 1880s, winning the junior sculling championship at the National Amateur Regatta in 1883. Unfortunately, when it became known that he was a professional pugilist, the National Rowing Association stripped him of both the title and his amateur status. The ring's revival created new opportunities for talented working-class men, however, and money-making opportunities were more compelling than the amateur ideal. The winter of 1883 found him teaching sparring at exclusive Cribb clubs in Boston and Baltimore. He took the ring name Jake Kilrain, fought Queensberry bouts in major East Coast and Midwest cities, and compiled a fine record. By 1887 Kilrain had grown weary of living in Sullivan's shadow, and Richard Kyle Fox agreed to back him, believing he now had the man to humble the Strong Boy.[52]

But Kilrain's rise coincided with Sullivan's run of trouble. Early in 1887 Fox designed a new heavyweight championship belt,—allegedly made from two hundred ounces of solid silver, with diamond and gold ornamentation. In return, the editor insisted that his offices arrange all title fights for the belt, that he be stakeholder, and that the *Gazette* have a representative at ringside. Meanwhile Kilrain published two cards challenging the champion for five thousand dollars a side and the belt. This was in May 1887, and because Sullivan's arm was still healing, he rejected the match. Citing six decades of American pugilism as precedent, Fox declared that a champion who refused a legitimate challenge relinquished his title. Thus on June 4, 1887, in a Baltimore theater, the editor of the *Police Gazette* awarded the belt to Kilrain and declared him champion.[53]

John L. contemptuously responded that he would fight once his arm was well and that when he won the "dog collar" from Kilrain, he would offer it as a boxing trophy to the bootblacks of New York. In retaliation against Fox, the champion's Boston friends had an even more elegant belt made, this one with three hundred ninety-seven diamonds and valued at eight thousand dollars. Mayor Hugh O'Brien, seven city councilmen, and four thousand Hub City residents packed the Boston Theater to present the belt and honor "Our John," as he was known locally. Sullivan then went to Europe, suffered the Mitchell fiasco, and returned only to have his health break down.[54]

Thus it was not until the champion's ability to defend his title grew doubtful that he took up Kilrain's challenge. The backers of the Strong Boy, whose physique had deteriorated badly, remanded him to the custody of William Muldoon, a champion wrestler, celebrity strongman, and health fetishist. He took Sullivan to his isolated country home in Belfast, New York, and put him under a strict regimen of diet and exercise, including rope jumping, dumbbell workouts, and farm labor. The champion shed years of dissipation and regained much of his lost vitality. Over and over, the press cited Sullivan's resurrection as an example of the fruits of industrious, moral, and purposeful living. "How inconsistent the pretended Christians are," trainer Muldoon complained. "They call us brutes and do not want us to give exhibitions lest we demoralize their cigarette-sucking, dwarfy puny offspring! We who would teach them an exercise beneficial to body and mind."[55]

Richard Kyle Fox bent every effort to stir up public interest. The *Police Gazette* condemned Sullivan as a drunken and swaggering braggart, while depicting Kilrain as a genteel family man, complete with high silk hat and polite manners. A letter to the *Boston Post*, written by a "Mother of Sons," praised Kilrain for his abstemiousness, modest demeanor, even temper, and good character. Perhaps, the writer speculated, Providence had sent him to knock out the bully Sullivan. But after their fight, she urged, Kilrain should quit the prize ring and go to work for an athletic club, "where he can train the rising generation in athletics and also in this fine art of keeping one's temper."[56]

Once again New Orleans was chosen as the most congenial staging ground for the battle. Despite new antiboxing statutes passed by the city council, a sympathetic mayor and dilatory law enforcement still made the Crescent City the best gathering place for the fancy. With Chief of Police David Hennessey's approval, gambler Bud Renaud arranged the excursion to the secret fight venue. The Southern Athletic Club offered its facilities for Kilrain's final training, while Sullivan fine-tuned at the Young Man's Gymnastic Club. Newspapers across the country gave unprecedented attention to the fight, covering the combatants' training, moods, and progress South. Reporters from every major daily made their way to New Orleans, the Associated Press sent representatives, and Western Union employed fifty special operators who telegraphed over two hundred thousand words of coverage. As the day of the fight approached, men poured into New Orleans in special trains, some chartered from New York by Richard Kyle Fox. Declared the *Picayune,* "The city is fighting mad. . . . Everybody had the fever and is talking Sullivan and Kilrain. Ladies discussed it in street cars, men talked and argued about it in places which had never heard pugilism mentioned before." On the night of July 7, 1889, after days of revelry, three trains left the Crescent City crammed with holders of ten- and fifteen-dollar excursion tickets.[57]

Governors of half-a-dozen Southern states vowed to prevent the battle, troops stood at the main railroad lines leading out of Louisiana, and the governor of Mississippi offered a one-thousand-dollar bounty for the arrest of Sullivan. But the train engineers stayed on little-used rural tracks to elude militia units. Before sunrise on a sweltering Delta morning, the cars from New Orleans unloaded their freight in Richburg, Mississippi. Five thousand citizens swarmed onto the land owned by Charles Rich, a sawmill proprietor, who had his men build a ring surrounded by rough-hewn bleachers. Pugs, gunslingers, and sporting men brushed up against influential society figures and members of exclusive athletic clubs. A timely bribe of two hundred fifty dollars kept a local magistrate from reading the riot act. By 10 A.M. both fighters were in the ring, and as the men stripped, the temperature soared past one hundred degrees. Mike Donovan, former middleweight champion, and Charlie Mitchell, the "bombastic sprinter" as Sullivan contemptuously called him, seconded Kilrain. Mitchell, always a volatile character, carried two guns, and he hired a private detective for protection, though precisely what he feared remains unclear. Mitchell even retained the services of famed gun fighter and gambler Bat Masterson to serve as timekeeper and bodyguard for the Kilrain party. Muldoon and Mike Cleary seconded Sullivan, and for referee both sides agreed on John Fitzpatrick, a New Orleans politician soon to be mayor.[58]

In black tights and white stockings Kilrain approached Sullivan's corner and wagered the thousand dollars given him by Richard Fox. The champion, in his usual green tights with the American flag round his middle, covered the side bet. The twenty-thousand-dollar purse, put up by Fox for Kilrain and by Boston gambler Charlie Johnston for John L., was the largest on record, topping the ten thousand dollars staked forty years earlier when Yankee Sullivan fought Tom Hyer. Partisans on both sides were confident, and so the odds stood even at fight time. The men were the same age and height, though Kilrain weighed one hundred eighty pounds, thirty fewer than the champion. Given his recent troubles, Sullivan appeared to be in excellent shape: "Neck firm, head set squarely on the shoulders, massive shoulder blades, great width of the chest, perfectly rounded, properly developed arms, and that grim savage determination that marked the man of strong animal courage and extraordinary physical endurance." Indeed, as he toed the scratch for the first round, the champion was like the strapping lad of old, moving as if he had springs under his shoes. "He was not the flabby Sullivan familiar to New Yorkers and Boston men of late. His feet bounded off the turf. His shoulders rolled with the old swaggering air of eight years ago. He looked the 'Boston Strong Boy' of early days as he sprang towards the center; his bent arms held low, his attitude careless, his head hanging a little forward as he glared at his adversary."[59]

Kilrain won the first fall by throwing Sullivan down and first blood with a sixth-round blow to the left ear. But the fight belonged to the Boston Boy. The challenger wrestled, backpedaled, and counterpunched to wear his opponent out. He succeeded only in angering the champion, who growled and cursed throughout the battle. Sullivan controlled the pace, stalking Kilrain, pressing, keeping him always off balance. "His old time ferocity seemed to come back," William Edgar Harding reported; "he rushed at Kilrain like a tiger at its prey. His eyes flashed, his lips were set and he seemed to become larger and more massive than he was." The battle lasted two hours and fifteen minutes. The July sun blistered Kilrain's pale back while Sullivan cut up his face and smashed his ribs. Kilrain survived seventy-five rounds by backing away and falling at light blows. Infuriated, Sullivan berated him: "Stand up and fight like a man"; "I'm no sprinter, I'm a fighter"; "You're a champion

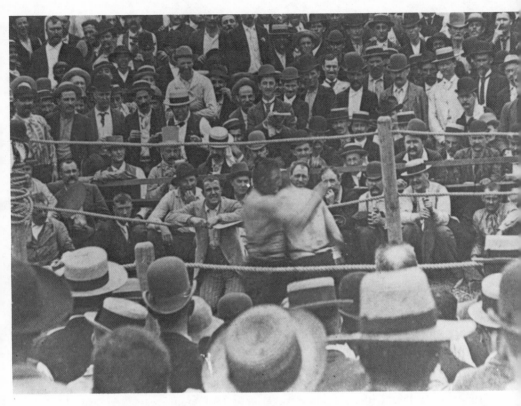

The last bare-knuckle championship fight, July 8, 1889. Sullivan and challenger Jake Kilrain fought seventy-five rounds in the mid-day sun of Richburg, Mississippi. Urban sports as well as lawyers, doctors, and even a college president looked on.

eh? A champion of what?'' Sullivan had words left over for Kilrain's second, Charlie Mitchell: ''I wish it was you I had in here, you sucker.''[60]

The only doubt about the outcome came in the forty-fourth round. A drink of cold tea spiked with whiskey made the champion vomit. Word quickly went round the ring that Sullivan's stomach was retaining the whiskey but rejecting the tea, a bit of humor that barely masked his partisans' alarm. Fighters often drank alcohol during especially difficult battles—Mike Donovan claimed a full quart of whiskey kept Kilrain going—so fans were surprised at Sullivan's sudden illness, and his friends feared that the tide now turned against him. But when Kilrain offered a draw, the champion barked ''No, you loafer,'' and punched him down again. By now Sullivan's left eye was closing, and his aging lungs blew hard, but repeated shots to the stomach, ribs, and neck left Kilrain in much worse shape. The final thirty rounds were more lopsided than the first forty-five. The fifty-fifth time they toed the scratch, Kilrain could barely defend himself. Ten rounds later it was five hundred dollars to fifty dollars on Sullivan and no takers. Before the seventy-sixth round could begin, Mike Donovan, fearing for his man's life, threw up the sponge. Still full of fight, Sullivan ran to Kilrain's corner and challenged Mitchell on the spot. Friends intervened to prevent serious bloodshed.[61]

Men at ringside seized everything as mementos of the great event, including Sullivan's hat, water bottle, and colors, bits of the ring posts and ropes, and souvenir to prove to themselves and others that they were eyewitnesses to history. The mania spread well beyound Richburg. "Never, during even a Presidential election, has there been so much excitement as there is here now, even when the brutal exhibition is over and it is known that Sullivan was successful and that seventy-five rounds were necessary to 'knock out' Kilrain." Thus the *New York Times* recorded its astonishment at the interest generated by the match. Many newspapers, including Joseph Pulitzer's *New York World,* gave all or most of their front page to the fight.[62]

The champion, never known for his humility, called the bout the best since Hyer's and Sullivan's 1849 match, and others were inclined to agree. Poets with serious pretensions memorialized the fight, among them Harry P. Keily, who dedicated his work to Sullivan's trainers:

> The referee now "Make ready" cries;
> Then all for battle quick prepare;
> Sullivan stands with brightening eyes;
> Kilrain transfixed with vacant stare.
> The seconds then disrobe their men,
> When lo two Hercules appear;
> Their like we ne're shall see again,
> Not if we lived a thousand years.
> Then all advance with friendly smile
> And grasp each other by the hand.
> 'Twas worth the journey—every mile—
> To see them so majestic, grand. . . ."[63]

But the jubilation over the great man's victory was best captured in countless songs and ditties. One bit of vaudeville doggerel caught on with special tenaciousness:

> His colors are the Stars and Stripes,
>   He also wears the green,
> And he's the grandest slugger that
>   The ring has ever seen,
> No fighter in the world can beat
>   Our true American,
> The champion of all champions
>   Is John L. Sullivan!

From high culture through folk culture, Americans lionized Sullivan. While Boston aesthetes followed the exploits of their city's champion, Texas blacks boasted that corn in the Lone Star State grew twenty feet high, "with stalks as big as the arm of John L. Sullivan when he whipped Kilrain." The American consul to Tahiti even claimed that on the Polynesian islands, natives knew of the Slugger's deeds.[64]

Although police chief Hennessey assured the boxers of legal immunity in New Orleans, the champion's party quickly left the Crescent City. In Tennessee, Nashville police broke in on Sullivan and Muldoon at a scheduled stop, arrested them, and took them off the train. Only a legal technicality and a sympathetic judge prevented their return to Richburg. Once in New York, Sullivan received his twenty-thousand-dollar stake money plus four thousand dollars in excursion profits. Awarded the *Police Gazette* championship belt, he had the "dog collar" appraised at one hundred seventy-five dollars and unceremoniously returned to Richard Kyle Fox.[65]

Mississippi governor Lowry still vowed to prosecute Sullivan. Having exploited the bout to sell newspapers, *Frank Leslies's* and other journals called for the fighters' extradition:

> All law-abiding citizens will sympathize with the efforts of Governor Lowry of Mississippi to vindicate the authority of the state as against the prize fighters who so recently defied it. . . . The spectacle of two bruised and battered ruffians dodging about the country, to escape the officers of the law, was in itself sufficiently demoralizing, without the addition, in print, of the story of their debaucheries and their low brutalities: and the two together, as illustrative of prevailing popular tendencies, certainly afford little ground for confidence as to the future dominance of the better forces in our life as a people.[66]

Spurred by a thousand-dollar bounty offered by the state of Mississippi, officials finally caught up with Sullivan, and Governor Hill of New York signed the requisition sending the champion back South. If proof were still needed of Sullivan's popularity, his return to Mississippi provided it. The journey resembled a royal progress more than the rendition of a criminal. His captors agreed not to bind him in irons or limit his movements, and in each city and at every train stop enormous crowds met and cheered their champion. An especially friendly gathering greeted the returning hero in Mississippi's capital city, Jackson, where Sullivan held a gala reception at his hotel.[67]

The state indicted him for the offenses of prize fighting and assault and battery. He was tried in Purvis, the seat of Marion County, and convicted of the first charge. His attorneys appealed on the grounds that the nature of the champion's crimes had not been adequately specified in the indictment, that the Sullivan-Kilrain battle was not a *public* fight because it did not disturb the peace and tranquility of an unwitting community, and that the law required two defendants who must be charged jointly. In a bit of very convoluted legal reasoning the court agreed, reversing the earlier decision and quashing the indictment. Perhaps the Great John L.'s mere presence influenced the judge to bend the law. The victory was a Pyrrhic one, however, because it cost Sullivan more in lawyers' retainers, court fees, and travel expenses than he cleared from beating Kilrain. He vowed never to fight again under the old prize ring rules. No one knew for sure at the time, but the world had witnessed the last bare-knuckle title fight.[68]

"The Champion of All Champions"

Sullivan wore his laurels lightly. Back on top as the greatest fighter alive, the "physical superior of all men," he had nothing more to prove.[69] He was too old, too successful, and too impulsive to maintain the intense discipline demanded by the ring; the good life beckoned again, and he followed. Once his legal difficulties were settled, the champion joined a theatrical troupe and toured in the melodrama *Honest Hearts and Willing Hands,* written expressly for him. Playing a blacksmith, he took off his shirt, pounded an anvil, beat a bully, and mutilated his lines. Critics hated it, the public loved it. More than ever, Sullivan was the consummate celebrity, one on whom the public spotlight shone so brightly that person and persona merged. Always a showman, he often had made little speeches to his fans after knocking out some hapless victim. The theater possessed all the old elements of display, pageantry, and fantasy which Sullivan the boxer loved. Besides, next to fighting itself John L.'s greatest talents lay in the show-business arts of self-advertisement and self-promotion. His troupe toured North America in the second half of 1890, then went overseas to Australia in 1891. In the three years following the Kilrain match the champion did not do any serious fighting, though he did spar against a young Californian named James J. Corbett.[70]

Time is always the athlete's sternest opponent. As his body begins to betray him, younger men come to the fore. Sports give poignant expression to the cycle of youth, maturity, and old age. The observant spectator watches a deeply moving drama containing lessons about his own mortality, but an athlete lives that drama. He travels a foreshortened life span, lasting a score of years if he is very lucky, less than a decade if he is not. In the end the skills that brought glory, fame, and wealth are dead, and in a symbolic sense so is he.

Sullivan's overseas tour was not a success. Australians were well acquainted with the ring, and they wanted to see first-class fighting, not second-rate acting. While the champion was away, hungry young boxers mocked his abilities, and when he returned to America, fans clamored to know if he dared renew his claim as the world's greatest fighter. Hurt by his supporters' loss of confidence and angered at the petty pretenders, he answered in his own distinctive way:

St. Paul, Minn., March 5, 1892 . . .
I hereby challenge any and all the bluffers who have been trying to make capital at my expense to fight me, either the last week in August or the first week in September, this year, at the Olympic Club, in the City of New Orleans, La., for a purse of $25,000 and an outside bet of $10,000, the winner of the fight to take the entire purse. . . .
I give preference in this challenge to Frank P. Slavin of Australia, as he and his backers have done the greatest amount of blowing. My second preference is that bombastic sprinter, Charles Mitchell, of England, whom I would rather whip than any man in the world. My third preference is James J. Corbett, of America, who has achieved his share of bombast. But in this challenge I include all fighters.
The Marquis of Queensberry rules must govern this contest, as I want fight, not foot-racing, as I intend keeping the championship of the world.
John L. Sullivan
Champion of the World.[71]

There it was. The next world heavyweight championship fight would be settled with gloves. Sullivan failed to mention the most formidable challenger of all, Peter Jackson, the great black Australian fighter. Partly because of the racist beliefs that he imbibed from the larger culture, and partly because of fear that his fans would desert him if he fought a black man, Sullivan continued to draw the color line, just as Americans were drawing it in countless new areas of social life during this era of Jim Crow.

Slavin, the Australian champion, had touring commitments he was unable or unwilling to break, and Mitchell hesitated at the size of the stakes. Young Corbett, however, who knew Sullivan's style firsthand, raised the money. Part of it came from the usual bookmakers and sporting men. But Mike Donovan also garnered a large portion of Corbett's cash through his contacts at the New York Athletic Club, where he obtained commitments from such wealthy socialites as Col. Frederick McLewee and Edward Kearney, Jr.[72] When putting up the stakes in New York, Corbett's manager, William Brady, allegedly remarked, "There are men, members of high-standing clubs right in this city, who will put up almost any amount on Corbett." Significantly, Brady was not an old-time boxer or ring man but a show-business entrepreneur, soon to become a motion-picture promoter, who saw prize fighting as an extension of the entertainment field. Indeed, he viewed the championship as a way to cash in on the real money afforded by the stage. Accordingly, Brady wrote a play, *Gentleman Jack,* expressly for Corbett to star in after he won the title.[73]

The Sullivan-Corbett fight differed from previous championship bouts in striking ways. Although the usual sporting men and pugs gathered for the signing of articles, they met not at the *Police Gazette* offices but in the *New York World* building. Respectable journals such as E. L. Godkin's *The Nation* bemoaned the decline of newspaper editors' moral stewardship. Godkin railed that the press pandered to the "offscourings of human society—gamblers, thieves, drunkards and bullies . . . persons whose manners and morals are a disgrace to our civilization." But Joseph Pulitzer and other new moguls of the print media understood the power of spectacles, and they wanted to capture Richard Kyle Fox's readership for their dailies. Indeed, to compete for the *Gazette*'s clientele they established separate sports sections, featuring stories on the likes of the great John L. In ten years, then, the *New York World* went from condemning the ring to calling itself "fistiana's authority." Mainstream papers had contained fight news for decades but Pulitzer's open commitment to arranging and covering bouts was a new departure for a family daily. Rearguard opposition notwithstanding, prize fighting now had powerful allies.[74]

Corbett's public persona also added a unique dimension to the ring. After attending college, he held a respectable job as a bank clerk; heavy

James J. Corbett, first title challenger under the Queensberry rules. Corbett's reputation was based on his abilities as a scientific boxer, not on barroom brawling. Betting odds initially gave him little chance against Sullivan.

labor for Corbett meant training, not putting bread on the table. He learned boxing in a sparring club rather than on the streets, and his reputation rested totally on glove fights under the Queensberry rules. No gang connections, lower-class drifting, or street fighting for Corbett. The newspapers called him "Handsome Jim," "Pompadour Jim," and eventually "Gentleman Jim." Clean-cut, intelligent, and highly skilled, Corbett in his public image denied the old equation of boxers with brutes.[75]

But the most striking thing of all about the Sullivan-Corbett fight was its business arrangements. Late in 1889 New Orleans' silk-stocking athletic clubs began sponsoring professional bouts, expanding old arenas and building new ones, all the while hiding behind the thin padding of five-ounce gloves. As one newspaper put it, "steady businessmen, society bloods, and in fact, all classes of citizens are eager and anxious to spend their wealth to see a glove contest." On March 14, 1890, the New Orleans city council authorized Queensberry fights, with the provisos that no liquor be served, that no bouts be staged on Sundays, and that promoters contribute fifty dollars to charity. The final legal obstacle fell when the Olympic Club defeated the old anti-prize ring statutes in court, establishing the right to hold glove fights to the finish for a purse.[76]

Thus on January 14, 1891, Jack Dempsey "the Nonpareil" and "Ruby" Robert Fitzsimmons fought with gloves for the middleweight championship and eleven thousand dollars. They battled in the Olympic Club's new thirty-five-hundred-seat arena on Royal Street, where police enforced a ban on gambling and drinking. Three hundred special ringside seats were reserved for the wealthiest fans. The *New Orleans Daily Picayune* called Fitzsimmons's victory a "scientific exhibition of the manly art of self-defense, free from the disorderly scenes which formerly surrounded the ring," while the *Times Democrat* compared boxing favorably with football, so popular just then on college campuses. Once the old gentlemen's clubs demonstrated the demand for "reformed" prize fighting, new ones devoted mainly to profit took out charters, built arenas, and staged bouts. Soon the New Orleans, West End, Columbia, and Metropolitan clubs were promoting fights not as genteel amateur affairs but as business ventures.[77]

All of this testifies to the transformation of boxing. Before the Queensberry championships many socially prominent New Orleanians, including members of the Young Men's Gymnastic Club and the Southern Athletic Club, had surreptitiously attended Sullivan's bare-knuckle fights in Mississippi. Lawyers, doctors, school board members, police commissioners, city officials, even one college president later acknowledged their presence in Richburg for the Kilrain match. As glove contests were now legal, these men *openly* planned to attend the upcoming bout.[78]

Sensing the large potential audience for the newly sanitized sport, clubs now competed with one another to sign up prominent contenders, offering handsome purses in the belief that gate receipts would exceed expenses. Boxing failed to become as rationalized and bureaucratically regulated as baseball or football; the corrupt underworld scent always lingered. Still, new promotional techniques shifted control away from gamblers to entrepreneurs. The de facto legalization of prize fighting in New Orleans and the transformation of the ring into something approaching a business gave unprecedented opportunities to promising young fighters, among them Robert Fitzsimmons, Arthur Upham, Billy Myer, Jimmy Carroll, Peter Mahar, Andy Bowen, Frank Slavin, and many others.[79]

New Orleans athletic clubs did more than simply attract new talent; they helped systematize boxing. Six weight classifications, which Richard Kyle Fox had informally recognized with championship belts, were standardized. Referees, now club employees, were empowered to stop bouts and award decisions if a fighter's life was endangered. Some clubs sponsored contests with a limited number of rounds and authorized the referee to declare a winner if the battle went the distance. All the old pugilistic categories—prize fights, sparring exhibitions, Queensberry contests—began to merge under the new order. Especially important, the challenge system, derived from dueling's code of honor, was eliminated. Club owners selected contenders, hired agents to negotiate their contracts, rented or built indoor arenas, and made all the local arrangements for matches. These changes ratified the fact that control of the ring had moved out of the old, honor-bound neighborhoods. Boxing was becoming commercial entertainment, more accessible than ever before to all classes.[80]

As the first heavyweight championship bout fought with gloves, promoted by an athletic club, and held in an urban arena, the Sullivan-Corbett fight put a seal of approval on these changes. Risking his title under the new order, Sullivan was the key player in this transition because he was by far the most prestigious figure in the boxing world. But although the champion had done so much to bring about the ring's transformation, he would always be remembered better as the last great bare-knuckler than the harbinger of the modern era. As the *New Orleans Picayune* put it, "it was the old generation against the new. It was the gladiator against the boxer."[81]

"Handsome Jim" Corbett had already bested Jake Kilrain, beaten the fine Jewish fighter Joe Choynski, and fought to a draw against the masterful Australian black, Peter Jackson. The challenger worked out in California with Mike Donovan and, by the time he left for New Orleans, felt sure that Sullivan would also fall. Meanwhile the champion packed the house for a few more performances of *Honest Hearts and Willing Hands,* trained lightly for the coming bout, and enjoyed a triumphal round of benefits all the way South.[82]

As both men arrived, the Crescent City was in an uproar. The Olympic Club not only built another new arena and put up the twenty-five-thousand dollar purse for the heavyweight bout on September 7, 1892, it arranged a lightweight title fight between Jack McAuliffe and Billy Myer on September 5 and a featherweight championship contest between Jack Skelly and George "Little Chocolate" Dixon for September 6. The *New York Herald* marveled that "the odium which rested upon the prize ring and the majority of its exponents a decade or two ago, because of the disgraceful occurrences connected with it, have in a measure been removed, until now the events on hand are of national and international importance." As the *Chicago Daily Tribune,* recalling the old sporting days, observed, "now men travel to great boxing contests in vestibule limited trains; they sleep at the best hotels . . . and when the time for the contest arrives, they find themselves in a grand, brilliantly lighted arena."[83]

The great pugilistic carnival sent a surge of excitement through the country. Grover Cleveland's and Benjamin Harrison's presidential campaign simmered on the back burner as boxing coverage boiled over onto front pages. MacAuliffe retained his lightweight title with a convincing knock-out in the fifteenth round. The following night, despite the controversy over a black fighting a white, Dixon thrashed Skelly in eight rounds. The fight may have demoralized Southern whites, and many resolved that a black man must never strike a white one again in the ring, but "Little Chocolate" retained his crown for seven more years.[84]

At last, on the night of September 7, ten thousand fans from all over the country swarmed the Olympic Club arena. The festive crowds in the French Quarter recalled Mardi Gras. Colorfully dressed sportsmen, solid planters, ragged black roustabouts, and Italian street vendors paraded the teeming thoroughfares. Merchants' windows were filled with pictures of the principals and replicas of their fighting colors. Until fight day betting had been light at three or four to one on Sullivan, as fans expected repeats of 1882 and 1889. Ominously, however, a surge of last-minute money for Corbett brought the odds close to even. "The most intense excitement prevailed throughout the city," declared the *Times Democrat*

The end of the bare-knuckle era, September 7, 1892. Before ten thousand fans in a New Orleans arena, Sullivan risked his title against Corbett under the marquis of Queensberry rules. From the *National Police Gazette*, September 24, 1892.

as New Orleans held its breath; "the streets were thronged with visitors of all classes, from the millionaire to the baker to the fakir. Politicians, lawyers, merchants and gamblers elbowed each other in all public places on comparatively equal terms."[85]

At ringside, former New Orleans mayor Guilotte announced the fighters' weights. Sullivan scaled in at two hundred twelve pounds, close to his size against Kilrain. But the Slugger's flabby body showed none of the tautness of three years earlier. Corbett, his hair as always in an impeccable pompadour, entered the ring in splendid condition, twenty-five pounds lighter and eight years younger than the champion. Urbane clubmen, respected professionals, and formally attired businessmen sat nervously at ringside until the usual introductions ended. But it was not only men—and a few elegant women—in the Crescent City who waited anxiously. In every metropolis excited fans gathered in theaters and newspaper offices to learn the results. On top of the Pulitzer Building in New York a red beacon was poised to signal when the fight went Sullivan's way, a white one for Corbett. Small towns were also caught up in the information network. Miners in Blocton, Alabama, for example, gathered at the local Odd Fellows lodge where, for fifty cents each, they heard the round-by-round telegraphic reports read aloud and shared for a moment in an instantaneous national culture. With hundreds of thousands on the edges of their seats, then, the bout began.[86]

The fight was no contest. Young Corbett circled, danced, jabbed, and countered, while Sullivan rushed his fleeting form and slugged the air. At first the crowd hissed the champion's running tactics but soon applauded his strategy. By the fifth round, having measured Sullivan's slow reactions, the Californian landed consistently. Fans grew ever more excited, sensing what was coming. Corbett probably could have ended the fight any time after the twelfth round, but he waited until the champion staggered with exhaustion. Then, in the twenty-first,

> he rushed in and planted blow after blow on Sullivan's face and neck. The champion, so soon to lose his coveted title, backed away, trying to save himself. He lowered his guard from sheer exhaustion, and catching a fearful smash on the jaw, reached to the ropes, and the blood poured down his face in torrents and made a crimson river across the broad chest. His eyes were glassy, and it was a mournful act when the young Californian shot his right across the jaw and Sullivan fell like an ox.

Youth, skill, and science, the newspapers said, over age, dissipation, and brute strength.[87]

The day after the fight William Lyon Phelps, professor of English at Yale, read the daily newspaper to his elderly father, a Baptist minister. "I had never heard him mention a prize fight and did not suppose he knew anything on the subject, or cared anything about it. So when I came to the headline CORBETT DEFEATS SULLIVAN, I read that aloud and turned the page. My father leaned forward and said earnestly, 'Read it by rounds.'" A few commentators welcomed Sullivan's defeat as the fitting end for a swaggering rowdy. Declared the *New York Times,* "the dethronement of a mean and cowardly bully as the idol of the barrooms is a public good that is a fit subject for public congratulations."[88]

But more sensitive observers saw larger significance in Sullivan's career. A young journalist named Theodore Dreiser remembered meeting the great man shortly after his last fight:

And then John L. Sullivan, raw, red-faced, big-fisted, broad shouldered, drunken, with gaudy waistcoat and tie, and rings and pins set with enormous diamonds and rubies—what an impression he made! Surrounded by local sports and politicians of the most rubicund and degraded character. . . . Cigar boxes, champagne buckets, decanters, beer bottles, overcoats, collars and shirts littered the floor, and lolling back in the midst of it all in ease and splendor his very great self, a sort of prize-fighting J. P. Morgan.

Here was Sullivan the hedonist, garish in every detail, flattered by hangers-on, luxuriating in the good life. With his own masculine prowess unquestioned, he gloried in leisure and excess.

> 'Aw, haw! haw! haw!' I can hear him even now when I asked him my favorite question about life, his plans, and the value of exercise(!), etc. 'He wants to know about exercise! You're all right, young fella, kinda slim, but you'll do. Sit down and have some champagne. Have a cigar. Give him some cigars, George. These young newspaper men are all right to me. I'm for 'em. Exercise? What I think? Haw! haw! Write any damned thing yuh please, young fella, and say that John L. Sullivan said so. That's good enough for me. If they don't believe it, bring it back here and I'll sign it for yuh. But I know it'll be all right, and I won't stop to read it neither. That suit yuh? Well all right. Now have some more champagne and don't say I didn't treat yuh right, 'cause I did. I'm ex-champion of the world, defeated by that little dude from California, but I'm still John L. Sullivan—ain't that right? Haw! haw! They can't take that away from me, can they? Haw! haw! Have some more champagne, boy.'
> I adored him. . . .

Crude, boisterous, gargantuan in his powers and his appetites, Sullivan was the perfect symbol for an expansive age.[89]

Within ten years of losing the title, having gained a hundred pounds and pawned his championship belt, he filed for bankruptcy. For a while his fortunes revived as he gave theater tours and temperance lectures and even collaborated on fight stories under his own by-line. Sullivan became a sort of elder statesman, brusque yet comical, always on hand for a championship bout. According to legend, his last years were painful ones, as heart disease, cirrhosis of the liver, and poverty debilitated his body and spirit. He died on February 2, 1918, and was buried in Roxbury.[90]

But it was Sullivan in his full powers that men remembered, the raw, bare-knuckled giant who challenged the world and beat all comers. At the turn of the century Ernest Thompson Seton, later the founder of the

Boy Scouts of America, had worried aloud that feminine influence coddled American youths and made them flabby. But Seton was reassured by the thought that he never met a boy who would not rather be John L. Sullivan than Leo Tolstoy.[91]

Looking back on his own boyhood, Vachel Lindsay also recognized the champion as the central symbol of his era:

> When I was nine years old, in 1889,
> I sent my love a lacy Valentine.
> Suffering boys were dressed like Fauntleroys,
> While Judge and Puck in giant humor vied.
> The Gibson Girl came shining like a bride
> To spoil the cult of Tennyson's Elaine.
> Louisa Alcott was my gentle guide . . .
> Then . . .
> I heard a battle trumpet sound.
> Nigh New Orleans
> Upon an emerald plain
> John L. Sullivan
> The strong boy
> Of Boston
> Fought seventy-five rounds with Jake Kilrain.[92]

Heroic strife broke through the sentimental clutter of lace and ruffles and curls. Sullivan rejected the routine world of work and family to live by his fists and his wits. If one may think of culture in terms of gender, then John L. Sullivan, the greatest American hero of the late nineteenth century, represented a remasculinization of America. To Lindsay, writing in the shadow of World War I, the Strong Boy of Boston embodied a lost era of genuine heroism, betrayed now by the complexity of modern life. To turn-of-the-century American men, Sullivan symbolized the growing desire to smash through the fluff of bourgeois gentility and the tangle of corporate ensnarements to the throbbing heart of life.[93]

Epilogue: The Manly Art

A third of a century after John L. Sullivan lost his title and ended the bare-knuckle era, Jack Dempsey, seventh holder of the heavyweight championship under the Queensberry rules, defended his crown against Gene Tunney. Billed as part of the nation's sesquicentennial celebration, the 1926 battle attracted 120,000 fans in Philadelphia, while millions listened to round-by-round radio coverage. At ringside sat movie stars including Charlie Chaplin, Tom Mix, and Norma Talmadge, sports heroes such as Babe Ruth, John McGraw, and Jacob Rupert, businessmen, among them Andrew Mellon, Charles Schwab, Vincent Astor, Harry Payne Whitney, and W. Averill Harriman, as well as governors, mayors, and cabinet secretaries. Elegant women—"classie dames" as fight promoter Tex Rickard called them—also watched the bout with their escorts. When Tunney won a surprise decision over Dempsey, the *New York Times* announced it with a three-tier banner headline across page one, followed by seven pages of front-section coverage.[1]

The path from the Boston Strong Boy's reign to Dempsey's and Tunney's was not a smooth one; prize fighting had its difficulties in the decades after Corbett became the first Queensberry titleholder. States legalized the sport then outlawed it as boxing leadership passed from city to city. When Jack Johnson—defiant, unbeatable, and black—became champion in 1908, Progressive Era racism caused another relapse of the ring. But the groundwork for pugilism's triumph in the 1920s and beyond was laid during the 1880s and 1890s. Gradually prize fighting found its place in the larger twentieth century landscape of big business, mass media, and corporate-capitalist ideologies.

Less than a century separated England's aristocratic boxing patrons from the rich and powerful of America who sat at ringside watching

Dempsey and Tunney. In the intervening years critics charged that the ring subverted republican virtue, threatened human progress, mocked evangelical piety, and destroyed the spirit of industry. But the Victorian cry that sports in general, and boxing in particular, fostered nothing but sloth and criminality grew increasingly hollow as the century wore on. Liberalized Christianity advocated less worldly asceticism, more active participation in secular life. Equally important, the advanced capitalist economy required adventurous consumers as much as cautious, self-controlled producers.

Boxing itself changed along with American society. One need only contrast Tom Hyer and Yankee Sullivan, barely escaping Baltimore authorities and then fighting at sunset on frozen turf before a few hundred friends, with James J. Corbett and John L. Sullivan, contending in an electrically illuminated arena in front of ten thousand fans from all social classes, to appreciate how far the ring had come. Boxing still had roots in the countless local clubs and gyms of ethnic neighborhoods. But now a sophisticated commercial structure channeled local talent into national entertainment markets. By the 1890s prize fighting was less tightly controlled at the local level, less dependent on the old saloon-centered bachelor subculture, less exclusively a part of working-class life. Boxing had become a business.

Athletic heroes added a new dimension to America's success ethic. On the simplest level, sports such as prize fighting embodied deep-rooted national mythology. Champion boxers fulfilled the American dream of personal achievement and unlimited individual opportunity. The ring was the sternest of meritocracies, for each man tested himself against all challengers, publicly risking injury and humiliation to make it to the top. Men from poor backgrounds, armed only with courage, muscle, and skill, became heroes because their hard-earned achievements reaffirmed the potential of American life. Few noticed that it was the lack of other opportunities which pulled men toward the ring. Far from deflating the myth of social mobility, the fact that most fighters possessed limited ability, suffered serious injuries, and left boxing as poor and obsure as when they began, only served to highlight the gaudy success of the few at the pinnacle. Winners in the most elemental competition, prize ring champions were new stars in the constellation of the self-made man.

But driving oneself toward fame and fortune is learned behavior. To be intensely, unrelievedly individualistic cut against the grain of the cultures from which so many prize fighters came. Boxing blended the cult of success with older loyalties and thereby kept men connected with their origins. Bruiser John L. Sullivan was an Irish *and* American champion, clever Benny Leonard was a Jewish *and* American champion, invincible Rocky Marciano was an Italian *and* American champion, brilliant Muhammad Ali was a black *and* American champion. The symbolism of the ring refracted the American ideal of individual achievement, of upward social mobility, through distinctive ethnic and working-class sensibilities; like other sports, boxing merged particularistic loyalties and modern values. This blending process has remained a constant function of boxing from the earliest bare-knuckle fights through today, as new groups of immigrants and their children have undergone the complex and halting process of acculturation.[2]

What changed by the late nineteenth century, however, was the fact that boxers were no longer heroes exclusively to working-class and ethnic peoples. Now America's growing white-collar population craved muscular demigods. Athletic idols were harbingers of transformation as the success ethic stretched to accommodate new social necessities. A society gearing toward mass consumption needed models of pleasure as well as labor. Leisure goods and grand spectacles offered vicarious escape from the corporations and bureaucracies engulfing social life; activities that once had been considered wasteful or immoral now became valued. Far from the paragons of productivity upheld by the old Victorian world, the new idols were celebrities, entertainers, people who produced nothing tangible but possessed personality and charisma. In a word, America's future heroes would be exemplars of play more than work.[3]

These cultural transitions were captured in the very words "the manly art." Like other skilled workers, bare-knuckle boxers practiced the "arts and mysteries" of their trade. Indeed, their ability to symbolize autonomous craftsmanship became ever more important as the old artisan system broke down. But on a more abstract level, prize fighting had some of the same social and cultural functions as the fine arts, especially the theater. Drama interprets daily life, helping us understand the world. Far from being purely escapist, the theater—indeed, all art—addresses the human condition, allowing us to transcend workaday consciousness and perceive reality anew. Art comments on mainstream culture, suggests alternatives to the way things are, reveals new human ideals and aspirations.[4]

The manly *art* functioned in precisely these ways. In the bare-knuckle days, when "prize fighter" and "pugilist" were terms of derision in polite society, every bout's celebration of violence, physicality, and "animal passions" defined by antithesis the competing cultural styles of the bourgeoisie and the working class. Boxing upheld aggressiveness, courage, and personal honor over safe and stable Victorian values; it offered a model of rough-cut masculinity in opposition to the domestic ideal; it glorified male beauty in an age deeply ambivalent about human corporeality. The ring was a place of freedom amidst the constraints of daily life. Its hard, unsentimental ethos grew out of the dangers and disappointments of working-class experience. But the ring could also embody ideals of restraint. Never as anarchic as its critics charged, prize fighting at its best exemplified rule-bound methods for settling personal differences. Boxers exhibited composure under pressure, unflinching fortitude, and heroic stoicism, all in the name of masculine prowess. The sporting fraternity measured bouts against their own aesthetic standards, which balanced in poetic tension cool self-control and hot-blooded passion. Potentially, then, each fight was a work of art, or more precisely a drama, staged according to tightly structured rules and illuminated by violence.[5]

Although the ring was transformed by the end of the nineteenth century, it still sometimes offered art sketched in blood. Prize fighting continued to resonate for street-corner men in male peer group societies; it upheld the old passion-filled displays of courage and honor. Occasional championship matches stirred men's imaginations with mythic meaning: the racial drama of Jack Johnson and Jim Jeffries, the taming of the brute by a skilled technician in the Dempsey-Tunney fights, the international battles of freedom versus fascism in the Joe Louis-Max Schmeling bouts.[6]

But what commercial sophistication gave in breadth of audience appeal, it sometimes took away in depth. Boxers were becoming celebrities, individuals who made careers out of offering repeatable spectacles to paying audiences rather than folk heroes of local communities. As the old Victorian ethos withered, prize fighting grew to be less the shared expression of an oppositional way of life than exciting entertainment sold in national leisure markets, similar to circuses, amusement parks, dime novels, and movies. The ring began losing its capacity to uphold alternative cultural standards. Increasingly, boxing matches provided vicarious thrills, temporary interludes from which men returned better adjusted to modern life. Sports in general and prize fighting in particular became absorbed into the hegemonic culture, and successful athletes were pointed to as proof that the social order still functioned smoothly, that ability and hard work were indeed rewarded. In a word, the ring's original antibourgeois message had been diluted, and pugilism lost some of its old expressive force.

If boxing's power as *art* grew problematic, so did the very meaning of the word *manly*. We rarely hear this term any more, yet it was quite common until the twentieth century. Manly had many nuances, but it is clear that bourgeois and working-class men often used the word differently. In *The Contrast*, Royall Tyler's 1787 play, Colonel Manly was frank, upright, brave, and independent. Similarly, Benjamin Franklin declared that a tract written by his grandfather exhibited "decent plainness and manly freedom." Almost a century later Horatio Alger wrote that Ragged Dick, one of his fictional characters, "would not steal, or cheat, or impose upon younger boys, but was frank and straight-forward, manly and self-reliant." These bourgeois examples all conjoined manliness with the values of self-possession and forthrightness, which in turn were linked to maturity. The concept implied adult autonomy, the opposite of childlike dependence. To be manly was to be responsible and socially useful, to have, in a word, what Victorians called "character."[7]

Although working-class men accepted the importance of independence, many rejected the stable bourgeois morality implied in such phrases as "manly self-reliance." In their usage, manliness had to do more with valor, strength, and prowess than with upright behavior. To be manly meant being not womanly—soft, sentimental, nurturant—more than being not childlike. Manliness on the urban streets was tied to honor, to one's status among peers; it inhered in an individual's reputation for toughness. Bravado, group loyalty, and defiance of outsiders were marks of leadership in this world. As exemplars of the manly art, pugilists resisted all slights. They avenged with blood insults to themselves and their cliques, and upheld a masculine ideal of elemental virility. For the fancy, then, bare-knuckled prize fighting was not merely entertainment but the expression of a way of life.

Toward the end of the century, however, this working-class ideal of masculinity took on a vicarious appeal for a middle and upper classes. Internalized self-control—a crucial component of bourgeois manliness—grew ever less satisfying in an age of diminishing autonomy. The business world, where men identified their interests with impersonal bureaucracies and attempted to ascend the corporate ladder, left them feeling cut off from the physical basis of life and isolated from each other. Not only clerks but even successful managers and professionals in massive new institutions felt adrift in a passional vacuum of dull routine. Here the old bourgeois ideal of manliness lost much of its appeal. But the very forces that rendered work unfulfilling also offered new forms of leisure as compensation, sports prime among them. The more that middle- and upper-class men sensed the artificiality and stuffiness of modern life, the more they were captivated by mass-produced images of virility. Where institutions now controlled so much of individuals' lives, sports heroes such as boxers seemed autonomous. More, they upheld the importance of human volition, of bold assertions of selfhood. Still tightly controlled in the working world, many bourgeois men turned to the pet sport of the urban underground as one vicarious escape from an oppressive environment.

The ring itself, ironically, was transformed in the process. Modern life compartmentalizes the ancient concept of honor, relegating it to those on the margins of society. Pool hustlers, pimps, juvenile delinquents, and gangsters, such outcasts help define normal behavior by violating social conventions. Acting out that which is considered deviant, they highlight what is acceptable. But they also fill a void, offering vicarious examples of fateful and honorable acts. Dangerous deeds, high-stakes risks, tests of strength and nerve, all are part of conventional society's fantasies, yet all are denied by daily life. The modern world is divided into safe and silent places on the one hand—home, shop, and office—and the underworld of criminals, sportsmen, and gamblers on the other.[8]

From the realm of danger, of risk taking, of elemental manliness, commercial fantasies are fashioned. The tedium and predictability of workaday life bring people to seek thrilling experiences and models of individuality in the rigidly segmented realm of play. Although fascinated by underworld ways, bourgeois culture does not become one of honor. Rather, its members consume *images* of honor. Examples of toughness, defiance, glamor, aggressive sexuality, and machismo are not merely tolerated; they are essential palliatives to the boredom and moral vacuity of modern life. Thus mass media sanitize then play back depictions of outlaw folk cultures. Criminals, six-gun heroes, urban detectives, rock stars, renegade cops, gamblers—all are glamorized, their images transformed into consumer commodities. All fulfill daydreams without altering life's realities.

On the urban streets the ring never completely lost its capacity to symbolize the violent ways of male honor. But although they still sprang from tough neighborhood subcultures, prize fighters, especially the most successful ones, were decreasingly representative of an oppositional way of life. Displays of manliness, courage, and prowess in the ring were now valuable commodities, marketable images, not threatening at all to middle-class ways. As of old, boxers' deeds spoke of elemental strife and bloodshed. But for many, perhaps most in the audience, the message was goods for sale, not hard-won knowledge of a brutal life. Successful fighters had been turned into celebrities, new models of success in a culture dedicated to fame, leisure, and consumption. And the *fancy*—the old sporting fraternity that had lived beyond the pale of respectable society—became *fans,* paying spectators in search of entertainment.[9]

Notes

Prologue. The English Prize Ring

1. Pierce Egan, *Boxiana, or Sketches of Ancient and Modern Pugilism* (London, 1812), pp. 408–20. Egan claimed that one quarter of the crowd was "of the *highest mould*," p. 409. For a fine discussion of the social diversity of the fancy, its special language and pastimes, see John Ford, *Prize Fighting: The Age of Regency Boximania* (South Brunswick, 1971), chap. 9.

2. Egan, *Boxiana*, pp. 360–71.

3. Ibid., p. 404

4. Pierce Egan, "Memoirs of Tom Molineaux," *The Fancy* I (1822): 492; Egan, *Boxiana*, pp. 360–71, 386–408; Ford, p. 39.

5. Egan, *Boxiana*, pp. 411–12.

6. Ibid., p. 412.

7. Ibid., p. 419.

8. George Borrow, *Lavengro* (London, 1921), p. 166; J. C. Reid, *Bucks and Bruisers: Pierce Egan and Regency England* (London, 1971), pp. 12–17. Writing of the reign of Richard Humphries as champion in the 1780s, Pierce Egan declared, "Royalty frequently witnessed the displays of the art, accompanied by Dukes, Earls, Honourables, etc. and men of the first distinction felt not ashamed of being seen in the *ring* or in acting as umpires at a boxing match." *Boxiana*, p. 104.

9. Pindar, *The Odes of Pindar*, trans. Sir John Sandys (Cambridge, Mass., 1978), pp. 79–80. Also see the tenth and eleventh odes in praise of boxers, pp. 111–25.

10. *The Iliad*, trans. Richmond Lattimore (Chicago, 1967), pp. 467–69; *The Odyssey*, trans. Robert Fitzgerald (New York, 1963), pp. 335–39. In the *Odyssey*, Odysseus, disguised as an impoverished old man, fought an insolent beggar while noblemen enjoyed the sport.

11. *The Aeneid of Virgil*, trans. Rolfe Humphries (New York, 1951), pp. 125–29.

12. Allen Guttmann emphasizes the sacred/secular dichotomy in *From Ritual to Record: The Nature of Modern Sports* (New York, 1978), pp. 16–26. On boxing in classical civilizations see, for examples, E. Norman Gardiner, *Athletics of the Ancient World* (London, 1930), chap. 15; Gardiner, *Greek Athletic Sports and*

Festivals (London, 1910), chap. 19; M. I. Finley and H. W. Pleket, *The Olympic Games: The First Thousand Years* (New York, 1976), pp. 37–42; H. A. Harris, *Greek Athletes and Athletics* (Bloomington, 1966), pp. 97–109; Nicolaos Yalouris, ed., *The Eternal Olympics; The Art and History of Sport* (New Rochelle, N.Y., 1979), pp. 216–25.

13. Teresa McLean, a historian of English medieval sports, makes no reference to boxing in *The English at Play in the Middle Ages* (Windsor Forest, 1983). T. B. Shepherd claims the January 1681 *Protestant Mercury* as the first newspaper to give an account of the ring: "Yesterday a match of boxing was performed before His Grace the Duke of Albermarle between the Duke's footman and a butcher. The latter won the prize, as he hath done many times before, being accounted, though a little man, the best at that exercise in England." *The Noble Art: An Anthology* (London, 1950), p. 88. A 1725 poem by Robert Byrum on the championship match between Fig and Sutton assumed that boxing fans knew the classics:

> To compare such poor dogs as Alcides and Theseus
> To Sutton and Fig would be very facetious.
> Were Hector himself with Apollo to back him,
> To encounter with Sutton—zooks how he would thwack him!

In a similar vein the caption on a mid-eighteenth-century print of Jack Broughton invited Pindar to revive and compare the English champion to his puny Greeks. Both are reprinted in Shepherd, pp. 91–95.

14. Dennis Brailsford, *Sport and Society, Elizabeth to Anne* (Toronto, 1969), pp. 198–216; Robert W. Malcolmson, *Popular Recreations in English Society, 1700–1850* (Cambridge, 1973), chap. 1; Ford, pp. 41–42, 88–93; and Eric Dunning and Kenneth Sheard, *Barbarians, Gentlemen and Players: A Sociological Study of the Development of Rugby Football* (New York, 1979), pp. 269–70. Also see the excellent essays in Neil McKendrick, John Brewer, and J. H. Plumb, eds., *The Birth of a Consumer Society: The Commercialization of Eighteenth Century England* (London, 1982). On the rise of sports in England see Richard D. Mandell, *Sport: A Cultural History* (New York, 1984), chap. 7.

15. Ford, chap. 6 and pp. 102–6, 119–20. Also see Reid, pp. 14–15; Egan, *Boxiana*, pp. 51–59; and Shepherd, pp. 88–90, 95–97.

16. Ford, esp. pp. 131–36; McKendrick, Brewer, and Plumb, esp. chaps. 1 and 6; John Ford, *Cricket: A Social History, 1700–1835* (Plymouth, 1972); and Malcolmson, pp. 42–43, 145–46.

17. William Hazlitt, "The Fight," in *The Complete Works of William Hazlitt* (London, 1933), 17: 79, 81.

18. Ibid., pp. 82–86. As was the custom, carrier pigeons released at ringside brought news of the fight's outcome back to London.

19. Pierce Egan, *Boxiana, or Sketches of Ancient and Modern Pugilism*, ed. John Ford (London, 1976), pp. 5–9, 132–34, 182–86; Ford, *Prize Fighting*, pp. 70–72, 78–79, 97, 166–87. Henry Hall Dixon wrote in *The Druid* that all of the magistrates in the county of Rutland attended the second Crib-Molineaux fight. Excerpted in Shepherd, p. 103.

20. Pierce Egan, from *Anecdotes* (1827), quoted in Shepherd, p. 95. On violence in English social life see Malcolmson, pp. 43–51; Lawrence Stone, *The Family, Sex and Marriage in England, 1500–1800* (New York, 1977), pp. 94–95; and Keith Thomas, *Man and the Natural World: Changing Attitudes in England, 1500–1800* (London, 1983), chap. 4.

21. Ford, *Prize Fighting*, pp. 10, 26, 31, 65–82; Egan, *Boxiana*, Introduction, pp. 2–3, 90–91, 108–12, 146–55, 219, 236, 263–64. Jack Slack's boxing skills inspired George Coleman and Bonnel Thornton to declare in 1754, "the sturdy English have been as much renowned for their boxing as for their beef; both which are by no means suited to the watery stomachs and weak sinews of the French. To this nutriment and this art is owing that long established maxim, that one Englishman can beat three Frenchmen. . . ." Excerpted in Shepherd, pp. 96–97.

22. Dunning and Sheard observe that in most traditional recreations, the gentry and aristocracy participated directly with the lower classes, though the barriers of inequality were clearly demarcated: "prior to the nineteenth century . . . the daily lives of the different classes were intertwined in a closer, more direct and personal manner than later became the case" (pp. 38–39).

23. This heterogeneity was captured in a miniature panorama drawn by George Cruikshank and accompanied by Pierce Egan's text. "A Picture of the Fancy" was fourteen feet long and two-and-one-half inches wide, came rolled up in a tiny box, and depicted all of the revelry and ritual that attended a great battle. For a description, see Reid, pp. 41–43.

24. George Borrow brilliantly evoked the complex interplay of individual and community pride: "Ah, there is nothing like the ring," an old barkeep muses. "I wish I was not rather too old to go into it. I often think I should like to have another rally—one more rally—and then—but there's a time for all things—youth will be served, every dog has his day, and mine has been a fine one. Let me be content. After beating Tom of Hopton there was not much more to be done in the way of reputation; I have long sat in my bar, the wonder and glory of this here neighbourhood. I'm content as far as reputation goes" (p. 491).

25. Reid, p. 22; Ford, *Prize Fighting*, pp. 26–28, 36–57; and Egan, *Boxiana*, pp. 464–67. Many of Egan's chapters have titles of the pattern "Joe Hood—The Weaver," "Bill Wood—The Coachman," and "George Ingleston—The Brewer."

26. A central theme in Malcomson, *Popular Recreations;* E. P. Thompson, *The Making of the English Working Class* (New York, 1966); Dunning and Sheard, *Barbarians, Gentlemen and Players.*

27. *The Fancy* 1 (1822): 504; Dunning and Sheard, pp. 269–72; Malcolmson, chap. 5; and Ford, *Prize Fighting*, pp. 9, 31, 166–87.

28. Cobbett, "In Defence of Boxing," *Political Register* (1805), reprinted in Shepherd, pp. 6–8; Thompson, *Making of the English Working Class*, pp. 225, 736; and Ford, *Prize Fighting*, p. 33. Of course the values of manliness, simplicity, and hardihood could readily be used to attack the decadence and luxury of the aristocracy.

29. Hugh Cunningham's *Leisure in the Industrial Revolution* (New York, 1980) provides a fine corrective to those who see a total eclipse of old sports in the Victorian era. Nonetheless, I believe Cunningham underestimates the damage done when social elites abandoned working-class recreations. For a fine discussion of

middle-class repression of leisure along with the "wholesome" alternatives proffered by Victorians, see Peter Bailey, *Leisure and Class in Victorian England: Rational Recreation and the Contest for Control, 1830–1885* (London, 1978).

30. Ford, *Prize Fighting*, pp. 136, 184, 188–89. By 1831 *Bell's Life in London* commented on the "prostrate state of pugilistic sports" and declared, "We think we may now fairly say we have recorded the last speech and dying words of the Fancy." The English ring was far from dead, and great matches in the future would excite widespread interest. But there was never again an era to match the one that ended with the first quarter of the nineteenth century. Quoted in *Spirit of the Times*, December 10, 1831.

31. Brian Harrison, "Religion and Recreation in Nineteenth Century England, " *Past and Present* 38 (December 1967): 98–125; Reid, pp. 70–72, 136–38; Bailey, chaps. 1 and 2; and Malcolmson, chaps. 6–8. For the simultaneous assault on bloodsports and cruelty to animals, see Thomas, chap. 4; Cunningham, chap. 1.

32. See Malcolmson, chaps. 6–8; J. H. Plumb, "The Acceptance of Modernity," in McKendrick, Brewer, and Plumb, pp. 316–34. Before the late eighteenth century English writers expressed little moral revulsion at the ancient gladiatorial games. But now, embracing a progressive view of history growing out of romantic, egalitarian, and revolutionary ideologies, many viewed all such spectacles, ancient as well as modern, with horror.

33. Cf. Elmer M. Million, "The Enforceability of Prize Fight Statutes," *Kentucky Law Review* 27 (November 1938): 164–67; anon., "Is Prize Fighting Legal?" *Law Times* 35 (April 28, 1860): 74.

34. Cunningham, chap. 1; Malcolmson, chaps. 5 and 6; Bailey, chap. 1; Ford, *Prize Fighting*, pp. 32–34; and Dunning and Sheard, pp. 41–43.

Chapter 1. Hats in the Ring

1. On Molineaux see Pierce Egan, *Boxiana, or Sketches of Ancient and Modern Pugilism* (London, 1812), pp. 360–71; Egan, "Memoirs of Tom Molineaux," *The Fancy* 1 (1822): 489–502; Frederick W. J. Henning, *Fights for the Championship: The Men and Their Times*, 2 vols. (London, 1903), 2: 30; and Paul Magriel, History of Boxing collection, mostly unsorted and unnumbered transcripts and photocopies of documents relating to the American prize ring in the nineteenth century, primarily selections from newspapers and periodicals; a private collection owned by Jim Jacobs of New York City. Some of these documents have been paginated, some contain bibliographical information, but many are of uncertain provenance. (Hereafter cited as Magriel ms.)

2. What is most interesting about U.S. press coverage of the Crib-Molineaux fights is that it differed hardly at all from reporting on championship battles not involving an American. On February 18, 1811, the *New York Evening Post* simply copied a round-by-round description from an English journal, adding no editorial comment. But six years later the *Evening Post*, on January 4, 1817, gave exactly the same treatment to a battle between Carter and Oliver, two English fighters. In other words, the American press sporadically reported the English ring and Molineaux's

fights with the same space-filling nonchalance. The *New York Morning Post* was typical; see, for example, October 8, November 12 and 28, December 6, 11, and 31, 1811.

3. A good comprehensive study of blacks in boxing remains to be written. For an informal and often inaccurate work, see Nathaniel Fleischer, *Black Dynamite,* 5 vols. (New York, 1938). Eugene Genovese argues that such fights occurred but offers no evidence. See Genovese, *Roll Jordan Roll: The World the Slaves Made* (New York, 1974), p. 569. On southern "boxing," more commonly called "rough and tumble," see Elliott J. Gorn, " 'Gouge and Bite, Pull Hair and Scratch': The Social Significance of Fighting in the Southern Backcountry," *American Historical Review* 90 (February 1985): 18–43. For Faulkner, see *Absalom! Absalom!* (New York, 1951).

4. David K. Wiggins, historian of antebellum black recreations, found no evidence of this pattern save for two WPA narratives. See his "Sport and Popular Pastimes in the Plantation Community: The Slave Experience" (diss., University of Maryland, 1979). The *American Turf Register* 2 (September 1830) reported a fight at New Jerusalem, Fairfax County, Virginia, between Lee Sims, a free black and a blacksmith by trade, and "the noted bully" Elias Grimsley. Sims won, declaring, "I'll let you know I'm a Jackson man, you d——d Adams son of a bitch." But most evidence indicates that in the early nineteenth century, southerners, white or black, rarely participated in the regular prize ring. For examples of legends and family memories of blacks fighting, see Richard M. Dorson, *American Negro Folktales* (Greenwich, Conn., 1967), pp. 132–35.

5. Jennie Holliman, *American Sports, 1785–1835* (Durham, N.C., 1931), p. 140; Magriel ms., pp. 54–56; Egan, *Boxiana,* pp. 360–71; and Egan, "Memoirs," pp. 489–502.

6. Egan, *Boxiana,* pp. 440–49. In occasional street fights Richmond avenged racial slurs uttered by his adopted countrymen.

7. Ibid., pp. 360–71; Egan, "Memoirs," pp. 489–502.

8. See Paul Magriel, *Bibliography of Boxing: A Chronological Checklist of Books in English Published before 1900* (New York, 1948); Magriel ms., pp. 62–63; and anon., *The American Fistiana* (New York, 1849). New editions of *American Fistiana* were also published in 1860 and 1873. Louise Jordan Walmsley, who studied the sports affiliations of prominent Americans, records no notice of Molineaux in her *Sport Attitudes and Practices of Representative Americans before 1870* (Farmville, Va., 1938). See also anon., *Famous Fights in the Prize Ring,* vols. 2 and 3 (n.d.), pp. 17–29.

9. *Boston Gazette,* March 5, 1733, reprinted in Frank Luther Mott, *American Journalism* (New York, 1962), p. 53. Mott claimed this was the first prize ring news published in America. Magriel found no earlier reports in his research. Carl Bridenbaugh, however, points out that in 1709 newly rich New York merchants and English colonial officials attempted to recreate the gay gentry life of the mother country, patronizing horse races, the theater, and even prize fights. Finding these activities offensive, townsfolk obtained orders from their council forbidding them. See Bridenbaugh, *Cities in the Wilderness: The First Century of Urban Life in America* (New York, 1938), p. 275. In the eighteenth century southern rough and tumble fighting was often called "boxing" and the practice had ties to the English

ring. But these "eye-gouging" matches scarcely resembled stand-up prize fighting. See Gorn, pp. 18–23.

10. *Royal American Magazine* I (June 1774); Holliman, pp. 139–40. Private Joseph Plumb Martin described a boxing match between two "drunken Irishmen" during the Revolution; only "lowbred foreigners" engaged in the practice, he concluded. *Private Yankee Doodle,* ed. George F. Scheer (New York, 1963), p. 129, quoted in Bonnie Sue Stadelman, "Amusements of the American Soldier during the Revolution" (diss., Tulane University, 1969), p. 92. Seventy-five years after the Revolution the *New York Clipper* (March 11, 1854) claimed that an English and an American soldier fought each other for £10 just before the Battle of Yorktown.

11. Magriel ms., p. 45; Douglass C. North, *The Economic Growth of the United States, 1790–1860* (New York, 1966), p. 23. As Jennie Holliman's *American Sports* reveals, sports tend to migrate not as disembodied ideas but as customs, carried by immigrants.

12. Robert Moreau de St. Méry, *Moreau de St. Méry's American Journey, 1793–1798,* trans. and ed. Kenneth and Anna Roberts (Garden City, N.Y. 1947), pp. 328–29.

13. Additional scraps of evidence support this conclusion. By 1805 the *New York Evening Post* assumed its readers were well enough acquainted with the terminology of the ring that it carried a tongue-in-cheek story, "Congressional Pugilism," describing a falling out between two members of the House of Representatives as a sixty-four-round struggle. With increasing frequency American newspapers reprinted detailed accounts of English fights in the 1810s and 1820s. Meanwhile, constables and aldermen did their best to prevent occasional surreptitious battles in New York City and Philadelphia. See *New York Evening Post,* December 13, 1805, in Magriel ms., pp. 50–51; *Port Folio,* February 1813, pp. 188–90; *American Register* 2 (1817): 273–76; *Philadelphia National Gazette,* July 8, 1823, Magriel ms; and John Thomas Scharf and Westcott Thompson, *History of Philadelphia, 1609–1884* (Philadelphia, 1884), p. 941.

14. *American Fistiana* (1849), p. 28, and (1860), p. 6; Magriel ms., pp. 72–74.

15. *New York Evening Post,* July 10, 1823, in Magriel ms., pp. 79–81.

16. Ibid.

17. Ibid.

18. Average income is from *Historical Statistics of the United States, Colonial Times to 1970,* 2 vols. (Washington, D.C., 1975), 1:163–64.

19. Indeed, even journalists were far from fully aware of boxing's spread. After a number of fights had already been staged in America, Charleston's *Southern Patriot and Commercial Advertiser,* October 29, 1824, still headlined its article on the Hammond-Kensett fight "First American Regular Milling Match." The story was taken from the *New York Emerald,* October 16, 1824.

20. Ibid. See also *New York Spectator,* October 17, 1824, in Magriel ms., pp. 83–84. *American Fistiana* (1860), p. 6, credited immigrants George Kensett and William Fuller with this American blossoming of English sporting life.

21. *American Fistiana* (1860), pp. 6–7; "Report of the Battle between George Kensett and Ned Hammond," in *The Life and Battles of Yankee Sullivan* (New York, 1854), pp. 88–89.

22. "Report of the Battle," pp. 88–90. This report was originally submitted to the *New York Evening Post,* but the editor rejected it, probably because of the usual hesitancy to cover the ring but also because the account contained a vehement attack on boxing critics.

23. Ibid.

24. *New York Spectator,* October 17, 1824, in Magriel ms., p. 83; Rowland Tappan Berthoff, *British Immigrants in Industrial America, 1790–1950* (Cambridge, Mass., 1953), pp. 5–6.

25. Berthoff, pp. 5–6; also see *Spirit of the Times,* February 20, 1836, a letter from "Our Liverpool Correspondent" dated January 1, 1836; Robert Malcolmson, *Popular Recreations in English Society, 1700–1850* (Cambridge, 1973), chaps. 6–8; Nat Fleischer and Sam Andre, *A Pictorial History of Boxing* (New York, 1975), p. 40; and *American Fistiana* (1860), pp. 8–9. For informal histories of Deaf Burke, see Nathaniel Fleischer, *The Heavyweight Championship* (New York, 1949), pp. 37–46, and Louis Golding, *The Bare-Knuckle Breed* (New York, 1954), pp. 168–74.

26. *American Fistiana* (1860), pp. 8–9; *New York Star,* cited in *Spirit of the Times,* July 2, 1836; and *Spirit of the Times,* February 27, 1836.

27. *New Orleans Daily Picayune,* May 10, 1837, in Magriel ms.; *American Fistiana* (1860), p. 9; *Spirit of the Times,* September 2, 1837, in Magriel ms.; and Earl F. Niehaus, *The Irish in New Orleans, 1800–1860* (Baton Rouge, 1965), pp. 59–60. Burke, incidentally, was of Irish ancestry, a fact that seems not to have mattered.

28. *Spirit of the Times,* August 22, September 2, 1837; *New York Morning Herald,* August 21, 1837.

29. In addition to the sources in note 28, the *New York Commercial Advertiser,* August 23, 1837, and the *New York Star,* August 22, 1837, also covered the fight. The *Advertiser* was less sanguine than the *Spirit of the Times,* condemning this "exhibition of brutality" put on by "two foreign vagabonds."

30. This was equally true of other forms of entertainment. During plays theaters were filled with talking, peanut chewing, banter between actors and audiences, not to mention an occasional riot. See David Grimsted, *Melodrama Unveiled: American Theater and Culture, 1800–1850* (Chicago, 1968); Peter George Buckley, "To the Opera House: Culture and Society in New York City, 1820–1860" (diss., State University of New York at Stony Brook, 1984), pt. 1.

31. Sources generally noted boxers' trades—see, for example, *American Fistiana* (1849).

32. Stephan Thernstrom's *Poverty and Progress: Social Mobility in a Nineteenth Century City* (New York, 1964) started a flood of studies documenting this mobility. For other examples, consult Frank Friedel, ed., *The Harvard Guide to American History,* 2 vols. (Cambridge, Mass., 1974), 1: 425, 437–38, and 2: 900. Walmsley, who surveyed the writings of several dozen prominent Americans before 1870 for *Sporting Attitudes and Practices,* found very little evidence of elite interest in pugilism and no involvement with prize fighting.

33. Two New Yorkers who had a falling out over money, for example, stripped, squared off, and settled their differences in front of a crowd on Broadway. *Spirit of the Times,* June 9, 1832.

34. On the theme of play as a formative influence on culture, see Johan Huizinga's *Homo Ludens: A Study of the Play Element in Culture* (Boston, 1950).

35. *American Fistiana* (1849), p. 29; *Spirit of the Times,* June 10, 1837; *American Fistiana* (1860), pp. 7–8; and *Spirit of the Times,* March 3, 1832. Often we know little more about particular fights than names and dates: Fearnon versus Spanish Lew in 1835, for example, or Jack Teal versus Jim "The Infant" Jeroloman in 1841. Because they arose over genuine social conflicts, bouts came in spurts, one challenge leading to another. *American Fistiana* (1849) recorded three fights in 1832, four each in 1835, 1838, and 1841, and virtually none in between. Newspapers reveal that many more fights took place.

36. McLane to Jack Langan, quoted in *American Fistiana* (1860), p. 8. McLane mentioned a few names of which *American Fistiana* was unaware, and the reverse was also true. Also see *American Fistiana* (1849), p. 29.

37. Anon., *The Complete Art of Boxing* (Philadelphia, 1829), was the very first book on pugilism published in America; see Magriel, *Bibliography of Boxing,* p. 14. The next work, appearing in the 1840s, was also a book of instruction, Owen Swift's *Boxing without a Master,* originally published in London in 1840.

38. *Columbian Sentinel,* February 10, 1798, in Magriel ms.; *Philadelphia Aurora,* August 15, 1815. Gabriel Furman, a New York attorney and amateur historian, observed that as of 1673, Boston authorities would not countenance a dancing school but permitted fencing lessons to be given. By the nineteenth century things were reversed, with dancing seen as a polite accomplishment and self-defense in the form of boxing condemned. See Furman's "The Customs, Amusements, Style of Living and Manners of the People of the United States from the First Settlement of the Country to the Present Time," typescript of an 1840s' manuscript, in the collections of the New-York Historical Society. Also see Mr. LeGuy's December 4, 1769, advertisement for fencing and dancing lessons in the *New York Gazette Mercury,* in Magriel ms., and Richard Lyneall's notice in the *New York Gazette Postboy,* January 3, 1757; Stewart Soren Brynn, "Some Sports in Pittsburgh during the National Period, 1775–1860," *Western Pennsylvania Historical Magazine* 51 (October 1968): 345–63, and 52 (January 1969): 57–59.

39. Holliman, p. 141; *National Intelligencer,* April 3, 1828.

40. *American Fistiana* (1849), pp. 29–30; Melvin Adelman, "The Development of Modern Athletics: Sport in New York City, 1820–1870" (diss., University of Illinois, 1980), p. 560; *Spirit of the Times,* April 20, 1832, and December 11, 1841; and *Boston Evening Transcript,* January 19, 1836, in Magriel ms. For other advertisements and descriptions, see Scharf and Thompson, p. 942; *Baltimore American,* November 23, 1825; *Spirit of the Times,* January 26, 1833, March 5, 1836, and July 2, 1836, May 26, 1832, and April 6 and 20, 1844.

41. *The Telescope,* June 25, 1825; *New York Evening Post,* December 14, 1826, in Magriel ms.

42. *American Fistiana* (1849), p. 29; *Baltimore American,* November 23, 1825, in Magriel ms., p. 86; *Columbian Sentinel,* November 1, 1826, in Magriel ms., p. 86; Holliman, pp. 146–47; and Scharf and Thompson, p. 942.

43. *National Intelligencer,* April 3, 1828, in Magriel ms., p. 92.

44. Egan, *Boxiana* 4, quoted in Magriel ms.; *Boxiana*, pp. 473–74; and Egan, "Memoirs," pp. 496–98.

45. Egan, *Boxiana* 4, quoted in Magriel ms.

46. For examples, see Fleischer and Andre, pp. 26–29; Magriel ms., pp. 66, 101–3. In his pioneering study of the sporting subculture John Dizikes also found a clear social distinction between patrons of sparring masters and supporters of the ring. See Dizikes, *Sportsmen and Gamesmen* (Boston, 1981), pp. 209–10.

47. Newspaper advertisement from an unspecified Charleston daily, December 15, 1824, Magriel ms., p. 105. On "Tom and Jerry" see Buckley, pp. 353–59.

48. Magriel ms., pp. 108–12; Holliman, pp. 141–46. For some examples of Fuller's advertisements, see the *New York Evening Post*, November 27, 1826; *Spirit of the Times*, October 13, 1832, and January 3, 1835; Adelman, p. 560. According to *American Fistiana* (1860), p. 7, Fuller beat Madden, and more significantly, the fight arrangements were made with "increasing regard for rules and precedents." Also see Holliman, p. 145; *Life and Battles of Sullivan*, p. 89. Fuller attended at least one other fight, at which he held the wagers of several individuals, but he refused to accept any official position as referee or umpire, fearing for his reputation.

49. *Charleston Mercury*, February 1, 1825. For other newspaper endorsements, see *New York Albion*, March 12, 1825, April 29, 1826; *New York Evening Post*, June 24, 1830; and *New York Enquirer*, November 22, 1826, all in Magriel ms. The equation of physical with moral health was just beginning at this early date; it would grow stronger as the century progressed.

50. Furman, pp. 302–3.

51. Letter to *New York Albion*, December 12, 1825, in Magriel ms., pp. 105–7. Also see Holliman, p. 146.

52. Holliman, pp. 141–44; *Spirit of the Times*, October 13, 1832, January 3, 1835; *New York Albion*, December 12, 1825; *New York Enquirer*, November 22, 1826; *New York Evening Post*, November 27, 1826, all in Magriel ms.

53. David Rothman treats social breakdown more as a metaphor than a reality in *Discovery of the Asylum* (Boston, 1971). Paul Johnson's study of Rochester makes a very convincing case for a real, not just a metaphorical, change in patterns of deference. See Johnson, *A Shopkeeper's Millennium: Society and Revivals in Rochester, New York, 1815–1837* (New York, 1978).

54. Robert Waln, *The Hermit in Philadelphia*, 2d ser. (Philadelphia, 1821), pp. 78–80, 187–93.

55. A point well made by Dizikes, chaps. 1, 2, 4, 5.

56. This is made clear in Owen Swift's popular sparring guide, *Boxing without a Master*. Advertisements on the front and back covers offered advice manuals on fashion, the art of conversation, bridal etiquette, tasteful dress, and decorous behavior, indicating that the publisher anticipated a socially conscious, upper-crust readership. According to Swift, it was the scientific basis of sparring which separated it from vulgar prize fighting. In life men must "live temperately, but not abstemiously," and sparring similarly moderated the excesses of the ring, substituting friendly rivalry for violent hatreds, physical excellence for simple brutality.

57. For two differing interpretations of the role of social class in early nineteenth-

century popular culture, particularly the theater, see Buckley, "To the Opera House," and Lawrence W. Levine, "William Shakespeare and the American People: A Study in Cultural Transformation" *American Historical Review* 89 (February 1984): 34–66.

58. *Spirit of the Times,* May 5, 1832; "Report of the Battle between George Kensett and Ned Hammond," in *Life and Battles of Sullivan,* p. 88.

59. R. Payne Knight, "Eulogy of Boxing and Cock Fighting," reprinted in *Literary Magazine and American Register,* October 1806, pp. 266–67.

60. Ibid.

61. Ibid.

62. "Nimrod on Boxing," in *Bell's Life in London,* reprinted in *New York Sporting Magazine,* November 1834, p. 188; *American Turf Register* 7 (June 1836): 457–61; and *Spirit of the Times,* August 22, 1837. Even the special vocabulary of the fancy seeped into everyday conversation: "Is a man bankrupt, he is 'floored' in town, but if a countryman, they become more agrarian, and now say he is 'grassed.' When a partner dies, he is 'done for'; and, if he runs away, 'bolted' expresses the rapidity of his motions." *American Turf Register* 7 (June 1836): 460. See also *Spirit of the Times,* January 8, 1842; Gorn, pp. 18–43. On the *American Turf Register* see Jack William Berryman, "John Stuart Skinner and Early American Sports Journalism, 1819–1835" (diss., University of Maryland, 1976).

63. Dizikes, pp. 210–12; Waln, pp. 78–80, 187–93.

64. Thomas Jefferson to J. Bannister, October 15, 1785, quoted in Henry Steele Commager, ed., *Living Ideas in America* (New York, 1951), pp. 557–58. *Nile's Illustrated Journal* condemned English society for encouraging men "to beat and abuse and possibly kill one another, as has frequently happened, in the presence of nobles and divines. . . . We are not yet fashionable enough for such things in the United States." Quoted in Dizikes, p. 211. Of course, republicanism (like Darwinism) was broad enough to justify many positions; as we have seen, republican values legitimated boxing for William Cobbett. On republicanism see J. G. A. Pocock, *The Machiavellian Moment: Florentine Political Thought and the Atlantic Republican Tradition* (Princeton, 1975); Bernard Bailyn, *The Ideological Origins of the American Revolution* (Cambridge, Mass., 1967); Gordon S. Wood, *The Creation of the American Republic* (Chapel Hill, 1969); Sean Wilentz, *Chants Democratic: New York City and the Rise of the American Working Class, 1788–1850* (New York, 1984); Robert E. Shalhope, "Toward a Republican Synthesis: The Emergence of an Understanding of Republicanism in American Historiography," *William and Mary Quarterly,* 3d ser., 29 (January 1972): 49–80; and John F. Kasson, *Civilizing the Machine: Technology and Republican Values in America, 1776–1900* (New York, 1976). For a critique, see John Patrick Diggins, *The Lost Soul of American Politics: Virtue, Self-interest, and the Foundations of Liberalism* (New York, 1984).

65. *Gazette of the United States,* January 23, 1790, p. 328, reprinted from the *Massachusetts Sentinel.* On these arguments see Dizikes, pp. 210–12.

66. "Of Boxing," *New York Magazine, or Literary Repository,* November 1794, pp. 656–58. For a spirited attack on "vulgar" mob behavior, on the rabble's alleged love of gossip, buffoonery, and violence, see The Wanderer, "Mobs—'Odi Profanum Vulgus,'" *Port Folio* 3 (April 11, 1807): 230, quoted from the *New York Emerald.*

67. "On Pugilism," *Literary Magazine and American Register,* June 1806, pp. 468–69. Also see Kasson, chaps. 1–3.

68. *New York Spectator,* July 15, 1823, in Magriel ms., p. 82.

69. *New York Evening Post,* July 10, 1823, in Magriel ms. The *Philadelphia National Gazette* copied an English paper's description of the 1823 battle between Tom Spring and William Neate to reveal the "debased" sporting tastes of the English public and the "barbarous" slang with which these scenes were described: "We doubt whether any other part of Christianity affords, in the ratio of the population, more scope for propagating Religion, than London;—and we are sure that none other could present a scene more adverse to the spirit of religion and civilization, then the Boxing Match, at which so many scores of the Fair Sex were assembled." Religion, tender sentiments, morality—all, the editor thundered, were overturned in the prize ring. Round-by-round coverage followed. *Philadelphia National Gazette,* July 8, 1823, in Magriel ms., p. 79. Editors occasionally expressed their astonishment at women being associated with the manly art in this era. A tongue-in-cheek report in the March 3, 1832, *Spirit of the Times* described two women challenging each other and squaring off in England in 1772. Nevertheless, such incidents seem to have been rare. In the Old World and the New, prostitutes were sometimes seen at ringside, but their sporadic appearance merely seems to have underscored male domination of the culture of the ring.

70. *Spirit of the Times,* May 12, 1832. In 1787 Thomas Jefferson declared in a letter to Edward Carrington, "Were it left to me to decide whether we should have a government without newspapers or newspapers without a government, I should not hesitate a moment to prefer the latter. . . ." Adrienne Koch and William Peden, eds., *The Life and Selected Writings of Thomas Jefferson* (New York, 1944), pp. 411–12.

71. *New York Evening Post,* December 14, 1826, in Magriel ms., pp. 90–91. Also see the *New York Evening Post,* July 10, 1823, versus December 11, 1826; or the *New York Spectator,* July 15, 1823, and October 17, 1824; all in Magriel ms., pp. 80, 82, 83, 87.

72. On the *New York Herald* see Don Carlos Seitz, *The James Gordon Bennetts, Father and Son* (New York, 1928); Richard O'Connor, *The Scandalous Mr. Bennett* (Garden City, N.Y., 1962); and Oliver Carlson, *The Man Who Made the News* (New York, 1942). Also see Alexander Saxton, "Problems of Class and Race in the Origins of the Mass Circulation Press," *American Quarterly* 36 (Summer 1984): 211–34; *New York Morning Herald,* August 21, 1837. On the penny press also see Michael Emery, *The Press in America: An Interpretive History of the Mass Media,* 4th ed. (Englewood Cliffs, N.J., 1978). On early sports journalism see John Rickard Betts, "Sporting Journalism in Nineteenth Century America, 1819–1900," *American Quarterly* 5 (Spring 1953): 39–56.

73. *Spirit of the Times,* May 19, 1832. The week before Porter reprinted without comment a note from the *Sporting Magazine:* ". . . far from looking on this beastly practice with any degree of toleration, we have always held it in deepest abhorrence. . . . The custom is looked upon, and justly so, as a stain upon the national character of England by her continental neighbors. Let us afford no reason to infer that we have inherited the vicious taste which encourages it." Also see Norris W. Yates, *William T. Porter and the Spirit of the Times* (Baton Rouge, 1957).

74. *Spirit of the Times,* February 20, 1836, August 22, 1837, September 2, 1837. While editor John Stuart Skinner modeled his journal on such English gentlemen's magazines as *Bell's Life in London,* he too hesitated when it came to blood sports, and he printed very little prize-fight news. For examples, see *American Turf Register and Sporting Magazine* 5 (February 1834): 310; 7 (June 1836): 457–61. On the American gentry see Dizikes, chaps. 4, 5.

75. *New Yorker,* October 6, 1838. Also see *Nile's Weekly Register,* August 14, 1830, September 21, 1833, August 27, 1836; *New York Mirror* 12 (March 7, 1835): 287, quoted in Frank Luther Mott, *A History of American Magazines* (New York, 1962), p. 482.

76. "The Boxer," from *Passages from the Diary of a Physician,* in *Spirit of the Times,* November 3, 1832, also reprinted in *Atkinson's Casket* 8 (February 1833): 66–67.

77. See sources in note 64 on republicanism.

78. The literature on Victorianism is extensive, but see especially Peter Gay, *The Bourgeois Experience: Victoria to Freud,* vol. 1: *The Education of the Senses* (New York, 1984); Kasson, chaps. 1 and 2; Daniel Walker Howe, *Victorian America* (Philadelphia, 1975); Daniel T. Rodgers, *The Work Ethic in Industrial America, 1850–1920* (Chicago, 1978), esp. chap. 1; and Karen Halttunen, *Confidence Men and Painted Women: A Study of Middle-Class Culture in America, 1830–1870* (New Haven, 1982).

79. *Spirit of the Times,* August 22, 1837, in Magriel ms. In *The Bourgeois Experience* Peter Gay brilliantly captures the Victorians' complex attitudes and unconscious conflicts about sexuality. Though his work is an excellent corrective to rigid stereotypes, the *public* culture of the nineteenth-century middle class still appears quite austere.

80. A brief story in the *New York Traveler* described a boy bringing dinner to his working father. Two well-dressed youths belittled his tattered garments: "The little fellow put down his kettle, and the spirit of the hero rising within him, he dropped his furless hat and went to his persecutors in a style of skill and bravery that would have done honor to a Fuller or a Blackburn with their best and brightest laurels won in pugilistic lore." Whistling "Yankee Doodle," the lad picked up the dinner pail and set off to bring his father both the meal and the story. *Spirit of the Times,* May 26, 1832, from *New York Traveler.* For a definitive but deterministic exploration of the modernizing process, see Richard D. Brown, *Modernization: The Transformation of American Life, 1600–1865* (New York, 1976).

81. *American Fistiana* (1849), p. 29. "Now gentlemen," he allegedly declared, "I've done my duty, and as you don't seem disposed to go, I'll stay and see it out."

82. John Rickard Betts, *America's Sporting Heritage, 1850–1950* (Reading, Mass., 1974), p. 38; *New Jersey Emporium and True American,* January 24, 1835, p. 2, cited from the *New York Courier and Enquirer.*

83. *Acts of the Fifty Ninth General Assembly of the State of New Jersey, Begun October 28, 1834* (Trenton, 1835), "A Further Supplement to the Act entitled 'An Act for the Punishment of Crimes,'" passed February 26, 1835, pp. 89–90; *New Jersey State Gazette* 6 (March 14, 1835): 3.

84. See references in note 64. In a civil action a New York court failed to uphold

a breach of contract suit brought against a steamship owner who agreed to transport spectators to and from a fight, then failed to provide the service. Charles Denny sold tickets labeled "Sparring Match" for one dollar each, paying William D. Norton $125 for use of the steamship *Bergen.* After the fight at Fort Washington Point spectators found the vessel gone, and Denny was forced to refund their ticket money. A jury refused to award damages to Denny because the original contract was for an illegal purpose and therefore void. *New York Commercial Advertiser,* January 13, 1836, in Magriel ms. For other laws, see State of Massachusetts, *Acts and Resolves Passed by the General Court of Massachusetts* (Boston, 1849), chap. 49, p. 31, "An Act to Prevent Prize Fighting"; State of Massachusetts, *Massachusetts Reports: Supreme Judicial Court of Massachusetts* 73 (Boston, 1883): 324-28; and State of New York, *Senate and Assembly Proceedings* (New York, 1858), pp. 35, 99, 149, 253, and (1859), pp. 120, 147, 504. On early statute and case law also see Elmer M. Million, "Enforceability of Prize Fight Statutes," *Kentucky Law Review* 27 (November 1938), pp. 152-55.

85. Dizikes, pp. 28-44, 71-73.

86. William Alcott, *The Young Man's Guide* (1836), p. 159, quoted in Peter Levine, "The Promise of Sport in Antebellum America," *Journal of American Culture* 2 (Winter 1980): 627; *Nile's Weekly Register,* May 31, 1823, quoted in Betts, *America's Sporting Heritage,* p. 11. On the work ethic see Rodgers, chaps. 1-3.

Chapter 2. The First American Champions

1. Anon., *The Life and Battles of Yankee Sullivan* (New York, 1854), pp. 9-11. Also see Ed James, *The Life and Battles of Yankee Sullivan* (New York, n.d.).

2. *Life and Battles of Sullivan,* pp. 18-15; *Spirit of the Times,* March 6, 1841, quoting from *Bell's Life in London;* Ed James, "Lives and Battles of the Irish Champions," contained in scrapbook of sports clippings, New York Public Library Annex; *New York Clipper,* July 5, 1856; and Thomas M. McDade, "Death in the Afternoon," *Westchester Historian* 46 (Winter 1970): 2. Alexander Johnston claims that larceny was Sullivan's crime in *Ten-and-Out* (New York, 1972), pp. 24-25. The deportation story is difficult to pin down. Whether or not Sullivan really was deported, the story was well known and contributed to his unsavory reputation. Years later it was also alleged that Sullivan quarreled with his wife one night and inebriated, he knocked a burning lamp onto the bed where she lay. Her clothes caught fire and she burned to death.

3. *Life and Battles of Sullivan,* p. 16.

4. Ibid., pp. 16-17; anon., *American Fistiana* (New York, 1860), pp. 10-11.

5. The *Sporting Chronicle,* quoted in *American Fistiana* (1849), pp. 8-11; Ed James, *The Life and Battles of Tom Hyer* (New York, 1879), p. 2. James claimed that McCleester and Hyer had clashed before over politics.

6. James, *Life and Battles of Hyer,* pp. 4-6, 30; *American Fistiana* (1860), pp. 12-13; *Life and Battles of Sullivan,* pp. 17-22. Secor published a challenge for a rematch and Sullivan declared his willingness to fight, but no battle ever resulted. See *Spirit of the Times,* March 5, 1842. The "dropping system"—falling without a

blow to end a round and avoid punishment—was illegal, but apparently Sullivan was quite good at feigning being hit or thrown.

7. *American Fistiana* (1860), p. 22.

8. *Life and Battles of Sullivan*, pp. 22–23; *American Fistiana* (1860), p. 13.

9. *Life and Battles of Sullivan*, pp. 23–24; *American Fistiana* (1860), p. 13; *Spirit of the Times*, September 3, 1842.

10. *Life and Battles of Sullivan*, p. 24; *Spirit of the Times*, September 3, 1842.

11. *American Fistiana* (1849), p. 2.

12. *New World* 5 (September 3, 1842): 158; *New York Express and New York Morning Express*, August 30, 1842, in Margriel ms. (clippings and excerpts of prize fight stories mostly from newspapers). Peter George Buckley's discussion of the development of the penny press is particularly helpful. See his "To the Opera House: Culture and Society in New York City, 1820–1860" (diss., State University of New York at Stoney Brook, 1984), pp. 359–63.

13. McDade, p. 1; Melvin Adelman, "The Development of Modern Athletics: Sport in New York City, 1820–1870" (diss., University of Illinois, 1980), p. 562; and *New York Herald*, extra ed., November 28, 1842, testimony of Jaspar J. Golden. Ethnic tensions ran particularly high in New York in 1842. A deep recession and Catholic demands for aid to parochial schools were two of the most salient causes of the rise of the anti-Catholic American Republican party. See Edward K. Spann, *The New Metropolis: New York City, 1840–1857* (New York, 1981), pp. 36–40; Robert Ernst, "Economic Nativism in New York City during the 1840's," *New York History* 32 (1948): 70–86; and Ira M. Leonard, "The Rise and Fall of the American Republican Party in New York City," *New-York Historical Society Quarterly* 50 (1966): 150–92.

14. *New York Herald*, extra ed., November 28, 1842, testimony of Harold Carpenter and George Lansing; *Spirit of the Times*, September 17, 1842; and McDade, p. 2.

15. *New York Herald*, extra ed., November 28, 1842, testimony of Jaspar J. Golden; McDade, p. 3; *New York Morning Express*, September 15, 1842, in Margriel ms.; *Spirit of the Times*, September 17, 1842.

16. *Spirit of the Times*, September 17, 1842.

17. *American Fistiana* (1849), pp. 15–16; McDade, pp. 2–3; *New York Herald*, extra ed., November 28, 1842, testimony of E. E. Camp; *Spirit of the Times*, September 17, 1842.

18. *Spirit of the Times*, September 17, 1842. Also see the *New York Commercial Advertiser*, September 15, 1842.

19. *Spirit of the Times*, September 17, 1842; McDade, p. 3–4; *New York Morning Express*, September 15, 1842.

20. *Proceedings of the Board of Aldermen of New York City* 23 (May 10–November 14, 1842) (New York, 1843), minutes of meetings on September 19, 1842, pp. 322–24. *New York Herald*, extra ed., November 28, 1842; *Westchester Herald* (no date given), quoted in McDade, p. 6. The *New York Evening Post* also covered the trial but not as well as the *Herald*.

21. *New York Herald*, extra ed., November 28, 1842.

22. McDade, p. 6.

23. *The Diary of George Templeton Strong*, ed. Allen Nevins and Milton Halsey

Thomas (New York, 1952), p. 185; *The Dairy of Philip Hone, 1828–1851*, 2 vols., ed. Allan Nevins (New York, 1927), 2: 620, 636–37; and Daniel T. Rodgers, *The Work Ethic in Industrial America, 1850–1920* (Chicago, 1978), p. 15. For a fine discussion of Hone's response to the social changes taking place in New York City during the 1830s and 1840s, see Allen Stanley Horlick, *Country Boys and Merchant Princes: The Social Control of Young Men in New York* (Lewisburg, 1975), pp. 34–39. For another attack on the *Herald* as the cause of McCoy's demise, see *New York Evangelist*, September 15, 1842, pp. 292–93.

24. *New York Herald*, extra ed., November 28, 1842; *Spirit of the Times*, September 17, 1842.

25. *New York Tribune*, September 17, 1842. The *Herald* claimed that McCoy's mother told him to return home victorious or not at all, a charge vehemently denied in the *New York Commercial Advertiser*, November 24, 1842, which accused Sullivan of being the main promoter of all recent prize fights.

26. *New York Tribune*, September 17, 1842. Also see *New York Sun*, September 14 and 15, 1842.

27. *New York Daily Tribune*, September 19, 1842.

28. The *New York Commercial Advertiser*, November 27, 1842, claimed that when McCoy was fouled early in the fight, his chief backer, Jack Harris—a "king gambler and harlot's paramour"—waved off the awarded victory. The newspaper alleged that McCoy was deliberately brought to the ring fatigued and improperly trained in a conspiracy by his backers "to win money on his premeditated defeat." A letter to the editor of the *Commercial Advertiser*, September 16, 1842 declared that the promoters were not men of character engaged in some lawful calling but predators, "living on their wits, keepers of gambling houses, and what is termed *fancy men* about town, who by their outrageous conduct, and vicious propensities, furnish the most baneful examples to the youths of our country."

29. *New York Daily Tribune*, September 19, 1842.

30. Benjamin Caunt, dated New York, December 20, 1841, to an unnamed correspondent, in Magriel ms.; *Spirit of the Times*, April 12, May 7, October 22, 1842.

31. *Spirit of the Times*, April 23, 1842. Also see ibid., October 22, 1842.

32. Ibid., January 21 and January 28, 1843.

33. Ibid., January 14, 1843; *American Fistiana* (1860), p. 15; McDade, p. 5. The *Herald*, for example, gave Freeman's and Perry's exploits about six inches of indifferent copy; January 27, 1843.

34. Freeman was not even mentioned in any edition of *American Fistiana*.

35. *American Fistiana* (1860), pp. 15–17; *Life and Battles of Sullivan*, p. 28. The *New York Herald* of February 9, 1849, also credited the Mexican War with attenuating interest in pugilism. Though many boxers enlisted to fight in Mexico, the conflict's late beginning and short duration hardly account for prize fighting's long hiatus.

36. *National Police Gazette*, October 8, 1845; *Spirit of the Times*, May 1 and April 3, 1847; and *American Fistiana* (1849), p. 30. *American Fistiana* (1849 and 1860), the *Police Gazette*, and *Spirit of the Times* during the 1840s contained much of the best coverage of the ring.

37. *American Fistiana* (1849 and 1860).

38. Advertisements in Alvin F. Harlow, *Old Bowery Days* (New York, 1931), pp. 300–301.

39. *Spirit of the Times*, December 12, 1846, January 2, 1847.

40. *American Fistiana* (1860, p. 16; *Life and Battles of Sullivan*, pp. 29–33, quoted from *New York Herald*, May 14, 1847; *Police Gazette*, May 8, April 3, and June 12, 1847; and John Rickard Betts, *America's Sporting Heritage, 1850–1950* (Reading, Mass., 1974), p. 56. The local country folk were at once fascinated and repelled by the invaders from New York. The commandant from the Harper's Ferry armory tried unsuccessfully to stop the fight, fearing his foundry workers would be lured away from their tasks.

41. *New York Herald*, February 6, 1849; *Police Gazette*, February 10, 1849, reprinted in *Spirit of the Times*, February 17, 1849; *American Fistiana* (1849), p. 27; *Life and Battles of Sullivan*, pp. 49–60; and *American Fistiana* (1860), p. 17.

42. Unspecified New York newspaper, quoted in *Life and Battles of Sullivan*, pp. 63–64; *Police Gazette*, February 19, 1849, quoted in *American Fistiana* (1849), p. 22.

43. Leonard Dinnerstein and David Reimers, *Ethnic Americans*, 2d ed. (New York, 1982), p. 156; Ray Allen Billington, *The Protestant Crusade, 1800–1860* (Chicago, 1938), p. 239; *Historical Statistics of the United States, Colonial Times to 1970*, 2 vols. (Washington, D.C., 1975), 1: 106; and Edward K. Spann, *The New Metropolis: New York City, 1840–1857* (New York, 1981), chaps. 2 and 4.

44. James, *Life of Hyer*, p. 1. One of the umpires at the fight, John J. Way, was also a butcher. On New York butchers, see Sean Wilentz, *Chants Democratic: New York City and the Rise of the American Working Class, 1788–1850* (New York, 1984), pp. 137–40.

45. *New York Herald*, February 7 and 9, 1849; *Life and Battles of Sullivan*, pp. 33–34; *American Fistiana* (1849), p. 2; and George W. Walling, *Recollections of a New York City Chief of Police* (n.p., 1890), pp. 40–41.

46. Reprinted in *American Fistiana* (1849), p. 3; *Life and Battles of Sullivan*, p. 34.

47. *American Fistiana* (1849), pp. 3–4.

48. Ibid.; *Life and Battles of Sullivan*, pp. 35–36.

49. *American Fistiana* (1849), pp. 3–4; *Life and Battles of Sullivan*, pp. 35–36.

50. *American Fistiana* (1860), p. 18; *American Fistiana* (1849), p. 15; *New York Herald*, February 9, 1849.

51. See references in note 50.

52. *Police Gazette*, story reprinted in *American Fistiana* (1849), pp. 10–11, 14–15. Also see *Spirit of the Times*, November 25, 1848.

53. *American Fistiana* (1849), pp. 10–15. *American Fistiana* (1860) reveals the ambiguity of the term prize fight. It lists hundreds of battles between 1850 and 1860, yet in many of these the primary motive appears to have been settling private scores.

54. *Police Gazette* story reprinted in *American Fistiana* (1849), pp. 11–14; *New York Herald*, February 9, 1849, quoted in *Life and Battles of Sullivan*, pp. 40–46. For other athletic regimens, see "Training for Running, Fighting or Health," *New York Sporting Magazine*, July 1833, pp. 219–22; *Spirit of the Times*, July 9, 1842.

Training philosophy owed much to British thought and practice as articulated by the Victorian boxing journalist Henry Miles. See Alan Lloyd, *The Great Prize Fight* (New York, 1977), chap. 11.

55. *American Fistiana* (1849), pp. 11–14; *Life and Battles of Sullivan*, pp. 40–46.

56. *Life and Battles of Sullivan*, pp. 40–46.

57. *Spirit of the Times*, February 3, 1849.

58. Among the fullest accounts are *Police Gazette*, February 10, 1849, reprinted in *Spirit of the Times*, February 17, 1849; *American Fistiana* (1849), pp. 22–28; and *Life and Battles of Sullivan*, pp. 50–60. Also see *New York Sun*, February 9 and 10, 1849.

59. Quoted in *Police Gazette*, February 10, 1949, reprinted in *Spirit of the Times*, February 17, 1849. Also see sources in note 58.

60. See sources in note 58.

61. *New York Herald*, February 8, 1849, reprinted in *Life and Battles of Sullivan*, pp. 60–61; James, *Life of Hyer*, p. 20; Betts, p. 33; and reports reproduced in *Life and Battles of Sullivan*, pp. 62–63. Also see *Spirit of the Times*, January 20 and February 3, 1849; *New York Herald*, February 6, 1849; *New York Sun*, February 7–11, 1849; *New York Tribune*, February 8 and 10, 1849; *New York Herald*, February 9, 1849; and *New York Commercial Advertiser*, February 8 and 10, 1949.

62. *Life and Battles of Sullivan*, pp. 60–61; James, *Life of Hyer*, p. 20; *American Fistiana* (1849), pp. 10–28.

63. *Spirit of the Times*, February 24, 1849.

64. From the "Colonel's Club" in the *Literary World*, reprinted in *Spirit of the Times*, March 10, 1849. The broadside ballad was a common form of news dissemination for three centuries in the Old World and the New. See Leslie Shephard, *The Broadside Ballad: A Study in Origins and Meaning* (London, 1962); and G. Malcolm Laws, *Native American Balladry* (Philadelphia, 1964).

65. See, for examples, accounts in *American Fistiana* (1849 and 1860); *New York Herald*, February 9, 1849; *New York Sunday Mercury*, February 25, 1849; and James, *Life of Hyer*, p. 20.

66. *Diary of Philip Hone*, p. 861; *New York Christian Advocate*, February 15, 1849.

67. *New York Evening Mirror*, February 7, 1849. *Bell's Life in London*, March 11, 1849, declared that recent immigrants transplanted the old spirit of the English ring in America; reprinted in *Spirit of the Times*, April 14, 1849.

68. Cf. *Spirit of the Times*, October 23, 1858, quoted in Adelman, p. 564; *New York Herald*, February 5, 7, 9, and 11, 1849.

69. See for example, William Riordan, *Plunkett of Tammany Hall* (New York, 1948), p. 86.

Chapter 3. The Age of Heroes

1. Letter signed "Reklaw," dated April 30, 1849, in *Spirit of the Times*, May 5, 1849. *Fistiana* was a yearly publication on the English ring written by Francis Dowling, editor of *Bell's Life in London*.

2. Anon., *American Fistiana* (New York, 1849 and 1860), reported six to seven times more fights in the decade after the Sullivan-Hyer battle than in the one before. Moreover, it is often difficult to tell from the descriptions when personal quarrels or even sparring matches ended and prize fights began. This absence of clear distinctions should caution us against imposing rigid categories. Prize fighting and street brawling were close kin, and the word "pugilism" was often applied indiscriminately to both.

3. See *American Fistiana* (1860), p. 34; *New York Daily Tribune*, October 22, 1858. On the saloon see Jon M. Kingsdale, "The 'Poor Man's Club': Social Functions of the Urban Working-Class Saloon" *American Quarterly* 25 (October 1973), pp. 472–89.

4. *American Fistiana* (1860), pp. 34, 77. On the working-class saloon see, for examples, Norman H. Clark, *Deliver Us from Evil: An Interpretation of American Prohibition* (New York, 1976), chap. 4; Jill Siegel Dodd, "The Working Classes and the Temperance Movement in Antebellum Boston," *Labor History* 19 (Fall 1978): 510–31.

5. John Rickard Betts, *America's Sporting Heritage, 1850–1950* (Reading, Mass., 1974), pp. 33, 57; Betts, "Sporting Journalism in Nineteenth Century America, 1819–1900," *American Quarterly* 5 (Spring 1953): 39–56. Betts' studies remain the standard works on nineteenth-century sports journalism.

6. The most thorough bibliography of pre-twentieth-century boxing is Paul Magriel, ed., *Bibliography of Boxing: A Chronological Checklist of Books in English Published before 1900* (New York, 1948). Also see Armand J. Lottinville, "A Bibliography of Boxing," *Research Quarterly* 9 (March 1938): 139–51; and Robert Henderson, ed., *Early American Sports*, 3d ed. (Rutherford, N.J., 1977).

7. Michael T. Isenberg, "John L. Sullivan and His America," manuscript draft (Annapolis, 1985), chap. 4, p. 16; *New York Clipper,* August 20 and September 10, 1853, January 21, February 25, March 18 and 25, April 22 and 29, 1854.

8. Duke of Wellington to Sir John Burgoyne, on the "National Defences of Great Britain," London, 1845, from *New York Clipper,* in Magriel ms.

9. Neil Harris, *Humbug: The Art of P. T. Barnum* (Boston, 1973); Robert Toll, *On with the Show: The First Century of Show Business in America* (New York, 1976), p. 26. Queen expressed such sentiments frequently. See, for examples, *New York Clipper,* July 23, August 13 and 20, 1853, October 24 and December 12, 1857, and January 22, 1859. For typical advertisements, see *New York Clipper,* September 16, 1854.

10. "Amusements," *New Englander* 9 (1851): 358, quoted in R. Hogan, "Sin and Sports," in Ralph Slovenko and James A. Knight, eds., *Motivation in Play, Games and Sport* (Springfield, Ill., 1967), pp. 124–25.

11. Junius Henry Browne, *The Great Metropolis* (Hartford, 1869), pp. 68–70. In addition to Hogan, pp. 121–49, see Clifford E. Clark, "The Changing Nature of Protestantism in Mid-Nineteenth Century America: Henry Ward Beecher's Seven Lectures to Young Men," *Journal of American History* 57 (March 1971): 832–46.

12. "The Good Time Coming," reprinted in *The Life and Battles of Yankee Sullivan* (New York, 1854), p. 97. The original "Good Time Coming" was written by Charles Mackay and set to music by Stephen Foster. The lyrics were a paean to

the coming era of social, moral, and religious perfection. See William W. Austin, *"Susanna," "Jeanie," and "The Old Folks at Home": The Songs of Stephen C. Foster from His Time to Ours* (New York, 1975), pp. 17–20. For a representative example of Queen's sporting values, see *New York Clipper*, September 2, 1854. For an incredibly bloody match between a pig and a dog, see *New York Clipper*, January 21, 1854.

13. This law even forbade Commonwealth citizens from staging fights in other states. See State of Massachusetts, *Acts and Resolves Passed by the General Court of Massachusetts* (Boston, 1849), chap. 49, p. 31; *New York Clipper*, September 27, 1856; *Massachusetts Reports, Supreme Judicial Court of Massachusetts* 73 (Boston, 1883): 324–28, "An Act to Prevent Prize Fighting"; *New York Clipper*, November 24, 1854.

14. *New York State Legislature, Eighty-Second Session*, 1859, chap. 37, "An Act to Prevent and Punish Prize Fighting," passed March 7, 1859, pp. 63–64 in Magriel ms.

15. A point made explicitly by the *New York Sunday Mercury*, March 7, 1853, after arrests on Riker's Island. Frank Queen believed magistrates were less concerned with justice than with shaking down boxers for part of their stake money. He pointed out that the laws kept doctors away from the ring, depriving fighters of medical attention. See, for example, *New York Clipper*, October 4, 1856, January 22, 1859. Ironically, the anti-prize-fight laws may have had a counteractive effect, diverting ring activities into underground channels and reinforcing feelings of rebellion against authority.

16. Dale Somers, *The Rise of Sport in New Orleans* (Baton Rouge, 1972), pp. 53–59. Many fights were held in parishes adjoining New Orleans to circumvent the law.

17. *American Fistiana* (1860), p. 23; *Spirit of the Times*, August 13, 1853.

18. *American Fistiana* (1860), p. 26.

19. Ibid. pp. 24–66, 70–72, 76, especially 52–53. For boxing in Pittsburgh, see Stewart Soren Brynn, "Some Sports in Pittsburgh during the National Period, 1775–1860," *Western Pennsylvania Historical Magazine*, 52 pt. 2 (January 1969): 63, 69.

20. *American Fistiana* (1860), pp. 24–66. The geographical mobility of American laborers in this era was nothing short of remarkable. See, for examples, Stephan Thernstrom, *Poverty and Progress: Social Mobility in a Nineteenth Century City* (New York, 1964); Thernstrom and Richard Sennett, eds., *Nineteenth Century Cities: Essays in the New Urban History* (New Haven, 1969).

21. *American Fistiana* (1860), pp. 26, 46, 53, 64, 66, 90–93. James Kelly, for example, was born in Ireland, migraged to England, then America, sailed to Australia to search for gold, returned to the United States, joined the gold rush to California, returned to New York. He fought all along the way, finishing his ring career against Ned Price in Point Albino, Canada. *American Fistiana* (1860), pp. 72–73.

22. William Tovee, for example, a cabinetmaker by trade, fought a few battles in the English ring late in the Regency Era. He migrated to New York in 1831, where his fortunes rose and fell as a tavern keeper and seller of furniture. He turned back to pugilism when hard times came and supported himself by giving sparring lessons and exhibitions, finally becoming the acknowledged master of ceremonies for most of the

glove displays held in the New York area. When old "Father Bill" died in 1883, he was known throughout the sporting world for the congeniality and good times he facilitated on the sparring stage. Tovee's career can be traced in the *New York Clipper.*

23. Ed Price to Frank Queen, Boston, December 11, 1859, printed in *American Fistiana* (1860), pp. 76–77. Price, incidentally, became an attorney when his boxing days were over.

24. Melvin Adelman, "The Development of Modern Athletics: Sport in New York City, 1820–1870" (diss., University of Illinois, 1980), pp. 569–81. On the general development of sports see Betts, *Sporting Heritage,* pt. 1, and Benjamin Rader, *American Sports: From the Age of Folk Games to the Age of Spectators* (Englewood Cliffs, N.J., 1983), pts. 1, 2; on urban street culture see chap. 4.

25. In the voluminous literature on the rags-to-riches motif John Cawelti's *Apostles of the Self-Made Man: Changing Concepts of Success in America* (Chicago, 1965) stands out.

26. For Morrissey's early life, see *New York Herald,* May 2, 1878; *New York Sun,* May 2, 1878; *New York Clipper,* May 23, 1878; *New York Times,* May 6, 1878; Ed James, *The Life and Battles of John Morrissey* (New York, 1879), pp. 3–4; Edward Wakin, *Enter the American Irish* (New York, 1976), pp. 116–18; William Edgar Harding, ed., *John Morrissey, His Life, Battles and Wrangles, from His Birth in Ireland until He Died a State Senator* (New York, 1881); *American Fistiana* (1860), p. 58; *New York Tribune,* May 2, 1878; David R. Johnson, "A Sinful Business: The Origins of Gambling Syndicates in the United States," in David Bayley, ed., *Police and Society* (Beverly Hills, 1977), pp. 28–29; Herbert Asbury, *The Gangs of New York* (New York, 1928), pp. 90–100; Alvin F. Harlow, *Old Bowery Days* (New York, 1931), p. 301; and M. R. Werner, *Tammany Hall* (New York, 1938), pp. 67–69. There is a book-length "biography" of Morrissey, Jack Kofoed's *Brandy for Heroes* (New York, 1938). It is thoroughly unreliable. Fred Harvey Harrington's forthcoming study of Morrissey therefore will be especially welcome.

27. James, p. 5; *New York Herald,* May 2, 1878; and anon., *The Lives and Battles of Tom Sayers and John C. Heenan, "The Benicia Boy"* (New York, 1860), pp. 57–58 (mainly a collection of English and American newspaper stories).

28. *Life and Battles of Sullivan,* p. 64; *American Fistiana* (1860), p. 20; *Spirit of the Times,* October 16, 1852; and James, pp. 5–6. Thompson's real name was Bob McLaren.

29. In addition to the sources in note 28 see Adelman, p. 565; Harding, p. 6. During these years Hyer alternately declared that he promised his parents he never would fight again and issued general challenges to all comers, and specific ones to particular fighters including William Perry, champion of England, for ten thousand dollars a side. However, Hyer never fought a regular prize battle after his 1849 fight with Sullivan. See *Spirit of the Times,* March 22–April 5, 1851.

30. *New York Daily Tribune,* March 10, 1855; *Life and Battles of Sullivan,* pp. 64–70; *American Fistiana* (1860), pp. 20–22. As Adelman notes in "Development of Modern Athletics," this early ethnic paradox is similar to the modern one where, for example, Joe Frazier is depicted by the press as the white man's boxer and Muhammad Ali as the militant black.

31. *New York Clipper,* October 15 and 22, 1853; *Life and Battles of Sullivan,* pp. 67–69. "The behavior of some of them while in the cars," the *Herald's* correspondent complained of the men going to the fight, "was not such as could be commended; and many acts of disorder, to use the mildest term, were perpetrated." *New York Herald,* October 13 and 14, 1853.

32. In addition to coverage by the *Herald* and the *Clipper* see James, pp. 6–12; *American Fistiana* (1860), pp. 20–22; *Life and Battles of Sullivan,* pp. 64–71; *New York Daily Tribune,* October 13 and 20, 1853; *New York Times,* October 11, 1853; *New York Evening Post,* October 13, 1853; and *Spirit of the Times,* October 22, 1853.

33. In addition to the above see the *Clipper,* October 22 and 29, and November 5, 1853. After the fight the *Clipper* received correspondence from as far away as Alabama, including an offer to back Sullivan in a rematch; November 26, 1853.

34. *Life and Battles of Sullivan,* p. 98; *New York Tribune,* October 13, 1853; *New York Evening Post,* October 13, 1853; and *New York Times,* October 14, 1853.

35. *Lives of Sayers and Heenan,* p. 56; Ed James, *Life and Battles of Tom Hyer* (New York, 1879), p. 22; James, *Life of Morrissey,* p. 11; and *New York Clipper,* July 22, 1854.

36. James, *Life of Morrissey,* p. 13; *New York Tribune,* November 2, 1877; and George Walling, *Recollections of a New York Chief of Police* (n. p., 1890), pp. 375–76.

37. Anon., *The Life of William Poole* (New York, 1855); Elliott J. Gorn, "The Killing of Butcher Bill" (paper read at the American Historical Association meetings, Chicago, December 1984). It was alleged that gangs led by Poole and Morrissey had once fought for control of the ballot boxes in an uptown precinct. See, for example, Matthew Hale Smith, *Wonders of a Great City* (Chicago, 1887), pp. 345–49.

38. *New York Sunday Mercury,* May 3, 1863; *Buffalo Commercial Advertiser,* August 1, 1857; and *New York Clipper,* August 8, 1857.

39. *American Fistiana* (1860), pp. 38–46; *New York Clipper,* August 8, 1857; *Philadelphia Sun,* August 4, 1857; *Philadelphia Evening Bulletin,* August 3, 1857; *New York Daily Tribune,* August 4, 1857; and *Buffalo Commercial Advertiser,* August 1, 1857.

40. For example, see *American Fistiana* (1860), pp. 46–49, 50–51; *New York Clipper,* October 17 and November 28, 1857.

41. *American Fistiana* (1860), pp. 58–59; Ed James, *The Life and Battles of John C. Heenan, the Hero of Farnborough* (New York, 1879), pp. 1–2.

42. *American Fistiana* (1860), pp. 58–59; James, *Life and Battles of Heenan,* pp. 2–4; *Lives of Sayers and Heenan,* p. 56.

43. *American Fistiana* (1860), p. 66; *Buffalo Republic,* quoted in *New York Daily Tribune,* October 20, 1858; and Allan Lloyd, *The Great Prize Fight* (New York, 1979), pp. 63–66.

44. *New York Tribune,* October 20 and 22, 1858; *New York Clipper* report, reprinted in *American Fistiana* (1860), pp. 58–61; *Frank Leslie's Illustrated Newspaper,* October 30, 1858; James, *Life of Morrissey,* pp. 13–19; and *Lives of Sayers and Heenan,* pp. 63–67.

45. See references in note 44. Fred Harvey Harrington points out in personal

NOTES TO PAGES 116–124

correspondence that boxing matches were often more orderly than political conventions.

46. See sources cited in note 44.

47. See the sources cited in note 44, and *American Fistiana* (1860), pp. 57–58; *Harper's Weekly* 2 (October 30, 1858): 690.

48. Harding, p. 14; *Buffalo Commercial Advertiser,* October 18, 1858, cited in *New York Tribune,* October 20, 1858; and *New York Daily Tribune,* May 2, 1878.

49. *New York Tribune,* October 20 and 22, 1858; *American Fistiana* (1860), pp. 58–61; and *Lives of Sayers and Heenan,* p. 63.

50. *New York Tribune,* October 22, 1858; *Frank Leslie's Illustrated Newspaper,* October 30, 1858; Lloyd, p. 36.

51. "The Prize Fight," *Harper's New Monthly Magazine* 18 (December 1858): 84–86. The literature on reform is voluminous, but for two seminal works on romantic perfectionism, see David Brion Davis, "The Emergence of Immediatism in British and American Antislavery Thought," *Mississippi Valley Historical Review* 49 (September 1962): 209–30, and John L. Thomas, "Romantic Reform in America, 1815–1865," *American Quarterly* 17 (Winter 1965): 656–81.

52. "The Prize Fight," *Harpers,* pp. 86–88; *Buffalo Republic,* quoted in *New York Tribune,* October 20, 1858; *New York Herald,* October 21, 1858, and *American Fistiana* (1860), p. 59.

53. *Troy Evening Transcript,* October 1858, quoted in *New York Tribune,* October 20, 1858 *New York Times,* quoted in Betts, *America's Sporting Heritage,* p. 57; *Harper's Weekly* 2 (October 30, 1858): 690.

54. *Lives of Sayers and Heenan,* pp. 64–67; James, *Life of Morrissey,* pp. 18–20; anon., *The Life of John Morrissey: From the Penitentiary to Congress* (n.p., n.d.), p. 7. The "Dead Rabbits" were a street gang of mostly Irish youths, accused of various criminal activities.

55. "Morrisy and the Russian Sailor," in M. C. Dean, comp., *The Flying Cloud and One Hundred Fifty Other Old Time Poems and Ballads* (Virginia, Minn., 1922). This broadside ballad has been recorded often. Hear, for example, Joe Heaney on *Irish Music in London Pubs,* ASCH Records FG 3575 (New York, 1965). D. K. Wilgus of the University of California, Los Angeles, has kindly supplied me with dozens of references to this ballad, as well as other songs about the Troy man, recorded in Ireland and America. Many of the songs of nineteenth-century pugilists could still be heard in Ireland well into the twentieth century.

56. Hubert Howe Bancroft's *Popular Tribunals* 2, pp. 1–9 and 267–83 in his *Collected Works* (San Francisco, 1887), is sympathetic to the vigilantes for their efforts to secure "civilized industry, agriculture, manufacturers, and the gentler arts of domesticity." The *New York Clipper* of July 5 and 12, 1856, doubted the vigilantes' claims, quoting California newspapers, Sullivan's alleged confession, and the coroner's report to throw suspicion on those who usurped the law. Also see Ed James, *The Life and Battles of Yankee Sullivan* (New York, n.d.), pp. 22–23. On the vigilantes see Robert M. Senkewicz, *Vigilantes in Gold Rush San Francisco* (Stanford, 1984).

57. *Spirit of the Times,* October 3, 1863, July 2, 1864; *New York Herald,* June 27, 1864; *New York Times,* June 27, 1864; Asbury, pp. 67–69, 100; and James, *Life of*

Hyer, p. 24. Dying young and destitute was almost the norm for these working-class men. In an informal sample of forty-nine prominent English and American bare-knuckle fighters by sports writer Arthur William Mann, half the men died before reaching the age of forty, four-fifths never turned fifty. Most were poor, and only about one out of five ever attained more than a modest living. From the papers of Arthur William Mann, Library of Congress; my thanks to Warren Goldstein for this reference. Michael T. Isenberg claims that forty-seven was the average age of death for bare-knuckle fighters, roughly typical for working-class men, but disturbingly low given the fact that most prize fighters began their adulthood as unusually healthy individuals who had survived childhood diseases. Isenberg, chap. 3, p. 38.

58. *American Fistiana* (1860), pp. 80–81; James, *Life of Heenan,* p. 4.

59. *New York Clipper,* no date given, quoted in *American Fistiana* (1860), pp. 80–81.

60. *New York Times* and *New York Herald,* no dates given, quoted in ibid.

61. Johnson, pp. 17–24. "Sinful Business" is well-researched and an impressive piece of work given the fugitive nature of the subject.

62. Ibid., pp. 28–43; Adelman, p. 584; anon., "The True Inwardness of Gambling," *New York Sun,* August 4, 1875, originally printed in the *Cincinnati Commercial;* and Donald J. Mrozek, *Sport and American Mentality, 1880–1910* (Knoxville, 1983), pp. 120–21.

63. In addition the sources cited in note 62 see *Biographical Dictionary of the American Congress* (Washington, D.C., 1928), in Magriel ms. (mainly a collection of contemporary newspaper reports); Leo Hershkowitz, *Tweed's New York* (Garden City, N.Y., 1977), pp. 149–55, 321–25; Werner, pp. 286–91; Myers, pp. 299–301; Wakin, pp. 116–18; and "Morrissey: A Remarkable Interview with the Great Expelled," *Brooklyn Daily Eagle,* August 2, 1875.

64. *New York Daily Tribune,* May 2, 1878. See also the *Nation* 4 (March 7, 1867).

65. Harrington, personal correspondence; *New York Herald,* May 2, 1878.

Chapter 4. The Meanings of Prize Fighting

1. Peter George Buckley, "To the Opera House: Culture and Society in New York City, 1820–1860" (diss., State University of New York at Stony Brook, 1984), pp. 505–10, raises this crucial issue in a very sophisticated way. We must be careful, however, not to read the present into the past. Today's celebrity possesses an aura of media-created intimacy which is fraudulent and alienating. We never personally touch the media-made celebrity, and he or she is oblivious to fans as individuals. But this was not the case for the first generation of great bare-knucklers.

2. Frederick Van Wyck, *Recollections of an Old New Yorker* (New York, 1932), pp. 100–114. On the development of sports in the antebellum era see Benjamin C. Rader, "The Quest for Subcommunities and the Rise of American Sports," *American Quarterly* 29 (Fall 1977): 307–21; Roberta J. Park, "The Attitudes of Leading New England Transcendentalists toward Healthful Exercise, Active Recreations, and Proper Care of the Body, 1830–1860," *Journal of Sport History* 4 (Spring 1977): 34–50; Melvin Adelman, "The Development of Modern Athletics: Sport in New

York City, 1820–1870" (diss., University of Illinois, 1980), esp. chaps. 9–11; John Rickard Betts, "Mind and Body in Early American Thought," *Journal of American History* 54 (March 1968): 790–801; Betts, "Sporting Journalism in Nineteenth Century America, 1819–1900"; *American Quarterly* 5 (Spring 1953): 39–56; Betts, *America's Sporting Heritage, 1850–1950* (Reading, Mass., 1974), pt. 1; Stephen Hall Hardy and Jack Berryman, " 'Public Amusements and Public Morality': Sport and Social Reform in the American City, 1800–1860" (paper presented at the annual meeting of the Organization of American Historians, Detroit, April 1–4, 1981); Peter Levine, "The Promise of Sport in Antebellum America," *Journal of American Culture* 2 (Winter 1980): 623–34; and Benjamin Rader, *American Sports: From the Age of Folk Games to the Age of Spectators* (Englewood Cliffs, N.J., 1983), pt. 1.

3. On the bourgeois response to the poor of mid-nineteenth-century cities see Paul Boyer, *Urban Masses and Moral Order in America* (Cambridge, Mass., 1978), pts. 2 and 3; Carroll Smith-Rosenberg, *Religion and the Rise of the American City* (Ithaca, 1971). For examples of Victorian responses to sports, see John Dizikes, *Sportsmen and Gamesmen* (Boston, 1981), chaps. 1–5, 8; Buckley, pp. 591–604; Edward K. Spann, *The New Metropolis: New York City, 1840–1857* (New York, 1981), pp. 164–73; and Rader, *American Sports*, pp. 30–43. Stow Persons captures the earnest tone of Victorian life in his *The Decline of American Gentility* (New York, 1973). On the growing bifurcation of American culture—elite vs. plebeian—see Buckley, esp. pp. 160–61. Excellent discussions of the underlying assumptions in Victorian culture are contained in Daniel T. Rodgers, *The Work Ethic in Industrial America, 1850–1950* (Chicago, 1978); Daniel Walker Howe, ed., *Victorian America* (Philadelphia, 1976); and Howe, *The Political Culture of the American Whigs* (Chicago, 1979).

4. For demographic change, see Spann, chap. 1; Amy Bridges, *A City in the Republic* (Cambridge, Mass., 1984), pp. 39–45; Sean Wilentz, *Chants Democratic: New York City and the Rise of the American Working Class, 1788–1850* (New York, 1984), pp. 18–24, 192; Allen Stanley Horlick, *Country Boys and Merchant Princes: The Social Control of Young Men in New York* (Lewisburg, 1975), chap. 1; George Rogers Taylor, "American Urban Growth Preceding the Railroad Age," *Journal of Economic History* 27 (September 1967): 309–39; Douglass C. North, *The Economic Growth of the United States, 1790–1860* (New York, 1966), pt. 2; and Philip A. M. Taylor, *The Distant Magnet: European Migration to the United States of America* (London, 1971), pp. 34–37. Frank Queen claimed that audiences for sparring matches ranged from dealers in Wall Street stocks to dealers in faro, from Broadway dandies to sellers of lozenges. However, he mentioned nothing of shopkeepers, businessmen, or industrialists. *New York Clipper,* February 4, 1854.

5. For a fine discussion of the moral economy of the old artisan culture, its rootedness in republican ideology and collective welfare, see Wilentz, chaps. 2 and 3. For change in the relations of work, see Wilentz, pp. 108–10, 119, 134; Paul Faler, *Mechanics and Manufacturers in the Early Industrial Revolution: Lynn, Massachusetts, 1760–1860* (Albany, N.Y., 1981), chap. 7; Bruce Laurie " 'Nothing on Compulsion': Life Styles of Philadelphia Artisans, 1820–1850," *Labor History* 15 (Summer 1974): 337–66; Susan Hirsch, *Roots of the American Working Class*

(Philadelphia, 1978), chaps. 1, 2, and 5; Joseph F. Kett, *Rites of Passage: Adolescence in America, 1790 to the Present* (New York, 1977), chap. 6; Bridges, chap. 3; and Paul Johnson, *A Shopkeepers' Millennium: Society and Revivals in Rochester, New York, 1815–1837* (New York, 1978), chap. 2. For a parallel transformation of white collar work, see Horlick, pts. 1 and 2. On wealth distribution see, for examples, Stephan Thernstrom, *Poverty and Progress: Social Mobility in a Nineteenth Century City* (New York, 1975); Edward Pessen, *Riches, Class and Power before the Civil War* (Lexington, Mass., 1973); and Lee Soltow, "Economic Inequality in the United States in the Period from 1790–1860," *Journal of Economic History* 31 (December 1971): 833–39.

6. For some of the social and cultural implications of the transformation from an artisan to an industrial economy, see the works by Wilentz, Johnson, Faler, Laurie, Hirsch, and Horlick cited above, in addition to Bruce Laurie, "Fire Companies and Gangs in Southwark: The 1840s," in Allen F. Davis and Mark H. Haller, eds., *The Peoples of Philadelphia: A History of Ethnic Groups and Lower-Class Life, 1790–1940* (Philadelphia, 1973), pp. 71–87; J. Thomas Jable, "Aspects of Moral Reform in Early Nineteenth Century Pennsylvania," *Pennsylvania Magazine of History and Biography* 102 (July 1978): 344–63; Susan G. Davis, "'Making Night Hideous': Christmas Revelry and Public Order in Nineteenth Century Philadelphia," *American Quarterly* 34 (Summer 1982): 185–99; Rodgers, pp. 15–22; Jill Siegel Dodd, "The Working Classes and the Temperance Movement in Antebellum Boston," *Labor History* 19 (Fall 1978): 510–31; David Montgomery, "The Working Classes of the Pre-Industrial American City, 1780–1830," *Labor History* 9 (Winter 1968): 3–22; and Karen Halttunen, *Confidence Men and Painted Women: A Study of Middle-Class Culture in America* (New Haven, 1982), esp. pp. 8–37.

7. The social stress created by the expansion of markets is a central theme in the work of Wilentz, Johnson, Faler, Laurie, Horlick, Rodgers, and Hirsch.

8. Laurie, Faler, Johnson, Dodd, and Wilentz all trace variations on this theme of "moral classes" within the working class.

9. Raised on the radical republicanism of the preindustrial city, editor George Wilkes also merged support for labor with interest in sporting events. See Alexander Saxton, "George Wilkes: The Transformation of a Radical Ideology," *American Quarterly* 33 (Fall 1981): 437–58. Wilkes's devotion to radicalism waned as his desire to acquire wealth grew. Wilentz argues that historians have exaggerated the inherent contradiction of labor radicalism and street life, pp. 255–56, 270–71, 326–35. Also see Bridges, p. 152; *Subterranean*, January 31, February 28, and May 23, 1846, and October 25, 1845.

10. As Buckley reveals in "To the Opera House," surprising numbers of these men migrated to California in search of adventure. War also provided a test of masculine honor. Several boxers and their backers signed an open letter to the *Subterranean* (July 11, 1846), for example, declaring their intention to enlist and fight in Mexico. For an alternative interpretation of sports and work, one emphasizing "congruence" between labor and leisure values, see Stephen M. Gelber, "Working at Playing: The Culture of the Workplace and the Rise of Baseball," *Journal of Social History* 16 (Summer 1983): 3–22. For two pathbreaking studies of

NOTES TO PAGES 133–134

nineteenth-century theater, see Robert Toll, *Blacking Up: The Minstrel Show in Nineteenth Century America* (New York, 1974), and David Grimsted, *Melodrama Unveiled: American Theater and Culture, 1800–1850* (Chicago, 1968).

11. Wilentz argues persuasively that the street culture was not purely traditionalist—seeking to restore the recreations of the past—but a hybrid, mixing old and new social and cultural patterns; pp. 53–60, 257–63. Also see Joshua Brown, "The 'Dead-Rabbit'–Bowery Boy Riot: An Analysis of the Antebellum New York Gang" (thesis, Columbia University, 1976), pp. 155–56; Spann, pp. 248–56; Hirsch, pp. 74–75; Howard B. Rock, *Artisans of the New Republic* (New York, 1979), pp. 295–319; Buckley, pp. 319–35; and Bruce Laurie, *The Working Peoples of Philadelphia, 1800–1850* (Philadelphia, 1980), pp. 53–58. For a particularly lurid account of working-class life on the Bowery, see Junius Henri Browne, *The Great Metropolis: A Mirror of New York* (Hartford, 1869), pp. 130–37, 326–31, 568–73.

12. Brown, Spann, Wilentz, Buckley, Rock, Hirsch, and Laurie all touch on these points. The desire to form voluntary associations was part of the larger tendency of Americans to band together in pursuit of specific goals, a tendency engendered by the atomization of market- and contract-based society. As Benjamin Rader observes, sports organizations such as early baseball clubs were another way that men countered social isolation with voluntary consocation. See "Quest for Subcommunities," pp. 355–69. The Irish also brought their heritage of secret societies and faction fighting—the poor man's tools for influencing elections and tempering the power of landlords and bosses—all of which fed the gangs, fire companies, political clubs, and other working-class institutions in American cities. See Brown, pp. 117–47.

13. Stonecutter and Bowery B'hoy David Broderick also opened a tavern, named it in honor of Mike Walsh's radical newspaper, and there entertained the editor along with the likes of Yankee Sullivan, William Poole, and John Morrissey. Another saloon keeper, Tom McGuire, a man whose roots were in the radical republicanism of the preindustrial city, grew to moderate wealth promoting prize fights as well as black-faced minstrelsy, and even grand opera in New York and San Francisco. J. Frank Kernan, *Reminiscences of the Old Fire Laddies and Volunteer Departments of New York and Brooklyn* (New York, 1885), pp. 114–19; Saxton, pp. 437–38, 442. For a typically judgmental account of these "degraded" characters, see Browne, *Great Metropolis*, chap. 6. On the centrality of the saloon to working-class culture see Jon M. Kingsdale, "The 'Poor Man's Club': Social Functions of the Urban Working-Class Saloon," *American Quarterly* 25 (October 1973): 472–89; Michael T. Isenberg, "John L. Sullivan and His America," draft manuscript (Annapolis, 1985), chap. 2, pp. 24–26; and Roy Rosenzweig, *Eight Hours for What We Will: Workers and Leisure in an Industrial City, 1870–1920* (Cambridge, 1983), pt. 2, chap. 2.

14. Laurie, *Working Peoples of Philadelphia*, pp. 58–62; Herbert Asbury, *Ye Olde Fire Laddies* (New York, 1930), pp. 154–55, 171–84; Wilentz, pp. 259–63; Laurie, "Fire Companies and Gangs in Southwark," pp. 71–87; Kernan, p. 19; Buckley, pp. 333–42; Adelman, pp. 569–74; Alvin F. Harlow, *Old Bowery Days* (New York, 1931), chap. 12; Alexander B. Callow, *The Tweed Ring* (New York, 1966), chaps. 1, 4, 5, 7, 8; Leo Hershkowitz, *Tweed's New York* (Garden City, N.Y., 1977), chaps. 1–6; Kett, pp. 90–93; and Ed James, "Lives and Battles of the Irish Champions" (1883), in a scrapbook of clippings on nineteenth-century American sports, New York Public Library Annex.

15. See, for example, anon., *London and New York: Their Crime and Police* (New York, 1853), reprinted from articles in the *New York Journal of Commerce*, February 1853; Harlow, chaps. 11 and 16; Herbert Asbury, *The Gangs of New York* (New York, 1928), pp. 37–45; Jerome Mushkat, *Tammany: The Evolution of a Political Machine, 1789–1865* (Syracuse, 1971), p. 208; Gustavus Myers, *The History of Tammany Hall* (New York, 1901), pp. 154–63; and M. R. Werner, *Tammany Hall* (New York, 1928), pp. 44–65.

16. Saxton, pp. 437–58, does a fine job of revealing the juncture of politics, street life, and working-class culture. Also see Kett, pp. 8–90; Wilentz, pp. 255–64, 300–301; Brown, pp. 60–61, 144–56; George G. Foster, *New York by Gaslight* (New York, 1850), chap. 12; Foster, *New York in Slices by an Experienced Carver* (New York, 1849), chap. 9; Laurie, *Peoples of Philadelphia*, pp. 151–58; Harlow, chaps. 11, 16; Asbury, *Gangs of New York*, pp. 37–45; Mushkat, p. 208; Meyers, pp. 154–63; and Werner, pp. 44–65. For an alternative interpretation of gang behavior— one stressing antisocial acts more than group norms—see Leonard Berkowitz, "Violence and Rule Following Behavior," in Peter Marsh and Anne Campbell, eds., *Aggression and Violence* (Oxford, 1982), pp. 91–101.

17. Spann, pp. 319, 326–29, 344–50, 352–53; Wilentz, pp. 255–64, 326–35; Brown, pp. 78–95; and Bridges, pp. 61–62, 110–13, 132–35. Rynders, for example, brought such fighters as Bill Ford and John McCleester to sixth ward primary meetings, trying to use muscle to broaden his political base beyond the fifth ward. Kernan, pp. 52–54. On violence as a political tool in artisan culture see Michael Feldberg, "Urbanization as a Cause of Violence: Philadelphia as a Test Case," in Allen F. Davis and Mark H. Haller, eds., *The Peoples of Philadelphia* (Philadelphia, 1973), pp. 56, 66. For ties between urban vice, gambling, and politics, see Haller, "Recurring Themes," the conclusion to Davis and Haller, pp. 277–90.

18. For more on street politics, see George Walling, *Recollections of a New York Chief of Police* (n.p., 1890), pp. 375–76; *New York Daily Tribune,* "The Poole Tragedy," March 10, 1855; Spann, 318–19; Fred Harvey Harrington, "Gamblers, Politicians and the World of Sport, 1840–1870" (a paper read at the Organization of American Historians meeting, April 8, 1983). As Buckley points out, several of the most influential individuals in working-class culture, such as editors George Wilkes and Mike Walsh, politician Isaiah Rynders, and promoter David Broderick, became wealthy men and ultimately cut themselves off from the very culture they helped create; pp. 406–9.

19. On nativism and politics in New York see Robert Ernst, "Economic Nativism in New York City during the 1840s," *New York History* 29 (April 1948): 170–86; Ira M. Leonard, "The Rise and Fall of the American Republican Party in New York City," *New-York Historical Society Quarterly* 50 (April 1966): 150–92; Spann, pp. 276–80, 334–39; Wilentz, pp. 315–25, 343–49; and Bridges, pp. 12, 30–33, 39–45, 92–98. Several historians have argued that ethnic conflict was the major formative influence in the politics of the antebellum era. For this "ethnocultural" school, see Michael F. Holt, *Forging a Majority: The Formation of the Republican Party in Pittsburgh, 1848–1860* (New Haven, 1969); Holt, *The Political Crisis of the 1850s* (New York, 1978); Joel H. Silbey, *The Transformation of American Politics, 1840–1860* (Englewood Cliffs, 1967); Robert Kelly, *The Cultural Pattern in American Politics: The First Century* (New York, 1979); Paul Kleppner, *The Cross of Culture: A Social*

Analysis of Midwestern Politics, 1850–1900 (New York, 1970); Kleppner, *The Third Electoral System, 1853–1892: Parties, Voters and Political Cultures* (Chapel Hill, 1979). Boxers affirmed the continuity of ethnic identity across generations in their ring names. Thus one black became "Young Molineaux" and a Jewish fighter called himself "Young Dutch Sam" after his English predecessor. Still, Irish and English immigrants dominated the sport. Adelman estimates that around 55 percent of pre–Civil War New York fighters were of Irish extraction, and most of the rest came from English stock; pp. 559–69.

20. Wilentz, pp. 137–39; Buckley, pp. 342–49; *New York Clipper,* April 29, 1854.

21. In addition to Wilentz and Buckley as cited in note 19, see Laurie, "Fire Companies," pp. 77–78; Jable, "Moral Reform," pp. 362–63.

22. For examples, see *New York Clipper,* December 10 and October 15, 1853.

23. The most comprehensive work on street culture is Buckley, "To the Opera House." It was the corrupting effects of street culture on youth which reformers feared most. See especially Halttunen, pp. 23–32.

24. On symbolic inversion see Barbara A. Babcock, ed., *The Reversible World: Symbolic Inversion in Art and Society* (Ithaca, 1978). Police Captain Petty referred to Norton's fifth ward clique as "a gang of rowdies composed of thieves, gamblers, pimps, bounty jumpers, fighters and rum sellers." The president of the police board called Norton "the champion of the desperate and dangerous classes," including thieves, prostitutes, and murderers. Other boxers also found success on their own terms. Ed Price became an attorney after retiring from the ring, building his practice with the aid of his street contacts, while Orville "Awful" Gardner—a few years after biting off part of William "Dublin Tricks" Hasting's ear in a brawl—was converted to Christianity and preached to others of his background in the language and style of the Bowery. Quotations from Edwin P. Kilroe, comp., "Skeleton Outline of the Activities of Michael Norton," New-York Historical Society manuscript dated April 1, 1938. See also Charles Lorring Brace, *The Dangerous Classes of New York and Twenty Years Work among Them* (New York, 1872), pp. 288–97; Spann, p. 346.

25. On "modern" personality see Richard D. Brown, *Modernization: The Transformation of American Life, 1600–1865* (New York, 1976), chaps. 5 and 6, and Wilbur Zelinsky, *A Cultural Geography of the United States* (Englewood Cliffs, N.J., 1973), chap. 2. My considerable intellectual debt to Clifford Geertz should be obvious in these pages. See his *The Interpretation of Cultures* (New York, 1973).

26. Contrast the behavior of men at a fight with Victorian propriety as elucidated by Howe et al. in *Victorian America* and by Halttunen in *Confidence Men and Painted Women.*

27. On gambling see Ann Fabian, "Rascals and Gentlemen: The Meaning of American Gambling, 1820–1890" (diss., Yale University, 1983).

28. On the centrality of gambling to the rise of sports see Harrington, "Gamblers, Politicians, and the World of Sports." Labor radical Mike Walsh seems to have taken a live-and-let-live attitude toward gambling; see *Subterranean,* December 27, 1845. The ring depended on professional gamblers for stake money and to facilitate wagering among other bettors. Jake Somerendyke, for example, was a regular at the Empire Club where fights were discussed and arranged. He earned his money from his expertise at the ring and track, handicapping horses and fighters and selling

"pools" to other gamblers. See Ed James, *The Life and Battles of Tom Hyer* (New York, 1879), p. 2.

29. Fabian, "Rascals and Gentlemen"; Harrington, "Gamblers, Politicians and the World of Sports." Also see Haller, "Recurring Themes," pp. 277–90.

30. On gender roles in Victorian America see Rader, *American Sports*, p. 34; Peter Stearns, *Be a Man: Males in Modern Society* (New York, 1979), chap. 5; Edward Anthony Rotundo, "Body and Soul: Changing Ideals of American Middle-Class Manhood," *Journal of Social History* 16 (Summer 1983): 23–38; Rotundo, "Manhood in America: The Northern Middle Class, 1770–1920" (diss., Brandeis University, 1982), chaps. 4–6; Mary P. Ryan, *Cradle of the Middle Class: The Family in Oneida County, New York, 1790–1865* (Cambridge, 1981); Charles E. Rosenberg, "Sexuality, Class and Role in Nineteenth Century America," in Joseph and Elizabeth Pleck, eds., *The American Man* (Englewood Cliffs, N.J., 1980), pp. 219–54; Michael Gordon, "The Ideal Husband as Depicted in the Nineteenth Century Marriage Manual," in Pleck and Pleck, pp. 145–57; Joe L. Dubbert, *A Man's Place: Masculinity in Transition* (Englewood Cliffs, N.J., 1979), chap. 2; Pleck and Pleck, "Introduction," pp. 14–15; Nancy F. Cott, *The Bonds of Womanhood: "Woman's Sphere" in New England, 1780–1835* (New Haven, 1977); Ann Douglas, *The Feminization of American Culture* (New York, 1977); William H. Chafe, *Women and Equality: Changing Patterns in American Culture* (Oxford, 1979), chap. 2; Peter Gabriel Filene, *Him/Her/Self: Sex Roles in Modern America* (New York, 1974), chaps. 1 and 2; and Nancy F. Cott and Elizabeth H. Pleck, eds., *A Heritage of Her Own: Toward a New Social History of American Women* (New York, 1979), chaps. 6–14.

31. Spann captures the male basis of this culture, pp. 344–50. Rotundo's dissertation is particularly helpful here, especially chaps. 2–6. Also see Jonathan Katz, ed., *Gay American History: Lesbians and Gay Men in the USA* (New York, 1976). Joseph H. Pleck, *The Myth of Masculinity* (Cambridge, Mass., 1981), pp. 140–42, uses the terms "traditional" and "modern" to differentiate male-centered from female-centered masculinity, a class-biased formulation. Peter Stearns is quite sensitive to the problem of how class and gender roles interact; pp. 41–46, 59–60, 62–63, 70–71.

32. Rader, *American Sports*, p. 34; Hirsch, pp. 54–55; Kernan, p. 165; Stearns, pp. 52–53, 85; Kingsdale, "The 'Poor Man's Club,'" pp. 472–89; Brace, pp. 286–97; Ned Polsky, *Hustlers, Beats and Others* (Chicago, 1967), especially pp. 31–37, 72–73, 85–115; Adelman, pp. 582–89; Boyer, chap. 7; and David R. Johnson, *Policing the Urban Underworld* (Philadelphia, 1979), especially pp. 29–40, 78–89, 126–81.

33. Carroll Smith-Rosenberg, "The Female World of Love and Ritual: Relations between Women in Nineteenth Century America," *Signs* 1 (Autumn 1975): 1–29; Isenberg, chap. 2, pp. 18–19.

34. *New York Clipper,* December 10, 1853. Joseph and Elizabeth Pleck point out that eighteenth-century men were intensely intimate in their interactions with one another. *American Man,* p. 13.

35. On the concept of honor see Bertram Wyatt Brown, *Southern Honor: Ethics and Behavior in the Old South* (New York, 1982), esp. pt. 1; Wyatt-Brown, *Yankee*

Saints and Southern Sinners (Baton Rouge, 1985); Edward L. Ayers, *Vengeance and Justice, Crime and Punishment in the Nineteenth Century American South* (New York, 1984), esp. chap. 1; Elliott J. Gorn, "'Gouge and Bite, Pull Hair and Scratch': The Social Significance of Fighting in the Southern Backcountry," *American Historical Review* 90 (February 1985): 38–42; Peter Berger et al., *The Homeless Mind* (New York, 1973), pp. 83–94; Julio Caro-Baroja, "Honour and Shame: An Historical Account of Several Conflicts," trans. R. Johnson, and Julian Pitt-Rivers, "Honour and Social Status," both in J. G. Peristiani, ed., *Honour and Shame* (Chicago, 1966), pp. 88–91, 19–77; and "Honor" in David Sills, ed., *The International Encyclopedia of the Social Sciences* 6 (New York, 1968): 503–10.

36. See references in note 32 above.

37. Brown, pp. 113–17; Bridges, p. 116; Spann, pp. 71, 25–28, 134–51. 306–19; Wilentz, pp. 117–19, 363–64; and Roger Lane, *Violent Death in the City* (Cambridge, Mass., 1979), pp. 59–64, 117–24. The human environment could be as threatening as the natural one. Mobbing and rioting were common, traditional forms of protest aimed at attaining particular social or economic goals. Moreover, street crime—though comparatively infrequent by modern standards—was perceived as growing out of control. See Michael Feldberg, "Urbanization as a Cause of Violence, Philadelphia as a Test Case," in Davis and Haller, pp. 53–69.

38. Wilentz, chap. 7, esp. 262–66; Leonard L. Richards, *Gentlemen of Property and Standing: Anti-Abolition Mobs in Jacksonian America* (New York, 1970). Traditional uses of violence is a pervasive theme in Buckley, "To the Opera House," and Brown "'Dead Rabbit'–Bowery Boy Riot." Also see Harlow, pp. 146–51; Charles N. Glabb and Theodore Brown, *A History of Urban America* (New York, 1967), pp. 87–88.

39. Even though the rules of the ring sometimes broke down, it was the *ideal* of fair combat which gave boxing symbolic power. After a barroom misunderstanding in 1859, John C. Heenan was set upon in the streets of Boston, kicked down from behind, shot at, and left bleeding with injuries to his back and knee. Contrast such brutality—not uncommon in street life—with the controlled passions of the ring. Ed James, *Life and Battles of John C. Heenan* (New York, 1879), p. 3. For a fascinating discussion of the verbal violence in English youth gangs, see Pater Marsh, "The Rhetorics of Violence," in Marsh and Anne Campbell, eds., *Aggression and Violence* (Oxford, 1982), pp. 102–17.

40. The best evidence indicates that violent spectacles such as boxing matches do not have a cathartic effect but tend to promote real violence. See, for examples, David P. Phillips, "The Werther Effect," *The Sciences*, July–August 1985, pp. 33–39; George Gaskill and Robert Pearton, chap. 10 of Jeffrey H. Goldstein, ed., *Sports, Games and Play: Social and Psychological Viewpoints* (Hillsdale, N.J., 1979), pp. 263–91; Goldstein, ed., *Sports Violence* (New York, 1983); and Richard G. Sipes, "War, Sports and Aggression: An Empirical Test of Two Rival Theories," *American Anthropologist*, n.s., 751 (February 1973): 64–86.

41. For an excellent survey of sociological theories on youth gang violence, see David Downes, "The Language of Violence," in Marsh and Campbell, *Aggression and Violence,* chap. 3.

Chapter 5. Triumph and Decline

1. *American Fistiana* (New York, 1860), pp. 82–85; Alan Lloyd, *The Great Prize Fight* (New York, 1977), chap. 7; *Bell's Life in London,* May 15, 1859, in *The Lives and Battles of Tom Sayers and John C. Heenan, "The Benicia Boy"* (New York, 1860), pp. 71–77; and Richard Calhoun, "The Great International Prize Fight of 1860," *World of Sport,* May 1984, pp. 40–45. Generally, Lloyd and Calhoun are the most reliable secondary sources on this fight.

2. *Lives of Sayer and Heenan,* p. 90; *Vanity Fair,* January 14, 1860, p. 45, in Magriel ms. (a collection primarily of comtemporary newspaper accounts of bareknuckle fights).

3. Oliver Wendell Holmes, "The Autocrat of the Breakfast Table," *Atlantic Monthly* 1 (May 1858): 881.

4. Melvin Adelman, "The Development of Modern Athletics: Sport in New York City, 1820–1870" (diss., University of Illinois, 1980), p. 566. Frank Luther Mott, historian of American journalism, claims that Heenan's fights were the sports highlights of the era. *A History of American Magazines* (New York, 1962), 2: 201; *American Journalism* (New York, 1962), p. 382. Also see William Edgar Harding, *John C. Heenan: Champion Pugilist of America* (New York, 1881), p. 5.

5. Lloyd, pp. 92–94. On this fascinating woman see John Dizikes, *Sportsmen and Gamesmen* (Boston, 1981), pp. 228–34; Claudia Johnson, *American Actress: Perspectives on the Nineteenth Century* (Chicago, 1984), chap. 8.

6. Several samples of the iconography of the ring are photocopied in the Magriel ms. Also see Nathaniel Fleischer, Sam Andre, and Nat Loubet, *A Pictorial History of Boxing,* rev. ed. (Secaucus, N.J., 1975), pp. 43–47.

7. Alexander Saxton, "George Wilkes: The Transformation of a Radical Ideology," *American Quarterly* 33 (Fall 1981): 445–46; *New York Times,* April 25, 28, 30, 1860. Newspapers carried debates and letters on the fighters' respective merits. See *Lives of Sayers and Heenan,* pp. 69–71, 91–94; John Rickard Betts, *America's Sporting Heritage, 1850–1950* (Reading, Mass., 1974), p. 39.

8. *Harper's Weekly* 4 (May 5, 1860), quoted in Betts, *America's Sporting Heritage,* p. 39.

9. Leslie's criticism is contained in the issue of December 31, 1859. For examples of how the illustrated newspapers covered the fight, see *Frank Leslie's Illustrated Newspaper,* March 24, 1860, and the *New York Illustrated News,* April 14, 1860.

10. Mott, *American Journalism,* p. 382. Each journal assured its readers that it alone could be counted on for authentic coverage, and the competition between papers was extremely fierce. The *New York Illustrated News* sent an engraver to do his work from artists' sketches on board the homeward-bound steamer *Vanderbilt.* American papers flooded London while tons of English journals were snatched up at American ports. Lloyd, pp. 133, 158–59.

11. See Prologue, above; Lloyd, pp. 14, 18–19. Robert W. Malcolmson, *Popular Recreations in English Society, 1700–1850* (Cambridge, Mass., 1973), makes a forceful case for the decline of ancient sports in the Victorian period, and writers on boxing in the era confirm his conclusions. Dennis Brailsford, *Sport and Society:*

Elizabeth to Anne (Toronto, 1969), argues that the decline of sports theory is greatly overestimated, that the working class was able to preserve its autonomous recreations. He clearly exaggerates in the case of boxing, but the tenacity of the working class in preserving old pastimes has too often been slighted by those who view modernization as an overwhelming, superorganic process.

12. See Lloyd, pp. 22–116.

13. Ibid. Morrissey denied revenge as a motive, implying that betting on Sayers was purely an investment. The former champion, incidentally, was accompanied to England by Dad Cunningham, slayer of Paudeen MacLaughlin, who was William Poole's murderer. Ed James, *The Life and Battles of John Morrissey* (New York, 1897), pp. 19–20.

14. Lloyd, pp. 111–25; see also undated passages from *London Sporting Life* in *Lives of Sayers and Heenan*, pp. 77–86.

15. *Clipper* quoted in *American Fistiana* (1860), p. 87; *Wilkes' Spirit of the Times,* January 21, 1860, quoted in Adelman, p. 566.

16. *Lives of Sayers and Heenan,* pp. 71, 91, quotation taken from a January edition of *Wilkes' Spirit of the Times; The Diary of George Templeton Strong,* ed. Allen Nevins and Milton Halsey Thomas (New York, 1952), Monday, April 3, 1860.

17. For example, see George Borrow, *Lavengro* (London, 1910), chap. 26; unattributed quotation in Lloyd, pp. 124–31, 157; *Famous Fights in the Prize Ring* (London, n.d.), p. 4; Ed James, *The Life and Battles of John C. Heenan, the Hero of Farnborough* (New York, 1879), pp. 5–6.

18. James, *Life of Heenan,* pp. 6–17. Lloyd, chaps. 20–23, persuasively synthesizes reports from the British and American press.

19. F. Locker-Lampson, *Fifty Famous Fights in Fact and Fiction,* quoted in T. B. Shepherd ed., *The Noble Art: An Anthology* (London, 1950), p. 147; Lloyd, pp. 155–57, 164.

20. William Makepeace Thackeray, "The Fight of Sayerius and Heenanus," reprinted in Shepherd, *Noble Art,* pp. 151–52.

21. One broadside by "Dilsey of London" had Heenan repeatedly declare "Erin go Bragh." Reprinted in J. N. Healy, *Old Irish Street Ballads* (Cork, 1969), 3: 16.

22. Quoted in William D. Cox, ed., *Boxing in Art and Literature* (New York, 1935), pp. 121–22; Foster Rhea Dulles, *America Learns to Play* (Gloucester, Mass., 1959), p. 146; Lloyd, p. 152; Adelman, pp. 568–69; and James, *Life of Heenan,* pp. 17–18.

23. All cited in Adelman, pp. 567–68. Also see Lloyd, pp. 158–59; *Lives of Sayers and Heenan,* p. 78; Harding, *John C. Heenan,* p. 5; and James, *Life of Heenan,* pp. 15–17. The passage of time made the English press as certain that Sayers was cheated as the American press was that Heenan deserved the belt.

24. "Heenan and Sayers," in M. C. Dean, comp., *The Flying Cloud and One Hundred Fifty Other Old Time Poems and Ballads* (Virginia, Minn., 1922), pp. 24–25.

25. The *New York Clipper* had to remind its readers who Charles Freeman was. See *Lives of Sayers and Heenan,* p. 90. Also see Adelman, p. 601, and Lloyd, p. 38.

26. Randy Roberts, *Jack Dempsey: The Manassa Mauler* (Baton Rouge, 1979), chap. 3. On boxing and militarism in the twentieth century see Jeffrey T. Sammons,

"America in the Ring: The Relationship between Boxing and Society circa 1930–1980" (diss., University of North Carolina, Chapel Hill, 1982).

27. Thomas Wentworth Higginson, "Physical Courage," *Atlantic Monthly* 2 (November 1858): 733–37.

28. For example, *American Fistiana* (1860), p. 17. The Sayers-Heenan bout continued to provide a living metaphor for men involved with the diplomacy of the Civil War. In England, Lord Palmerston wrote to his foreign secretary on June 13, 1862, that British mediation between the warring sides would be like "offering to make it up between Sayers and Heenan after the Third Round." Henry Adams, in England with his father, Ambassador Charles Francis Adams, Sr., also used a boxing metaphor to explain the situation of the summer of 1862 to his brother, Charles, Jr.: "You see we are stripping and squaring off, to say nothing of sponging, for the next round." From Brian Jenkins, *Britain in the War for the Union*, 2 vols. (Montreal, 1974), 2: 166–76; *The Letters of Henry Adams*, ed. J. C. Levenson et al. (Cambridge, Mass., 1982), 1: 167–69.

29. The argument that sports prepared men for war received fullest expression at the end of the century. See Donald J. Mrozek, *Sport and American Mentality, 1880–1910* (Knoxville, 1983), chap. 2.

30. Lawrence Webster Fielding, "Sport on the Road to Appomattox: The Shadow of Army Life" (diss., University of Maryland, 1974), pp. 48, 106–10, 155, 172–74. According to Fielding, the Union armies were generally more interested in sports than the Confederates.

31. Ibid., pp. 106, 306, 313, 321, 345, 346, 366, 385, 392, 397, 411, 414, 487, 491.

32. Augustus Buell, *The Cannoneer* (Washington, D.C., 1890), pp. 54–55. See also Alexander Hunter, *Johnny Reb and Billy Yank* (New York, 1905), p. 98. The 1873 edition of *American Fistiana* stressed the pugnacity of the Irish soldiers. Frank Wilkeson recalled that the battery next to his was manned by Irishmen who "indulged in a fist fight almost nightly." They eventually persuaded some of Wilkeson's comrades to participate in their melees. *Recollections of a Private Soldier* (New York, 1887), p. 24.

33. Buell, pp. 54–55, 274–77.

34. *American Fistiana* (1873), pp. 100–101.

35. Fielding, pp. 329, 462, 308; Alfred Davenport, *Camp and Field Life of the Fifth New York Volunteer Infantry* (New York, 1879), p. 103, quoted in Fielding, p. 308; Edmund Randolph Brown, *The Twenty Seventh Indiana Volunteer Infantry in the War of the Rebellion, 1861–1865* (Monticello, In., 1899), p. 87, quoted in Fielding, p. 305.

36. A point well made by Fielding, pp. xi–xii.

37. J. H. Worsham, *Foot Cavalry,* cited in Fielding, pp. 199–200, 202–3, 487.

38. Note by Private George E. Smith, quoted in Fielding, p. 441. See also Alan T. Nolan, *The Iron Brigade* (Madison, Wisc., 1975), pp. 184–85; Fielding, pp. 202–3.

39. Johan Huizinga, *Homo Ludens: The Play Element in Culture* (Boston, 1950), esp. chap. 1.

40. *American Fistiana* (1873), pp. 101, 103, 104. *Fistiana*, p. 103, reported a

highly "artistic" fight in which Joe Coburn and Bill Clark put on the gloves and fought for half an hour, each clean hit ending a round, until Coburn won eleven hits to ten. Ed James, sports editor of the *Clipper*, refereed this bout on January 28, 1863.

41. For examples see *American Fistiana* (1873), pp. 117, 119–21, 123–24. On male frontier life see Elliott West, *The Saloon on the Rocky Mountain Mining Frontier* (Lincoln, Neb., 1979).

42. *American Fistiana* (1873), pp. 96, 117–18, 124; West, pp. 85–87. In 1851, five hundred patrons paid $2.50 each to watch Matthew Tracy and Bill Blackwood pummel each other at Storm's Ranch, California. Four years later, twenty-five hundred spectators, including "a number of gayly dressed females," spent five dollars apiece and saw Con Orem battle Patsy Marley at Last Chance Flat, Montana Territory. Also see Robert K. DeArment, *Bat Masterson, The Man and the Legend*, (Norman, Okla., 1979), pp. 72, 218–19, 339–43; Fleischer, Andre, and Loubet, *Pictorial History*, p. 79.

43. *New York Sunday Mercury*, May 10, 1863; accounts taken from the *Sporting Life*, the *Sportsman*, and the *Illustrated Sporting News*, cited in *Famous Fights in the Prize Ring* (London, n.d. [ca. 1870s]), pp. 173–75.

44. In addition to the sources in note 43 see William Edgar Harding, *Champions of the American Prize Ring* (New York, 1880), pp. 39–44; Harding, *Prize Ring Heroes* (New York, 1889), pp. 78–80; James, *Life of Heenan*, pp. 18–19; Mott, *American Journalism*, p. 382; and Dizikes, p. 225. As was common, some enterprising rogues published a bogus extra edition of *Wilkes' Spirit of the Times* with an early but false report of the Heenan-King fight. See *American Gentleman's Newspaper*, December 26, 1863.

45. *New York Times*, May 6, 1863. See also the *New York Sunday Mercury*, May 3 and 10, 1863; *Wilkes' Spirit of the Times*, May 16 and 23, 1863; *New York Illustrated News*, May 16, 1863; *American Fistiana* (1873), pp. 106–8; and *New York Herald*, May 6, 1863.

46. See references in note 45. On rough and tumble fighting on the Southern frontier see Elliott J. Gorn, " 'Gouge and Bite, Pull Hair and Scratch': The Social Significance of Fighting in the Southern Backcountry," *American Historical Review* 90 (February 1985): 18–43.

47. *New York Clipper*, quoted in *American Fistiana* (1873), p. 106; see also *New York Herald*, May 6, 1863.

48. See references in note 45. Coburn's colors were emerald green, McCoole's green-and-white check with a red, white, and blue border.

49. *New York Sunday Mercury*, May 3, 1865.

50. *American Fistiana* (1873), pp. 128, 136; E. B. Mitchell, *Fencing, Boxing and Wrestling* (London, 1893), pp. 143–44; *Boston Theatrical News*, June 4, 1870, *Sporting Times and Theatrical News*, May 21 and 28, 1870, all in Magriel ms.; and *New York Clipper*, quoted in *American Fistiana* (1873), pp. 145–47.

51. Categories (heavyweight, lightweight, etc.) were used intermittently and without precision during the bare-knuckle era. Chandler weighed 136 pounds, Harris 137. Nat Fleischer regards this as the first middleweight championship bout, in *Ring Record Book* (New York, 1968), p. 17. The quotation is from the coverage in

American Fistiana (1873), pp. 128–31. Also see "The Dooney Song," published by T. C. Boyd (San Francisco, n.d.), from the collection of Daniel W. Patterson, University of North Carolina, Chapel Hill; *American Fistiana* (1873), pp. 103, 116–17, 134, 136, 144; Herbert Asbury, *Gangs of New York* (New York, 1928), pp. 184–85; *Wilkes' Spirit of the Times,* November 14, 1863, in Magriel ms.

52. Huizinga's central thesis in *Homo Ludens* is that agonistic play is the font of culture.

53. *American Fistiana* (1873), pp. 98, 101, 108–10. *American Fistiana* refers to the "increased vigilance of the myrmidons of the law" during the 1860s, p. 101. Also see *Wilkes' Spirit of the Times,* May 23, 1863. Fight crowds occasionally roughed up the local officials.

54. On the changing nature of politics see Peter George Buckley, "To The Opera House: Culture and Society, 1820–1860" (diss., State University of New York at Stony Brook, 1984), pp. 408–9; Adelman, pp. 573–74; and especially Amy Bridges, *A City in the Republic* (Cambridge, Mass., 1984), chaps. 7, 8.

55. *American Fistiana* (1873), pp. 123, 136–37, 144, 150. See also *American Gentleman's Newspaper,* October 24, 1863; *Wilkes' Spirit of the Times,* December 23, 1865, and February 15, 1868.

56. For an excellent reinterpretation of Gilded Age culture, see Alan Trachtenberg, *The Incorporation of America: Culture and Society in the Gilded Age* (New York, 1982).

57. *New York Clipper,* quoted in *American Fistiana* (1873), pp. 70–71.

58. *American Fistiana* (1873), p. 151. On labor in this era see, for examples, Trachtenberg, chap. 3; Daniel T. Rodgers, *The Work Ethic in Industrial America, 1850–1920* (Chicago, 1978), chaps. 2 and 6; Melvin Dubofsky, *Industrialism and the American Worker, 1865–1920* (New York, 1973); David Montgomery, *Workers' Control in America: Studies in the History of Work, Technology and Labor Struggles* (Cambridge, 1979); and Herbert G. Gutman, *Work, Culture and Society in Industrializing America* (New York, 1972).

59. *American Fistiana* (1873), pp. 103–4, 120, 129, 142–43; *Wilkes' Spirit of the Times,* May 23, 1863; and *New York Clipper,* June 10, 1871. Henry L. Ferguson, *Fisher's Island, New York, 1614–1925* (New York, 1925), contains a fine description from the point of view of a local community invaded by a fight crowd. Fay Fox, daughter of Robert Fox who owned Fisher's Island, left a vivid recollection of a bout on the sleepy island: "Have I mentioned this episode of my early days, a prize fight? There were two but the first one was the important one. A farm hand came rushing around to the front piazza to tell my father that two or three hundred men were being landed from two big schooners near North Hill. Father ordered his horse and, followed by every man on the premises, set out to investigate matters. The big field just below the Twin Hills was the scene of action. All the women and children, too frightened to be left behind, followed on and from the Twin Hills we looked down upon a scene, one which I have never forgotten. Sentinels were on the watch for an approaching steamer with officers of the law, and the affair was not one of pure enjoyment for fear of liability to arrest." Ferguson concluded that the ground the fight took place on was still known as the "battlefield" during the 1920s. My thanks to Willie MacMullen for this reference.

60. *St. Louis Democrat,* May 11, 1870, quoted in *Sporting Times and Theatrical News,* Boston, May 28, 1870, in Magriel ms.

61. *American Fistiana* (1873), pp. 148–51. The estimates of profit and loss come from the *New York Clipper,* December 16, 1871, in a letter signed "Justice" and dated December 11, 1871. Also see *Clipper,* January 28 and May 20, 1871; Alexander Johnston, *Ten and Out* (New York, 1927), pp. 45–57. Sources estimate that each party took home $800.

62. *American Fistiana* (1873), pp. 102, 119, 148; Harding, *Champions of the Prize Ring,* pp. 25, 31–32; Johnston, p. 49; and Michael T. Isenberg, "John L. Sullivan and His America," manuscript draft (Annapolis, 1985), chap. 5, pp. 14–15.

63. *American Fistiana* (1973), pp. 99, 110–11, 115, 132, 140, 152–55. Also see *Wilkes' Spirit of the Times,* August 21, 1869; Johnston, p. 50.

64. *The American Gentleman's Newspaper,* October 24, 1863; *American Fistiana* (1873), pp. 112, 121–22, 140–42; Johnston, pp. 45–49; Wells Drury, *An Editor of the Comstock Lode* (New York, 1936), pp. 88–89; A. K. McClure, *Three Thousand Miles through the Rockies* (Philadelphia, 1869), pp. 422–25; "The Pacific City Fight," *The Palimpsest* 2 (June 1921): 182–89; and Nathaniel Fleischer, *The Flaming Ben Hogan* (New York, 1941).

65. *American Fistiana* (1873), pp. 119, 121–22; *Wilkes' Spirit of the Times,* January, 1868; and *Wilkes' Spirit of the Times,* October 10, 31, 1868.

66. *New York Clipper,* December 4, 1869; *American Fistiana* (1873), pp. 153–55.

67. For examples of the literature on crime among the "dangerous classes," see Charles Loring Brace, *The Dangerous Classes of New York* (New York, 1872); New York State, *Report of the Select Committee Appointed by the Assembly of 1875 to Investigate the Causes of the Increase of Crime in the City of New York* (New York, 1876), pp. 8–10, 12–24, 37–38, 85–89; Herbert Asbury, *The Gangs of New York* (New York, 1928); Arthur Pember, *The Mysteries and Miseries of the Great Metropolis* (New York, 1874), pp. 2–12; and Peter Stryker, *The Lower Depths of the Great Metropolis* (New York, 1866). On the rise of weapons see Roger Lane, *Violent Death in the City* (Cambridge, Mass., 1979), pp. 59–63. Lane argues that per capita violent crime rates probably dropped in this era.

68. Harding, *Champions of the Prize Ring.* See Paul Magriel, *Bibliography of Boxing: A Chronological Checklist of Books in English Published before 1900* (New York, 1948), pp. 20–25, for several titles under Harding's and Price's names, as well as others probably written by one of them but published anonymously. All of these biographies have the same reverential tone as *Champions of the Prize Ring.* Harding described Hyer, for example, as a "generous, whole souled man and a 'thorough American,' " pp. 7–8.

Chapter 6. "Fight Like a Gentleman, You Son of a Bitch, If You Can"

1. Rising interest in athletics was far from purely American. In England and France sports received great attention from upper- and middle-class men in colleges, prep schools, and athletic clubs. Though I concentrate here on developments in the

United States, therefore, the growth of sporting interest should be seen as a trans-Atlantic phenomenon. The literature on the Gilded Age is immense, but I have found Alan Trachtenberg's *The Incorporation of America: Culture and Society in the Gilded Age* (New York, 1982) particularly useful. This chapter's title is from a quotation attributed to John L. Sullivan after Charlie Mitchell spiked him during their 1887 fight on the estate of the baron de Rothschild.

2. On the historiography of the play movement see Stephen Hardy and Alan G. Ingham, "Games, Structures and Agencies: Historians on the American Play Movement," *Journal of Social History* 17 (Winter 1983): 285–301. As Donald J. Mrozek observes, physical educators and doctors interested in sports shared an emphasis on scientific methods, efficiency, management of the body, and rational expertise—all pregnant values during this era. Mrozek, *Sport and American Mentality, 1880–1910* (Knoxville, 1983), pp. 67–68.

3. Gunther Barth, *City People: The Rise of Modern City Culture in Nineteenth-Century America* (New York, 1980), pp. 195–96; T. DeWitt Talmage, *Sports That Kill* (New York, 1875), pp. 20–22, 46–47; Talmage, *Abominations of Modern Society* (New York, 1872), pp. 154–85; R. Hogan, "Sin and Sports," in Ralph Slovenko and James A. Knight, eds., *Motivation in Play, Games and Sports* (Springfield, Ill., 1967), pp. 125–26; Roy Rosenzweig, *Eight Hours for What We Will: Workers and Leisure in an Industrial City* (Cambridge, Mass., 1983), pt. 3; Joseph F. Kett, *Rites of Passage: Adolescence in America, 1790 to the Present* (New York, 1977), pp. 189–208; Benjamin Rader, *American Sports: From Folk Games to the Age of Spectators* (Englewood Cliffs, N.J., 1983), pp. 146–69; Gerald Franklin Roberts, "The Strenuous Life: The Cult of Manliness in the Era of Theodore Roosevelt" (diss., Michigan State University, 1970), chap. 3; Mrozek, pp. 203–10; Guy Lewis, "The Muscular Christianity Movement," *Journal of Health, Physical Education and Recreation* 5 (May 1966): 27–42; Richard A. Swanson, "The Acceptance and Influence of Play in American Protestantism," *Quest* 11 (1968): 58–70; Stephen Hall Hardy, *How Boston Played: Sport, Recreation and Community, 1865–1915* (Boston, 1982), chaps. 3 and 4; and Daniel T. Rodgers, *The Work Ethic in Industrial America, 1850–1920* (Chicago, 1978), chap. 4.

4. The development of sports in this era is well summarized in Rader, *American Sports*, pt. 2, and John Rickard Betts, *America's Sporting Heritage, 1850–1950* (Reading, Mass., 1974), chaps. 4–8. On the erratic but still rising average income between 1860 and 1880 see *Historical Statistics of the United States, Colonial Times to 1970*, 2 vols. (Washington, D.C., 1975), 1: 165. Also see John Modell, "Patterns of Consumption, Acculturation and Family Income Strategies in Late Nineteenth-Century America," in Tamara Hareven, ed., *Family and Population in Nineteenth-Century America* (Princeton, 1978), and Joseph S. Zeisel, "The Workweek in American Industry, 1850–1956," in Eric Larrabee and Rolf Myersohn, eds., *Mass Leisure* (Glencoe, Ill., 1958), pp. 145–53. Also see Herbert G. Gutman, "Work Culture and Society in Industrializing America, 1815–1919," *American Historical Review* 78 (June 1973): 531–87.

5. Among the clearest statements of sports as a manifestation of modernization are Melvin Adelman, "The Development of Modern Athletics: Sports in New York City, 1820–1870" (diss., University of Illinois, 1980); Allen Guttmann, *From Ritual to*

Record: The Nature of Modern Sports (New York, 1978); and Alan Geoffrey Ingham, "American Sport in Transition: The Maturation of Industrial Capitalism and its Impact on Sport" (diss., University of Massachusetts, 1978). For sport and business, see especially Peter Levine, *A. G. Spalding and the Rise of Baseball: The Promise of American Sport* (New York, 1985), chap. 5. For a case study of one prominent turn-of-the-century sport, see Richard Hammond, "Progress and Flight: An Interpretation of the American Cycle Craze of the 1890s," *Journal of Social History* 5 (Winter 1971): 235–57.

6. On the rise of commercialized leisure see, for examples, Trachtenberg, pp. 122–39; Barth, chap. 5; Lewis A. Erenberg, *Steppin' Out: New York Nightlife and the Transformation of American Culture, 1890–1930* (Westport, Conn., 1981); Robert Toll, *On with the Show: The First Century of Show Business in America* (New York, 1976); Francis G. Couvares, "The Triumph of Commerce: Class Culture and Mass Culture in Pittsburgh," in Michael H. Frisch and Daniel J. Walkowitz, eds., *Working-Class America: Essays on Labor, Community and American Society* (Urbana, Ill., 1983), pp. 123–52; Rosenzweig, chaps. 7 and 8; Perry Duis, *The Saloon: Public Drinking in Chicago and Boston, 1880–1920* (Urbana, Ill., 1983); Jon M. Kingsdale, "The 'Poor Man's Club': Social Functions of the Urban Working-Class Saloon," *American Quarterly* 25 (October 1973): 472–89; Lary May, *Screening Out the Past: The Birth of Mass Culture and the Motion Picture Industry* (Chicago, 1980), chaps. 1 and 2; and especially John F. Kasson's outstanding *Amusing the Million: Coney Island at the Turn of the Century* (New York, 1978).

7. The history of Fox and the *Police Gazette* awaits scholarly treatment, but see Betts, *America's Sporting Heritage,* pp. 61–63; Betts, "Sporting Journalism in Nineteenth Century America," *American Quarterly* 5 (Spring 1953): 39–56; Gene Smith and Jayne Barry Smith, eds., *The Police Gazette* (New York, 1972) pp. 14–18; Edward Van Every, *The Sins of New York as Exposed by the Police Gazette* (New York, 1930); Van Every, *The Sins of America as Exposed by the Police Gazette* (New York, 1931); and Barth, pp. 83–109.

8. These themes are treated with special perceptiveness in Warren I. Susman, *Culture as History: The Transformation of American Society in the Twentieth Century* (New York, 1984), esp. chaps. 8–11, 14. Also see Zeisel, pp. 145–53; Modell, "Patterns of Consumption"; T. J. Jackson Lears, *No Place of Grace: Antimodernism and the Transformation of American Culture, 1880–1920* (New York, 1981), esp. chaps. 1, 3; and D. H. Mayer, "American Intellectuals and the Victorian Crisis of Faith," *American Quarterly* 27 (December 1975): 585–603.

9. Erenberg, *Steppin' Out,* is the authority here. See esp. chaps. 1, 3, pp. 233–38.

10. Ibid.; Herbert Asbury, *The Gangs of New York* (New York, 1928), pp. 244, 261, 273, 276; Normal R. Clark, *Deliver Us from Evil: An Interpretation of American Prohibition* (New York, 1976), chap. 4; and Trachtenberg, chap. 4.

11. In addition to the sources in note 10 see Michael Isenberg, "John L. Sullivan and His America," manuscript draft (Annapolis, 1985), prologue, pp. 11–13. For contemporary accounts of Harry Hill's and similar establishments, see Edward Crapsey, *The Nether Side of New York; or, The Vice, Crime and Poverty of the Great Metropolis* (New York, 1872), pp. 161–62; James D. McCabe, *Lights and Shadows*

of New York Life (Philadelphia, 1879), pp. 600–604; anon., *The Snares of New York* (New York, 1879), p. 179; Mathew Hale Smith, *Wonders of a Great City; or, the Sights, Secrets and Sins of New York* (Chicago, 1887), chaps. 2, 17; Samuel A. Mackeever, *Glimpses of Gotham, and City Characters* (New York, 1887), pp. 59–60; John H. Warren, Jr., *Thirty Years Battle with Crime* (Poughkeepsie, N.Y., 1874), chaps. 14–16.

12. Van Every, *Sins of New York,* pp. 199–219; Isenberg, prologue, pp. 11–13; Barth, chap. 6; Toll, chaps. 7, 8, 10; Erenberg, chaps. 1, 3.

13. On the play movement see references in note 3 and especially Hardy and Ingham, pp. 285–301.

14. Kett, pp. 173–81; Rader, *American Sports,* pp. 70–86; Guy Lewis, "The Beginning of Organized Collegiate Sport," *American Quarterly* 22 (Summer 1970): 229–29; Betts, *America's Sporting Heritage,* pp. 209–23; John A. Lucas and Ronald A. Smith, *The Saga of American Sport* (Philadelphia, 1975), chaps. 12–15; Christopher Lasch, "The Corruption of Sport," *New York Review of Books* 24 (April 28, 1977), reprinted in his *The Culture of Narcissism* (New York, 1979), pp. 181–219; Lasch, "The Moral and Intellectual Rehabilitation of the Ruling Class," in *The World of Nations: Reflections on American History, Politics and Culture* (New York, 1974), chap. 7; and Christian Karl Messenger, *Sport and the Spirit of Play in American Fiction: Hawthorne to Faulkner* (New York, 1981), chaps. 6–8.

15. Rader, *American Sports,* pp. 50–68; Benjamin Rader, "The Quest for Subcommunities and the Rise of American Sports," *American Quarterly* 29 (Fall 1977): 364–66; Betts, *America's Sporting Heritage,* chap. 6; Lucas and Smith, chap. 10; Hardy, chap. 7; Mrozek, pp. 118–29; Joe Willis and Richard Wettan, "Social Stratification in New York City Athletic Clubs, 1865–1915," *Journal of Sport History* 3 (Spring 1976): 45–63.

16. Mrozek is particularly good on sports and upper-class regeneration, pp. 19–27. His discussion of the rise of a male aesthetic among elites (chap. 7) is also quite fine. On the development of a "masculine primitive" ethic see Edward Anthony Rotundo, "Manhood in America: The Northern Middle Class, 1770–1920" (diss., Brandeis University, 1982), chaps. 7 and 9.

17. In addition to the citations in note 16 see Lears, pp. 47–58; Stow Persons, *The Decline of American Gentility* (New York, 1973), pp. 274–75, 285–87; Kett, pp. 162–73; Elizabeth H. and Joseph H. Pleck, eds., *The American Man* (Englewood Cliffs, N.J., 1980), pp. 24–25; Edward Anthony Rotundo, "Body and Soul: Changing Ideals of American Middle-Class Manhood, 1770–1920," *Journal of Social History* 16 (Summer 1983): 28–33; and Franklin Henry Giddings, *Democracy and Empire* (New York, 1901), pp. 317–18.

18. The classic statement of these phenomena is John Higham, "The Reorientation of American Culture in the 1890s," in John Weiss, ed., *The Origins of Modern Consciousness* (Detroit, 1965), pp. 25–48. Higham dates this shift too precisely—it began before the Civil War and accelerated toward the end of the century. Moreover, though he purports to write about *American* culture, his examples come mostly from the upper and middle classes. Nevertheless, it is a seminal essay. Also see Roberts, chap. 4. On Sandow see Toll, pp. 297–99; Mrozek, pp. 220–24.

19. Lasch, "Rehabilitation of the Ruling Class," pp. 83–87. George M. Fredrickson,

The Inner Civil War: Northern Intellectuals and the Crisis of the Union (New York, 1965), pp. 217–25; Dudley A. Sargent, *Outing* 5 (February 1885): 379. Sargent's diary, incidentally, reveals a rather strenuous daily regimen. My thanks to John Kneebone for excerpts culled from the Harvard Archives.

20. James Turner, *Without God, Without Creed: The Origins of Unbelief in America* (Baltimore, 1985); Meyer, pp. 585–603; John Cawelti, *Apostles of the Self Made Man* (Chicago, 1965), p. 5; Adelman, pp. 679–94; Karen Halttunen, *Confidence Men and Painted Women: A Study of Middle-Class Culture in America, 1830–1870* (New Haven, 1982), pp. 201–10. Also see Norbert Elias and Eric Dunning, "The Quest for Excitement in Unexciting Societies," in Gunther Luschen, ed., *The Cross-Cultural Analysis of Sports and Games* (Champaign-Urbana, Ill., 1970), pp. 31–51. Lodge, speaking before a Harvard alumni dinner in June 1896, is quoted in Mrozek, p. 28.

21. See David Brion Davis, "Stress Seeking and the Self-Made Man in American Literature: 1894–1914," in Samuel Klausner, ed., *Why Man Takes Chances* (Garden City, N.Y., 1968), pp. 108–13. Roderick Nash argues that the "discovery" of the wilderness as a font of national virtue occurred at the end of the nineteenth century because primitivism seemed an antidote to civilization. "Natural" life, like virile athletic activity, was a counter to the softness of commercialism. See Nash, "The American Cult of the Primitive," *American Quarterly* 18 (Fall 1966): 517–37.

22. On social Darwinism see Richard Hofstadter, *Social Darwinism in American Thought, 1860–1915* (Philadelphia, 1944); Fredrickson, pp. 192–94, 213–25; Lasch, "Rehabilitation of the Ruling Class," pp. 80–99; Mrozek, chaps. 2 and 7; Lears, chap. 1; Trachtenberg, chap. 3.

23. In addition to the references in note 22 see especially Mrozek, pp. 28–53. On Anglo-Saxon racism see John Higham, *Strangers in the Land: Patterns of American Nativism, 1860–1925* (New York, 1970), chaps. 6 and 7.

24. Lears, pp. 107–17. Lears' analysis builds on Lasch's "Rehabilitation of the Ruling Class," pp. 84–87. Sports, as Lears points out, were part of a larger martial ideal that beguiled many upper-class men.

25. Francis A. Walker, "College Athletics," *Technological Quarterly* 6 (July 1983): 1–16. On purposeful play see esp. Rosenzweig, pp. 140–52.

26. Oliver Wendell Holmes, Jr., "The Soldiers Faith," in Max Lerner, ed., *The Mind and Faith of Justice Holmes* (Boston, 1943), pp. 18–21.

27. Halttunen, pp. 201–10; Rotundo, "Manhood in America," chap. 4; and Susman, *Culture as History,* Intro. Jeffrey P. Hantover identifies this transformation of work as the key element in the rise of Boy Scouts of America. See his "The Boy Scouts and the Validation of Masculinity," in Pleck and Pleck, pp. 285–310. For an interesting discussion on the rise of the new middle class, see Stuart M. Blumin, "The Hypothesis of Middle-Class Formation in Nineteenth Century America: A Critique and Some Proposals," *American Historical Review* 90 (April 1985): 299–338. Also see Peter N. Stearns, *Be a Man: Males in Modern Society* (New York, 1979), pp. 96–112; Peter Gabriel Filene, *Him/Her/Self: Sex Roles in Modern America* (New York, 1975), pp. 68–76. Filene points out that the number of salaried white-collar workers multiplied eight times between 1870 and 1910, jumping from one-third to two-thirds of the entire middle class. Many of these new jobs were filled by women.

28. Pleck and Pleck, pp. 14–28; Stearns, pp. 75–78, 96–112; Rotundo, "Body and Soul," pp. 28–33; Rotundo, "Manhood in America," chaps. 4–6; Filene, chaps. 1–3; Joe L. Dubbert, *A Man's Place: Masculinity in Transition* (Englewood Cliffs, N.J., 1979), chaps. 2–6; Roberts, "The Strenuous Life," chap. 4; Rupert Wilkinson, *American Tough: The Tough-Guy Tradition and American Character* (Westport, Conn., 1984); and David G. Pugh, *Sons of Liberty: The Masculine Mind in Nineteenth Century America* (Westport, Conn., 1983). See Peter Gay on the subtleties of male fears of female power: *The Bourgeois Experience, Victoria to Freud*, vol. 1: *The Education of the Senses* (New York, 1984), pp. 179–82, 188–213. The masculine crisis is nicely summarized in Patrick Miller, "The Manly Ideal and National Character in late Nineteenth Century America" (paper presented at the tenth American Studies convention, San Diego, Calif., November 3, 1985).

29. All of the works mentioned in note 28 discuss these fears of feminization. Also see Henry James, *The Bostonians* (Harmondsworth, 1976), p. 290, and Ernest Thompson Seton, quoted in Pleck and Pleck, p. 25. On medical views of women see Carol Smith-Rosenberg and Charles Rosenberg, "The Female Animal: Medical and Biological Views of Woman and Her Role in Nineteenth Century America," *Journal of American History* 60 (September 1973): 332–56.

30. See references in note 28 for male fears of "new women." Ironically, just as bourgeois males discovered the joys of savagery, Irish working-class men were being urged by Catholic religious and lay leaders to acquire the classic Victorian virtues. In novels, sermons, and tracts manliness was redefined as being a good provider, a stable worker, and a devout churchgoer. "Real men" attended mass and shunned drunkenness. See Colleen McDannel, "Catholicism and the Irish Male: Gender and Ethnicity in Late Nineteenth-Century America" (paper read at the tenth American Studies Association meetings, San Diego, Calif., November 3, 1985).

31. Pleck and Pleck, Introduction, pp. 21–28; Filene, pp. 86–94; Rotundo, "Body and Soul," pp. 37–38; Rotundo, "Manhood in America," chap. 8; Stearns, pp. 110–12; Hantover, pp. 285–301; Kett, p. 173; Dubbert, chaps. 2–6; Miller, "Manly Ideal."

32. Although disgusted by professional prize fighting, Thomas Wentworth Higginson praised sparring as fine exercise and cited the example of a New York clergyman who saved himself by administering a "timely cross-counter and flying crook" to an assailant. Higginson, "Saints and Their Bodies," *Atlantic Monthly* 1 (March 1858): 592.

33. Oliver Wendell Holmes, Sr., "Autocrat of the Breakfast Table," *Atlantic Monthly* 1 (May 1858): 881.

34. Ibid. A few young men, including Francis Parkman, sparred at Harvard in the antebellum years. Isenberg, chap. 3, p. 25.

35. Theodore Roosevelt, "Professionalism in Sports," *North American Review* 15 (August 1890): 187. Also see Isenberg, chap. 3, pp. 25–26.

36. On the era of Jack Johnson see Randy Roberts, *Papa Jack: Jack Johnson and the Era of White Hopes* (New York, 1983); Al-Tony Gilmore, *Bad Nigger: The National Impact of Jack Johnson* (Port Washington, N.Y., 1975).

37. Roosevelt, p. 191.

38. Wayne Andrews, ed., *The Autobiography of Theodore Roosevelt*, condensed

ed., (New York, 1958), pp. 30–31. Also see Theodore Roosevelt, *Letters,* ed. Elting
E. Morrison, 8 vols. (Cambridge, Mass., 1951–54), 6: 1103; 8: 962; Michael
Donovan, *The Roosevelt That I Know* (New York, 1909), chap. 1. On the young
Roosevelt see David McCullough, *Mornings on Horseback* (New York, 1981), and
Edmund Morris, *The Rise of Theodore Roosevelt* (New York, 1979).

39. Pennsylvania, for example, saw renewed efforts against sparring and prize
fighting, testimony to pugilism's growing popularity. See J. Thomas Jable, "Aspects
of Moral Reform in Early Nineteenth Century Pennsylvania," *Pennsylvania Maga-*
zine of History and Biography 102 (July 1978): 191.

40. Famous names come up often in Isenberg's descriptions of Sullivan's fights.
Also see Donald Barr Chidsey, *John the Great* (New York, 1942), p. 78; anon., *The*
Modern Gladiator (St. Louis, 1892), p. 383.

41. G. Stanley Hall, *Life and Confessions of a Psychologist* (New York, 1923),
pp. 578–79.

42. See Messenger, p. 95, chaps. 5, 6, 10; Elizabeth Johns, *Thomas Eakins: The*
Heroism of Modern Life (Princeton, 1983), pp. 43, 47; and Carl S. Smith, "The
Boxing Paintings of Thomas Eakins," *Prospects* 4 (1979), pp. 403–20. Paintings by
Eakins embodied the new masculine aesthetic of the upper and middle classes. The
romantic versus the realistic dichotomy is an enduring one, finding recent expression
in such popular motion pictures as *Rocky* and *Raging Bull.* On the estrangement of
intellectuals from bourgeois culture, see Christopher Lasch, *The New Radicalism in*
America, 1889–1963 (New York, 1967).

43. On Victorian didacticism see, in addition to the sources mentioned in note 42,
Howe, "American Victorianism as a Culture," pp. 507–32, and Walter Edwards
Houghton, *The Victorian Frame of Mind, 1830–1870* (New Haven, 1957). Smith
notes that Eakins and other American students in Paris in the late 1860s were familiar
with boxing for exercise and for settling quarrels, pp. 405–6.

44. John Lawrence Sullivan, *Life and Reminiscences of a Nineteenth Century*
Gladiator (Boston, 1892), p. 273. For a parody of this work, see John L.
Sluggervan, *De Recommbrances of a 19-Cent Scrapper* (New York, 1892). Also see
Betts, *Sporting Heritage,* p. 165; *Frank Leslie's Magazine,* March 31, 1883, p. 86,
November 29, 1884, p. 227, quoted in Frederick L. Paxon, "The Rise of Sport,"
Mississippi Valley Historical Review 4 (September 1917): 150; Isenberg, chap. 3, pp.
23–27; and Rader, *American Sports,* p. 56. Rotundo, "Manhood in America," pp.
309–10, reports an increased number of street fights among young gentlemen.
Magriel's and Lottinville's bibliographies document a large number of new boxing
lesson manuals in these years.

45. Michael Donovan, *The Science of Boxing* (New York, 1893), pp. 19–21;
Donovan, *Roosevelt I Know,* p. 146; James E. Sullivan, *Life and Battles of James J.*
Corbett (New York, 1892), p. 13; and *Bacon's Dictionary of Boston,* 1886, in
Magriel ms. (a collection of newspaper reports on bare-knuckle fights).

46. Reverend Brobst's sermon is quoted in anon., *The Modern Gladiator* (St
Louis, 1892), pp. 191–93.

47. G. Stanley Hall, *Youth: Its Education, Regimen and Hygiene* (New York,
1911), pp. 93–95.

48. Daniel L. Dawson, "With the Gloves," *Lippincott's Monthly Magazine* 49

(January 1892): 97–100; A. Austin, "Theory and Practice of Boxing," *Outing* 15 (March 1890): 412, 419.

49. Charles E. Clay, "A Bout with the Gloves," *Outing* 9 (January 1887): 359–60. This is the first part of Clay's series; see also parts 2 and 3 in 9 (February 1887): 469–77, and 10 (April 1887): 26–31.

50. Duffield Osborn, "A Defense of Pugilism," *North American Review* 46 (April 1888): 434–35.

51. John Boyle O'Reilly, *The Ethics of Boxing and Manly Sports* (Boston, 1888), chaps. 13, 15; *The Science of Self-Defense* (Philadelphia, 1900), intro. Professor E. D. Cope agreed that the ring must be taken back from the "vicious classes" and reformed for the educated elite. Cope believed that anti-prize fight legislation contributed to effeminization and sentimental delicacy among men. See "The Effeminisation of Man," *Open Court* 7 (October 26, 1893): 38–47. Boxing's rise to semirespectability was affirmed by Eadweard Muybridge's photographing pugilists as part of his 1887 university-sponsored scientific motion studies. See *Muybridge's Complete Human and Animal Locomotion*, 4 vols. (New York, 1979), 2: 682–709.

52. See especially Cope, "Effeminisation of Man," p. 3847.

53. Maurice Golesworthy, comp., *Encyclopedia of Boxing* (London, 1975), pp. 194–95; Isenberg, chap. 3, pp. 27–28.

54. O'Reilly, *Ethics of Boxing* pp. 5–6, made the argument for reduced violence under the Queensberry rules, and it has been repeated ever since. Certainly comparing accounts of fights under the old London Prize Ring rules and the new Queensberry rules does not reveal any lessening of the brutality. The quotation about the Dixon-Skelly fight is from the *New Orleans Weekly Times Democrat*, Sept. 7, 1892.

55. Dr. Allan J. Ryan recently argued that "removing the gloves would make boxing a sport of jabs and defense and it would deemphasize the knockout punches. It is a change that would save lives and preserve the sport." Ryan goes on to say that today's ten-ounce glove, soaked with perspiration by the late rounds of a fight, makes the fist into a club. See his editorial in *Physician and Sportsmedicine* 11 (December 1983): 49. The medical literature on Boxing injuries is voluminous, but one conclusion is clear: the more punches to the head a man takes over his career, the greater is the likelihood of severe brain damage, though it may not manifest itself until years after he retires. See, for examples, R. J. Ross, M. Cole, and J. S. Thompson et al., "Boxers—Computed Tomography, EEG, and Neurological Evaluation," and Council on Scientific Affairs Report, "Brain Injury in Boxing," both in *Journal of the American Medical Association* 249 (January 14, 1983): 211–13, 254–57; MacDonald Critchley, "Medical Aspects of Boxing, Particularly from a Neurological Standpoint," *British Medical Journal*, February 16, 1957, pp. 357–66; F. J. Unterharnscheidt, "Head Injuries after Boxing," *Scandinavian Journal of Rehabilitation Medicine* 4 (1972): 77–84; J. A. N. Corsellis, C. J. Bruton, and Dorothy Freeman-Browne, "The Aftermath of Boxing," *Psychological Medicine* 3 (1973): 270–303; and Robert J. McCunney and Pearl K. Russo, "Brain Injuries in Boxers," *Physician and Sportsmedicine* 12 (May 1984): 53–64. My thanks to Dr. Tom Virgets for these references. On the general topic of violence in sports see Jeffrey H. Goldstein, ed., *Sports Violence* (New York, 1983).

56. Golesworthy, pp. 194–95; Clay, p. 30; Dawson, "With the Gloves," p. 101.

Dawson argued that the chief advantage of the Queensberry rules was to shorten bouts, putting a premium on offensive skills rather than endurance.

Chapter 7. The End of the Bare-Knuckle Era

1. John Boyle O'Reilly, *The Ethics of Boxing and Manly Sports* (Boston, 1888), pp. 75, 79. Sargent's evaluation was also published as an appendix to Sullivan's autobiography, *The Life and Reminiscences of a 19th Century Gladiator* (Boston, 1892).

2. Unspecified newspaper quoted in Sullivan, *Life and Reminiscences*, p. 14. The autobiography appears to have been ghostwritten with Sullivan's aid. Despite enormous gaps and factual errors, it contains valuable details on important events, especially Sullivan's tours. Sullivan has been the subject of several popular biographies, often highly imaginative and unreliable. In addition to Donald Barr Chidsey, *John the Great* (New York, 1942), see R. F. Dibble, *John L. Sullivan: An Intimate Narrative* (Boston, 1925); Nathaniel Fleischer, *The Boston Strong Boy: The Story of John L. Sullivan, the Champion of Champions* (New York, 1941); and Fleischer, *John L. Sullivan: Champion of Champions* (New York, 1951). See also the chapters on Sullivan in Bohun Lynch, *Knuckles and Gloves* (London, 1922), and Louis Golding, *The Bare-Knuckle Breed* (New York, 1954).

3. Michael T. Isenberg, "John L. Sullivan and His America," draft manuscript (Annapolis, 1985), chap. 1; Sullivan, *Life and Reminiscences*, pp. 21–22. For Sullivan's early life, see also anon., *Famous Irish Fighters in the Ring* (London [ca. 1892]), pp. 1–3.

4. Sullivan, *Life and Reminiscences*, pp. 23–25. Sullivan claimed he attended Boston College for sixteen months, where he studied for the priesthood. The story is almost certainly fictitious. Michael T. Isenberg, whose excellent biography of Sullivan is forthcoming, informs me that a thorough check of college records reveals no trace of John L. Isenberg estimates that Sullivan had roughly the equivalent of an eighth- or ninth-grade education.

5. Ibid. On the social and economic limitations placed on the Boston Irish see Isenberg, chap. 1, pp. 11–12, 20–23, chap. 2, pp. 3–6; Stephen Thernstorm, *The Other Bostonians: Poverty and Progress in the American Metropolis, 1880–1970* (Cambridge, Mass., 1973), chaps. 6, 7.

6. Sullivan, *Life and Reminiscences*, pp. 24–25; Isenberg, chap. 2, pp. 1–2, 18–19, 24–30.

7. Isenberg, chap. 1, pp. 32–33; Sullivan, *Life and Reminiscences*, pp. 24–27; and Stephen H. Hardy, *How Boston Played: Sport, Recreation and Community, 1865–1915* (Boston, 1982), pp. 168–72.

8. Sullivan, *Life and Reminiscences*, pp. 28–31; Michael Donovan, *The Roosevelt That I Know* (New York, 1909), pp. 40–44; and Isenberg, chap. 1, pp. 32–33.

9. Isenberg, chap. 4, pp. 9–11; Sullivan, *Life and Reminiscences*, pp. 38–42.

10. Sullivan, *Life and Reminiscences*, pp. 40–45; Isenberg chap. 4, pp. 23–33.

11. Sullivan, *Life and Reminiscences*, pp. 44–46; Edward Van Every, *The Sins of New York as Exposed by the Police Gazette* (New York, 1930), p. 261; William

Edgar Harding, *John L. Sullivan, the Champion Pugilist* (New York, 1883), pp. 10–12; and Isenberg, prologue, p. 13.

12. See references in note 11 and Isenberg, chap. 4, pp. 23–28; for average wages, see *Historical Statistics of the United States, Colonial Times to 1970*, 2 vols. (Washington, D.C., 1975), 1: 165.

13. The story of the Sullivan-Ryan fight is well told by Isenberg, chap. 4, pp. 28–38; Sullivan, *Life and Reminiscences*, pp. 45–52; and *Famous Irish Fighters*, pp. 2–3.

14. William H. Adams, "New Orleans as the National Center of Boxing," *Louisiana Historical Quarterly* 39 (1956): 93; C. Vann Woodward, *Origins of the New South* (Baton Rouge, 1951), p. 171.

15. For coverage of the Sullivan-Ryan fight, see especially the *National Police Gazette* for the weeks before and after February 7, 1882. *Gazette* sports editor William Edgar Harding reprinted these stories in his biographies. Also see Sullivan, *Life and Reminiscences*, pp. 70–76; Dale Somers, *The Rise of Sport in New Orleans* (Baton Rouge, 1972), pp. 162–65; and Van Every, p. 263. Reverend Flynn is quoted in Somers, p. 166. José Martí, *The America of José Martí*, trans. Juan de Onís (New York, 1953), p. 118. Martí considered the ring absolutely barbarous.

16. *New Orleans Times Democrat* and *New Orleans Picayune*, February 2–7, 1882; Martí, p. 120.

17. Martí, p. 117; Isenberg, chap. 4, pp. 28–36. Obviously, Martí got a few of his details wrong.

18. Isenberg, chap. 4, pp. 32–36; *Famous Irish Fighters*, p. 3; Somers, p. 166; Sullivan, *Life and Reminiscences*, pp. 78–85; anon., *The Modern Gladiator* (St. Louis, 1892), p. 27; William Edgar Harding, *Life and Battles of John L. Sullivan* (New York, 1891), pp. 32–41; and Harding, *John L. Sullivan*. The last two sources reprint *Police Gazette* reports. Also see *New Orleans Times Democrat* and *New Orleans Picayune*, February 8, 1882.

19. See references in note 18. Ryan's ring experience was in fact not much broader than Sullivan's.

20. See references in note 18. On the Ryan fight see Isenberg, chap. 4, pp. 35–38.

21. See references in note 18; *New Orleans Times Democrat*, February 8, 1882; Isenberg, chap. 4, pp. 35–38.

22. *New York Times*, quoted in Somers, p. 167.

23. Harding, *John L. Sullivan*, pp. 13–25; Frank Luther Mott, *American Journalism* (New York, 1962), p. 487; Hardy, pp. 168–75; Van Every, p. 265; Sullivan, *Life and Reminiscences*, pp. 92–94. The *New Orleans Times Democrat* was obviously proud that the fight went so well yet editorialized against the "disgusting display."

24. Sullivan, *Life and Reminiscences*, pp. 94–95; Frederick L. Paxson, "The Rise of Sport," *Mississippi Valley Historical Review* 4 (September 1917): 150; and John A. Lucas and Ronald A. Smith, *The Saga of American Sport* (Philadelphia, 1975), p. 300. Nat Fleischer, America's leading boxing journalist for fifty years, declared he knew of no other fighter "getting such a grip on the popular imagination," not even Jack Dempsey or Joe Louis. Fleischer, *Boston Strong Boy*, p. 1. Sport historian John Rickard Betts called Sullivan "the first of our legendary sporting heroes." Betts,

America's Sporting Heritage, 1850–1950 (Reading, Mass., 1974), p. 165. Benjamin Rader agrees that Sullivan was "probably the first truly national sports hero." Radar, *American Sports: From the Age of Folk Games to the Age of Spectators* (Englewood Cliffs, N.J., 1983), pp. 101–3.

25. Sullivan, *Life and Reminiscences*, pp. 97–98; *Famous Irish Fighters*, pp. 5–6. The precise number of Sullivan's fights is open to question, but his autobiography clearly exaggerates. I defer to Isenberg on this point, whose research indicates that Sullivan fought forty-six prize bouts and forty-two exhibitions against real boxers (not including members of his touring groups). Even these more modest numbers give Sullivan many times more ring experiences than any of his predecessors. Isenberg, personal correspondence.

26. Again, The *Police Gazette* is the most important source on Sullivan's glove fights, but also see Sullivan, *Life and Reminiscences*, pp. 97–98; *Famous Irish Fighters*, pp. 5–6; and especially Isenberg, chap. 5.

27. Sullivan, *Life and Reminiscences*, pp. 99–103; Harding, *Life of John L. Sullivan*, pp. 42–46; *Famous Irish Fighters*, p. 6; and Isenberg, chap. 5, pp. 6–9.

28. Sullivan, *Life and Reminiscences*, pp. 103–17.

29. Quoted in ibid.; Isenberg, chap. 5, pp. 16–17, 26–30. When Sullivan rendered Mitchell defenseless in the third round, police officers stepped in to end the carnage.

30. Sullivan, *Life and Reminiscences*, pp. 103–30, 132–56, chaps. 9–10; Nathaniel Fleischer, *All Time Ring Record Book* (Norwalk, Conn., 1942), pp. 24–25, 41–42; and *Famous Irish Fighters*, p. 7. Sullivan estimated his earnings at half a million dollars as of 1889.

31. Sullivan, *Life and Reminiscences*, pp. 103–56. Again, Isenberg has followed the progress of Sullivan's tours with admirable scholarship and corrected the record. Sullivan claimed in his autobiography that fifty-nine challengers from the audience stood before him on the tour, a grossly exaggerated estimate. Isenberg, prologue, pp. 23–24.

32. Isenberg tells the story of the grand tour brilliantly. See chap. 6. Also see Robert Toll, *On with the Show: The First Century of Show Business in America* (New York, 1976), pp. 61–79, for the logistics of circus touring, which he likens to a "moving factory." On the centralization of the theater see Jack Poggi, *Theater in America: The Impact of Economic Forces* (Ithaca, 1968), pp. 3–8, 26–27; Gunther Barth, *City People* (New York, 1980), chap. 6.

33. Foster Rhea Dulles, *America Learns to Play* (Gloucester, Mass., 1959), p. 263; Isenberg, prologue, pp. 23–24, chap. 6; Betts, *America's Sporting Heritage*, pp. 79, 207, 242–43; Fleischer, *Ring Record Book*, pp. 24–25; Sullivan, *Life and Reminiscences*, pp. 221, 281; and Harding, *John L. Sullivan*. Early books such as *American Fistiana* contained a page or two of advertising, usually for their publishers' other works. By contrast, the Spalding Athletic Library's *Boxing: A Perfect Treatise on the Science of Self-Defense* (New York, 1893) contained forty-two pages of text and twenty-two of advertising.

34. See, for example, *Modern Gladiator*, pp. 383–84. With tables of statistics, Nathaniel Fleischer's *Ring Record Book* gives a good sense of this blossoming of the ring.

35. On the new acceptance of previously taboo entertainment see especially Lewis A. Erenberg, *Steppin' Out: New York Nightlife and the Transformation of American Culture* (Westport, Conn., 1981); John Kasson, *Amusing the Million: Coney Island at the Turn of the Century* (New York, 1978); and Lary May, *Screening Out the Past: The Birth of Mass Culture and the Motion Picture Industry* (Chicago, 1980).

36. Sullivan, *Life and Reminiscences*, pp. 241-44.

37. One is reminded of the nineteenth century's fascination with the "sublime," the artistic merger of terror and beauty, danger and security. See Perry Miller, *The Life of the Mind in America; From the Revolution to the Civil War* (New York, 1965).

38. Isenberg, chap. 5, pp. 18-25, 32-37; Dulles, pp. 226-28; Donovan, chap. 4; and *New York Morning Journal*, April 1, 1885. See also Isenberg's discussion of the "urban manhood culture," chap. 2, pp. 24-30, and Perry R. Duis, *The Saloon: Public Drinking in Chicago and Boston* (Urbana, Ill., 1983).

39. *Boston Globe*, August 9, 1882; Somers, p. 173; and William Edgar Harding, *The Life and Battles of Jake Kilrain* (New York, 1888), p. 17.

40. John D. McCallum, *The World Heavyweight Boxing Championship* (Radnor, Penn., 1974), p. 10; Herbert Gutman, "Work, Culture and Society in Industrializing America, 1815-1919," *American Historical Review* 78 (June 1973): 564; William V. Shannon, *The American Irish* (New York, 1963), pp. 95-102; and *New York Tribune*, December 30, 1887, p. 4, cited in Paxson, pp. 150-51. The *Tribune* editor condemned Sullivan's unmitigated coarseness and brutality yet marveled at his fearlessness in the ring.

41. Roy Rosenzweig, *Eight Hours for What We Will: Workers and Leisure in an Industrial City, 1870-1920* (Cambridge, Mass., 1983), p. 75.

42. Abraham Cahan, *Yekl, and the Imported Bridegroom and Other Stories of Yiddish New York* (New York, 1970), pp. 2-3; Barth, *City People*, chap. 5, esp. pp. 186-91; and Isenberg, chap. 2.

43. Charles Dana as cited in *Modern Gladiator*, pp. 189-90.

44. The newspapers, especially the *Police Gazette*, were filled with stories of the champion's sprees. Accounts of Sullivan's style of living within the bachelor subculture are readily found in *Modern Gladiator*, pp. 73-87, 216-17, 337-66. Chidsey's *John the Great* contains many stories with a core of truth and a great deal of embellishment. Also see Isenberg, chap. 2.

45. Isenberg, chap. 5, pp. 28-32; Fleischer, *Ring Record Book*, pp. 24-25, 41; Harding, *Life of John L. Sullivan*, pp. 49-52; and Sullivan, *Life and Reminiscences*, chap. 5.

46. Isenberg, chap. 5, pp. 24-28, and chap. 7, p. 20; *National Police Gazette*, cited in Van Every, p. 268; *Famous Irish Fighters*, pp. 9-10; and Sullivan, *Life and Reminiscences*, chap. 5. A few months later, numerous magnates and politicians came to watch Sullivan battle Alf Greenfield; see Isenberg, chap. 7, p. 11.

47. Isenberg, chap. 5, pp. 9, 14, 27, 31; chap 7; p. 12, 43-44. Zulma Steele, *Angel in Top Hat* (New York, 1942), pp. 269-70; and John Thomas Jable, "Sports Amusements and Pennsylvania Blue Laws" (diss., Pennsylvania State University, 1974), pp. 99-104. Officials foiled most of Bergh's efforts. In Philadelphia local clergymen exerted pressure on Mayor Smith, but despite magisterial efforts, many

fights went on. Former New York police chief George Walling stopped an 1884 match in Madison Square Garden when it became clear that Sullivan was going for a knockout. No policeman except Walling would testify before a grand jury that the exhibition was indeed a prize fight, and the case was dismissed. Walling, *Recollections of a New York Chief of Police* (New York, 1890), pp. 373–74.

48. Fleischer, *Ring Record Book*, pp. 24–25, 41; *Famous Irish Fighters*, p. 10; and Sullivan, *Life and Reminiscences*, chap. 9. E. B. Mitchell, *Fencing, Boxing and Wrestling* (Longon, 1893), pp. 140–47, for example, argued that glove fighting proved nothing, that only bare-knuckle fights were real battles. On Sullivan's drinking see especially Isenberg, chaps. 5 and 6. On his divorce, see Isenberg, chap. 7, pp. 20–24, 46–48.

49. Harding, *Life of Kilrain*, p. 17; *Famous Irish Fighters*, pp. 11–14; Sullivan, *Life and Reminiscences*, chaps. 9–10; Harding, *Life of John L. Sullivan*, pp. 74–80; and *Modern Gladiator*, pp. 95–97.

50. Sullivan, quoted in Harding, *Life of Sullivan*, pp. 76–80; also see references in note 49.

51. Harding, *Life of Kilrain*, pp. 7–18; Sullivan, *Life and Reminiscences*, chaps. 9–10; and *Famous Irish Fighters*, pp. 12–14.

52. Harding, *Life of Kilrain*, pp. 5–7; Fleischer, *Ring Record Book*, p. 40. The Baltimore Cribb Club charged $15 for membership and $10 for twenty lessons from Kilrain. For a well-written popular account of the fight, see James A. Cox, "The Great Fight: Mr. Jake vs. John L. Sullivan," *Smithsonian* 15 (December 1984): 153–68. Isenberg, chaps. 9 and 10, is the best source on these years.

53. Harding, *Life of Kilrain*, pp. 18–19, 32–33. The *Police Gazette* now called him "ex-champion" Sullivan.

54. Harding, *Life of Kilrain*, pp. 18–19, 32–33; Isenberg, chap. 7, pp. 44–46; Sullivan, *Life and Reminiscences*, pp. 175–76; and Hardy, pp. 173–76. *Police Gazette* reports for the Kilrain-Smith fight are reprinted in Harding, *Life of Kilrain*, pp. 7–10, 19–40. Each having a belt now, Sullivan and Kilrain sailed for England, both fought for the "Championship of the World," both received a draw, and both claimed that the English had robbed them, just as they had robbed John C. Heenan a generation earlier.

55. See references in note 54. On Sullivan's and Muldoon's preparations see *Modern Gladiator*, pp. 219–62, 330.

56. Quoted in Harding, *Life of Kilrain*, p. 29. For months the *Police Gazette* hyped the fight. See also Gene Smith and Jayne Barry Smith, eds., *The Police Gazette* (New York, 1972), p. 16.

57. Adams, "New Orleans as the National Center of Boxing," pp. 93–95; Somers, pp. 168–70; Donovan, pp. 110–13; *Famous Irish Fighters*, p. 14; *New Orleans Picayune*, July 8, 1889; and Betts, *America's Sporting Heritage*, p. 73.

58. Somers, pp. 172–74; Donovan, chap. 8; *Famous Irish Fighters*, p. 14; *New York World*, July 9, 1889; *New Orleans Picayune*, July 8, 9, 1889; *New Orleans Times Democrat*, July 9, 1889; Sullivan, *Life and Reminiscences*, chap. 10; Harding, *Life of John L Sullivan*, pp. 80–92; McCallum, pp. 14–15; Robert K. DeArment, *Bat Masterson: The Man and the Legend* (Norman, Okla., 1979), pp. 339–41; and Cox, "The Great Fight," pp. 154–55.

59. The quotations are from Harding, *Life and Battles of John L. Sullivan* and

Famous Irish Fighters, both of which relied heavily on the *New York World* for their accounts. Excellent coverage also appeared in the *Police Gazette* and *New Orleans Picayune* for the weeks before and after the fight.

60. Harding, *Life of John L. Sullivan*, p. 88; account from an unspecified Boston newspaper in Prize Fighting scrapbook, Widener Library, Harvard University, Cambridge.

61. Sullivan's remarks are quoted in the detailed report of the *Modern Gladiator*, pp. 139, 143, 150, 156, 160. Also see Harding, *Life of John L. Sullivan*, pp. 80–92; *Famous Irish Fighters*, pp. 15–16; Donovan, chap. 8; Sullivan, *Life and Reminiscences*, pp. 207–12; McCallum, pp. 14–15; and Cox, "The Great Fight," p. 166.

62. *New York Times*, July 9, 1889. The *Times'* use of "knock out" is indicative of the influence of the Queensberry rules, for the term and concept were borrowed from glove fighting. *New York World*, July 9, 1889; Somers, p. 173.

63. *Modern Gladiator*, p. 356. Keily's poem is reprinted on pp. 321–24.

64. The song circulated widely. See Fleischer, *Boston Strong Boy*, p. 1. D. K. Wilgus has kindly loaned me several broadside ballads on Sullivan. Significantly, by the 1880s songs about fighters seem to have been less numerous than in the days of Morrissey, Hyer, and Yankee Sullivan. Perhaps this indicates prize fighting's growing distance from the folk life of the streets, the ring's institutionalization as part of commercial culture. The Magriel ms. (a collection of newspaper reports of bare-knuckle fights) contains several cartoons from unspecified sources parodying well-bred Bostonians fawning over Sullivan. See also George P. Rawick, ed., *The American Slave: A Composite Autobiography* (Westport, Conn., 1977), suppl. ser. 1, vol. 11: *South Carolina*, p. 103; Dulles, p. 227; and *Modern Gladiator*, p. 353.

65. *Modern Gladiator*, pp. 196–97, 194–95; Donovan, p. 131; and Sullivan, *Life and Reminiscences*, pp. 213–16.

66. *Frank Leslie's Weekly*, July 27, 1889.

67. Sullivan, *Life and Reminiscences*, pp. 217–19; Betts, *America's Sporting Heritage*, p. 142.

68. Brame and Alexander, *Reports of Cases Decided by the Supreme Court of Mississippi, October Term, 1889, and April Term, 1890* (Philadelphia, 1890), pp. 345–56; Sullivan, *Life and Reminiscences*, pp. 219–21; Elmer A. Million, "The Enforceability of Prize Fight Statutes," *Kentucky Law Review* 27 (November 1938): 155; and Jeffrey Thomas Sammons, "America in the Ring: The Relationship between Boxing and Society, circa 1930–1980" (diss., University of North Carolina, Chapel Hill, 1982), pp. 7–14.

69. This is Mike Donovan's phrase in *Roosevelt I Know*, p. 187.

70. Fleischer, *Ring Record Book* pp. 24–25, 42; Sullivan, *Life and Reminiscences*, pp. 221–28, chap. 11; Chidsey, chap. 17; and Isenberg, personal correspondence. On the concept of celebrity see Daniel J. Boorstin, *The Image: A Guide to Pseudo-Events in America* (New York, 1978), chap. 2; and Warren I. Sussman, *Culture as History: The Transformation of American Society in the Twentieth Century* (New York, 1984), chaps. 8, 14.

71. Chidsey, chap. 18; Sullivan, *Life and Reminiscences*, chaps. 11–12; challenge quoted in William Edgar Harding, *Life and Battles of James J. Corbett* (New York, 1892), pp. 25–26. Sullivan claimed that stage commitments prevented him from fighting.

72. Donovan, pp. 148–68; Harding, *Life and Battles of Corbett*, p. 27. According to Donovan, Corbett later sought advice from Kearney on investing in Bronx real estate, p. 190.

73. Harding, *Life and Battles of Corbett*, p. 27; Dulles, p. 210; and especially Alan Woods, "James J. Corbett: Theatrical Star," *Journal of Sport History* 3 (Summer 1976): 162–75. Joe Choynski and Peter Jackson also had attained sufficient celebrity status to appear in *Uncle Tom's Cabin*, managing to spar during the adaptation of this abolitionist work.

74. In addition to the *New York World* itself see Betts, *Sporting Heritage*, pp. 63–68, 377; "A Point in Journalism," *The Nation* 56 (March 23, 1893): 209–10. For an excellent discussion of the development of the urban popular press, see Barth, chap. 3. Isenberg, chap. 12, is the authority on the Corbett fight.

75. See, for examples, James Edward Sullivan, *The Life and Battles of James J. Corbett* (New York, 1892), chaps. 1–2; and Harding, *Life and Battles of Corbett*, chap. 1 and p. 44; Isenberg, personal correspondence. The reality of Corbett's life was less attractive than his press image, for he was a deeply moody and even brutal man. For an example of the Corbett image, see Nathaniel Fleischer, *An Informal History of Heavyweight Boxing from 1719 to the Present Day* (New York, 1949), chap. 10.

76. Adams, "New Orleans as the National Center of Boxing," pp. 96–100; *New Orleans Daily States*, January 3, 1890, quoted in Somers, *Rise of Sport*, p. 174.

77. See Somers, pp. 174–91; Adams, "New Orleans as the National Center of Boxing," pp. 96–100; *New Orleans Daily Picayune*, January 19, 1891; *New Orleans Times Democrat*, January 16, 1891.

78. Men from all these professions attended the Sullivan-Corbett fight. They testified in favor of such matches in "State of Louisiana vs. The Olympic Club," Henry Demis, reporter, *Reports of Cases Argued and Determined in the Supreme Court of Louisiana* 46, pt. 2, 1894 (New Orleans, 1895): 952–57. See also vol. 77, 1895 (New Orleans, 1896): 1096–99; Sammons, pp. 7–14.

79. Somers, pp. 174–91; Adams, "New Orleans as the National Center of Boxing," pp. 96–100. As Melvin Adelman points out, the gambler promotes his man, the entrepreneur promotes the whole spectacle: "The Development of Modern Athletics: Sport in New York City, 1820–1870" (diss., University of Illinois, 1980).

80. This interpretation is taken from Somers's excellent discussion, pp. 174–91; Harding, *Life of John L. Sullivan*, and *Life and Battles of Corbett* also discuss fight arrangements. Also see Adams, "New Orleans as the National Center of Boxing," pp. 96–100.

81. *New Orleans Picayune*, September 8, 1892.

82. Donovan, chaps. 9, 10; Somers, pp. 183–84. Newspapers spilled incredible amounts of ink for weeks before and after the battle. See especially *Police Gazette, New York World*, and *New Orleans Picayune*.

83. *New York Herald*, August 28, 1892, quoted in Somers, *Rise of Sport*, p. 179; *Chicago Daily Tribune*, September 8, 1892, quoted in Betts, p. 77.

84. Somers, pp. 179–83; Adams, "New Orleans as the National Center for Boxing," pp. 101–5. A crowd of cheering blacks greeted Dixon outside the arena and heralded him as their champion. The following day the *Times Democrat* called

the fight a mistake, and the *Picayune* declared that the Olympic Club had "learned its lesson."

85. Somers, pp. 179-83; Adams, "New Orleans as the National Center for Boxing," pp. 101-5; *New Orleans Picayune,* September 7, 8, 1892; *New York World,* September 7, 8, 1892; *New Orleans Times Democrat,* September 7, 8, 1892; and Isenberg, prologue, p. 21.

86. The *Blocton [Ala.] Courier,* September 2, 1892, claimed that "this is a spirit of entertainment which should be encouraged." My thanks to Charles E. Adams of the University of Alabama for this reference.

87. Somers, pp. 183-85; *Chicago Tribune,* September 9, 1892; Harding, *Life and Battles of Corbett,* chap. 7; quoted from Sullivan, *Life of Corbett,* p. 35; Harding, *Life of John L. Sullivan,* pp. 92-102; and James Connors, *Illustrated History of the Great Corbett-Sullivan Ring Battle* (Buffalo, 1892). Connors's book used illustrations and symbols to indicate the location of each punch, claiming that Sullivan received 141 blows to the head and 45 to the body. Lieut. Col. A. A. Woodhull also saw the fight as proof that speed and agility—which, he pointed out, the army could train men for—were superior to brute strength, and that force must be made effective through intelligence, an important lesson for modern armed forces. Donald J. Mrozek, *Sport and American Mentality, 1880-1910* (Knoxville, 1983), p. 56.

88. William Lyon Phelps, *Autobiography with Letters* (New York, 1939), p. 356; Adams, "New Orleans as the National Center of Boxing," pp. 104-5; and *New York Times,* September 8, 1892. Needless to say, San Franciscans were ecstatic and Bostonians saddened.

89. Theodore Dreiser, *A Book about Myself* (New York, 1922), pp. 150-51.

90. Dibble, chaps. 5-8; also see George Bellows's painting, "Introducing John L. Sullivan." On Sullivan's last years, see especially Isenberg, chaps. 13 and 14.

91. Seton quoted in Joseph and Elizabeth Pleck, eds., *The American Man* (Englewood Cliffs, N.J., 1980), p. 25. See also Joseph F. Kett, *Rites of Passage: Adolescence in America, 1790 to the Present* (New York, 1977), p. 23; Rader, p. 103; Isenberg, prologue.

92. Vachel Lindsay, "John L. Sullivan, the Strong Boy of Boston," in Mark Harris, ed., *Selected Poems of Vachel Lindsay* (New York, 1963), p. 13.

93. Christian K. Messenger, *Sport and the Spirit of Play in American Fiction: Hawthorne to Faulkner* (New York, 1981), pp. 93-95.

Epilogue. The Manly Art

1. Elliott J. Gorn, "The Manassa Mauler and the Fighting Marine: An Interpretation of the Dempsey-Tunney Fights," *Journal of American Studies* 19 (April 1985): 28-31; Randy Roberts, *Jack Dempsey: The Manassa Mauler* (Baton Rouge, 1979), pp. 228-29.

2. This interpretation is eloquently put forth by Lawrence Levine for Afro-American expressive culture in *Black Culture and Black Consciousness: Afro-American Folk Thought from Slavery to Freedom* (New York, 1977). See especially the sections of Jack Johnson, Joe Louis, and the Epilogue, pp. 429-37, 441-45.

3. See T. J. Jackson Lears, *No Place of Grace: Antimodernism and the Transformation of American Culture, 1880–1920* (New York, 1981), chap. 3; Warren Susman, *Culture as History: The Transformation of American Society in the Twentieth Century* (New York, 1984), chaps. 8, 11, 14.

4. Cf. Victor W. Turner, "Liminal to Liminoid in Play, Flow and Ritual: An Essay in Comparative Symbology," *Rice University Studies* 60 (Summer 1974): 52–92.

5. Testifying at the trial of William Poole's alleged murderers, Johnny Ling, a saloonkeeper, used the word "artists" to describe skilled gamblers and pugilists who won by playing within the rules. *New York Times,* December 7, 1855.

6. On boxing in twentieth-century street gangs see William Foote Whyte, *Street Corner Society* (Chicago, 1943).

7. See Edward Anthony Rotundo, "Manhood in America: The Northern Middle Class, 1770–1920" (diss., Brandeis University, 1982), chap. 2; Benjamin Franklin, *The Autobiography of Benjamin Franklin* (New York, 1944), p. 11; and Horatio Alger, *Ragged Dick* (New York, 1962), pp. 43–44.

8. Cf. Erving Goffman, "Where the Action Is," in his *Interaction Ritual* (Garden City, N.Y., 1967), pp. 266–69.

9. Peter Tamony, an amateur linguist, argues in personal correspondence that "fancy," not "fanatic" as most dictionaries claim, is the source of the word "fan." He makes a persuasive case.

Index

The abbreviation "pf" means "prize fighting"

"Muscular Christianity," 180. *See also* Sports
Myer, Billy, 243

Nation, The, 239
National honor and pf, 20–22, 80, 149, 152, 157–159
National Intelligencer, 48
National Police Gazette, 83, 88, 89, 175, 181, 184, 203, 211, 213, 215, 222, 236, 239, 244. *See also* Fox, Richard Kyle
Neale, Ned, 32
Neate, William, 25–26
Neighborhood focus of pf, 39–40, 132–136
Nelson, J. A., 165
New Englander, 102
New Jersey Emporium and True American, 66
New Jersey State Gazette, 67
New Orleans Daily Picayune, 100, 232, 241, 242
New Orleans Times-Democrat, 215, 241, 243–244
Newspapers:
  British influence on, 40–41
  coverage of pf: Coburn-McCoole fight, 168, 169; conventions re, 39; first instance of, 39; focus on corruption, 176–177; Heenan-Sayers fight, 149–151; increase in, 41–42, 121–122; Morrissey-Heenan fight, 120–122; profits, concerns re, 61–62; J. L. Sullivan–Corbett fight, 239, 243–244; J. L. Sullivan–Kilrain fight, 232, 235; J. L. Sullivan–Ryan fight, 213–214, 215; Y. Sullivan–Hyer fight, 92–94
  criticism of pf, 59–63, 73, 78–79, 111–112, 120–122, 223
  hypocrisy of, 61
  interviews with fighters, 215
  nostalgia for early days of pf, 177
  sparring, attitude toward, 48–49
  sporting newspapers, 181
  sports coverage by, 100, 181
  support for pf, 42, 58, 81, 100–104, 200–201, 239. *See also National Police Gazette; New York Clipper*
  See also specific titles
New World, 73
New York Athletic Club, 186, 190, 199
New York Clipper, 100–103, 111, 114, 116, 169, 171, 176. *See also* Queen, Frank
New Yorker, 63
New York Evening Mirror, 96
New York Evening Post, 39, 49, 61, 111
New York Herald, 42, 44, 62, 78, 83, 100, 125, 243. *See also* Bennett, James Gordon

New York Illustrated News, 151
New York Illustrated Times, 93
New York Magazine, 60
New York Mercury, 169
New York Morning Express, 73
New York Spectator, 61
New York Sporting Magazine, 58
New York Sun, 94, 213
New York Sunday Mercury, 95
New York Times, 100, 112, 122, 125, 144, 150, 157, 215, 235, 245, 248
New York Tribune, 78–79, 100, 111, 117, 120, 127
New York World, 235, 239
Night clubs, 182
Night fights, 37, 38, 211, 243–245
Nile's Weekly Register, 68
Norris, Frank, 197
North American Review, 201
Norton, Michael, 138, 172

O'Baldwin, Ned, 169, 170, 172, 173
O'Brien, Hugh, 231
O'Donnell, Pat, 47
O'Donnell, Tom, 81, 89–90, 91
Oelricks, Herman, 197
O'Hagan, Jim, 47
Olympic Club, New Orleans, 238–245
Olympic Club, San Francisco, 199
O'Neal, Hugh, 165
"On Pugilism," 60
Oral culture of pf, 98–99
O'Reilly, John Boyle, 201–202
Orem, Con, 165, 174
Organized athletics, 180
Origins of pf in America, 36–47
O'Rourke, M., 162
O'Rourke, Samuel, 44, 100
Osborn, Duffield, 201
Outing, 201
Outlawing of pf, 11, 107–108
  effect on corruption in pf, 171–172
  in England, 32
  fighters' political involvement and, 135
  ineffectiveness of, 104
  in Massachusetts, 103–104
  in New Jersey, 66–67
  in New York, 104
  reforms and, 228
  in the South, 212–213
  J. L. Sullivan-Kilrain fight, and, 236–237
  See also Prevention of fights attempted; Trials of fighters
Overs, George, 70

Paddock, Tom, 151
Palmerston, Lord, 152